JONATHAN BARDON was born in Dublin in 1941 but has lived and worked in Belfast since 1963. He is author of several books on Irish history, most notably *A history of Ulster* (1992) and, most recently, *A history of Ireland in 250 episodes* (2008), based on BBC Radio Ulster broadcasts. He has written radio and television historical documentaries for BBC, UTV, RTÉ and Channel 4. He was chairman of the Northern Ireland Community Relations Council between 1996 and 2002 and was awarded the OBE for services to community life in 2003.

All Children Together was asked to make two programmes for the BBC in 1975. The first was a *Platform* programme for Radio Ulster in March '75, and following this, ACT was given air-time to broadcast its vision and hopes for the development of shared schools in Northern Ireland through a *Community Access* programme broadcast on BBC 2 in May of the same year.

These photos show key ACT players deep in discussion, as follows:
In the group photo, back row (from left): Margaret Kennedy, Brian Mulholland, Kathleen Lindsay, Breige Cunningham (left) and Bettie Benton.
Front row (from left): Thelma Sheil, Bill Brown.

TOP PHOTOGRAPH: Facing the group: Cecil Linehan (left) and Tony Spencer.

THE STRUGGLE FOR SHARED SCHOOLS IN NORTHERN IRELAND

The history of All Children Together

JONATHAN BARDON

ULSTER
HISTORICAL
FOUNDATION

To the parents who entrusted their children
to the new concept of integrated education and to
the teachers who were brave enough to step out
and support them but, above all, to the children
who made our vision a reality by just going to
school together in Northern Ireland
and to their children and grandchildren

The ACT logo was originally developed by Thelma Sheil and
Bettie Benton. When Rowel Friers designed the name of our
newsletter, *ACT-LETT*, he also incorporated the two little children,
who were used from then on.

First published 2009
Ulster Historical Foundation
49 Malone Road, Belfast BT9 6RY

Printed by Cromwell Press Group
Design by Dunbar Design

Contents

Preface

I warmly congratulate All Children Together on the publication of its history. I am filled with admiration for the tenacity and dedication of the movement's founders and members in their long campaign to promote integrated education in Northern Ireland. In 1974, when the region was bitterly divided on religious lines and engulfed in violence, parents could only send their children to publicly funded schools which were, in effect, either Protestant or Catholic. Yet national opinion-poll surveys in 1967/8 had found that 64 per cent of adults in Northern Ireland favoured integrated schools.

This history chronicles how ACT faced seemingly insurmountable resistance from the establishment to educate children of all religions and no religion together; how it succeeded in persuading Westminster to pass enabling legislation (the Dunleath Act) in 1978; how, taking great risks, it set up Lagan College in 1981; how it convinced government in 1989 to release funding to enable parent groups wishing to do so to found integrated schools; how it responded assiduously to official education reports; and how, despite many vicissitudes, the movement developed at an impressive pace. I understand that, by September 2008, there were 19,183 pupils in 62 integrated schools in Northern Ireland.

Throughout its existence ACT has been concerned with human rights, particularly those of children. This too has been my own lifelong concern, more formally during my term as UN high commissioner for human rights (1997–2002) and subsequently during my involvement with Realizing Rights: the Ethical Globalisation Initiative. The mission of Realizing Rights is to put human rights standards at the heart of global governance and policy making. Surely ACT's achievement of making it possible for children in a deeply divided region to be educated together is a major victory for human rights in Northern Ireland. Another part of Realizing Rights is strengthening women's leadership. A striking feature of

ACT Directors meet President Mary Robinson in Áras an Uachtaráin in December 1991, close to the first anniversary of her installation as president of Ireland.
FROM LEFT: Gavin Ross, Bettie Benton, Bill Brown, Thelma Sheil, President Robinson, Doreen Budd, Sister Anna, Margaret Kennedy, Cecil Linehan.

this book is that it makes it clear that the driving force in ACT, from the outset, was a group of ordinary women, not previously prominent in public life, determined to do the best for their children.

I had the pleasure of receiving the directors of ACT in Áras an Uachtaráin on 1 December 1991, close to the first anniversary of my inauguration as president of Ireland. I learned then with pleasure of the close association the organisation had with the integrated movement in the south. I am pleased now to wish this book every success.

MARY ROBINSON

Introduction

This story has relevance for divided societies in countries far from Ireland's shores. It is a true example of the David and Goliath story, of the power of ordinary people to challenge church and state, and to transform societies … the pioneers of the integrated education movement [are] among the first genuine peace people.

BRIAN MAWHINNEY[1]

I was born, brought up and educated in Northern Ireland. In many ways I was raised in an exceptionally vibrant society, punching above its weight in the United Kingdom by producing remarkably talented scientists, artists, poets, musicians, entrepreneurs and public figures. However, it was, and continues to be, blighted by bitter division, the origins of which go far back into the island's history. Distrust, ignorance and the surfacing of ancient hatreds played a central role in the eruption of terrible violence from 1969 onwards.

By the end of 1985, just as I was about to take up a post as a government minister in the Northern Ireland Office, a total of 2,515 people – innocent civilians, members of the security forces and paramilitary activists – had met with violent deaths in what were euphemistically known as the Troubles. The UK Conservative government was then primarily concerned to bed down the Anglo-Irish Agreement of November 1985 in an effort to reduce the death toll and to seek long-term solutions to the region's acute problems.

My main ministerial responsibility in Northern Ireland was education. It did not take me long to become aware of a small but energetic group of parents who believed that, as long as children were educated apart, there would be little hope of healing the festering wounds. These parents were members of a movement started in the early 1970s, named All Children Together. In many ways the views they held were close to my own. Back in 1975, long before I had any reason to believe that one day I would be Northern Ireland's minister of education, I had written in a book co-authored with Ronald Wells the following words: 'How bright the prospects for peaceful coexistence in Ulster can be while children are educated separately is a matter of considerable doubt.'[2] In addition, the leading activists in ACT – Catholic and Protestant – were all, like me, committed Christians.

Jonathan Bardon makes it clear in this book that valiant efforts had been made long before to educate the children of Ireland together. Lord Edward Stanley, as Irish chief secretary, created a public system of education in 1831, 40 years before one came into being across the Irish Sea in Great Britain. However, his ambitious scheme to provide government-funded integrated elementary education for every class and every denomination across the whole of Ireland was steadily undermined by all the leading churches. Almost a hundred years later, in 1923, Lord Londonderry, appointed Northern Ireland's first education minister, made a fresh attempt to set up a primary education system where Catholic and Protestant children would be educated together. Howls of protest from church leaders and politicians greeted his bill and, though it was passed, virtually everyone involved in education refused to make their schools integrated. The terms of the act were altered, almost surreptitiously, and Londonderry was left with no choice but to resign.

The great expansion of education provision and funding in Northern Ireland after the Second World War, for all its benefits, actually extended the time Protestant and Catholic young people spent in educational institutions being educated separately. Not until the Northern Ireland secretary of state William Whitelaw masterminded the setting up of the power-sharing executive at the end of 1973 was a new effort made to make it possible, for those who wanted it, to have their children educated together. Remarkably, Basil McIvor, the moderate unionist MP appointed minister of education in the power-sharing executive, got approval in the Northern Ireland assembly for his shared-schools plan in April 1974. Immediately after that, of course, the devolved power-sharing administration collapsed in the wake of the Ulster Workers' Council strike. Basil McIvor, who subsequently became a member of ACT and chaired Lagan College for quarter of a century, made his extensive archive of writing available before his death in 2004. In February 1974, some three months before the power-sharing executive fell, the Labour Party was returned to power in Britain and Northern Ireland. That government's attempts to restore devolution came to nothing and it was now up to direct-rule ministers appointed in London to grasp the McIvor nettle. Jonathan Bardon has thoroughly mined government files recently opened under the 30-year rule. They demonstrate that, faced with a kaleidoscope of problems in Northern Ireland and strong opposition from church leaders, government ministers shrank from any serious attempt to put into effect the shared-schools plan approved by the assembly in 1974.

Meanwhile, members of ACT refused to be discouraged. Starting out as a handful of mainly Catholic housewives in County Down they steadily gathered support from both sides of the community. Frustrated by government inaction, members of the ACT executive drafted a private member's bill in 1977. Put forward by the Alliance peer, Lord Henry Dunleath, the bill became law in 1978. To ACT's great disappointment, the Dunleath Act failed to yield results. The problem was that it depended on church leaders and school managers taking the initiative and this they failed to do.

Undaunted, ACT decided to set up an integrated secondary school in Belfast. The courage those involved showed, the energy they expended and the financial risks they ran is vividly chronicled throughout this book. It all began when this first integrated school, Lagan College, was opened with just 28 pupils in a scout hall in south Belfast in September 1981.

The Conservatives had returned to power in 1979 and, as under-secretary in the Northern Ireland Office, Nicholas Scott was in charge of education from the outset. He proved more receptive than his predecessors to determined lobbying from ACT. He issued a memorable circular in June 1982 saying that everyone involved in education had:

> an inescapable duty to ensure that effective measures are taken to ensure that children do not grow up in ignorance, fear or even hatred of those from whom they are educationally segregated.[3]

He followed this up by providing funding for contact schemes between segregated schools and by campaigning openly for education managers to seize the opportunities provided by the Dunleath Act.

When asked to return in an official capacity to my native province in September 1985 I became parliamentary private secretary to Tom King, the newly appointed Northern Ireland secretary of state. The furious response of many in Northern Ireland to the Anglo-Irish Agreement, signed at Hillsborough on 15 November 1985, certainly ensured that I was able to withstand tirades from critics when I was appointed a minister in January 1986. I had no illusions about how my appointment would be received in the high-octane atmosphere that then existed in the province. My principal responsibility was education and, when not on the Stormont estate or at Westminster, much of my time was spent in Rathgael House, the Department of Education's offices in Bangor, County Down. I now had a unique opportunity to make a difference.

It is clear that members of ACT consider that I did make a difference and a beneficial one too. *In the firing line*, my memoir published in 1999, describes the pioneers of the integrated-education movement as 'among the first genuine peace people'.[4] Surviving largely on donations and support from the Joseph Rowntree Charitable Trust and the Nuffield Foundation, Lagan College needed immediate help. Twice I increased the school's capacity and provided a considerable amount of new money for new buildings. The condition of a second integrated school, Hazelwood College in north Belfast, was even more perilous. What was needed was an easing of the criteria for deciding when a school was educationally viable – not only for Hazelwood but also for the whole integrated-education movement.

Facing much critical, sometimes sulphurous, opposition, I forged ahead to put through the Education Reform (Northern Ireland) Order 1989. The main part of the legislation was the introduction of the national curriculum to Northern Ireland, with appropriate adaptations to suit the region. It also included a statutory responsibility on the Department of Education to encourage integrated education and the provision of grant aid to integrated schools from an early stage in their development.

An argument constantly advanced from the early days when ACT first put forward their ideas on shared schools, critics argued that integrationists were planning to force parents into non-denominational schools. In fact, all the papers and reports of the movement make it clear that the intention was to create the opportunity *only* for those parents who wanted their children educated together to have their own schools. That has always been my own view. In truth I had no ability to overturn the existing education system, but as a Christian and a Conservative I supported the principle of parental choice.

I believe that it is entirely appropriate for Christians to play an active part in the country's political processes. It is very evident in this book that the pioneers of the integrated-education movement, and most of those who continued to lead it, were motivated by strongly held Christian beliefs. Indeed, that does much to explain their radicalism. Like them I firmly believe that integrated schools in Northern Ireland's divided community are a powerful force for reconciliation and a testament to the great Christian virtue of hope.

When I presented my education-reform proposals I realised that there was one glaring omission, huge in its importance but so unthinkable that no one believed it even worth mentioning. There was no agreed syllabus for religious education. I had a strong sense that it was my Christian duty to see that a core religious-education syllabus was created. With Tom King's total support I launched the proposal and – as I had warned him – there was a row. 'Normally gracious clergy said uncharacteristically harsh things,' I recalled in my memoir.[5] Eventually I did get agreement. ACT fully supported my plan. After all, they had built up considerable prowess in this field as they, with advice from St Bede's School in Surrey, had painstakingly put together a common religious-education programme for Lagan College.

Immediately after the 1992 general election, Prime Minister John Major asked me to move from the Northern Ireland Office to become minister of health back in London. Naturally I could not keep abreast of the day-to-day developments in education in Northern Ireland. Nevertheless, I have never lost touch and I follow news of the development of the integrated-education movement in my home province with keen interest. In June 2008 I spoke in Belfast at a meeting of the All-Party Parliamentary Committee on Northern Ireland. To those in the integrated-education movement I said:

> The work you do is very, very important. It may appear slow and you may think progress is very limited, but at some stage your work will bring about a tipping point in society. I do not know how many schools

that tipping point will be: 100 schools? 200 schools? But you will then be seen to be The Answer; and your work will be mainstream. So always be conscious of just how important your work is – and keep at it.[6]

In taking on the task of writing the history of ACT, a historian of Bardon's stature shows what an important role this movement for reconciliation through education holds in the story of Northern Ireland's Troubles and, more importantly, its way out of conflict. This story has relevance for divided societies in countries far from Ireland's shores. It is a true example of the David and Goliath story, of the power of ordinary people to challenge church and state, and to transform societies.

RT HON. THE LORD MAWHINNEY KT

1
Failing to educate
all children together

I do not know of any measures which would prepare
the way for a better feeling in Ireland than uniting
children at an early age and bringing them up in the
same school, leading them to commune with one
another and to form those little intimacies and
friendships which often subsist through life.

DR JAMES DOYLE, ROMAN CATHOLIC BISHOP OF KILDARE
AND LEIGHLIN, 1826

Ireland's children divided

Three attempts at establishing integrated education have been made since
the early nineteenth century by determined people endeavouring to rid
Ireland of its divisive system of education. The third and present attempt
has been a battle not entirely won. To understand and put in context this
latest attempt to enable Catholic and Protestant children to sit and learn
together in the same classroom, it is necessary to go back two centuries.
This book chronicles the history of All Children Together, an organisation
in Northern Ireland which played a pivotal role in giving parents the
opportunity to choose integrated education for their children.

   During its long and often strained relationship with Britain, Ireland was
usually a rather belated recipient of beneficial advances made on the other
side of the Irish Sea. A notable exception, surprising as it will be to many,
is that Ireland had a state system of education long before one was
provided in England. However, despite the earnest desire of Bishop Doyle
for schools in Ireland where Catholic and Protestant children could be

educated together (quoted above), the establishment of these was prevented, in the main, by the actions of churches and churchmen for over 150 years.

Before it voted itself out of existence in 1800, the Irish parliament had debated the setting up of a national system of education. After the Act of Union in 1801, the Commission of Irish Education Enquiry sat between 1806 and 1812 and its recommendations on elementary education were developed by the commission of 1824–7, which issued no fewer than nine reports. Meanwhile, the Society for Promoting the Education of the Poor of Ireland – better known as the Kildare Place Society – was operating as the first organisation in Ireland that had the aim of providing elementary education of a non-denominational nature. From 1814 the government supplemented this charity's voluntary subscriptions with grants and by 1831 there were 1,629 schools funded or assisted by the society.[1] Then in 1819 Daniel O'Connell, fast becoming the most prominent campaigner for Catholic emancipation, accused the Kildare Place Society of proselytism because it insisted on compulsory Bible reading for all children, 'without note or comment'. In fact the organisation was moving away from its strict non-denominational stance and gave grants to Protestant proselytising societies from 1820. Decisive action to put into effect the cascade of the commission's recommendations had to wait for the return of the Whigs to power at Westminster in 1830 after decades in opposition.[2]

The architect of the national-school system was the dynamic Lord Edward Stanley, the new chief secretary for Ireland. On 9 September 1831 he told the House of Commons that parliamentary grants to the Kildare Place Society must be withdrawn because although 'five-sixths of Ireland are Roman Catholic, two-thirds of the whole benefit go to Protestant Ulster'. The national system of education he was creating was not the outcome of an act of parliament. Instead, on the instructions of the chief secretary, the National Education Board was set up to administer funds allocated annually by parliament. The board, made up of commissioners nominated by the different religious denominations, was to provide a system of combined 'literary' and separate religious education. In a letter to the board's first president, the duke of Leinster, Stanley explained that no pupil would be required to receive any religious instruction to which his or her parents objected, and the clergy of each denomination were to be given the opportunity of giving religious instruction to the children of their respective creeds. The system was to be one 'from which should be banished even the suspicion of proselytism'. Stanley added that the board would be required to look with 'peculiar favour' on applications to aid schools made jointly by Catholics and Protestants.[3]

Government-funded integrated elementary education

So began an ambitious scheme to provide government-funded integrated elementary education for children of every class and every denomination across the whole of Ireland. It was all the more remarkable that its progenitor, Stanley, was a devout Anglican and a fervent upholder of the established church in Ireland – indeed, he resigned soon afterwards because his government decided to divert some of the funds collected as tithes. Could state-sponsored integrated education work? After Stanley had gone the commissioners adhered closely to his injunction not to have children of different denominations educated separately at public expense. The words the commissioners generally used for Stanley's principle were 'undenominational', 'general', 'combined', 'united' and 'mixed', but today's educationalists would unhesitatingly accept that they intended the national schools to be 'integrated'.

The 'New Reformation' and the 'Catholic Renewal'

The 1830s – and, indeed, the whole of the nineteenth century – were a particularly unpropitious time to attempt the education of all children together. For the first time since the seventeenth century there was a concerted drive to convert Irish Catholics to Protestantism. The 'New Reformation', with its emphasis on faith, the literal truth of the Bible and the rejection of eighteenth-century rationalism, affected every Protestant sect. The Evangelical Revival swept across even the loftiest ranks of the established church (united with the Church of England by the Act of Union 1801, then becoming the Church of Ireland again after disestablishment in 1869) in surging waves throughout the century, the highest crest – heavily influenced by the religious revival in the United States – breaking in 1859. Meanwhile the Catholic Church, shaking off its eighteenth-century deference, gained confidence with every decade. The Catholic Renewal ensured that mass was no longer just to be served to the better off in private houses but to all in the hundreds of chapels being erected across the island. Tens of thousands of adults previously on the fringes of the Catholic Church were baptised and confirmed. Discipline was tightened up and the authority of the hierarchy strengthened.[4]

Modern analysts can discern many similarities between the Protestant Evangelical Revival and the Catholic Renewal. Both displayed intense religious fervour and a triumphalist assertiveness. Both made faith the cornerstone of their beliefs and laid new emphasis on regular prayer, private devotions, participation in church services and Sunday instruction for children. Both embraced a fervent puritanism and were opposed to sexual permissiveness, strong drink and 'pernicious' literature. Both accepted infallibility – one of the Pope and the other of the Bible as God's word – and both adopted English 'Victorian morality' with a greater enthusiasm than the English themselves. And yet most Catholics and Protestants were acutely aware of what divided them.

Sectarian conflict in Ulster

In the late eighteenth century fierce sectarian conflict was largely confined to County Armagh and its borderlands. The routing of Catholic Defenders at the battle of the Diamond in north Armagh in September 1795 was followed by the formation of the Orange Order, an association of lodges pledged to defend 'the king and his heirs so long as he or they support the Protestant Ascendancy'.[5] In the nineteenth century Catholics and Protestants alike were pushed out of over-populated mid-Ulster by the collapse of the domestic linen industry and potato-harvest failures. They were drawn to the rapidly growing industrial centres of Belfast, Londonderry and Portadown. Here, where the low-paid majority – both Catholic and Protestant – eked out a wretched existence in brutalising conditions, religious hatreds had ample opportunity to fester. Though repeatedly condemned by bishops and priests, poorer Catholics joined secret oath-bound sectarian organisations such as the Rockites and Ribbonmen. One Ribbon Society oath included these words:

> I, A.B., Do Swear in the presence of My Brethren and by the Cross of St Peter and of Our Blessed Lady that I will Aid and Support Our holy Religion by Destroying the Hereticks and as far as my power & property will Go not one Shall be excepted … [6]

The prophecies of Pastorini (a pseudonym of the clergyman Charles Walmesley) foretold the violent destruction of Protestant churches in 1825. Cheap editions circulated freely as the year of doom approached and, when it passed quietly, 1844 was fixed as the new date when the 'locusts from the bottomless pit' – the Protestants – would meet their end. Following the activities of evangelical missionaries, Protestant communities were attacked, notably in County Limerick. The Orange Order became stronger and stronger in the nineteenth century, its leadership dominated by Anglican clerics.[7] The order successfully resisted government attempts to suppress its activities and, especially in Ulster, its parades and demonstrations were often the occasion of conflict and death. The most notorious incident occurred at Dolly's Brae near Castlewellan in 1849, where Orangemen killed some 50 Ribbonmen with no loss to themselves. Sectarian conflict was at its worst in Belfast in the second half of the century, the most severe riots being in 1857, 1864, 1872 and 1886.

A 'supreme despotic board'

Meanwhile, Stanley's principle (that national schools were to be non-denominational in character), which underlay the religious regulations for such schools, was being steadily undermined. The most sustained attack came at first from the Presbyterians. The assault was led by Rev. Dr Henry Cooke, who had crushed those refusing to subscribe to the Westminster Confession (a seventeenth-century catalogue of Presbyterian doctrine) at the 1827 Presbyterian Synod. 'Its first essential feature,' Cooke declared of the National Education Board, 'is a supreme despotic board. Three parts Protestant establishment, two parts Roman Catholic, one part Unitarian and one part Church of Scotland ...'[8] Presbyterians had benefited greatly from grants from the Kildare Place Society and realised they could not afford to opt out of the national-school system. They therefore doggedly campaigned to have the rules altered. In particular, they objected to the commissioners' rules regarding the use of the Bible and condemned the book of scripture lessons the board circulated for use during the hours of combined instruction. The Presbyterians insisted that the Bible be read during ordinary school hours. For years the commissioners refused to bend but in 1837 they made a major concession: religious instruction could thenceforth be given at any time during the school day – not, as before, only at the beginning or the end of the day. In the end the commissioners allowed 'non-vested' schools – schools not built with their aid but given grants to pay for books and teachers' salaries – to emerge. These were, in effect, denominational schools run by Presbyterian ministers and elders.

Anglicans (members of the established church) did not attempt to negotiate with the commissioners but instead flooded Westminster with petitions and voiced their objections in both houses of parliament. They objected to priests using the schoolrooms to teach what they called 'the peculiar dogmas, the superstitious rites, the intolerant sentiments, the blasphemous fables, the dangerous deceits, and, in a word, all the errors of popery'. Anglican clergy attempted to create their own schools and, because they attracted substantial donations and endowments, they flourished for some time. These diocesan schools were open to children of all faiths, though all pupils were required to read the Authorised Version of the Bible. By 1849 there were 1,868 Anglican diocesan schools with 111,877 pupils, 37,857 of them Catholics and 15,562 Protestants who were not Anglicans. In the end, however, the established church found the financial burden too heavy and began to seek ways of entering into the national-school system.

One consequence of Anglicans setting up their own diocesan schools was that over much of Ireland the newly established national schools were entirely Catholic in their intake. At first the Catholic Church did not oppose non-denominational schools and three members of the hierarchy were outspoken supporters of national schools: James Doyle, bishop of Kildare and Leighlin; William Crolly, bishop of Down and Connor; and Daniel Murray, archbishop of Dublin and one of the National Education Board commissioners. Members of the hierarchy had, after all, taken a lead in demanding a state-funded national education system. Certainly the new system was better than the one it replaced, whereby government funds could be used to fund proselytising schools.

Gradually the attitude of the Catholic Church changed in favour of denominational schools. In 1836 the Christian Brothers withdrew from the system because of the insistence that religious instruction be kept to specific hours and because crucifixes and statues could not be permanently displayed. Then in 1837 Archbishop John McHale began condemning the commissioners, in particular Archbishop Murray, in letters to the press.

McHale did not have the support of a majority of the hierarchy but the Vatican became involved; in July 1838 the Sacred Congregation of Propaganda gave a negative answer to the question of 'whether, considering the nature and the form of the system of national education in Ireland, the participation of Catholics therein could be tolerated'. This directly opposed resolutions strongly in favour of national schools that had been adopted by the bishops at their annual general meeting earlier in the year.

The commissioners were in a weak position. They had made major concessions to the Presbyterians. Above all, they had largely ignored the regulations laid down by Lord Stanley, which strongly encouraged joint applications by Protestants and Catholics and clearly stated that any applications coming from one denomination only must be investigated. The diocesan schools siphoned off Anglicans from schools intended for a mixed intake, particularly in the three southern provinces. By 1852 only 175 out of a total of 4,795 national schools were jointly managed. In addition, more than three-quarters were exclusively under clerical management. By 1867 only 680 out of 6,349 schools had mixed staffing arrangements. The 'non-vested' status had originally been created to satisfy Presbyterians but most schools in this category were Catholic. In short, by the middle of the century the national-school system had become denominational. In 1865, Isaac Butt, who five years later was to launch the Home Rule movement, wrote the following:

> Walking down King's-Inn-street, the passenger may see, divided by a narrow line, two separate buildings, both bearing the inscription of 'national school'. On the one side of the line is a school under the management of the ladies of a convent; on the other side is the school of a presbyterian church. Not a single protestant child attends the one – not a single Roman Catholic child the other.[9]

Denominational secondary and technical education: the Powis Commission and after

Meanwhile, the numbers of secondary schools continued to grow. Most of these were built and maintained by the churches and other bodies without state aid. The royal schools in Ulster, founded in 1608, were supported by fees and by income from lands confiscated in the plantation of Ulster; diocesan secondary schools were supported by some of the established church's income; but the great majority depended on pupils' fees, charitable donations, the religious orders and endowments.[10] Then, in July 1869, the Irish Church Act disestablished the Anglican Church in Ireland and on 1 January 1871 the Church of Ireland came into existence as a voluntary body. This was to lead to the first serious step towards state-supported secondary education.

The Royal Commission on Primary Education, under the chairmanship of Lord Powis, produced eight volumes of evidence and conclusions in 1870. Included in its 129 conclusions and resolutions were the introduction of the payment of part of teachers' salaries according to results, and compulsory attendance for all children of school age who were not at work. The commissioners also recommended that schools become denominational, with no state or government religious regulations whatever. It took years for the recommendations to be put into effect and some were ignored altogether. The Catholic hierarchy, for example, opposed compulsory schooling. One outcome was that £1 million from the endowments of the disestablished church was to be distributed to intermediate (secondary) schools. The Intermediate Education Board set standards and examinations and gave grants to secondary schools based on examination results. No attempt was made to ensure that schools receiving grants had a mixed intake of pupils.[11]

The Intermediate Education Board had no say in the appointment of teachers or managers and had no control over the schools for the whole period of its existence until 1923. Though in many parts of the island Catholics could be found attending Protestant schools and a very small number of Protestants could be found attending Catholic schools, education at primary and secondary level was entirely denominational at the beginning of the twentieth century. The Department of Agriculture and Technical Instruction for Ireland was set up in 1899, with a grant of £55,000 a year to be invested in technical instruction. Local authorities levied a rate of two pence in the pound for technical instruction. Belfast was then Ireland's largest city and the third most important port (after London and Liverpool) in the United Kingdom, at that time the greatest trading state on earth. It was therefore not surprising that Belfast Corporation's Municipal College of Technology, opened in 1902, was the finest of its kind in Ireland.[12] All the staff were Protestant, however, and the ethos of the college was so denominational that the Ulster Volunteer Force used its premises in 1913–14 (Sir Edward and Lady Carson visited the UVF bakery there in 1914). Even though the college was supported by rates paid by the population at large, it was then alien territory for Catholics. The Catholic Church therefore set up a trades school, run by the Christian Brothers, in Hardinge Street – which, of course, did not receive public funding.

The Catholic hierarchy had condemned Sir Robert Peel's 'godless' Queen's Colleges founded in 1846 in Belfast, Cork and Galway. By 1908 these problems were resolved following the creation of the National University and Queen's University. Queen's University in Belfast succeeded in being non-denominational: Catholic bishops lifted their ban as a new department of scholastic philosophy was created and the proportion of Catholic students there rose from 5 per cent in 1909 to 25 per cent in 1915.[13]

Ireland's education system lags behind

For much of the nineteenth century Ireland had been well ahead of the rest of the United Kingdom in the state provision of primary education. By the early twentieth century Ireland was falling behind. In spite of further legislation in 1892, compulsory attendance was erratically enforced. Too many schools were dilapidated and overcrowded, teachers were poorly paid and inspectors (paid only a little more than half the salaries of their English counterparts) lacked the power to insist on improvements. In Belfast, for example, some 4,000 children of school age did not go to school and one school in Ballymacarrett had over 400 pupils in a building designed for 209. Then followed the Home Rule crisis, the First World War and the turbulent and violent events that led to partition in 1921.

'Religious instruction in a denominational sense during the hours of compulsory attendance there will not be': the Londonderry Act 1923

Northern Ireland came into being in May 1921 with Sir James Craig as prime minister of the first devolved region of the United Kingdom. Intense intercommunal conflict had been raging in Ulster since the spring of 1920 and the primary concern of the new government was the restoration of order. At the same time, however, it had to show it could govern in other respects. Much would have to be done very rapidly. The administrative hub of British rule in Ireland under the union had been Dublin; Belfast, given recognition as a city only in 1888, possessed very few experienced in serving in, let alone managing, even the smallest government department.

Charles S.H. Vane-Tempest-Stewart, the seventh marquess of Londonderry, had made considerable personal sacrifices by joining the Northern Ireland government. One of the richest men in the kingdom, occupying a place at the dazzling centre of London society, he turned down the offer to become air minister to join Craig and his colleagues as minister of education in 1921. Back in Ulster he looked oddly out of place and out of time. Lady Spender remarked that 'he apes his ancestor the great Lord Castlereagh, wears a high black stock over his collar and a very tightly fitting frock coat, and doesn't look as if he belongs to this century at all'.[14] Determined to uphold the union his forebear had forged, Londonderry threw himself enthusiastically into the task, and won the devoted support of his civil servants in spite of his tendency to address them like domestics and to emphasise points by striking his ministerial table with his riding crop.

Charles S.H. Vane-Tempest-Stewart, the seventh marquess of Londonderry, joined the first government of Northern Ireland in June 1921, as leader of the senate and minister of education. Lord Londonderry was responsible for the Education (Northern Ireland) Act 1923 which endeavoured to introduce a system of secular schools, controlled for the first time by local education authorities. The act, known as the Londonderry Act, pleased no one. The Protestant churches secured amendments in 1925 and compulsory Bible instruction in 1930. The Catholic Church refused to allow its schools to be governed by this legislation.

The Catholic hierarchy opposes the Londonderry Act

Londonderry had no doubt learned much from his father, who had been president of the English Board of Education during the crucial years 1902–05, when schools were being placed under local-authority control. Full powers for education in Northern Ireland were not transferred from Dublin until February 1922. In addition, around a third of Catholic primary-school teachers refused to recognise the new ministry in Belfast and were paid salaries by the provisional government in Dublin until October 1922. The Catholic clergy refused to nominate representatives to a committee created by Londonderry in September 1921 and chaired by Robert Lynn, the unionist MP and newspaper editor. The Lynn Committee issued an interim report in June 1922 recommending a new system of elementary education, largely financed by rates and administered by the main local authorities. Londonderry duly put forward a bill based, with one important exception, on the Lynn recommendations. Modelled on the system operating in England since 1902, the legislation did not at first appear particularly controversial.

'Religious instruction in a denominational sense during the hours of compulsory attendance there will not be,' Londonderry declared in 1923, overruling one of the main recommendations of the Lynn Committee.[15] The marquess, like the architects of the national schools the previous century, set out to create a system of elementary schools drawing pupils from all parts of the community. He now faced the intense hostility of both the Catholic and Protestant churches. The managers of Catholic schools had stated their opinion in 1921 that 'the only satisfactory system of education for Catholics is one wherein Catholic children are taught in Catholic schools by Catholic teachers under Catholic auspices'.[16] The Catholic Church, however, had lost the opportunity to protect its interests. Catholics had declined the invitation to serve on the Lynn Committee and for almost a year around a third of Catholic schools refused to cooperate with the Northern Ireland government.

Protestant opposition was slower in coming. In part this was due to the complexity of the Education Bill, which Londonderry steered through parliament in 1923 with remarkable ease, considering the outcome. The act incorporated the Lynn Committee's recommendations that the state pay all teachers' salaries in elementary schools, which were to be in three categories: first, those fully maintained by local authorities and the state; second, 'four-and-two' schools (where the management committee was made up of four persons nominated by the managers or trustees, and two by the local education authority), which were eligible for capital grants and got half the cost of repairs, equipment, heating, lighting and cleaning; and third, the voluntary schools, which got only a contribution towards heating, lighting and cleaning. Londonderry spoke hopefully of having schools where children of different faiths might study and play together

"BIG BOGEY" IN IRELAND.

CARDINAL C–LL–N. "HUBBABOO, ME DARLINTS! GO BACK, GO BACK! YE MUSTN'T BE 'IN THE LIONS' DEN' WID THE LIKES O' THIM WICKED 'SWADDLERS,' ANYHOW! AN' YOU DO, I'LL ANATHEMATISE YE, &c. &c."

Cardinal Paul Cullen opposes interdenominational education. In fact Ulster Presbyterians were the first to oppose 'mixed' national schools. Cartoon by Sir John Tenniel, *Punch*, 18 September 1869.

and allowed denominational religious instruction only outside hours of compulsory attendance. He pointed to Section 5 of the Government of Ireland Act 1920, which made it illegal 'either directly or indirectly to establish or endow any religion', or to set religious tests for teachers maintained out of public funds.

'Protestants awake'

'Protestant teachers to teach Protestant children' was the watchword of clergy who resented their loss of control over teaching appointments and campaigned for Bible instruction in state schools. Led by Rev. Dr William Corkey, manager of nine schools in the Shankill area of Belfast, the campaign gathered strength. The United Education Committee of the Protestant Churches, founded in 1924, saw its opportunity as a general election approached early in 1925. The committee met the Belfast County Grand Orange Lodge and leading politicians on 27 February; a provincial conference was called for 5 March and a stirring handbill was distributed. With the title 'Protestants awake' written in large red letters, the handbill denounced the Londonderry Act, arguing, for example, that 'the door is thrown open for a Bolshevist or an Atheist or a Roman Catholic to become a teacher in a Protestant school'.[17]

On 3 March Londonderry gave a press conference reaffirming that his Education Act would not be changed. The United Education Committee's protest meeting on 5 March was impressively attended and – while the minister was in England – Sir James Craig capitulated and an amending bill was rushed through the Northern Ireland parliament with such speed that it had received royal assent by 13 March. Henceforth clergy could advise on the appointment of teachers; education authorities could take a candidate's religion into account when making a teaching appointment; and teachers were compelled to give 'simple Bible instruction' as part of their contractual duties. Not surprisingly, Londonderry resigned the following year to take on what were for him more congenial opponents – his mining employees in the Durham coalfield.

Bible instruction:
the 1930 act

Corkey and his followers were not yet satisfied and such was the vehemence of their campaign that the principal Protestant and Catholic teachers' unions jointly opposed it. Once again an impending general election, in 1929, gave the United Education Committee its opportunity. James Caulfeild, fifth Viscount Charlemont and Lord Londonderry's more compliant successor, hastily prepared a new bill. This time the Catholic Church did not stand aside. Joseph Devlin, now leading ten nationalists in the Northern Ireland Commons, argued that Catholic schools were worse off than before partition; Catholic bishops threatened to invoke Section 5 of the Government of Ireland Act 1920; the Ancient Order of Hibernians held monster protest meetings across the six counties on Saint Patrick's Day, with 10,000 attending at Omagh; and the *Irish News* published a letter, surrounded by a funereal black band, from the bishop of Down and Connor, Dr Daniel Mageean:

> In view of the attack on Catholic interests in education by the bill now
> before the parliament of the Six Counties, I would ask the clergy of this
> diocese to say in the mass the prayer Pro qua-conque Necessitate ...
> and I would request the laity to join with the priest in praying that God
> may guide and help us in this hour of danger.[18]

The bishop's threat was enough and on 8 May 1930 the prime minister announced at an Orange luncheon in Warrenpoint that an additional clause in the Education Bill would provide 50-per-cent grants for the building and extension of privately managed elementary schools.

The Reformed churches, which had asserted that 'the Protestant cause was in great peril', had triumphed nevertheless. They were able to ensure that only Protestant teachers would be appointed to schools wholly funded by the state and local authorities and that in such schools it was the duty of education authorities to provide Bible instruction in compulsory attendance hours as long as the parents of at least ten parents demanded it. The act's additional clause greatly improved the position of Catholic schools but it was clear the provisions of the Government of Ireland Act 1920 had been flouted. The Education Act 1930 allowed two school systems to operate, the Catholic one partly funded from local and central government sources, and the fully funded one attended almost exclusively by Protestants because 'simple Bible instruction' was in effect mandatory. The reading of any version of the Bible without denominational comment was unacceptable to Catholics, and Dr Mageean explained further:

> We cannot transfer our schools. We cannot accept simple Bible teaching. I wish to emphasise this point. Simple Bible teaching is based on the fundamental principle of Protestantism, the interpretation of sacred Scriptures by private judgement.[19]

Flouting the Government of Ireland Act 1920

The Westminster government was deeply unhappy and, when the bill was in draft, Charlemont and his senior officials were summoned to the Home Office in London. There the permanent secretary, Sir John Anderson, considered that obligatory Bible teaching 'would certainly be regarded by Roman Catholics as unacceptable and constituting a preference in violation of Section 5'. In the end, however, Westminster could not face withholding assent and it was left to a Northern Ireland attorney-general, John MacDermott, to declare in 1945 that the 1930 legislation broke the terms of the Government of Ireland Act 1920.

Had nationalist politicians and the Catholic Church complained to London the matter almost certainly would have been referred to the judicial committee of the Privy Council. In fact, the Catholic hierarchy felt it had done well in the circumstances, retaining complete control over Catholic schools. Bishops could have chosen to opt for 'four-and-two' status, as some Protestant schools had done, but this would have meant sharing management with Catholic laity, which they were not then prepared to do. The result of this total insistence on clerical control in the great majority of Catholic schools was that a generation of Catholic children suffered from inadequate and outmoded facilities by comparison with their Protestant peers. But even if Catholic schools had accepted 'four-and-two' management, as did some schools run by the Christian Brothers and a few in County Fermanagh with considerable success, they still would have been disadvantaged. There is no doubt that Westminster had allowed the unionist government with its unassailable majority to discriminate against Catholics in education provision.

The 1947 act:
'a betrayal'
'utterly unjust treatment'

Meanwhile, governments both in London and Belfast shrank from the responsibility of funding post-primary education for all children. The oldest secondary schools, the royal schools in Dungannon, Enniskillen and Armagh, had been established by James I and funded by plantation land grants. Most of the prestigious grammar schools had been founded in the nineteenth century: apart from bequests, all depended on fees paid by pupils. Apart from exemptions from certain rates and taxes, these schools received no government help but in the interwar years education committees awarded a limited number of 'scholarships' to provide free places to able pupils.

It was not until towards the end of the Second World War that the United Kingdom legislated to ensure compulsory secondary education for all. Applauding the Education Act 1944, commonly known as the Butler Act, the Presbyterian General Assembly resolved that 'any less a measure of reform in Northern Ireland than that now secured for England would be disastrous to the well-being of the people'.[20] Lieutenant-Colonel Samuel Hall-Thompson, the minister of education, duly published his proposals in December 1944 but three long and rancorous years were to pass before the main elements of the Butler Act were applied to Northern Ireland.

At this time the Catholic Church in Ireland was strongly opposed to an extension of state control in areas which it believed to be the responsibility of families and of the individual. Despite complete devotion to the church, ministers of the Fianna Fáil and interparty governments in Dublin were frequently locked in tense conflict with the Catholic hierarchy over plans to extend public services. The hierarchy's condemnation of the Mother and Child Scheme had led to the high-profile resignation of the Republic's minister for health, Dr Noël Browne, in 1951 – an event which provided many northern Protestants with further proof that the Republic was a clericalist state they never wanted to join. Hall-Thompson set out to be more generous than before to Catholic schools: he proposed to increase capital grants to them from 50 to 65 per cent, to provide books free of charge and milk and meals for necessitous children. Far from being satisfied with these plans, Catholic leaders condemned them as putting their schools under severe pressure to join the state system, particularly as the expansion of secondary education would require a great increase in expenditure. Expense could be saved by placing Catholic schools under 'four-and-two' committees, but the bishops rejected this option because it was 'but an instalment to the complete transfer of our schools'. They demanded 100-per-cent funding on the grounds that state schools were in effect Protestant schools.

'One aim of the White Paper is further to ostracise the Catholic voluntary schools,' T.J. Campbell, the nationalist leader, declared at Stormont. All the Catholic bishops in Northern Ireland denounced the proposals in their Lenten pastorals, Cardinal MacRory condemning the spending of so much public money and 'the utterly unjust treatment of a large portion of the population on account of their religious convictions', and Dr Mageean observing that 'from bitter experience' he knew 'what happened in other countries when the state took control of youth'.[21]

It was Protestant opposition, however, which caused Hall-Thompson most trouble when his Education Bill was published in September 1946. The bill set out to scrap the 1930 act's insistence on Bible instruction, seeking only compulsory collective worship and religious instruction in state schools, and it also included a conscience clause for teachers not willing to give religious instruction. Campaigners, organised by the United Education Committee of the Protestant Churches, wheeled into action with packed and angry protest meetings in Belfast, Bangor, Newtownards, Portadown and Derry. In particular, they opposed concessions to Catholics and, while refusing to admit that state schools were denominational, demanded that these schools keep their Protestant ethos.

All over Northern Ireland the protest campaign continued. At St Jude's church hall in Belfast, for example, Rev. Prof. Robert Corkey claimed that state schools would be thrown open to 'Jews, Agnostics, Roman Catholics and Atheists'. A former Northern Ireland minister of education, dismissed for inattention to his duties in 1944, Corkey was interrupted by cries of 'Nonsense!' and 'Tommy-rot!' but most of his listeners warmly applauded him, one person accusing the hecklers of being communists. On 8 November 1946 the Church of Ireland dean of Belfast launched an appeal at the Wellington hall for a £20,000 fighting fund. 'There are no sacrifices we will not make, in order that our Protestant form of inheritance will be made secure', he declared. The next day Hall-Thompson was howled down at a meeting of the Ulster Women's Unionist Council when he said that 'in the state schools the religious instruction must be undenominational'. So great was the uproar that Lady Clark asked to be excused from the chair, the minister left early and members of the audience sang 'Derry's walls' to mark their triumph.[22]

Hall-Thompson also faced strong opposition from his own side at Stormont. In the Senate William Wilton argued that under the conscience clause 'the education authority will have to appoint a teacher without regard to his religious views. He may be a Jew – although I am not saying anything against Jews – he may be a Roman Catholic, or even a member of the IRA.' Herbert Quin, unionist MP for Queen's University, declared: 'I feel there has been a betrayal of Protestantism.' Nevertheless, Hall-Thompson had his way and his bill became law in 1947.[23]

The traditionalists had their revenge two years later: Hall-Thompson proposed to pay Catholic teachers' national insurance and superannuation but the prime minister, Lord Brookeborough, cut the ground from under him by attending a protest meeting of the Grand Orange Lodge in Sandy Row and promising to amend the scheme. Not surprisingly, Hall-Thomson resigned. The new minister was Harry Midgley, who had vituperatively opposed increased funding for Catholic schools.[24]

Remarkably little had been said either in Stormont or outside it about the major features of this postwar education revolution. In the main Hall-Thompson's legislation mirrored the 1944 Butler Act. Pupils would leave elementary school at 11 years old; selected by a qualifying examination, the most able 20 per cent would proceed to grammar schools and the remaining 80 per cent would go on to intermediate or technical schools. The traditional grammar schools successfully resisted direct control and preserved their identity largely intact. All continued to charge fees and to take in a proportion of pupils who had not passed the qualifying examination; yet all obtained grants from the state and were not therefore 'public schools' in the British sense.

The Education Act 1947 took time to be implemented. Even the Belfast Education Committee, more energetic and enlightened than the Belfast Corporation itself, spent two years devising a scheme to put the act's 120 provisions into effect. The counties of Armagh and Tyrone did not have a single intermediate school until 1954 and Fermanagh had none until

1955. The school-leaving age was not raised to 15 until 1957.[25] The system remained strictly segregated. Children were now at school for longer and therefore officially separated on religious lines for longer than before. Apart from at Queen's University, it was only in some rural technical schools and in the growing further-education sector – quietly and unobtrusively – that young people of all creeds were being educated together.

'United in working together'?

Northern Ireland enjoyed all the benefits of the welfare state thanks to growing subventions from the treasury in London. The result was that by the end of the 1960s the region had an apparently flourishing system of compulsory education for children up to the age of 16, which then compared very favourably with that in the Republic of Ireland. GCE A-level and O-level results were higher than the United Kingdom's average. However, Northern Ireland did not create comprehensive schools and the proportion of pupils leaving secondary schools without any qualifications whatsoever was consistently higher than in any other part of the United Kingdom.

Segregated schools remained the order of the day. On Good Friday 1966 the prime minister, Captain Terence O'Neill, expressed the hope that Catholic and Protestant children could be educated together but, recognising that this was a long-term prospect, expressed the wish that those involved might at least be united in working together – in a Christian spirit – to create better opportunities for their children, whether they come from the Falls Road or from Finaghy. Because the Catholic Church remained determined that its schools should retain their voluntary status the cost of education fell more heavily on the Catholic minority than on the rest of the region's population, though O'Neill succeeded in increasing building grants to voluntary schools from 65 to 80 per cent in 1968. Segregation added very considerably to the cost of providing education. In a BBC Northern Ireland *Spotlight special* in 1977, Jeremy Paxman (who began his broadcasting career in Belfast) memorably demonstrated that a modest mid-Ulster town had four second-level schools – a voluntary grammar, a voluntary secondary, a maintained grammar and a maintained secondary. There was some mixing in the prestigious grammar schools: most of these were Protestant, such as Methodist College and Belfast Royal Academy, but the Dominican College at Portstewart had a considerable intake of Protestants also. Some of these schools could, at a pinch, claim to be 'mixed' but there was no serious attempt in any of them to make adjustments in the ethos and governing bodies to accommodate the minority intake.

The storm breaks

In 1969 the Cameron Commission concluded that the emergence of a civil-rights movement in Northern Ireland owed much to the expansion of the Catholic middle class, largely a result of the Education Act 1947, who were less ready to acquiesce in the situation of assumed (or established) inferiority and discrimination than was the case in the past. Though it needed qualification (the percentage of Catholics classed as 'unskilled' rose from 20 to 25 per cent between 1911 and 1971) there was much truth in this assertion. Young educated Catholics, fresh recruits to the middle class, sought radical reform rather than the perpetuation of a simple demand for an end to partition. By now the age of television had come into its own. Popular action could attract immediate worldwide attention and the year 1968 provided numerous examples: the peaceful defiance of Prague as the Soviet tanks rolled in; demonstrations against the Vietnam War; the continuing campaign for black civil rights in America; and the students' revolt in Paris. By the end of the year Northern Ireland, an apparently quiet backwater of the United Kingdom, was catapulted by the media into a position of global prominence. The region's age-old problems would be exposed to examination by an audience of a size not thought possible just a few months previously.

The shared experience of the horrors of the Blitz in 1941 had brought a slight easing in tensions but Northern Ireland remained a bitterly divided society. This corrosive bitterness surfaced during, for example, the 1949 elections, marches on the Longstone Road in south Down in the 1950s, the Divis Street riots in 1964 and the UVF murders in 1966. Such episodes rarely attracted interest outside the region. Unionist governments between 1921 and 1963 had not created the divisions in the people they ruled but they had done little to assuage them. O'Neill was the first prime minister to state clearly that reconciliation was a central part of his programme.

However, despite his mould-breaking gestures of conciliation, O'Neill eventually created intense frustration within the minority by his inability to deliver thoroughgoing reform. Meanwhile, more and more loyalists became convinced that he was conceding too much and turned against him. Quite suddenly, when images of the Derry civil-rights march of 5 October 1968 flashed across the world, Northern Ireland was destabilised. The sectarian dragon had been fully reawakened and the region was plunged into a near-revolutionary crisis, characterised by bitter intercommunal conflict and protracted violence and destruction.

The killing began in earnest in August 1969 and reached its peak in the two years following the imposition of internment in August 1971. The violence was accompanied by the biggest enforced movement of population in Europe since 1945–6. Was there anything that could be done to assuage the hatreds, suspicions and fears long etched into folk memory? How could the task of attempting to close over the fissures running across Northern Ireland's society begin? A few were coming to the conclusion that the education of children apart was approaching the root of the problem. These people were to be the founders of All Children Together.

2

McIvor's shared-schools plan, 1974

I don't see a wholesale shift to shared status, but I
hope that over the years there will be a gradual
growth, which would embrace existing schools as well
as new ones. I also hope that a start could be made
before the end of this year on shared schools at the
nursery schools level ... Successive Ministers of
Education in Northern Ireland have tried to grasp
this nettle of integrated schools but did not get
very much support for it. I feel I must get on
with the task.

BASIL McIVOR, 1974[1]

The power-sharing executive

'I remember vividly, at the last meeting of the negotiations on 22
November, seeing tears coursing down Willie's face at the moment he
knew his mission had been accomplished.'[2] So wrote Basil McIvor,
recalling the reaction of Secretary of State William Whitelaw to the
agreement at Stormont in 1973 which led directly to the
intergovernmental conference at Sunningdale and Northern Ireland's first
experiment in power-sharing. Elected in February 1969 for the new
constituency of Larkfield in south Belfast, McIvor was firmly on the liberal
wing of his party. He knew many of his constituents were suspicious of his

support for reform but he resisted attempts to win him over to the new Alliance Party, formed in 1970. In September 1971 the prime minister, Brian Faulkner, had appointed him minister of community relations, a post which had been created in 1969 on the initiative of Jim Callaghan when he was home secretary. 'The most I could hope to do,' McIvor wrote later, 'was to make people realise they had a problem, that it was a soluble problem but that only they could solve it.'[3]

Northern Ireland had entered the most violent phase in its history when Faulkner introduced internment in August 1971. The one-sided application of imprisonment without trial united nationalists in intense opposition. Very early on Monday, 9 August thousands of soldiers set out in arrest squads, each accompanied by an RUC Special Branch officer to identify suspects. By 7.30 a.m. 342 men had been seized. Terrible violence followed. The death toll for 1971 had been 180; 497 died in 1972, the worst year of the Troubles; and 263 died in 1973. In the spring of 1972 Edward Heath's Conservative government concluded that control of security must pass to Westminster. McIvor supported Faulkner in resigning rather than accepting this reduction of power and remained a close ally of the former Northern Ireland premier. They accepted the principle of power-sharing and played a key role in the Sunningdale Conference in December 1973.

Basil McIvor, politician and lawyer. Called to the Bar, Northern Ireland 1950; unionist MP for Larkfield, Northern Ireland parliament 1969–72; minister of community relations 1971–2; minister of education in the Northern Ireland power-sharing executive 1974; resident magistrate 1976–93; chairman, Board of Governors, Lagan College, Belfast 1981–2004; joined ACT following the collapse of the power-sharing executive 1974; awarded OBE 1991.

When the power-sharing executive began work on the last day of 1973, McIvor was the new minister of education. The high hopes of Sunningdale rapidly gave way to gloom when a Westminster general election in February 1974 made it clear that the great majority of Protestants in Northern Ireland were opposed to the executive. Gerry Fitt, the SDLP leader and deputy chief executive, was elected for west Belfast but all the remaining newly returned MPs for Northern Ireland were unionists opposed to power-sharing. McIvor was acutely aware that the time available for implementing educational change was likely to be exceedingly short. The most immediate task was to work out the relationship between the Department of Education and the new education and library boards. An overhaul of teacher training was widely considered overdue and campaigns to replace the '11-plus' qualifying examination were gaining ground.

'I feel I must get on with the task'

Could education make any contribution to reducing the bitter divisions fuelling the violence? McIvor's short spell as minister of community relations had caused him to ask this question more often than before and his brief included 'a detailed investigation of the role of education in the promotion of community harmony, and the development of pilot experiments, after consultation with interested parties, in integrated education'.[4] Meanwhile, the Joseph Rowntree Memorial Trust had invited Sir John Wolfenden to conduct a study of ways in which the educational system might help to create better understanding between the two communities in Northern Ireland. The report was not released but some form of integrated education was certainly among Wolfenden's recommendations.

McIvor had been one of those consulted by Wolfenden; he asked his permanent secretary, Arthur Brooke, to have his civil servants investigate and report back on the possibility of shared schools within the system.[5] With a speed not then usual in the department's home, Rathgael House, the report, together with a draft 'shared-schools plan', was ready by the end of April 1974. Attempting to cope with mounting opposition to the Sunningdale agreement and well aware that its days were numbered, the executive had to squeeze the item onto its permanently packed agenda. McIvor did not even get the opportunity to lobby members of the executive beforehand.

The scheme was to establish a third category of school (in addition to controlled and maintained) to be known as a 'shared school'. It was to be available to Catholic and Protestant parents alike who wished to see their children educated together. McIvor had written already to the leaders of the main churches to explain the proposals. Just before going into the executive meeting to present his scheme, the minister got a telephone message from Cardinal Conway warning him not to interfere with the schools. On the way in he mentioned this to Faulkner, who said he should carry on and that he would have his support.

The executive unanimously approved and welcomed the scheme,

McIvor recalled, 'with the exception of John Hume, who was less than enthusiastic'.[6] Immediately afterwards McIvor held a press conference and that evening, 30 April 1974, John Wallace reported for the *Belfast Telegraph*: 'Mr. McIvor declared his own basic belief that the mixing of schoolchildren would contribute to the reduction of community tension.' McIvor continued:

The Northern Ireland Executive
Office of Information Services
News Release

Stormont Castle, Belfast, BT4 3ST.   Telephone Enquiries: Belfast 63011
Ulster Office, 11 Berkeley Street, London W1X 6BU   Telephone Enquiries: 01-493 0601

STORMONT CASTLE, BELFAST
30 April 1974

MINISTER OF EDUCATION
STATEMENT ON MIXED SCHOOLING

I wish to put to the Assembly a suggestion to facilitate the provision of schools catering for children of different denominations.

First, I must declare my basic belief that the mixing of schoolchildren would contribute to the reduction of community tension in Northern Ireland.

Although I realise that the Churches have some hesitation about mixed schooling, I ask them earnestly to consider the very special needs of Northern Ireland and to join with a power-sharing Executive in a constructive approach to meeting these needs; and I, of course, as Minister of Education, must do everying that I can to help.

One of the grounds for the hesitation of the churches is an understable anxiety about the religious upbringing of their children in schools not under their own management. The management of schools is, however, a matter that we in the Assembly can do something about.

Under the present law, 50 per cent of the management committee of (State) controlled primary and intermediate schools are representatives of "transferors". Since in the past it was the Protestant Churches that transferred their schools, the de facto position is that these schools have 50 per cent Protestant Church management. The Roman Catholic Church in the past opted not to transfer its schools, with the result that now most Roman Catholic primary and intermediate schools are "maintained" schools; this gives them two-thirds membership of the management committee, freedom over the appointment of staff, and payment from public funds of all capital and running costs, except 20 per cent of new capital expenditure.

'I wish to put to the Assembly a suggestion to facilitate the provision of schools catering for children of different denominations' – this was the opening sentence of McIvor's shared school plan, announced on 30 April 1974, when he was minister of education in the short-lived Northern Ireland power-sharing executive. The plan had a budget of £13 million for schools, provided Catholic and Protestant churches shared in their management.

I don't see a wholesale shift to shared status, but I hope that over the years there will be a gradual growth, which would embrace existing schools as well as new ones. I also hope that a start could be made before the end of this year on shared schools at the nursery schools level ... Successive Ministers of Education in Northern Ireland have tried to grasp this nettle of integrated schools but did not get very much support for it. I feel I must get on with the task.[7]

McIvor realised 'that the churches had some hesitation about mixed schooling but he asked them earnestly to consider the very special needs of Northern Ireland and to join with a power-sharing executive in a constructive approach to meeting those needs'.[8]

By coincidence, leaders of the main churches were meeting together at a hotel in Ballymascanlon, County Louth. They had been informed beforehand of the minister's scheme but they were not prepared for the announcement of the plan on the evening news. Cardinal Conway was interviewed and guardedly said he could not comment on the plan – he had not discussed it with McIvor and he was not quite sure what was in the minister's mind. A spokesman at the cardinal's residence said:

The Catholic Bishops ... shall, of course, examine very carefully what the Minister has said but one hopes he realises that very grave issues are involved. One must regret the implication that it was the denominational schools which caused the present trouble. This is an alibi which ought to be discarded.[9]

The Church of Ireland gave the proposals a tepid welcome; the Presbyterians provided solid approval; and only the Methodists provided warm backing for them.

Church reactions

Dr Michael Ramsay, the Church of England archbishop of Canterbury, gave his approval within hours of the scheme's publication – he was sure that jointly controlled schools could go a long way towards easing the bitterness between the two communities. His sister church, the Church of Ireland, was more cautious. Its Education Board had called for experiments in integrated schooling but had also concluded that integration could only come when the two main divisions in the community were ready for it. The board felt that the best place to start was with shared sixth-form teaching and added, 'We envisage as socially desirable the schooling together of young children at nursery level in 'mixed' areas.'[10]

The Presbyterian Church had already passed a resolution in favour of the integration of schools at its 1971 General Assembly. Now the moderator, the Rt Rev. Dr John Orr, announced that the Presbyterian Church would be fully prepared to examine the proposals 'with great interest, would feel encouraged by them, and would hope to participate fully in negotiations that would bring the children of our torn community more closely together in mutual trust and understanding'. He was certain that 'integrated education would best serve the social, economic and educational needs of the community'.[11]

In short, the Methodist Church had wholeheartedly supported the plans; the Presbyterians had given them a broad welcome; the Church of Ireland had been cautious and circumspect in its support; and the Catholic Church was hostile. In a detailed analysis entitled 'No power sharing by the church?', John Cooney, the education correspondent for the *Irish Times*, observed of the church summit conference the previous Wednesday:

> All solemnly examined progress reports on a variety of church and social issues; all studiously avoided mention of the overnight proposal of the Northern Ireland Executive for shared schooling. Mr. McIvor had caught the churchmen with their ecclesiastical frocks around their ankles. That day's conference may go down in Irish church history as a classic example of the collective dilatoriness of the churches in face of the current Northern Ireland crisis. Not only did they not take the initiative in proposing some scheme of joint schooling in the period between the first part of their 'summit' last September, and the reconvening last week; they did not even find time to discuss the northern Executive proposal ... the co-chairman of the conference, Cardinal Conway, had evaded making any press comment on the proposal ... In other words, as Fr. John Harriott, an English Jesuit, recently observed, the Northern Irish Catholic Church is unwilling to make any concession on such a negotiable an issue as education.[12]

Cardinal Conway continued to avoid expressing his views in public and it was left to others in his church to rule out McIvor's scheme. In fact, only a month previously Dr William Philbin, bishop of Down and

Connor, had warned Catholic parents that if their children were educated in non-Catholic schools they could not expect to be confirmed. Indeed, in his speech to the assembly introducing the scheme, McIvor referred to Dr Philbin's 'unfortunate statement'. Fr Denis Faul, principal of St Patrick's Academy, Dungannon and a fearless critic of both republican militants and the security forces, stressed 'the right of Catholics to educate their children in schools that are guaranteed by their trustees and their staff to reflect the total value system and atmosphere of their homes and chapels':

> An oppressed community, which has been and is still the recipient of much social and legal injustice and which has lacked any great wealth, showed its scale of values when it invested the equivalent of £25 million in school in the last 25 years and is still continuing to do so.[13]

The Rt Rev. Msgr Mullally, vicar-general of the diocese of Down and Connor, said that, as far as the Catholic conscience in education was concerned, he did not see how the 'enormous difficulties' inherent in the scheme could be overcome.[14]

Canon Padraig Murphy of St John's Catholic Church on the Falls Road in Belfast got an opportunity to express his views when he was interviewed for the *Belfast Telegraph* by Ted Oliver. Described by Oliver as 'a big man – six foot three – with an ear for music and a fine tenor voice', Murphy believed that:

> If you had shared schools now the problem would be that you would have people actively opposed to the Catholic Church. What would happen as regards the crib at Christmas? Every Catholic school has a crib to show the children what Christmas is all about. I think there would be no crib in an integrated school because some people would say it was Catholic … then the next thing to go would be the Crucifix. And where would you stop after that?[15]

He was certain that commitment to Christianity had been weakened by state control of education. 'Conscientious Protestant clergymen and teachers have admitted to me,' he continued, 'that one of the worst mistakes they ever made was in agreeing to come into a state system early in the century.'

> They have admitted that the product of the state school is not often a deeply-committed Protestant. I say that without offence and I want to

stress that. The Protestant religion has suffered as a result of handing over the responsibility of religious teaching in schools to the state. The commitment has been weakened and diluted … we are being invited to make the same mistake.[16]

The canon looked forward to 'two co-equal religious communities facing each other' which 'could unite to act as a buttress against atheism'. He believed that children of different religions should be educated apart and that youth clubs, debates, sport and music (he was a patron of the Northern Ireland Youth Orchestra) would provide sufficient contact.[17] The *Sunday News*, which attracted readers from both sides of the divide, was scathing about Canon Murphy's initial response to the shared-schools plan, describing it as 'a declaration of medieval theology'. 'It is no use, Basil McIvor,' it advised, 'coaxing people like these. Lay down the law, impose stiff penalties, and stand up to them.' This columnist was almost a lone voice, not only in advocating draconian compulsion, but also in criticising McIvor's plan to manage shared schools with clergy from the main denominations – 'why on earth you propose to perpetuate and strengthen clerical domination of our failed education system I will never understand'.[18]

Reaction of teachers' unions and political parties

The principal teaching unions did not hesitate to support the shared-schools plan. Brian Thom, chairman of the Ulster Teachers' Union (largely representing staff of controlled schools), told the press that he was confident that his organisation would go along with the minister's proposals. Gerry Quigley, general secretary of the Irish National Teachers' Organisation (an all-island body favoured by staff of maintained schools), reminded reporters that he and his organisation were on record as advocating mixed schools as early as 1969.[19]

And what about the politicians? 'But how many people in the North really want integrated education?' Conor O'Clery asked in the *Irish Times* the morning after McIvor had announced his scheme. He continued: 'From ruffled reaction within the Assembly and outside it there is no mass movement in its favour … if there is any move, it will obviously have to be very tentative and very slow.' Support in the assembly was polite, sometimes warm but never rapturous. Some anti-Sunningdale unionists took the opportunity to take a swipe at either their opponents or the Catholic Church. 'I welcome this announcement,' John Taylor said. 'However, I note with despair, the evident opposition to Mr. McIvor's suggestion by some of the more bigoted of his supporters within the SDLP.'[20]

The party most likely to be divided by the shared-schools plan was the SDLP. It was essentially the constitutional voice of the Catholic minority; a high proportion of its leading members had been educated in the region's most prestigious Catholic grammar schools; and several spokesmen were or had been teachers in Catholic schools. At the same time the party was a coalition which included some Protestants, former members of the Northern Ireland Labour Party and the Republican Labour Party, and former civil-rights activists – all of whom were likely to welcome any move towards integrated schooling.

At its conference in December 1973 the SDLP had voted on a motion to investigate the possible benefits of integrated education and the 69 votes in favour and 42 against revealed significant opposition, particularly as few expected rapid and dramatic changes in Northern Ireland's education system when so many other acute problems had to be tackled. When McIvor put his proposals to the executive he was given complete support for the final draft of his statement. However, as John Wallace put it in the *Belfast Telegraph*, 'All the parties in the Executive knew they risked criticism, none more so perhaps than the SDLP, for publicly advocating the idea without first of all having canvassed the Church leaders for their views'.[21]

When McIvor took his statement to the assembly it became obvious that some SDLP deputies were uncomfortable. Seamus Mallon, assembly member for Armagh, described the minister's speech as 'inaccurate in its claims' and 'superficial in its approach to a highly sensitive area of community life'. Mallon referred to a recent speech made by McIvor in Craigavon in which he referred to Tullygally Primary School as a pilot scheme in integrated education. Rather, Mallon believed, children from one side of the sectarian divide had been forced to attend the school because work on their own had not been completed; consequently, McIvor's speech had drawn facile conclusions about a scheme which did not exist. 'I don't know whether it would, as the Minister suggested, relieve community tension,' Patrick O'Donoghue, assembly member for south

Down, observed. 'I would hope we will not have any sudden or instant solutions to this problem.' However, another SDLP speaker, Hugh News, also an assembly member for Armagh, welcomed the minister's statement without reservation as 'a step in the right direction'.[22]

Several members of the assembly took the opportunity to criticise the Catholic Church. The pro-assembly unionist, Lord Brookeborough, assembly member for north Down, said that integration at school level had been operating for years in Fivemiletown before it had been 'broken up' by the Catholic Church, which had established separate schools. Lord Dunleath of the Alliance Party welcomed the minister's statement and supported the freedom of parents to choose 'without the sanctions which are operated by the Roman Catholic Church'.[23]

On 8 May McIvor presented the 1974/5 estimates for the Department of Education, which included a major scheme to make provision for nursery schools across the region. In his speech he said that all involved in the education service had 'a role to play in moving our society back to a position of stability … to minimise the long-term effects of the mindless violence and destruction'. This provided Mallon with the opportunity to mend fences. He welcomed the way in which the minister had approached the problem through his shared-schools recommendations; and the concept of shared schools, as outlined by McIvor, was 'one to be welcomed' and was 'one which did not make the mistake of trying to impose a new system or which sought to adapt a system which was possibly too involved to be adapted properly'.[24]

He was in favour of pilot schemes but 'these would have to be clearly defined as pilot schemes from the start.' Brian Canavan, SDLP assembly member for Derry, said that integrated education would be a powerful force in repairing the terrible wounds which the community had suffered. Aidan Larkin, SDLP member for mid-Ulster, said that the integration of grammar and secondary schools was the really important development required. He asked for an unequivocal statement of commitment to the principle of comprehensive education. Mallon attacked the '11-plus' system, describing it as 'educationally unsound' and 'a total and unmitigated disaster'.[25]

Considering that the very existence of a power-sharing executive was anathema both to militant republicans and to an undoubted majority of unionists, McIvor's shared-schools proposals generated considerable debate and more interest than might have been expected. 'The arguments going on just now,' Robert Fisk reported for *The Times*, 'are on an infinitely larger and braver scale than in the past.' He continued:

> A little more than a year ago, for instance, a report by the advisory council for education in Northern Ireland said that 'it would be unrealistic to expect the introduction of integrated schools in the near future'. The document, which was examining the reorganisation of secondary education in Ulster, then continued to suggest 'further progress … towards a reduction of barriers'. In a manner which might even be described as pussyfooting, joint careers exhibitions, leavers' conferences and seaside holidays seemed to be the best that the advisory council could offer for teachers who wanted to prevent the bitter sectarian conflict in their society.[26]

A voice for the laity

McIvor, described by Fisk as 'a quiet and academic Protestant', asked parents in particular to express their views. 'Some teachers too feel,' Fisk observed, 'that the Catholic Church could find itself on the losing side if it does not take note of its own flock.' A County Armagh headmaster, with a mixed intake in his school, put it bluntly to Fisk, saying that 'if the Church insists on this conflict, then a lot of Catholic parents could well decide on their own freedom'. Fisk continued:

> Some Catholic parents already seem set – albeit against their will – on this very same journey. In North Down just now a group of them under the name of All Children Together are trying to provide ways of providing religious education for their children outside the Catholic school system. Their efforts have incurred what amounts to a prohibition from the Bishop of Down and Connor; if their children do not receive their religious education at Catholic schools and remain instead at state ones then those children will not be confirmed.[27]

Cecilia Linehan (known to all as Cecil), then chairman of All Children Together (at that stage a group of Catholic-only parents which had indeed been meeting since the early 1970s to work out ways of instructing their children in the Catholic faith outside the Catholic school system) listed for Fisk arguments many parents and members of ACT were making: 'It is obvious if Mr McIvor's plan is to get off the ground then the lay people will have to make their feelings known. When is it going to be accepted that the laity are part of the church?' She continued:

> Parents want to have more say in the way schools are run. If clergymen
> do not want to co-operate, let parents and lay people get on with the
> job. People are always saying that the system of integrated education
> would not work in parts of Belfast – but why should it be started in
> Belfast? One man at Maynooth said the other day that the system would
> not work in working-class areas but what does he know about the
> working-class?[28]

Cecil Linehan was given an opportunity to comment in detail on the
minister of education's plan in the *Irish Times*. McIvor's statement, she
began, 'if not very specific in outline, is serving a useful purpose, by
keeping discussion alive'. It possibly created the climate 'where Churches
will be forced to come together because the laity wishes them to'. She
continued:

> It is doubtful whether there will be any dialogue between the Church
> leaders and people until a sizeable proportion of the Catholic laity is
> involved. And it is doubtful whether many will make their true feelings
> felt unless they cease being afraid – afraid of incurring clerical wrath on
> the one hand, and of their children losing their religion if removed from
> segregated schools, on the other.[29]

An important part of her thesis was that Catholic clergy had not yet
understood the implications of the Second Vatican Council and in
particular of the *Declaration on Christian education*.

> But fear of pastor seems a strange sentiment in the post-conciliar
> Church where one would expect to find increased communication,
> greater emphasis on parish councils and activities and a recognition of
> the role of the laity. One wonders in how many Catholic homes and
> houses have the documents of Vatican II been discussed and one
> wonders how much progress can be made without such discussion.
> How else can we say to each other 'the Church is keenly aware of her
> very grave obligations to give zealous attention to the moral and
> religious education of all her children. To those large numbers of them
> being trained in schools which are not Catholic She needs to be present
> with Her special affection and help[?]'
>
> This was said nine years ago in the declaration on Christian
> Education of the second Vatican Council. Where is that special affection
> and help? Why is it given in other countries, but not in Northern
> Ireland?[30]

More people than ever before had been getting in touch with ACT and Linehan made it clear that neither she nor the members of the ACT movement were anti-clerical but simply opposed to clergy remaining in control of schools. 'If, and this is the crux of the matter,' she continued, 'parents felt the Church was with them and no longer disapproving or doubting their sincerity, their offers to participate and help would just pour forth.'

> We could then be in sight of Catholic children growing up in Northern Ireland fully committed to their religion and integrated into society. Their religion would be precious to them, in no way connected with the way their parents vote at elections and not causing them to lurk in the shadow of the gunman. They would grow up also trusting other people and if there is one commodity in very short supply in Northern Ireland, it is trust.[31]

In his article, 'No power sharing by the church?', also in the *Irish Times*, John Cooney was more acerbic. An important factor in bringing the churchmen to the conference table in Louth 'had been growing realisation that their performance during the Northern crisis had lacked public credibility'.

> However, it would seem that the churchmen have not sufficiently come to terms with the central importance of sectarianism in the pattern of violence. This psychological incapacity to acknowledge the nature of violence has prevented the churches from committing themselves fully to eradicating 'tribal religion'. A test of their ecumenical seriousness would have been to consider creating a shared school system in order to dismantle a basic reinforcement of tribal religion: the segregated school system ...
>
> Clearly, the absence of any mention of the proposal on the debating floor of the Dundalk conference was a result of the wish of the Protestant Churches not to embarrass or clash with the Roman Catholic Church on education – especially in view of the fact that the co-chairman of the conference, Cardinal Conway, had evaded making any press comment on the proposal ...
>
> This reaction of the Northern Catholic Church is, on the surface, puzzling. Most people of good will who are sick of the violence are not arguing that the segregated school system is a sole or absolute cause of the violence or even that it is a cause of violence. Some would argue that it is a contributory factor and many more, in the words of Mr.

McIvor, would take the view that 'the mixing of school children would contribute to the reduction of community tension'.[32]

Cooney added that the proposal was coming from the first ever Protestant–Catholic administration in Northern Ireland and that denominational religious teaching would be provided within the shared-schools system. He continued:

> This raises the question as to why on the one hand the Northern Catholic Church should be in favour of the Unionist political system giving way to power-sharing but on the other hand it wants to maintain a divided education system. Is this not the mentality of a ghetto Church that is steeped in the thought of the Catholic Church before Vatican II and Pope John?
>
> In the light of the Council the traditional argument that the Catholic school system is necessary for the maintenance of Catholicism no longer sounds so convincing – as witness the dissidence within that Church from the All Children Together movement.
>
> The whole spirit of the Second Vatican Council and the shared communal experience of violence provide more than sufficient warrant for a positive response by the Catholic Bishops to the McIvor proposal. But, as yet, like the Bourbons, the Northern Irish Catholic Church has learned nothing and forgotten nothing.[33]

The fall of the power-sharing executive in May 1974

Sadly, the prospect of being able to send their children, if they wished, to shared schools was not the most immediate concern of parents in Northern Ireland. Could the region's first experiment in power-sharing possibly survive? Harold Wilson, the British prime minister, had visited Northern Ireland on 18 April and declared that there could be no alternative to the Sunningdale agreement. The initiative, however, was passing to others. The assembly clearly no longer represented the views of the people; this had been plain since the February general election. Loyalist politicians talked of ways of toppling the executive but they could come to no agreement on whether a strike or a boycott should be attempted, or at what point extra-parliamentary pressure should be applied. In the end their hands were forced by a group of Protestant workers calling themselves the Ulster Workers' Council.

On Monday, 13 May 1974 four assembly members – Ian Paisley, John

Taylor, Ernest Baird and Austin Ardill – met the UWC and were told bluntly: 'We've got the strike organised – it begins tomorrow at six when the vote is taken in the Assembly.' On Tuesday, 14 May the assembly passed an amendment expressing faith in power-sharing by 44 votes to 28. At 6.08 p.m. Harry Murray and Bob Pagels, representing the UWC, informed journalists at Stormont that a strike would begin in protest against ratification of the Sunningdale agreement.

For 15 days a self-appointed junta in league with loyalist paramilitaries made an entire region of the United Kingdom ungovernable. For much of this period most of the people of Northern Ireland had been deprived of electricity, gas, transport, fresh food, piped water, employment and other facilities taken for granted in any western-European state. There was widespread intimidation and violence. Car bombs, driven in and planted by the UVF in Monaghan and central Dublin, killed or mortally wounded a total of 32 people and injured at least another hundred. Only the toppling of the democratically elected power-sharing executive prevented the region from sliding into further chaos.

On Monday, 27 May Hugo Patterson, the official spokesman for the Northern Ireland Electricity Service, told Barry Cowan in a BBC interview: 'This shutdown is on, it's complete, it's final, it's irrevocable ... We are past the point of no return.'[34] At 1.20 p.m. Faulkner resigned and a loyalist demonstration at Stormont became a massive victory rally. As McIvor later acknowledged, 'the Executive was not brought down by the strikers alone. The majority of Protestants simply did not want the Executive and were passive supporters of the strike.'[35] The opponent of Sunningdale, John Taylor, told McIvor that the shared-schools plan 'was the only creative idea that emanated from the powersharing Executive'.[36] In 1977 Faulkner wrote to McIvor and said that although power-sharing had cost him his political career, 'at least we had laid an educational foundation stone, if nothing else'.[37] The direct-rule ministers who replaced the executive showed little inclination to attempt the introduction of McIvor's plan. But, for the first time, integrated schools seemed an achievable objective and not just a dreamer's fantasy.

3

The formation of All Children Together

I do not think we can talk about peace and
reconciliation without talking about children – our
children. They are our hope for the future – our
citizens of tomorrow. But how can we become one
community, one people, when our children continue
to grow up separately?

BETTIE BENTON, 1974[1]

In 1982, Thelma Sheil, in a dissertation presented to the Ulster
Polytechnic (now the University of Ulster), described how she met Bettie
Benton in Bangor, County Down, Northern Ireland, as they waited for
their children outside Ballyholme Primary School and became involved in
the movement which eventually became All Children Together. Sheil said:

> In the stormy climate of civil unrest in the early 1970s, the two mothers
> often discussed the worsening situation and were distressed by the
> increasing polarisation of the two communities in Northern Ireland.
> They speculated on how the country might benefit if more Protestant
> and Roman Catholic children had the opportunity to make early
> friendships by going to school together. They both became involved in
> the Parent Teacher Association of the school and served together on the
> committee, the Catholic mother, Mrs Elizabeth Benton, becoming
> Chairman.[2]

In the late 1960s, several Catholic parents in the north-Down area were
sending their children to state-controlled schools – in effect, Protestant

schools. These parents faced this problem: how would they obtain religious instruction for their children and, have them prepared for the sacraments of first holy communion (usually made at age seven or eight in the Catholic Church) and confirmation (made at age eleven or twelve)? In the words of Thelma Sheil:

Although they were not attending Roman Catholic schools, Mrs Benton and other Catholic parents wanted their children brought up in the fellowship of their Church and prepared for their First Communion and Confirmation. They were having difficulty in obtaining any help from the Church as they strove to instruct their children in the tenets of the Catholic faith. A small group of Roman Catholic parents in Bangor had come together and formed a Sunday School and were taking turns in instructing their children.

On 24th March, 1972, a letter appeared in the local press from a Mrs Cecilia Linehan of Holywood advocating that integrated education 'should be encouraged where possible'. She suggested that centres of religious education should be set up to help Catholic parents (like herself) whose children were not attending Catholic schools. She invited interested parents to contact her. Mrs Benton did so and told her about the Bangor Catholic Sunday School. It was agreed that a meeting should be arranged with the other people who had contacted Mrs Linehan and Mrs Benton's group. Subsequently a meeting took place in June, 1972, at which it was agreed, to co-operate together, ideally with the help of the Roman Catholic Church, to provide religious instruction for their children, and that the desirability of integrated education would not be forgotten.[3]

This group met regularly for the purpose of tackling the immediate problem of religious education of their children.[4]

INTEGRATION – HERE

2370/3/1972

Sir,—Most people intending to "stick it out" in Northern Ireland, I am sure, must be wondering in what way we can help our children.

One solution often put forward is to integrate the schools. While I do not regard integrated education as anything like a panacea for all our ills, I do think it should be encouraged where possible.

For a variety of reasons, I, as a Catholic parent, will not be sending my children to a Catholic school. This leaves my husband and myself with the responsibility for the religious education of our children. (We do not have Sunday Schools as most Protestant Churches do). I suggest, therefore, that the setting-up of centres of religious education, staffed by trained catechists, would be a great help to Catholic parents who feel as we do. No Catholic parent decides to send his or her child to a non-Catholic school without some degree of soul-searching. I would be most grateful, therefore, to hear from any other interested parents on the premise that a problem shared is a problem halved.—Yours, etc.,

C. F. LINEHAN (Mrs.)
26 My Lady's Mile,
Holywood.

Following the publication of this pivotal letter, Cecil Linehan was contacted by Bettie Benton and learnt of the parent-run Sunday school in Bangor. From this meeting All Children Together was formed.

Thelma Sheil had been delighted to meet Bettie Benton, a kindred spirit from across the religious divide. Cecil Linehan, seeking help with the religious education of her own children, the eldest of whom was due to start at a non-Catholic school the following September, had known nothing of the Bangor Sunday school until Benton had responded to her letter in the press in March 1972. From the combined struggle of the Catholic parents who wanted to have freedom of choice in school, supported warmly by Thelma and other Protestant neighbours and friends (particularly Margaret Kennedy of Bangor and Bill Brown of Holywood respectively), Northern Ireland's first movement for integrated education emerged.

Catholic clergy at this time were fully aware that some Catholic children in the diocese of Down and Connor were attending non-Catholic schools. Parents had asked for help with the religious instruction of their children but this had not been provided. Instead, children were either given private tuition or instructed by their parents. Until 1969 children made their first confession and first holy communion with the other children of the parish at the age of seven or eight. The sacrament of confirmation was conferred by the bishop when he visited the parish every three years. Children not attending Catholic schools were examined beforehand by the local clergy to make certain they were properly prepared for the reception of the sacraments.

Then, in 1969, the diocese changed its policy. Cards were issued to every child prior to acceptance for confirmation. These cards were only given to children attending the local Catholic schools or obtained directly from the bishop himself, if he considered that the child's attendance at a non-Catholic school was a 'special' case and therefore acceptable to him. All parents were advised to provide in writing to the bishop their reasons for choosing a school which was not a Catholic one. This would then be investigated by the local parish clergy.

Why did some Catholic parents not send their children to Catholic schools? Firstly, some Catholic parents, in sympathy with the nascent philosophy of All Children Together, believed that if their children had the chance to grow up in school with Protestant children, 'fear and mistrust would diminish, and understanding grow through familiarity with the religious affiliation and cultural traditions of the "other" community'.[5] Then there were 'mixed' (now known as interchurch) families. In those years, some interchurch marriages were conducted in the sacristy or porch of a Catholic church, thus keeping the Protestant family and clergy out of the main body of the building, signalling the Catholic Church's disapproval of the 'mixing' taking place. Once children appeared, Catholic partners were often anxious to seek compromise by choosing non-Catholic schools. In some cases, where parents were serving in the police or in the armed services, children had to be taken away from Catholic schools because of the hostility shown them by fellow pupils. And then there were families where a child, parent or sibling suffered from poor health. Such families were unable to travel the long distances required in some areas to reach a Catholic school.

The bishop of Down and Connor at the time, Dr William Philbin, accepted some cases for confirmation for medical reasons and a very few cases from interchurch marriages, if it could be proved that the well-being of the marriage in question depended on it. It seemed that virtually no other reasons were considered valid. The bishop's response to letters from parents generally consisted of a terse reminder of their duty under canon law to send their children to Catholic schools, as per Canon 1373, which stated that Catholic children must not attend non-Catholic, neutral or mixed schools – that is, schools open to non-Catholics.

As it was very clear that no help with religious instruction would be coming from the church, the Sunday schools continued. The parents' catechism classes followed the syllabus prescribed at the time by the Catholic Education Advisers in Ireland. By 1972 the number of parents and classes had grown to the extent that most parts of north Down and parts of east Belfast were covered. The largest group was in Bangor, which had pre-communion, communion and pre-confirmation classes, with smaller groups in Holywood and Newtownards. Professional help on a part-time basis was sought, particularly for children due to make their confirmation. At first one or two teachers from Catholic schools were prepared to assist, 'but they were always nervous'[6] and had dropped out by 1973, fearing reprisals from church authorities should they wish to apply for a post in a Catholic school at a later date. And so the parents themselves had to become Sunday-school teachers, each taking it in turn to hold a class weekly in their own house. In addition to regular parents' meetings, the parents organised special services for children prior to the reception of first holy communion and confirmation.

This small white four-fold was the first information leaflet ACT sent to Catholic parents who had asked about catechism classes for their children not in Catholic schools. Several other leaflets followed.

A growing sense of community

The children in the Sunday-school classes attended many different primary schools. At a gathering at the end of the year, parents were able to tell each other how welcome their children had been made to feel by Protestant teachers, parents and pupils. Some Protestant headteachers had offered a room apart should a priest or teacher be willing to come to the school to give the Catholic children denominational instruction. One Protestant teacher gave the entire class a day off homework the day a Catholic child made his first holy communion. The same teacher came to the church with her husband for the ceremony; it was the first time they had ever been in a Catholic church. 'The Catholic child's presence in the class brought the whole life of the Catholic parish alive to the school in a way it had never been before'. There was a growing realisation among the Catholic parents that there was 'something very good going on here'.[7]

Then the blow fell. The bishop of Down and Connor usually visited the parishes of north Down in the spring. In 1973, however, confirmation was postponed until the autumn, when a letter from Bishop Philbin was read out at all Sunday masses. The letter stated that the sacrament of confirmation would not be administered to Catholic children attending non-Catholic schools.

> It was a blanket ban, based on the type of school the child attended. There would be no examination beforehand, nor any opportunity afforded to parents to discuss the family's reason for choice of school. Several of the children concerned had attended Catholic primary schools all their lives, and, had the Bishop administered the sacrament in the spring as had been his usual custom, they would have been confirmed with their primary classmates. However, he refused to confirm those who had moved on to non-Catholic post-primary schools.[8]

The founding of All Children Together

ACT co-founders Cecil Linehan (right) and Bettie Benton at the Linen Hall Library Exhibition, 1995.

The violence of the year 1972 – which witnessed Bloody Sunday, the Abercorn bomb, Bloody Friday, the fall of Stormont and the Claudy bomb – had claimed 497 lives in Northern Ireland. Despite hopes raised by the election of the Northern Ireland assembly and a reduction of violent deaths by around 50 per cent in 1973, the region was by any European standards traumatised and fractured by bitter sectarian and political conflict. Against this backdrop of violence the parents of the children attending the Sunday classes continued to meet. In November 1973 they assembled for a special meeting and formed a group which was named, in the words of Bettie Benton, All Children Together. As already stated, the group's immediate aims were to secure the religious education of their children, ideally with the help and guidance of the church.

> The parents' group often talked about the desirability of integrated education in Christian schools. Gradually the idea formed of a movement to campaign for such schools to be provided as a third choice for parents in Northern Ireland who [were] … faced with a straight choice between Roman Catholic or State (Protestant) schools. ACT was under way.[9]

Before entering into a dialogue with the clergy, the parents felt that they needed to scrutinise the documents of the Second Vatican Council, which was held in the years 1962 to 1965. In the introduction to the *Declaration on Christian education*, the council stated that 'certain basic principles promulgated by the Sacred Synod will have to be … applied by Episcopal conferences to varying local conditions'.[10] The parents were not slow to conclude that Northern Ireland then possessed conditions which varied in a most extreme way from the norm of comparative peace and stability in the rest of western Europe. It certainly seemed reasonable to parents in ACT to argue that the community divisions in Northern Ireland constituted a very specific example of 'varying local conditions'.

The *Declaration on Christian education* also stated that the church:

> must be present with her own special affection and help for those children who are being taught in non-Catholic schools … especially by the efforts of those priests and laymen who teach them Christian doctrine in a manner suited to their age and background and who provide them with spiritual aids … suitable to their requirements of time and circumstance.[11]

Parents who read the declaration, noting that they 'have the right to determine the kind of religious education that their children are to receive', concluded that the bishop had a duty to respect their decisions regarding choice of schools and to discuss their concerns with them. The 'Decree on religious freedom' seemed to stress this point even more when it said:

> since the family is a society in its own right, it has the right to live its own domestic religious life under the guidance of parents. Parents,

moreover, have the right to determine the kind of religious education that their children are to receive.[12]

Irrespective of what the documents of the Second Vatican Council said, all the parents' efforts to arrange a meeting with the bishop were turned down. He continued to refer them to canon law with the added comment that the parents were misreading the Second Vatican Council documents.

Local Catholic clergy were also approached but meetings with them yielded no results. Once again parents were told that they could expect no help with religious education and that confirmation would continue to be withheld as there was no certainty that the children would continue as Catholics in later life since they were not attending Catholic schools. What was most disheartening to the parents was that there appeared to be no attempt to understand their 'sincere concern for their children's spiritual well-being[;] neither was there any expressed interest on the clergy's behalf in the engagement of their Catholic parishioners with members of the Protestant community'.[13] Interestingly, however, some parish clergy did inform a few Catholic families who had moved to the north-Down area about the existence and location of the parent-run catechism classes.

Approach to the Vatican

In April 1974 the ACT parents decided to write to the prefect for the Congregation for the Sacraments and Divine Worship in Rome. Along with copies of correspondence with Bishop Philbin, a written appeal was ready to be forwarded to the Vatican by June. It detailed what the parents had been doing since 1969 to make sure their children had been provided with Catholic religious instruction. A copy of the appeal was also sent to the papal nuncio in Dublin, Dr Gaetano Alibrandi.

By the beginning of 1975 there had been no response from Rome and so another letter was sent. The papal nuncio gave a brief reply, advising the ACT parents that they must be guided by their bishop. He turned down a request to discuss the issues with him in person. Then, in the summer of 1976, through a mutual friend, one of the parents met Msgr Cormac Murphy-O'Connor, then rector of the English College in Rome. In September he was sent a copy of the appeal and he advised the parents to send the whole dossier again to Dr Alibrandi in Dublin, with a request that the issue be taken up at the 'highest level in Rome' and that the nuncio's advice should also be sought on the possibility of sending the dossier to the Congregation for the Clergy.

Meanwhile, Dr Philbin, bishop of Down and Connor, continued to refuse confirmation to children not instructed in Catholic schools. In a radio interview on 3 October 1976 he was asked the following question:

'Is it right to pressurise Catholic parents into sending their children to a Catholic school, in a way to coerce them into doing it, by, for example, refusing them certain sacraments – refusing for example confirmation – if these children are not brought up in a Catholic school?' The bishop replied:

It's not a question of depriving children of anything they're entitled to at any particular stage. It's a question of having the proper preparation for each of the sacraments given them. And confirmation is different from sacraments like penance or baptism or the eucharist in that it postulates a certain knowledge of what one is committing oneself to when a child has reached a certain stage of discretion.[14]

On 21 March 1977 a small group of ACT mothers, Catholic and Protestant, held a silent 'pray-in' outside the Catholic church in Newtownards where the bishop was administering the sacrament of confirmation. The mothers involved were protesting because the bishop of Down and Connor, Dr William Philbin, had refused to administer the sacrament of confirmation to some Catholic children not attending Catholic schools.

Bettie Benton (right) and Cecil Linehan holding placards outside the Catholic church in Newtownards.

Cecil Linehan pointed out the inconsistencies in this reply:

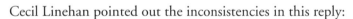

If it is a question of having the proper preparation given for the sacrament, one would have thought children would not be refused without being examined first to see if they were ready to receive the sacrament. A contrary case occurred this year when a child who had attended a state primary school all her life transferred to a Catholic school for her secondary education. She was admitted to Confirmation.

The inconsistencies are confusing. If a child fulfils the requirements in Church law to receive the sacrament, has the bishop the right to lay down a condition of attendance at a Catholic school? Is it right to refuse children without examining them to see if they are adequately prepared? Is it Episcopal policy which is at stake or the spiritual well-being of young people approaching adolescence at a difficult time in a difficult situation?[15]

On 21 March 1977 a small group of ACT mothers, Catholic and Protestant, held a silent 'pray-in' outside the Catholic church in Newtownards where the bishop was administering the sacrament of confirmation. The mothers involved issued this explanation for their action:

We are here to pray for the Bishop of Down and Connor, Dr Philbin, who has refused to administer the sacrament of Confirmation to some Catholic children who are not attending Catholic schools. It is not our role to condemn nor to judge but merely to say to the world [that] we want our children to be able to grow up together as Christians in Christian schools. Christ said 'Suffer little children to come unto me'. If He was here to-day would He have refused the Holy Spirit to our children?[16]

It was later explained to ACT members: 'In deciding to pray outside the church on that Monday morning, we did so, Catholic and Protestant alike, out of positive attitudes to our children and the community in which we live rather than out of any negative attitude toward the Catholic hierarchy'.[17] One of the mothers and then secretary of ACT, Bettie Benton, said:

> her two sons had been refused Confirmation, along with others, by the Roman Catholic Bishop of Down and Connor, Dr William Philbin. She said it was because they attended a State grammar school in the town where most of the boys were Protestant. She said there was not a suitable Roman Catholic school within 14 miles but in any case, she wanted her children to be educated with children from other faiths.[18]

In a paper prepared soon afterwards for the Catholic weekly paper, *The Tablet*, entitled 'The Irish school debate', Cecil Linehan, then chairman of ACT, describing the parent-run Sunday schools, said:

> We all find that taking on this responsibility has done us good; that we have become more aware of 'our inalienable duty as parents'. Nonetheless, while realising that parish clergy could not possibly have time to run Sunday schools for our children we would dearly love an end to the feeling of being 'second-class Catholics' because of our choice of school. We would welcome (and indeed we know

scéala éireann

vo cum slóine vé asus onóra na héireann

Dé Céadaoin, Márta 23, 1977

Today: Mass of the Day in Lent.
St. Turibius, bishop.
St. Victorian, martyr. | Tomorrow: Mass of the Day in Lent.

DENYING THE SACRAMENTS

IT must be presumed that Dr. Philbin, Bishop of Down and Connor, has weighty reasons for refusing to admit some children in his diocese to Confirmation. But it is very undesirable that these reasons should not be made public and be discussed in public, for it is a serious and public thing to deny the Sacraments to a believer.

In the present case, there is the added fact that the Catholic Church has placed a definite stress in her teaching on the adolescents' need of the strengthening power of this Sacrament to meet the crises of growing up.

Further, and most important, the present dispute takes place in a part of the country where all Christians have an obligation to avoid anything which could lead to still more false understandings and hardening of attitudes between them.

It would seem then, that anything which has even the appearance of Catholic or, more precisely, episcopal absolutism or arrogance must be scrupulously avoided. Anything which reinforces prejudices that can only see the Roman Catholic Church as a dyed-in-the-wool authoritarian body belies its true nature and does injury to truth and to our separated brethren.

The episcopal style which Bishop Philbin has employed in this, as in other cases, seems to be very strong on authority and weak on explanation. Such a style harks back to an Ireland of 40 years ago and makes the Second Vatican Council seem like an irrelevancy.

We seem to have a case of what the current issue of *The Tablet*, in a reference to present-day Irish religious attitudes, describes as "that harsh and literal integralism in religion (which) forms a mentality which is ill at ease with itself and irreconcilable with others."

If one feels, then, that in the North, on the Catholic side, the time for such hard-faced Catholicism is over, maybe Bishop Philbin is no longer the man to occupy such a pivotal position as he does in the Church structure there.

The Confirmation issue is a very serious one for the children and their parents. But for the Catholic community of Down and Connor as a whole, the issue is broader and yet more serious. Is a church which acts in this way, the Catholic Church they want their separated brethren to love and be reconciled to? Is not the human face of the Catholic Church in the diocese of Down and Connor the fundamental issue?

The refusal of the sacrament of confirmation was very widely publicised and commented on in the press. Here is just one example, an editorial entitled 'Denying the sacraments' in the Dublin-published *Irish Press*, printed two days after the 'pray-in'.

there is a great need for) counselling and advice at diocesan or parish level for Catholic families whose children attend non-Catholic schools.[19]

Meeting the nuncio

On the further advice of Msgr Murphy-O'Connor, an updated version of the appeal was sent to Dr Alibrandi in June 1977, with a direct request to him:

> as the Pope's representative in Ireland, to bring these matters, namely the lack of help with religious education and the withholding of the Sacrament of Confirmation, to the highest level in the Vatican.[20]

The parents regretted that their activities might have resulted in adverse publicity for the church, but pointed out the gravity of their situation:

> Having failed over a period of more than eight years to obtain an interview with their Bishop, Dr Philbin, the number of Catholic families [wishing to join the Sunday classes] grows steadily, yet there is apparently neither compassion for the parents nor concern for the spiritual well-being of the children … We feel the continuation of the present policy is perpetuating some of the community tension in this province.[21]

By return of post the parents received a cheering reply from the papal nuncio: 'I can assure you that this situation is already well-known to me, and in fact I am doing what is possible to remedy it. I am always at your disposal if you wish to see me.'[22]

'I will send them in the Diplomatic Bag': an end to the controversy?

A small group of ACT parents duly travelled to Dublin on 3 October 1977 to see the papal nuncio. Cecil Linehan remembered it as 'a most cordial and productive meeting'. The parents were able to describe all the problems they were experiencing and the fact that there had been no response from the Vatican. Dr Alibrandi suggested writing to Cardinal Baggio and the Congregation for the Clergy. 'Send the letters to me,' he said. 'I will send them in the Diplomatic Bag.'[23]

The nuncio suggested that either Dr Ryan, bishop of Dublin, or Dr Daly, bishop of Derry, could be asked to confirm the children as it was already their practice not to exclude any child from the sacrament. One of the fathers present said that the parents felt very strongly that their children should be confirmed in their own diocese and asked, 'Could His Holiness be asked to instruct the bishop to confirm the children?'

'Yes,' the nuncio responded. 'Write in detail to the Vatican. Tell them that Dr Ryan and Dr Daly confirm Catholic children in non-Catholic schools and ask that Dr Philbin should act likewise. The most important thing', he added, 'is that the children were brought up as Catholics, knew their prayers, and that as parents, you remain steadfast in your wish to bring your children up in the faith'.[24] The parents were also welcomed at Ara Coeli in Armagh to a very friendly meeting with the late Cardinal Tomás Ó Fiaich and it seemed that doors which for so long had been firmly closed were indeed beginning to open. On 19 February 1978, just four days before the bishop was due to confirm the parish children, an announcement appeared in the parish bulletins in Bangor and the neighbouring parishes of Newtownards and Holywood, saying:

> parents of post-primary children who have not been confirmed at the usual age are requested to notify a priest of the parish before the 4th Sunday of Lent so that preparatory arrangements may be made for their reception of the sacrament at an early date.[25]

Four years in all had elapsed from the time the first appeal to the Vatican was made until the issue was finally resolved. On 3 June 1978, Bishop Philbin held a special confirmation ceremony. Among those confirmed were many children from whom the sacrament had been withheld because of their attendance at non-Catholic schools.[26]

The long-running dispute ends up in court

However, the dispute had hit the headlines and several newspapers were suggesting that the fact that the bishop was arranging 'special' confirmation ceremonies for children who had not been confirmed at the usual age was an indication that he had been reprimanded by the Vatican – 'just malicious lies', the bishop's secretary remarked.[27] Meanwhile, the bishop's office issued a press statement to counter newspaper reports:

> Dr. Philbin had never refused to confirm children who attended non-Catholic schools simply because they did not attend Catholic schools. The Sacrament had only been denied, and would continue to be denied, to those children who persisted in attending non-Catholic schools and

who demanded to be confirmed as of right without adequate preparation.[28]

This, of course, was unfair: some children had been at Catholic primary schools all their lives until transferred to second-level schools; the children in the Sunday school had been given exemplary religious instruction and preparation and neither the bishop nor his diocesan adviser had examined any of the children. Conor O'Clery, under the headline 'Vatican pressure ends ban by bishop', wrote the following report in the *Irish Times* on 14 March 1978:

On 14 March 1978, an *Irish Times* journalist, Conor O'Clery, wrote a report under the headline 'Vatican pressure ends ban by bishop'. Almost at once, Dr William Philbin, Catholic bishop of Down and Connor 1962–82, announced his intention to sue the *Irish Times* for libel. The case was heard in the High Court in Dublin in May 1981. This picture shows Bettie Benton and Cecil Linehan, ACT co-founders, leaving the High Court, having given evidence on behalf of the *Irish Times*, 15 May 1981.

PHOTO COURTESY OF THE
Irish Times

> The Bishop of Down and Connor dropped his rigid opposition to confirming Catholic children in state schools in Northern Ireland because of the Vatican's conclusion that he was acting contrary to Canon Law … after detailed submissions from an English priest, who was working in close liaison with the Papal Nuncio, Dr Alibrandi, and the Archbishop of Armagh, Dr Tomás Ó Fiaich, during the last months … Dr Alibrandi, and Dr O Fiaich, who last year described the situation in Down and Connor as 'a tragedy', were involved in following up the closely researched submission made by the English priest, which resulted in the opinion expressed by the Vatican.[29]

Shortly afterwards, Bishop Philbin announced his intention to sue the *Irish Times* for libel. The case was heard in the High Court in Dublin in May 1981[30] and the bishop was awarded damages of IR£12,000 against the *Irish Times*.[31] Bishop Philbin maintained that he had always intended to confirm these children.

'Special' confirmations

Following the first 'special' confirmation in June 1978, another 12 children from the ACT Sunday school were due to be confirmed in 1979, and although parents wrote to the bishop of Down and Connor seeking information on when the next 'special' confirmation would take place, their letters remained unanswered for several months. Still receiving help from the nuncio in Dublin, Dr Alibrandi, and on his advice, the entire confirmation class and their families eventually travelled to Derry in June 1980, where they were welcomed from the altar by Bishop Edward Daly and the children were duly confirmed. Thereafter 'special' confirmations were conducted in the diocese of Down and Connor every two years. This was a vast improvement on the previous situation, though many parents still felt their children were being made to feel like second-class citizens because these so-called 'special' confirmations were held apart from the usual parish confirmations. 'Why,' asked the parents, 'do our children have to be separated for the reception of the sacraments just because they do not attend Catholic schools?'[32]

Formal steps taken towards ACT becoming interdenominational – 1974

During the early 1970s, while the Catholic parents had been having all this trouble with religious education and the confirmation issue, more and more Protestant parents were expressing a wish to join ACT. As has been noted, Thelma Sheil and Margaret Kennedy felt they were members of ACT long before it officially became an interdenominational movement. Sheil in particular remembers Bettie Benton suggesting 'All Children Together' as the name for the organisation, while together they designed the ACT logo on Thelma's ancient typewriter, which became completely worn out from typing ACT documents (including the appeal the Catholic parents sent to the Vatican). Even before Basil McIvor had announced his shared-schools plan in April 1974, ACT was well on its way to becoming an interdenominational organisation.

Bill Brown, Margaret Kennedy and Thelma Sheil – three Protestant parents involved in the work of ACT even before it became formally interdenominational.

An article in the *Belfast Telegraph*, written by Linehan in April 1974 on behalf of the movement, outlined the philosophy of ACT. She quoted Dr James Doyle, Catholic bishop of Kildare and Leighlin, who had stated in 1826:

> I do not know of any measures which would prepare the way for a better feeling in Ireland than uniting children at an early age and bringing them up in the same school, leading them to commune with one another and to form those little intimacies and friendships which often subsist through life.[33]

Linehan contrasted Dr Doyle's attitude with that of the Catholic Church in 1974, which insisted that Catholic children must attend Catholic schools. She outlined the historical background of the education system, explaining the emergence of a denominational structure. Turning to the present day, she noted that Dr Philbin considered that ACT members were disobeying Canon 1373 by not sending their children to Catholic schools. Linehan pointed out that the documents of the Second Vatican Council on Christian education, religious freedom and the apostolate of the laity justified integrated schooling: they reminded parents 'of their role as the primary and foremost educators of their children' and also of the important part played by the family in Christian education. She ended by stressing the fact that although Catholic parents had sent their children to non-Catholic schools for a variety of reasons (such as conscience, geography, health, safety) they all had within them 'the feeling akin' to that expressed by Dr Doyle in 1826.[34]

Two of the first Protestants to become involved with this lively group of Catholic parents were Rev. Bill Brown, an ordained Presbyterian minister from Holywood, and Margaret Kennedy, a teacher and a member of the Church of Ireland. Brown had become the adviser on religious education for the South-Eastern Education and Library Board (SEELB). He was impressed by Linehan's contributions to discussions of the board – of which she was a member; she, in turn, was heartened by the support he gave her and invited him to meet the Catholic parents who were due to meet in the Strathearn Hotel in Holywood, County Down. 'You'd be very interested,' she said. He was. The meeting was addressed by Fr Des Wilson – 'not as radical then as he subsequently became'. Later, at a conference run by ACT in 1974, Brown persuaded a fellow Presbyterian, Carrie Barnett, to give advice to the Catholic parents on religious-education teaching techniques. He recalls a feeling of 'delicious irony' as Carrie held up visual aids to help the parents impart Catholic doctrine to their children. Bettie Benton, Cecil Linehan and Carrie Barnett were all southerners; Bill Brown felt that as outsiders they carried 'less baggage', had 'a different way of networking' and less fear of disapproval than those who had spent all their lives in Northern Ireland.[35]

Margaret Kennedy first met Linehan at an Alliance Party meeting and soon became a staunch ACT activist. At first she was 'on the sidelines', mainly because she did not want to make things more difficult for Catholic parents in their dealings with the church. A move to teach in Cookstown in County Tyrone did not reduce her involvement and, when she later took a post in a Belfast secondary school, she found that her involvement in integrated education attracted some disapproval from the higher echelons of management – 'so I kept my head low'. She was a committed and active member of the Church of Ireland and was at pains to observe that 'we weren't anticlerical and we weren't anti-Church'.[36]

Linehan's article in the *Belfast Telegraph* in 1974 had marked a significant step towards the formation of ACT as an interdenominational movement. The fact that it recorded the bishop's refusal to confirm some children not attending Catholic schools received extensive publicity and brought the whole ACT movement to a much wider audience. The bishop's announcement refusing confirmation had 'politicised us to a certain extent', Linehan commented. The willingness of the two women, Benton and Linehan, as devout Catholics, to confront the hierarchy seemed presumptuous to some fellow parishioners and remarkably courageous to others. 'We harnessed a sort of fury,' Linehan recalled, 'particularly amongst those parents who had invested so much time and care in providing religious instruction to children due to be confirmed.' They had all expected that 'the day would come when the children would be quizzed' and some were so well taught that they 'were practically ready for PhDs' in religious instruction. Rebuffed by the clergy, they became fired with a zeal to widen the scope of their groups to campaign for shared schools.[37]

Having read the article on ACT in the *Belfast Telegraph*, Tony Spencer got in touch with ACT. He, his wife Rosemary and his daughters had not been involved in the Sunday schools. Tony was a senior lecturer in sociology at Queen's University, an Englishman and a devout Catholic.

Why ~~Mon Nov 11. '74~~
B 33
integration?

A.C.T. (All Children Together), a group of Catholic parents in Northern Ireland who support integrated education, is to hold a seminar in Queen's University, Belfast, at the end of this month on "Interdenominational Schools —Why? How? the Way Ahead."

The speakers will include Mr. Bill Browne, religious education advisor to the South-East Area Board, the Rev. Des Wilson, Professor John Berkeley and Mr. Liam McCollum. The seminar opens at 10 a.m. on November 30th in the Presbyterian Community Centre.

A.C.T., which has about 70 members, voted at its September meeting to open membership to Protestants. The group's chairman, Mrs. Cecilia Linehan, says that about 40 Protestants have taken up the offer. "We put it to our members that in view of the requests for membership from other groups we should go inter-denominational, while not forgetting that our primary purpose is to provide for the religious education of our own children. We have decided to hold open meetings once a quarter to discuss issues of interest to all denominations."

ACT leaders convened a special meeting to put to the original Catholic parents a proposal that All Children Together should become interdenominational. Originally called for 15 May 1974, the meeting had to be postponed to the autumn of that year due to the violence associated with Ulster Workers' Council Strike. The meeting was reconvened and, following some debate among the original Catholic parents, ACT became interdenominational in September 1974.

He was extremely well informed on *Humanae vitae* and other documents emerging from the Second Vatican Council and had no hesitation in confronting what he regarded as the outdated conservatism of the Irish Catholic clergy. Linehan 'put it down to English Catholic confidence'.[38]

ACT's founding principles on becoming interdenominational – 1974

The early months of 1974 seemed to offer bright prospects of cooperation and progress in spite of the continued intensity of political and intercommunal violence. From 1974 on, more and more Protestant parents expressed a desire to join the movement, to examine together with Catholic parents the possibility of developing integrated schools for all children. The McIvor shared-schools proposals of April 1974 appeared both exhilarating and revolutionary to the ACT parents. The plan, with a budget of £13 million for schools provided Catholic and Protestant churches shared in their management, created another wave of parents looking for a forum from which they could challenge the ongoing separate and, many believed, sectarian nature of Northern Ireland's schools.

The ACT leaders decided to put to a meeting of the original Catholic parents a proposal that ACT should become interdenominational. Originally called for 15 May 1974, the meeting had to be postponed until the autumn of that year owing to the violence associated with the Ulster Workers' Council strike. When it did take place the following September, some of the Catholic parents felt it was a move away from the original aims of providing catechism classes for Catholic children in non-Catholic schools and trying to ensure that they received the sacrament of confirmation with their peer group in the local parishes. However, after some debate, agreement was reached and, in September 1974, ACT became interdenominational, retaining the basic principles on which the movement was founded in February 1974:

Name: The name of the movement shall be All Children Together.

Aims and Objects: The All Children Together movement seeks changes in the education system of Northern Ireland which will make it possible for parents who so wish to secure for their children an education in shared schools acceptable to all religious denominations and cultures, in which the churches will provide religious education and pastoral care.

The movement shall be non-party political and non-sectarian.[39]

Later these three principles were incorporated unchanged into the constitution ACT formally adopted at its inaugural general meeting on 29 January 1977.

In time the movement published a manifesto outlining its credo, describing ACT as 'a movement for the advancement of integrated education in Northern Ireland', and quoting the observation made by Bishop Doyle in 1826. This quotation, referred to by Cecil Linehan in her *Belfast Telegraph* article in 1974, has been repeated in all ACT's documents since then.

ACT's credo stated:

- WE BELIEVE and support these views expressed 150 years ago.
- WE BELIEVE that the high degree of religious segregation in the Northern Ireland education system is an obstacle to the solution of Northern Ireland's problems.
- WE BELIEVE that parents have the fundamental right to choose the kind of education that shall be given to their children.
- WE BELIEVE that the educational system of Northern Ireland has permitted excessive representation of the churches and their clergy in both Catholic maintained and Protestant controlled schools and that such high representation is unnecessary from an educational viewpoint.
- WE BELIEVE the essential role of the clergy in schools is in the religious education of children.[40]

Reasons for establishing integrated schools

ACT's reasons for wishing to establish integrated schools were based on three main principles:

1 The right of parents freely to choose the type of school they want for their children as enshrined in the *Universal declaration of human rights*,[41] the *Declaration on Christian education* of the Second Vatican Council,[42] and the Education and Libraries (Northern Ireland) Order 1972.[43]

2 The development of intercommunity trust: ACT members listened to speakers on the prejudice-reduction work of the eminent sociologist

Gordon Allport, which suggested that contact between diverse groups over a long period of time with common goals on an equal footing and on a voluntary basis *does* reduce fear and mistrust.[44] They believed they could see in their own experience and that of their children a positive community aspect from sharing schooldays. Integrated schools were never going to solve Northern Ireland's problems, nor had they caused them in the first place, but because young people continued to be separated from the ages of five to nineteen years, parents did believe that Northern Ireland society was being held back from healing itself.

3   A commitment to Christian unity. As most of the founding members of ACT were committed members of individual Christian churches, they had a strong motivation to work for Christian unity. They believed that establishing schools where children from differing religious affiliations and cultural traditions could be educated together would be a powerful witness in a divided Christian land.

Botlie

No. 008

ALL   CHILDREN   TOGETHER

A.C.T. on

" INTER-DENOMINATIONAL SCHOOLS

WHY ?

HOW ?

THE WAY AHEAD "

* *

PRESBYTERIAN COMMUNITY CENTRE
Queen's University, Belfast.
SATURDAY, NOVEMBER 30th   9.30 a.m. – 5.30 p.m.

Admission by THIS programme only

The programme for ACT's first Seminar held on 30 November 1974 and entitled: 'Interdenominational schools: why? how? and the way ahead'. The Seminar was oversubscribed.

Depression – yet hope

The Ulster Workers' Council strike in May 1974, the appalling violence which accompanied it, the dashed hopes of so many and the consequent collapse of the power-sharing executive in May 1974 appeared to destroy all hope of moving forward. 'That's the end of you now,' someone said to Linehan at the time.[45] The reverse proved true. Amidst all this gloom and despair there were some pleasant surprises in store for ACT, the most pleasurable being that over the summer of 1974 Basil McIvor accepted an invitation from the ACT executive to join the movement. Not only did this bring a high-profile name to the emerging movement but it also helped to give it a sense of public recognition. By the end of September 1974 over 40 Protestant members had joined.[46] Then, in November, when ACT organised a conference entitled 'Interdenominational schools: why? how? and the way ahead', there was a further pleasant surprise – the conference was completely oversubscribed.

The themes discussed at and the speakers participating in the 1974 conference were:

1   'Parents' rights in education' – Liam McCollum, barrister and prominent member of the moderate Alliance Party of Northern Ireland.

2 'The importance of an integrated sector in education and social structure in Northern Ireland' – Tony Spencer, senior lecturer in sociology, Queen's University, Belfast.

3 'Christian love' – Fr Des Wilson, St John's parish, Belfast; Prof. Barclay, head of church history, (Presbyterian) Assemblies College, Belfast.

4 'A common religious-education syllabus' – John Greer, University of Ulster.

5 'Denominational instruction' – Michael McKeown, chairman, Catholic Parents' Sunday School, Bangor, County Down; Sr Agnes Devlin, Institute of Religious Education, Mount Oliver, Dundalk, County Louth;[47] Carrie Barnett, Sunday-school organiser, Presbyterian Church in Ireland, Belfast.

6 'Two cultures, one people' – Bill Brown, adviser in religious education, SEELB and vice-chairman, ACT; Victor Leitch, principal, Omagh High School, County Tyrone.

All the speakers that day spoke with passion and commitment to the ideal of shared schools for Catholic and Protestant children in Northern Ireland, especially as so many parents had expressed their wish to see such schools develop, but it is worth referring to some of the more salient themes.

Liam McCollum, a leading barrister in Northern Ireland and an Alliance Party candidate for the 1974 election to the Northern Ireland assembly, talked about the rights of parents, the state and the churches to insist upon minimum standards of moral and religious education but asked, 'Have the churches in their sphere any greater right? If so, such a right conflicts with parents' right to choice and which should prevail?' The ensuing years were to demonstrate that he was right to highlight the tension which would arise between churches insisting on their rights and parents seeking to educate their children together.

'Speak to your clergy'.
ROWEL FRIERS, COURTESY YVONNE FRIERS

Tony Spencer, senior lecturer in sociology at Queen's University, supported the demand for a third, integrated sector. This need arose from the characteristics of Northern Ireland's education system and those of its social structure, which are unique within the world of plural Christianity, although there are similar cases involving non-Christian religions in other parts of the world. Social psychology suggested that prejudice between members of two groups was likely to be diminished if they experienced face-to-face social interaction of a cooperative nature, in the pursuit of shared goals, especially if it was over a long period of time with equality of status.[48] Strong mutual reinforcement of home and school was normally a necessary condition of the internalisation of a system of values in children. Values such as tolerance and respect for the 'out-group' and its culture and rights were most likely to be transmitted to the children of parents who already embraced these values if their children were educated in schools institutionally structured to cherish them.

In many respects the most interesting contribution was by Michael McKeown, chairman of the Catholic Parents' Sunday School in Bangor, which could be regarded as the birthplace of ACT. He explained how over five years his group had been providing religious instruction and confirmation preparation for children from five families who – for various reasons – had been attending state schools. The Sunday school had been formed because no help had been forthcoming from either clergy or teachers from Catholic schools. This self-help group had obtained appropriate literature and had largely used parents themselves to give the instruction. Numbers had continued to grow and now there were 36 children with four classes, two teachers and parents attending on a rota system. Instruction was given in parents' houses and the group met regularly to monitor progress and arrange the sharing of responsibility.

Bill Brown, adviser in religious education in SEELB, called for a total review of Northern Ireland's educational system in his address, 'Two cultures, one people'. In the context of the internecine violence then raging in the region he examined the origins of the conflict, pointing out that the quarrel was not solely between England and Ireland. The roots of the Troubles were to be found in the seventeenth-century plantation, when a permanently divided society emerged, a pattern continued and strengthened in our own time by separate schooling. Two cultures had evolved with their loyalties slanted either towards London or Dublin, and schools reinforced this orientation by curriculum, sport and ethos.

Victor Leitch, principal of Omagh High School, took up this theme of two cultures. His experience was particularly valuable because his state school had an unusual mix of both Protestant and Catholic pupils. He warned that schools are not powerful agents of social change – the 'shared' elementary schools of the nineteenth century had, after all, produced the bigots of the 1920s and 1930s. Nevertheless, he believed that shared schools, committed to a policy of cultural integration, would provide a far wider education for all children. He suggested that there are, in effect, four cultures rather than two, because of sharp divisions between middle-class and working-class people, both Protestant and Catholic. Middle-class Protestant parents could enjoy Irish writing and music, for example, but working-class Protestants rejected any identification with Irish culture and turned towards the 'mainland' in search of roots.

Outcome of the 1974 conference

The overwhelming consensus arising from the conference was that all present shared a deep desire to create shared Christian schools. At the end of the day, three recommendations were passed, namely:

1 There was a need for a third interdenominational sector within the educational system of Northern Ireland.

2 Where a new school was planned, the Department of Education, the education and library boards and the churches should consult parents in the area before commencing negotiations.

3 The churches should increase their pastoral care to families, initiate the preparation of a joint religious curriculum and make plans to open adult centres of religious education on an interdenominational basis.

These recommendations were sent to government departments, churches, education and library boards and all other interested bodies.

The movement becomes known

During 1975, the movement was given two opportunities to publicise its

These prints were created for ACT by the cartoonist Rowel Friers for the 1975 BBC Open door programme and show parents trying to open the door to shared schools against the opposing force of clergy of all denominations; and trying to arouse politicians from a general state of inertia on the issue of parental rights in the region's education system.

YVONNE FRIERS

All Children Together trying to open the door to integrated education in Northern Ireland.

views when it was asked by the BBC to make two programmes: the first a *Platform* programme for Radio Ulster; the second an *Open door* programme for BBC2. These programmes were important developments in the movement's growth, eliciting a tremendous correspondence and public debate in the press. The movement was becoming well known and members of the ACT executive found themselves recognised as authorities on integrated education, often being asked to comment when the subject was being debated.

'ACT on shared schools' – a discussion document, 1976

ACT spent the next year gathering all the views expressed at the conference, opinions expressed as a result of the BBC programmes and other submissions made by its members into a discussion document. The document was published subsequently at a special press conference called for the purpose in Corrymeela House, Belfast in June 1976. Entitled 'ACT on shared schools', the document defined a shared school as 'one in which those of differing religious and cultural backgrounds share at all levels, in management, staffing and pupils'. It also dealt with all aspects of shared schools, including finance, composition of boards, church involvement in school management, staffing – especially in relation to senior posts – a shared religious-education curriculum and historical and cultural studies. Much of what was set down there in 1976, especially in relation to shared religious education and cultural and historical studies, was a clear precursor to the cross-curricular themes of education for mutual understanding and cultural heritage later introduced into the Education Order (Northern Ireland) 1989.[49]

This was ACT's first policy document setting out its beliefs on parental involvement in school management, the role of the churches in schools, especially in pastoral care, and the importance of our shared cultural inheritance – all themes later introduced in the Education Reform (Northern Ireland) Order 1989.

'Speak to your MP'.
ROWEL FRIERS, COURTESY YVONNE FRIERS

ACT also gave an undertaking to organise two further conferences – one on religious education in interdenominational schools, with case studies of existing schools in other countries, the second on the problems associated with bringing two cultures together.

1976 conference – postponed

The 19/4 conference had made it clear that the question of how religious education should be provided in shared schools and colleges was a particularly difficult and important one, which had to be addressed directly. So, true to the promise given at the end of the 1974 conference, ACT decided to bring experienced practitioners in religious education together to discuss the issue and booked the Presbyterian Community Centre at Queen's University, Belfast for Saturday, 3 April 1976. Through the good offices of the Joseph Rowntree Trust, ACT had received a grant to defray the expenses of the seminar, so considerable energy and resources were expended in identifying suitable speakers and the eventual line-up was impressive.

The topics and speakers for the 1976 conference were to have been:

1 'Aims and objectives of religious education', Fr David Konstant, director, Westminster Religious-Education Centre.

2 'Developments in shared education throughout the world', Rev. Robert Williams, Church of Ireland Education Board.

3 'Cooperation at teacher-training level', Rev. Terence McCaughey, Presbyterian chaplain to Trinity College, Dublin.

4 'Religious education for young children in state schools in Northern Ireland', Kathleen Lindsay, head of 'infants' in a state primary school in Bangor, County Down and member of the ACT executive.

ACT ON SHARED SCHOOLS

AT
BELFAST TEACHERS CENTRE
Upper Crescent, Belfast, 7.

ON
TUESDAY, 27TH. JANUARY, 1976

AT
7·30 pm

PROGRAMME at DOOR (inc tea) 30p

5 'Pastoral care for Catholic children attending non-Catholic schools', Sr Winifred Wilson, Brook Green Pastoral Centre, London.

6 'An interdenominational school in action', Larry Finnegan, principal, Sutton Park School, Dublin.

ACT continued its work of campaigning for shared schools right throughout 1975 and 1976 with a series of public meetings.

In the pre-conference literature, ACT posed a series of ten questions on the teaching of religious education for the conference to study:

⚥ ALL CHILDREN TOGETHER ⚥
A.C.T.   ON
"RELIGIOUS   EDUCATION
IN
SHARED SCHOOLS AND COLLEGES"
AT
PRESBYTERIAN COMMUNITY CENTRE
QUEENS UNIVERSITY BELFAST
SAT. 3 APRIL 1976 9.30AM–5.30PM
ADMISSION BY PROGRAMME ONLY
£2·00 (INC. LUNCH)
AVAILABLE FROM:
HON. SEC. A.C.T.,
174 GROOMSPORT RD.,
BANGOR BT20 5PL

The ACT seminar of 1976 had to be cancelled as two of the main speakers, Fr David Konstant of the diocese of Westminster, and Sr Winifred Wilson, who provided pastoral care for Catholic children in that diocese not in Catholic schools, were prevented by episcopal pressure from speaking at the conference.

all Children Together
Invite you to
Seacourt Teachers Centre
Princetown Rd. Bangor
TO SEE
A.C.T.
on
Shared Schools
(Reshowing of B.B.C.
Open DOOR)
followed by a Discussion
Programmes at door 30 P.
Thurs 20 Nov. 75 at 7.30 PM.

1   Is Northern Ireland's segregated school system producing committed Christians? We rival Cyprus alone in the Christian world in the extent to which our school population is divided along religious lines.

2   Are schools an important factor in passing on religious beliefs and practices? Surely children learn first and foremost in the home – at the mother's knee?

3   It is said that a common syllabus of religious education will lead to a watered-down Christianity – but will it?

4   How would Catholic parents cope if the Catholic school was not the source of doctrinal instruction for their children?

5   What sort of religious education do children in state schools receive?

6   Should religious education be given by 'specialists'? Is it time we stopped expecting all teachers to give religious education?

7   What is it like in a school where Catholic and Protestant sit down together day after day for all their subjects – religious education included?

8   Do teachers have to be educated in separate teacher-training colleges?

9   Do other countries in the world have shared schools and colleges?

10   What is the aim of religious education anyway?[50]

These were serious questions which would have to be addressed honestly by anyone genuinely interested in integrated education in Northern Ireland. But the conference never took place. Why? It became clear that the Catholic hierarchy in Ireland made representations across the Irish Sea, causing the two leading Catholic speakers to withdraw.

The *Belfast Telegraph* reported on 30 March 1976 on the 'Puzzle of priest who changed his mind':

The Roman Catholic priest who withdrew from a conference on mixed schools in Ulster had originally said he would be 'delighted' to attend, it was revealed today. Father David Konstant, Director of the Westminster Religious Education Centre in London, had said in January that he would be very pleased to address a seminar on shared schools scheduled for April 3. But a statement released by the Catholic Press and Information office in Dublin yesterday said Father Konstant would be unable to attend because he felt he had 'insufficient experience of the situation in Northern Ireland' to make a helpful and constructive contribution.[51]

The ACT honorary secretary, Bettie Benton, explained why the conference had been postponed:

> We have had to postpone the conference because Father Konstant and his colleague Sister Winifred Wilson have not been able to attend. There was no point in continuing with no one to represent the viewpoint of the Catholic Church. We have no criticism of Father Konstant and in fact have the deepest regard for him. But the question why he cannot attend still remains since only two months ago he was extremely enthusiastic about the whole idea. He was to have talked on the aims and objectives of religious education which are about the same everywhere, and so I cannot see how the Dublin statement makes sense. No specialist knowledge of Northern Ireland would be needed to lecture on that topic.[52]

Father Konstant said that he was unable to elaborate on his earlier statement but was very sorry he could not attend:

> The Dublin Press statement applies to both Sister Wilson and myself, and is a personal decision. It is a very difficult situation, but I am afraid that at the moment neither Sister Wilson nor myself can come to the 'All Children Together' seminar. The statement said that in the present circumstances I could not make a helpful and constructive contribution. Should the circumstances change then I may be able to do so.[53]

Cecil Linehan (ACT chairman), Bill Brown (vice-chairman) and Bettie Benton (honorary secretary) issued a statement cancelling the seminar, explaining:

> In the sad circumstances of the forced withdrawal of the two Catholic speakers, we feel that the meeting would be unbalanced and that we have no option but to postpone it to a later date. How can there be rational debate on Shared Christian Schools here, while one of the essential partners in 'sharing' not only prevents such debate taking place, but also stifles freedom of speech? This is completely in contrast to the co-operation between Christian Churches in the creation of Christian

Belfast Telegraph, Tuesday, March 30, 1976   9

Puzzle of priest who changed his mind

THE ROMAN Catholic priest who withdrew from a conference on mixed schools in Ulster had originally said he would be "delighted" to attend, it was revealed today.

Fr Konstant had originally said he would be delighted to attend the ACT seminar but a statement released by the Catholic Press and Information Office in Dublin later said he would be unable to attend as he felt he had 'insufficient experience of the Northern Irish situation to make a helpful and constructive contribution'.

Schools in Britain and other places throughout the world. However 'we must be about our children's business' and a new date will be arranged for this important discussion.[54]

ACT continues to communicate its philosophy – despite all the obstacles

This enforced cancellation of the 1976 seminar may have been a serious wake-up call for ACT, giving the leaders an increased realisation of the strength of the forces ranged against them. Yet, despite the obstacles, ACT continued its work, holding seminars and conferences right through the years 1976 to 1991, and again in 1999. These became regular and much-valued resources for the whole integrated-education movement.[55] Benton would later comment that she:

> looked upon these seminars and conferences as 'bricks' that built up the movement, which was continually consolidating its knowledge of integration and investigating how it could best be adapted to Northern Ireland's special needs.[56]

ACT was also involved in submitting its ideas on education to government working parties and investigating committees and from 1977 to 1996, a total of 26 submissions were made.[57] In addition, from 1977 to 1997, a newsletter entitled *ACT-LETT: News from All Children Together* was sent bi-annually to all members and education providers.[58]

An immense amount of passion, commitment and effort was required before ACT was able to set up Northern Ireland's first integrated school, Lagan College, in the autumn of 1981. On the cover of her thesis, submitted in 1982 and entitled 'The story of All Children Together and the founding of Lagan College', Thelma Sheil wrote:

> It was winter, 1981, dark and cold and with little hope for a better future.
> Hatred and death stalked the land. A small light glimmered. Nurtured and protected from the storms it flamed and grew stronger. Now it burns clearly, a bright light and a ray of hope in a dark corner of Europe.
> This is the story of that light and of the people that kindled the flame.[59]

It is hard to believe that all the members of the ACT executive had homes and families and that most of them had jobs to hold down as well as keep up with the ever-increasing demands of a movement for integrated education about which they all felt passionately.

ACT-LETT

No. 1.   Vol. 1.

News   from   All   Children   Together.   Jan. '77.

Chairman's Letter.

Dear A.C.T. Supporter,

Since its formation almost three years ago the ALL CHILDREN TOGETHER movement has had tremendous support from people all over the province and from a large number outside the province too. We have tried to keep in contact with anyone who has contacted us or shown an interest in the movement.

The main work of the movement has been directed towards making the Education Authorities aware of the public demand for integrated or Shared Christian Schools. This has involved us in organising conferences and meetings; in making radio and television programmes and in writing for papers and journals. We have endeavoured at all times to give whatever help we could, where we could, with parents particular problems.

Because of the volume of support pledged to us we feel we can say legitimately that ALL CHILDREN TOGETHER expresses the views of the very large numbers in this province who wish to see children of all denominations and cultures sharing their schooldays from an early age.
A.C.T. on Shared Schools

In June of this year, the movement produced an important discussion document entitled "A.C.T. on Shared Schools."

This document is the result of many months research and is a consensus of the view expressed to us regarding the form of Shared Schools desired by the majority of parents in Northern Ireland. (contd. over leaf)

Inaugural General Meeting. Jan. 29 '77.

Presbyterian Community Centre
Queen's University, Belfast

AGENDA

11.00 a.m.
(1) Opening remarks of Chairman.
(2) Adoption of Constitution.
(3) Election of Officers & Committee.
(4) Determination of Annual Subscriptions.
(5) Appointment of Auditors.
(6) Any other business.

12.30 - 1.15   Lunch Break.

1.30 p.m. Afternoon Session :
   "The Cowan Report -
    Its Implications for A.C.T."
    Introduced by Bill Browne.
                    Vice-Chairman.

3.30 p.m.   Close.

Shared Schools for Northern Ireland .....
What do the PEOPLE think?

A voice from the past ....

"I do not know of any measures which could prepare the way for a better feeling in Ireland, than uniting children at an early age and bringing them up in the same school, leading them to commune with one another and to form those little intimacies and friendships which often subsist through life"

Dr. Doyle, R.C. Bishop of
Kildare and Leighlin, 1826.

A voice in the wilderness you may think, but is it?

In 1967 and 1968 two surveys carried out in Northern Ireland by National Opinion Poll found that:-

64% of adults favoured integrated
65% of youths   " schools
69% of Catholics   "

Six years later in 1973, an Opinion Poll carried out by the Sunday Times/ Fortnight newspapers found these figures in reply to the following question - "How would you feel about your children, or children you know, going to a school attended by pupils and taught by teachers some of whom were Catholic and some Protestant?"

	All	R.C.	P
Strongly in favour	31%	34%	28%
In favour	31%	30%	31%
Don't mind/willing to accept	24%	21%	29%
Against	10%	10%	10%
Strongly against	3%	3%	3%

These Opinion polls in 1967, 1968 and 1973 show that a majority of people in both sections of the community WANT SHARED SCHOOLS. The Sunday Times Fortnight poll shows that 86% of people in Northern Ireland want Shared Schools for their children.

Yet an analysis of the present school population shows approximately 99.5% of Protestant children in State schools and 98% of Catholic children in Catholic schools.

The divide is almost complete. Only 13% of the people wish to see Catholic and Protestant children divided so. Yet this 13% appears to be able to deprive a majority of parents in Northern Ireland of the right to have their children playing together and learning together in school.

Will you help us to achieve our aims?

Will you become an active member of

ALL CHILDREN TOGETHER?

Achievement of our Aims.

i)   To demand that the Department of Education and the Area Boards introduce Shared Schools NOW, in development areas, in rural areas where duplication may already be uneconomic and especially in areas where 'sharing' already exists at all levels throughout the community.

ii) To press for integrated teacher training colleges - the only section of post-school education in Northern Ireland which remains segregated.

iii) To oppose the establishment of sectarian nursery schools.

iv) To seek to change the present legislation, which in effect perpetuates a sectarian system of education.

v)   To urge the Department of Education and the Area Boards to consult with parents on educational matters and before taking decisions regarding new schools.

vi) To press for more involvement of parents and teachers in the management of schools.

vii) To promote a new curriculum involving a common pattern of religious and moral education, and of historical and cultural studies.

viii) To seek co-operation with local clergy in the provision of religious education and pastoral care.

1

From 1977 to 1997, ACT's newsletter, *ACT-LETT,* was sent (usually biannually) to all members, churches, institutes of education and libraries in Ireland, the UK and overseas. Note the encouraging opinion polls conducted in 1967 and 1973.

4
Direct-rule dilemmas

It needs to be explained to the Armagh Three that there is no question of compulsion. The intention would be to provide the opportunity of shared schools only for those Catholics who wished to use them for their children. The Cardinal calls in aid Canon Law, but Catholic clergy outside Northern Ireland seem to be able to reconcile shared schools and Canon Law.

ROGER DARLINGTON, POLITICAL ADVISER TO THE SECRETARY OF STATE FOR NORTHERN IRELAND, 1976 [1]

A 'genuine and honest attempt'

Loyalists had been primarily responsible for the collapse of the power-sharing executive in 1974. This, undoubtedly, had been the main news story in Northern Ireland that spring. The executive had barely been given time to find its feet and one of its few achievements had been to give legislative support to Basil McIvor's shared schools. That initiative – like so many others – now began to run into the sand. In the case of shared schools the most effective opposition had come not from Protestants but from the spiritual leaders of the Catholic community.

Eugene McEldowney had been a teacher in a Catholic grammar school in Belfast. Now he was a journalist and was on his way to becoming a highly successful fiction writer. His views on the churches' position on integrated education are of great interest. In August 1974 McEldowney reflected at length in the *Education Times* on McIvor's shared-schools plan and the hierarchy's opposition to it. He began:

> On the sound principle that the best way to defeat an opponent's argument is to misrepresent either the argument itself or the motives behind it, poor old Basil McIvor has been accused by various Catholic apologists of playing politics, dodging the real education issues in Northern Ireland and even, shades of Lenin, planning to take their schools away from them.[2]

He continued:

> Now Basil McIvor may have been up to any or all of these things, but there are a few people around who would prefer to give him the benefit of the doubt and to accept his proposals for shared schools at their face value, that is, as a genuine and honest attempt to provide a third option to the growing number of parents in Northern Ireland who wish to have their children educated outside the narrow constraints of the dual sectarian system which exists at present. The former minister also clearly felt that by providing such schools there would inevitably be a reduction in community tension.[3]

He concluded that half the trouble was that these apologists had 'never paused to read exactly what it was that McIvor was proposing'. Had they done so, he observed, much of the wild talk about state takeovers and threats to cultural heritage would have appeared ridiculous, 'even to themselves'. The real cause of the 'hysterical reaction' lay in the fact that for some time now, the Catholic Church had seen in the prospect of integrated education a very real threat to its monopoly on education for Catholics:

> The Church's dilemma has been how to oppose integrated education without at the same time appearing, in the view of the present Northern turmoil, to be completely antediluvian. As a result they have found themselves for some time in the position where they oppose integration on principle and then search around for reasons to excuse or justify their position.
>
> For a long time their main arguments centred on the twin principles set out by Cardinal Conway in his 1970 pamphlet 'Catholic Schools': first that there was no evidence to suggest that Catholic schools were contributing to the violence in Northern Ireland, and second, that Catholic education meant more than merely teaching Religious Instruction in the classroom and concerned the whole religious formation of the young Catholic.[4]

The first argument, McEldowney believed, was 'a complete red herring', as no one had seriously suggested that separate schooling was actually *causing* the violence. What many were suggesting was that integrated education might be a means of destroying some of the more harmful myths which had flourished for years among both communities. 'The brave opposition of a handful of Northern Catholics who have drawn attention to their Church's ambivalent attitude to religious education in other countries and to the comments of Vatican II on education' had done much to weaken Conway's second argument. The result was that there had been a search for fresh arguments to defend the church's monopoly on education. He summed up a new one as follows:

> It is not healthy for the State to have a monopoly in education. It can lead to totalitarianism. We should welcome and encourage diversity in our society and appreciate different points of view. One of these is the Catholic sub-culture. Hands off our schools.[5]

He also quoted another argument, recently printed, that the McIvor proposals were an attempt 'to systematically set about to dismantle the twin cultures of Ulster, to root out and destroy the idealism and patriotism inherent in both of them with a hybrid "para-culture" at once foreign and incomprehensible'. McEldowney thought that these arguments could easily be turned around to *support* the McIvor proposals:

> If diversity is so laudable, then what possible objection can there be to having more and not fewer types of schools? If maintaining parental choice in education is a worthwhile objective, then why scream blue murder at suggestions to provide Northern parents with a real choice instead of the phoney or non-existent choice they have at present?
>
> As for the suggestion that the shared schools proposals were really an attempt to produce a hybrid para-culture, the reverse would appear to be the truth. The shared schools, under joint Catholic–Protestant management would surely guarantee, not that any of the Ulster cultures would be submerged or dominated, but that both would be accorded equal recognition, and that both groups of children would have equal access to both cultures. And if there has been any single factor in contributing to the Northern tragedy, it has surely been that majorities in both communities have felt themselves cut-off and alienated from the other community.[6]

McEldowney was certain that Basil McIvor was not attempting to ram anything down anybody's throat:

The emphasis in the proposals lay heavily on consultation and co-operation. Indeed, in his remarks to the Northern assembly, the former minister made it clear that he understood the anxiety of the churches concerning the religious upbringing of their children and was keen to consult fully with all the interested parties before even proposals for legislation could be formulated.[7]

McIvor had stated clearly: 'Obviously the vast bulk of our schools will continue as they are at present.' He had felt that his scheme would be particularly appropriate for nursery schools, none of which the Catholic Church had yet been able to bring under its sphere of influence. McEldowney ended his article with these observations:

> But, of course, the opponents of integration are not really interested in argument. They have decided on educational monopoly. Pluralism for Catholic parents will extend as far as the local Catholic school under threat of withholding the sacraments for their offspring should they be tempted elsewhere. It is really very hard to know which is saddest, the clerical cant or the mental confusion which has been the general reaction to Basil McIvor's very modest proposals.[8]

What would Westminster do now?

The collapse of the executive left Westminster with no alternative but to restore direct rule. Like Edward Heath before him, Harold Wilson had the complete support of the opposition at Westminster in attempting new solutions. For example, the bill legalising elaborate new machinery to extend direct rule went through the Commons in a single day in mid-July 1974 without any division. There was all-party backing, too, for legislation winding up the Northern Ireland assembly and replacing it with the elected Constitutional Convention, 'to consider what provisions for the government of Northern Ireland would be likely to command the most widespread acceptance throughout the community there'.[9] The 'Irish dimension' was quietly sidelined but Westminster remained wedded to power-sharing as the only acceptable outcome.

At Westminster, the general election of October 1974 returned a Labour government. Once again British politicians hoped that a silent majority in Northern Ireland would yield a moderate centre strong enough to deliver community government. London was whistling in the wind: the convention election in Northern Ireland on 1 May 1975 saw the defeat of

Brian Faulkner's party, giving little cheer to Merlyn Rees, the new secretary of state. The majority of unionists had no intention of power-sharing but did accept the return to direct rule.

For Merlyn Rees, the top priorities were a reduction in violence (which to some extent he achieved) and attempts to restore power-sharing. Roland Moyle, the MP for Lewisham and minister of state, had been appointed as minister with responsibility for the environment and education in Northern Ireland. He planned a major shake-up of secondary education in the region, with comprehensive education well to the fore, and produced a consultative document on the matter. Stan Orme, the left-wing MP for Salford, who joined Rees at Stormont as minister of state with responsibility for commerce and manpower services, was a noted advocate of comprehensive education.

Sir Kenneth Bloomfield. Permanent secretary to the power-sharing executive in 1974; following its collapse, he became in turn permanent secretary for the Department of the Environment, the Department of Economic Development, and finally head of the Northern Ireland civil service on 1 December 1984. As head of the civil service, he was the most senior advisor to successive secretaries of state for Northern Ireland and other ministers on a wide range of issues. Sir Kenneth retired in 1991.

Moyle seems to have shown little enthusiasm for the shared-schools plan approved by the assembly. Little of note on this topic seems to have been raised in government circles until early in 1975. On 15 January, Ken Bloomfield, a senior civil servant who had worked closely with the power-sharing executive, wrote a long letter to the permanent secretary at the Department of Education, A.C. Brooke. It was a letter prompted by a meeting with the ministers of state where an increase in the grant to maintained schools had been proposed:

Personal and Confidential
Office of the Executive
A.C. Brooke Esq. C.B.
Department of Education

Dear Arthur …

I tried to introduce the thought that the prospect of such an increase might present an opportunity to open out the wider issue of relaxing the rigidity of sectarian education. This suggestion found no favour at all with Mr. Moyle, or with Mr. Orme who was in the Chair. They took the line that the increase in grant was an inescapable decision, based on considerations of straightforward parity ...

I do not, of course, suppose for one moment that we can or should move swiftly from a system of segregated to a system of integrated education. Any such belief would be naïve. What does worry me is that we may be attaching to the views of the Catholic hierarchy in general and those of the Cardinal Archbishop in particular a degree of binding authority which is exaggerated in modern conditions. I gather that one reason for the virtual abandonment by our present Ministers of the idea of shared schools advanced by the Executive is that the Cardinal has made clear his extreme displeasure about the way that suggestion was floated without prior consultation with him. On past experience, however, any such consultation would have revealed an extreme lack of enthusiasm if not actual hostility to the idea. One would therefore have faced the very difficult choice of whether to drop the idea in deference to the Cardinal's doubts, or pursue it after he had made clear his lack of enthusiasm. For the first time, and with significant support of the first Catholic party to be in government in Northern Ireland, it was decided to take a different tack – to go public, and possibly reach out to the views of the Catholic community, which are not necessarily synonymous with those of the Cardinal or the Clergy. Personally, I believed at the time that this step was both courageous and right; however, it now seems to be so much water under the bridge.[10]

He referred to the proposal to increase grants, which would give Catholic schools financial parity with those in Great Britain. 'Can it be doubted that an inevitable result of this will be a further entrenchment of segregation?' Bloomfield asked. He put forward two reasons why the shared-schools plan should be revived. One was 'the extreme difficulty of the overall public expenditure position'. 'If ever there was a time,' he declared, 'when we needed to be thinking in terms of avoiding duplication and making a maximum use of available facilities, this is that time.' His second argument was that, even with the increase in grants, plans to step up the level of education provision – and the need to make provision in the Poleglass development (a major Housing Executive scheme linking west Belfast with Lisburn) – 'could be frustrated by the inability of the Church to raise the money'. 'Is it not the case,' he asked, 'that, while the academic standards of many Catholic schools are high, they are sometimes spartan as far as fringe activities and amenities are concerned – for example, that the take-up of school meals is sometimes inhibited by lack of dining facilities?'[11]

Bloomfield did not think that radical change in the present system was likely but at the very least the Department of Education could do more:

> to encourage a range of developments which might have the effect of working towards a more open and co-operative system. I have in mind fields like teacher training,[12] nursery education, shared sixth form colleges, shared campuses and specialised facilities. Beyond that, I wonder whether we should not consider some form of wider enquiry into the education system.[13]

He concluded that he had expressed his views with diffidence 'and only because of my interest in the wider political and social environment'. He had discussed this question thoroughly with his colleague in the Executive Office, Maurice Hayes, 'whose insight into these matters I value, and he is strongly of the view that the time is right to explore the possibility of even some limited movement'.[14]

Of the variety of suggestions for some 'movement' perhaps the one proposing shared teacher training had most appeal in the Department of Education. No progress was made, however, in implementing McIvor's shared-schools plan. Indeed, in September 1975, Roland Moyle made his position clear in an address to the annual conference of the Northern Ireland Association of Education and Library Boards at Newcastle, County Down. The press statement issued by the Department of Education stated:

> Mr. Moyle referred to integrated schooling. He told of views coming into the Department on the idea of 'shared schools' put forward by [the] former Minister of Education, during the term of office of the former Executive, and said: 'I am bound to say that there was not a substantial degree of agreement in favour of the idea. Bluntly, on the views that the Department has received, I am not given a mandate to change the law.
>
> 'In any case my own reflections lead me to doubt if this is a matter on which it would be useful or desirable to lay down hard and fast general rules or proceed by way of regulation. Such an approach might well be counter-productive. Circumstances, as your President has pointed out, differ from area to area and from school to school. What might be successful in one situation might not work at all in another. In different areas people have different views.

'These are the factors which should inform policy and administrative action. It is upon this basis that I intend to act for the future.'[15]

Lobbying the government

Integrated education virtually disappeared as an item for consideration either on the Stormont estate or at the Northern Ireland Office in London until Sir Nigel Fisher – Conservative MP for Surbiton and a decorated war hero – tabled a written question in the House of Commons on 22 January 1976. He asked the secretary of state for Northern Ireland:

> if he will encourage the provision of shared schools in Northern Ireland for children whose parents desire this, as a way of integrating the denominations and promoting better community relations in the next generation.[16]

The written reply was given not by secretary of state Merlyn Rees but by the minister with responsibility for education, Roland Moyle:

> It is our policy not to attempt to force any integrated school arrangement in any particular case but nevertheless to encourage those who provide schools to consider the possibility as the occasion allows.[17]

Hardly an encouraging response to Sir Nigel. It was the summer of 1976 before there was any sign that the government was prepared to open discussion once more on integrated schooling. This, when it came, appears to have been wholly due to external pressure. One included strong support from the Presbyterian General Assembly when it met in June 1976. The *Belfast Telegraph*'s headline for 7 June was: 'Presbyterians say "yes" to integrated schools – breakthrough must be found, assembly told'. The report continued:

> Experiments in integrated education were given the full backing of the Presbyterian General Assembly yesterday. A resolution recommending experiments in certain schools was unanimously passed by members.
>
> The Assembly's education secretary, the Rev. J.T. Simpson, said while it would be foolish to suggest that all Presbyterians 'were falling over themselves' to encourage mixed schooling, a breakthrough must be found, and the education board was prepared to throw in its lot. Mr. Simpson said that the resolution was compiled before the former Minister of Education, Mr Basil McIvor, put forward his proposals.
>
> 'We feel that there must be a breakthrough in community

development in this country if we are not going to have two communities, separated and isolated for ever more', said Mr. Simpson. Although religion has to be excluded, there were four other areas where progress could be made – work, housing, recreation and education. Take any one of these areas out of life and integration was crippled from the start, he warned.

NURSERY

Mr. Simpson said experiments in mixed schooling should begin at nursery and sixth form level. The education board was in favour of the churches being adequately represented on school management committees and was convinced that religious education should be a subject in the school curriculum, with opting-out rights protected.[18]

Rev. J.C. Faulkner, from Moy, sounded a note of caution. He said he had great sympathy with those who wanted to keep church schools and that he would be reluctant to put pressure on the Catholic Church. 'I am a little doubtful,' he said, 'that if you wash all the children in the same water they will all come out equally clean. I want to see integration but I am not sure that schools should be used to do it.' Nevertheless, he voted in favour. The religious-education adviser on the North-Eastern Education and Library Board (NEELB), Rev. W.E. Davison, suggested that integration should start in the training colleges and then work from there.[19]

Members of All Children Together welcomed this support but they were to find that warm words and resolutions led to little positive practical action. Bettie Benton, the indefatigable honorary secretary, sent the minister of state a copy of 'ACT on shared schools' with this note:

> We would welcome an opportunity to discuss the document with you and members of your Department when you have had time to consider it. At a time when the re-organisation of secondary education seems imminent we would urge that the religious and cultural integration of our children should also be taken into account.[20]

The private secretary to Roland Moyle, A.S. Pidduck, replied on behalf of her minister on 8 July:

> I think you know it is not Government policy to attempt to force any integrated school arrangement in any particular case, but nevertheless to encourage those who provide schools to consider the possibility as the

occasion arises: there is no legal reason at present why pupils of any religion can not attend any school in Northern Ireland. Some months ago the Department embarked on a series of consultations with interested parties and these revealed that there was not a substantial degree of agreement in favour of the idea. The Government therefore felt there was not sufficient support to justify legislation.

You will be aware that the Secretary of State has recently been asked to arrange a conference to take preliminary soundings among the major interested parties in order to see what basis exists for reopening discussions in this way. In the circumstances there would be no point in a meeting as you suggest.

It has been noted that All Children Together has asked education authorities and churches to consider your document. Mr. Moyle would be interested to see the outcome of this consideration. I think I should perhaps add that present thinking on reorganisation of secondary education has not been taking into account the integration aspects.[21]

Following this somewhat less than encouraging letter, pressure on the government that summer was also being applied by the British Irish Association. At its conference in Oxford in early July 1976, Brian Garrett and Lady Patsie Fisher, both members of All Children Together, organised a petition in favour of integrated education which was duly delivered to the secretary of state. Brian Garrett, a Belfast solicitor, a member of the Standing Advisory Committee on Human Rights and past chairman of the Northern Ireland Labour Party, had for a long time been an eloquent advocate of liberal reform. Lady Fisher, originally from Donaghadee, daughter of the north-Down unionist MP Sir Walter Smiles and wife of Sir Nigel Fisher MP, was the co-founder of the Women Caring Trust, a charitable organisation which did stalwart work for women and children in Northern Ireland by arranging respite breaks for women in areas with high levels of violence and joint holidays for Catholic and Protestant children.

Sir Nigel himself wrote to the secretary of state on 5 July:

Dear Merlyn

Patsie has told me about the Conference at Oxford last weekend and of your kind reference in your own speech to a point she had made in her little contribution about the possibility of shared schools in Northern Ireland.

I did put down a written question to you on January 22nd on this subject and received an answer from Roland Moyle. I wonder if this matter could now be followed up? There is of course no question of forcing any integrated school arrangement, but there are a large number of parents of both denominations in Northern Ireland who would be prepared to accept shared schools and indeed wish they could be organised.

I realise the practical difficulties involved but I should be most grateful if you could have the matter looked at carefully in the office, as I do think it would be a most constructive step and would do something to lessen the perpetuation of hatred into the next generation.

The Office will no doubt be aware that in the days of the power-sharing Government at Stormont the idea of shared schools was agreed in principle by all the political leaders including the Catholics in the SDLP and the Alliance Party. I have this information on the personal authority of Brian Faulkner and I think this should be correct, so that politically there should be no difficulty and the problem is really to persuade the Churches to co-operate.[22]

The records seem to indicate that, after more than two years of stasis, the question of integrated education was returning to agendas. In a long minute, entitled 'Note for the record – shared schools', Moyle's private secretary, John Pitt-Brooke, summarised recent discussions. He noted about McIvor's plan that 'it was found that there was insufficiently broad support for the idea to justify going ahead with it. The proposal was therefore allowed to drop.'[23] He continued:

The matter was raised again at the recent Oxford Conference by Lady Fisher on behalf of All Children Together. In his winding up speech on that occasion the Secretary of State said that there would be a 'conference' set up to discuss the idea further.

When the Secretary of State [Merlyn Rees] had dinner with Ministers and Officials in Stormont House on 15 July this was discussed and the following conclusions were reached:

a That the Government should not organise a conference directly.
b That consideration be given to inspiring some independent body to mount a properly prepared conference (e.g. QUB Institute of Education).
c That no conference should take place for about 3 months, since it is important that the public debate on the Consultative Document [on the re-organisation of secondary education] should not get mixed up with such a hot potato.

d It would be possible to discuss the format of an independent conference with the varied interests in the intervening period.

Mr. Moyle was in agreement with these and in particular was most keen this discussion on shared schools should be kept separate from the proposed public debate on secondary reorganisation.[24]

Members of ACT would have been quite astonished if they had known that men in high places were paying such close attention to their proposals.

Much foot dragging ... or monumental indecision?

A detailed minute of that dinner was written by Private Secretary N.R. Cowling the following day:

Confidential. Mr. Pitt-Brooke. PS/Mr. Moyle
1 The Secretary of State had a discussion at dinner in Stormont House last night touching upon the recently re-opened question of shared schools. Mr. Concannon, Mr. Dunn, Mr. Kidd, Mr. Slinger, Mr. Cowan, Dr. Hayes, and Mr. Macdonald were present. The Secretary of State would like to have an early word with Mr. Moyle. The way his mind is working is:
2 The Secretary of State would like a background paper to be prepared by the Department summarising the Basil McIvor proposals in the Assembly; the reaction at the time; and representations since the Oxford conference.[25]

It is quite clear from this minute, therefore, that it was Merlyn Rees himself who decided that the government should not itself sponsor a conference on shared schools. The process of 'preliminary consultation' began when Moyle, and his parliamentary under-secretary, Ray Carter MP, met Lady Fisher, Brian Garrett (who had to rush back from a family holiday in Devon to be there) and Joan Robbins, a leading member of the English Catholic laity – inaccurately described by Pitt-Brooke as 'the three leading members of the All Children Together movement' – at Stormont on 22 July. Lady Fisher hoped that the minister would follow up the suggestion that there should be a further conference on the matter. Moyle replied that he had 'noted the resurgence of public interest in shared schools and was open to suggestions about how best to proceed'. Lady Fisher expressed the hope that the creation of shared schools would do something to break down sectarian tension in Northern Ireland and would make a small contribution towards bringing about peace.[26]

Brian Garrett gave the minister a paper which set out two broad objectives:

a   To make maximum use of facilities within existing educational systems involving sharing of specialist teachers, equipment, out of school activities, etc.

b   To enable those parents who wished (and Mr. Garrett said that these were at the present not many) to send their children to an integrated school.[27]

Garrett wanted the conference to be organised by the government and chaired either by the minister or the secretary of state. He sought a standing conference, meeting regularly over a three-month period, attended by the government, educational administrators, teachers and – if possible – parent representatives. Its purpose would be to identify attitudes and encourage public discussion.[28]

Moyle's response was not particularly encouraging. He was worried that if a conference was set up 'those participating might be forced into expressing their position publicly at the outset and subsequently not being able to move from it because of the public commitment which had been given'. Progress was already being made in sharing facilities (justified by local circumstances) and 'this progress might be jeopardised if there were an acrimonious debate on the matter which would heighten sectarian feeling rather than lessen it'.[29]

And what about McIvor's shared schools? Moyle dismissed this proposal out of hand: he said that 'there would obviously be strong objections to this suggestion and that to discuss it in the public arena would only make those who objected stand even firmer on their positions'. Clearly the minister was thinking about objections from the Catholic hierarchy. This prompted Brian Garrett to say that he 'did not feel that Cardinal Conway spoke with the backing of the Catholic community, nor did he accept that the cardinal was in any way bound by canon law to oppose the scheme'.[30] Here the delegation was not united. With Brian Garrett and Lady Fisher was Joan Robbins, co-founder with Lady Patsie Fisher of the Women Caring Trust, a devout English Catholic and a member of the International Committee of the National Board of Catholic Women. According to a minute signed by T. Cowan, Robbins said, unhelpfully, that she felt that there was little possibility of progress towards:

providing a third type of school acceptable to both Protestant and Roman Catholic parents ... In this connection she explained the point of view of the Roman Catholic Hierarchy that only in exceptional circumstances should a Roman Catholic child attend a school not under Roman Catholic management.[31]

She was in favour, however, 'of developing and extending co-operation between schools in what they termed "the two systems"'. Cowan continued:

> The visitors were firmly of the opinion that whatever conference was held should be under the auspices of the Government and should not be by invitation only but should be open to the public at large. On the other hand they appeared to be unable to say how in a public conference the taking up of 'party positions' could be avoided or how the attendance of a representative cross-section of the public could be obtained. One possibility appeared to be that the conference might take the form of a series of meetings under a series of chairmen and lead to the publication of a report.[32]

Yet more indecision

Moyle responded that he had not yet decided whether or not to hold a conference. Garrett replied sharply that he had a letter from the Northern Ireland Office assuring him that the government intended to hold a conference. Towards the close of a very disheartening meeting, Garrett said:

> He felt the Minister ought to know that he had the backing of many influential newspapers in Great Britain and Northern Ireland – notably the *Belfast Telegraph*, the *Sunday Times* and the *New Statesman*, and that editorial pressure would be brought on the Government to be seen to act on shared schools.[33]

According to the *Belfast Telegraph*, Garrett indicated there was now more willingness to open discussion amongst all interested parties. A conference could clear the air and its conclusions should be made public. After the meeting at Stormont the three delegates held a press conference. Brian Garrett gave a more upbeat account than the Department of Education minutes would warrant. According to the *Belfast Telegraph* he said:

> 'There is a definite willingness to push the idea of a conference. The

issue now is how best to convene it. The speed with which we were asked to see the Minister on the shared schools issue indicates it has his priority …'

'We favour a revolving chairmanship of interested parties from the Education and Library Boards, parents, teachers and clergy. Very important too is the publication of the conclusions of the conference to clear the air on the shared schools subject generally', added Mr. Garrett.

Lady Fisher said it was now time to identify what people's objections were to shared schooling. Parents had to have a choice in the matter, she added.[34]

To the *Irish News* correspondent Garrett emphasised that there was no intention to force integrated schools on parents.

'All of us expect that maintained schools would remain', he said, adding that the conference to discuss shared education would have to be a 'substantial' one called under the aegis of the Secretary of State …

It is emphasised that the right of parental choice in education would be regarded by the conference as primary and Mr. Garrett said there was no intention on the part of anyone to harry parents into positions not of their own choosing.[35]

Legislation for comprehensive education forced through in Westminster

Choice was the theme of Jim Callaghan's speech in the House of Commons that same day as the bill to enforce comprehensive education in Britain was passing over its last hurdle. 'The choice of education of children was the right of parents and nobody else,' Callaghan said. Ian Gow from the opposition Conservative benches asked the prime minister to repeat his earlier statement that 'decisions for the education of children ought to be taken by their parents and not by the State'. Callaghan responded:

This is certainly my view, and it is the view of the great majority of people in this country who now have a greater freedom of choice and a wider curriculum of subjects than they have ever had in the past.[36]

The unamended bill was forced through the Commons by guillotine and passed at third reading by 134 votes.[37] The Labour government was now keen to extend the comprehensive system to Northern Ireland and it was clear that ministers regarded the demand for integrated education as something which would muddy the waters.

When he received a copy of Pitt-Brooke's 'Note for the record', Roger Darlington, political adviser to the secretary of state at the Northern Ireland Office, was clearly appalled that Moyle had not made any commitment on a conference:

> It was my impression from a comment made by the Secretary of State at Oxford on 4 July 1976, and from my conversations with the Secretary of State and the Minister of State in the office on 8 July 1976 that we were prepared to hold a conference, and I thought that consultations were being held to determine the principal features of such a conference, such as the date, venue and form … In any event, how can the Government decide on the one hand not to hold a conference, and then on the other hand consult interests about the form of a conference to be organised by someone else? If others are to mount the conference, then they will decide its form.[38]

Consulting the hierarchy

The Department of Education decided to begin the process of consultation by meeting the Catholic bishops. Just before that meeting, on 23 July 1976, Cardinal Conway received a letter from Hugo Young, chairman of the Education Committee of the Catholic Institute for International Relations in London. The committee had clearly been moved by public pronouncements made by the Irish higher clergy on shared-schools proposals. The letter reads as follows:

> Dear Cardinal Conway
>
> I am writing on behalf of the Executive Committee of the Catholic Institute for International Relations. As you know the CIIR has for some years taken an active interest in the problems of Northern Ireland. We have tried to explain to English Catholics the background of the situation and the roots of the conflict. We have also attempted to highlight the responsibility of people in this country and particularly the British Government in the deteriorating situation in the Province. Our primary concern, however, has been the role the Church, both in England and Ireland, in helping to ameliorate the situation.
>
> In all our work on Northern Ireland one of the questions most frequently raised has been the attitude of the hierarchy to the vexed

matter of shared schools. On the one hand, Catholics in this country point to our own system of Catholic schools to show that such schools are not a divisive influence within the community. On the other hand, equally committed Catholics feel that in a society as divided as Northern Ireland any way of helping to bridge the communal divide must be explored. They therefore suggest that ways should be found of ensuring that Catholic and Protestant children can be educated together and therefore come to know and understand each other better. Given the movement of population in Northern Ireland, it is obvious that there can be no overnight change, but experimental projects might be initiated which would be an indication of the Church's good faith.

For our part we feel that this whole question is open and for this reason warrants further discussion and research. We certainly do not feel that Church schools are a primary cause of violence in the Province. Furthermore, we feel that the effect of the immediate abolition of such schools would make the respective communities even more frightened and enclosed. We do feel however that this is an area which deserves greater discussion and more rigorous analysis.

We would therefore like to take this opportunity to express our feelings on the conference proposed to discuss this question. Although we understand that the conference is little more than an idea at the moment, we hope very much that you, or your representative, will take an active part in the conference both to explain the Church's policy on this matter and to listen to the various points of view. Such a conference, we feel sure, will prove a worthwhile initiative.

We do not have any great expectations about what such a gathering might achieve. We feel however that an open exchange of views on this matter can only have a positive effect.[39]

This appeal had no effect. A few days later Roland Moyle, accompanied by senior civil servants, drove down to Armagh to meet Cardinal Conway, Bishop Philbin and Bishop Daly. The minister began by making it clear that he had made no decision in favour of shared schools, as Pitt-Brooke's 'Note for the record' makes clear:

Mr. Moyle began the meeting by explaining that the issue of shared schools had once more become a focus of public interest and that there was now pressure for the setting up of a conference. Mr. Moyle added that the idea of shared schools was instantly appealing to people of good intention who knew nothing about the realities of Northern Ireland, and foremost among such people were the middle-class English journalists whom Brian Garrett numbered amongst his allies. As far as he himself was concerned, the Minister confirmed that he had taken no decisions but was merely taking preliminary soundings among interested parties; however there would be pressure on him to set up a conference and, given the Roman Catholic Church would be expected to attend such a conference, he asked for the Cardinal's views.

Cardinal Conway's attitude was one of complete intransigence. He dismissed the idea as trivial, irrelevant, and without popular support; he would not participate in any conference on the matter which would be set up by liberals for liberals and would be so constructed as to put the Catholic hierarchy 'in the dock' (he described Lady Fisher's scheme as an 'ambush'). He affirmed that his church attached the very highest importance to Catholic children continuing to be educated in Catholic schools – this was embodied in Canon Law, had been endorsed by the Vatican Council, and was the only way in which a stable environment could be created where children could learn about the meaning of life and the rules of principled human conduct. He thought that to take a child from a Catholic home and educate that child in a non-Catholic school would create tension between the home and school environment which could be only harmful to the child. This might not be the case in middle-class areas such as Holywood (both Cardinal Conway and Bishop Philbin spoke with particular scorn of Holywood as a kind of North Down Hampstead) but it certainly applied in the big housing estates, where Catholic schools were a great force for peace – teaching love, non-violence, and the importance of the family; it would be folly to destroy this and replace it by an unwanted and disruptive system of shared schools. Summing up, the Cardinal said they would object to shared schools, would not attend an open conference to discuss them, and would wage a campaign to fight a proposal which set out to relax the hold of the Catholic Church on the education of its own children. He said that he was sure that all his clergy supported his views.[40]

The minister was right to refer to the cardinal's words as a 'frank statement'. He then referred to Brian Garrett's two-tier suggestion, sharing facilities in the first stage and promoting integrated schools in the second. Bishop Philbin said that he did not object to the sharing of facilities and extra-curricular activities 'where specific circumstances necessitated such arrangements' but he 'could not endorse it as a principle to be generally applied'. Then the bishop of Derry intervened:

Bishop Daly then made the same points as the Cardinal but with even more vigour. He referred to a meeting with some children educated in non-Catholic schools whom he had asked about the meaning of Christmas – they had variously replied that it was to celebrate the birth of Santa Claus and the death of Christ. If Christian values were to be protected, he concluded, then Catholic schools must be retained. In England children were taught about all religions – including Buddhism and even Communism – this could only be confusing and children in Northern Ireland wanted stability and not confusion. Furthermore he suggested the Minister would find that when pressed the Protestant churches would be similarly opposed to this scheme – indeed the only people in favour were the 'minute crowd in Holywood'.[41]

The cardinal and bishops reiterated their opposition to a conference which they felt sure would be 'divisive and would do nothing to help sectarian feeling'.[42]

When he read the 'Note for the record', Roger Darlington, political adviser to the secretary of state, wrote from London to John Pitt-Brooke an acid commentary on the meeting with the three prelates:

Confidential Subject: Shared Schools

The intellectual level of the arguments against shared schools mounted by the Armagh Three was pathetic. Children at Catholic schools would give equally varied answers to the questions about the nature of Christmas, but in any event religious knowledge does not equal religious morality. Although there are some comparative religion lessons, I doubt whether there are any English schools actually teaching Buddhism and Communism, since the 1944 Education Act prevents such an approach, as the controversy over the 1974 Birmingham Agreed Syllabus showed only too well.

I grant that the Armagh Three have a kind of negative power, but was it Stalin who asked 'How many battalions has the Vatican?' Put another way, how seriously should we take this predictable opposition from the leading members of the Catholic hierarchy in Northern Ireland? On 29 July 1976, in the House of Commons, David James MP – himself a Catholic – asked us not to be deterred by such hostility. I understand that three opinion polls in Northern Ireland over the last 10 years have shown a majority in both communities in favour of shared schools for those parents who want them.

It needs to be explained to the Armagh Three that there is no question of compulsion. The intention would be to provide the opportunity of shared schools only for those Catholics who wished to use them for their children. The Cardinal calls in aid Canon Law, but Catholic clergy outside Northern Ireland seem to be able to reconcile shared schools and Canon Law.[43]

Darlington had attached the letter from Hugo Young to the cardinal (referred to and quoted above) and pointed out that the executive of the Catholic Institute for International Relations included several eminent Catholic clerics.[44] 'I am no authority on Canon Law,' Darlington added, 'but I would suggest that the Cardinal's interpretation is out of step with that of many of his co-religionists elsewhere in the United Kingdom.'

The political adviser did agree that limited progress would be obtained from a conference at this time. He observed that he was under no illusions about the impact or the take-up of shared schools. He thought that the impact would be marginal and long term; he referred to American studies that demonstrated that black and white children had already formed false stereotypes of their opposite numbers before attaining school age. Take-up, he felt, would be extremely small at first, 'largely confined to the middle class parents so despised by the Cardinal, and they might run the risk of excommunication'.

Finally, Roger Darlington urged the government not to avoid the growing demand for integrated education:

> Government cannot absolve itself in the field of educational choice. If there are signs of genuine interest amongst parents in the possibility of shared schools, the Government should not allow itself to be dictated to by the Roman Catholic hierarchy.[45]

He implied that the government itself should organise a conference and keep the interest in shared schools alive.

> I am sure that it would be wrong of the Government to let the renewed interest in shared schools collapse. I am inclined to the view that it would be wrong too for the Government to pass the buck to someone else to organise a conference, since sooner or later it comes back to the Department of Education in Northern Ireland.[46]

The minister of state had decided that there had been enough consultation. During the last week in July 1976, Moyle provided this answer to a parliamentary question:

> It is not the intention of the Government to deprive parents of the right

to have children educated in accordance with their religious choice. A proposal for shared school governing bodies was made by Mr. Basil McIvor, Minister for Education in the power sharing executive, in May 1974.

Consultation on this proposal subsequently did not reveal sufficient support to warrant legislation. I have noted a recent renewal of interest in similar proposals to those put forward by Mr. McIvor and I am at present reviewing how these might be further considered.[47]

Unfair sampling

Darlington was clearly unhappy about this:

The consultations have been confined to three individual supporters of the proposal and three leading members of the Catholic hierarchy in Northern Ireland. Surely this is too narrow a sample as a basis for decision-making and we ought to conduct further consultations with bodies such as the teachers' unions, the Church leaders, the political parties in Northern Ireland, the Northern Ireland Members of Parliament and, if possible, parent organisations from both communities.[48]

One civil servant, I.M. Burns, was also unhappy that the secretary of state had gone back on the assurance he had given at Oxford that he would hold a conference. He wrote to Pitt-Brooke on 9 August:

I think I should record as one of those present at the Oxford Conference I understood the Secretary of State to then give a clear undertaking that a conference would be convened to discuss the question of shared schools. I am in no doubt that the meeting as a whole understood the Secretary of State to give this assurance. He had been pressed to take some action, and when he said he would hold a conference he was loudly and spontaneously applauded by the meeting. I am not sure how widely known is the undertaking which he gave at Oxford but there is undoubtedly a danger that if no conference is held the Secretary of State will be seen to have gone back on his word.[49]

But the minister was preoccupied with the consultative document on secondary reorganisation. Department of Education officials were understandably anxious that the issues of secondary reorganisation and shared schooling would become mixed up. One senior civil servant, Patrick Carvill, put together a paper presented in August:

COMPREHENSIVE EDUCATION: INTEGRATION

Although the Minister has been at pains to emphasise that he sees integrated education as an entirely separate issue from comprehensive education, it is clear that the Press and other pressure groups will continue to try to link the two issues. They may find a certain amount of ammunition in the various references in the Consultative Document to possible integrated arrangements for senior pupils. Although there are only a few instances where these suggestions are tentatively put forward, their existence cannot be denied, and I think it is therefore worthwhile to be clear about just what is said. I have therefore had all the references to integrated education in the Consultative Document extracted and set out on the attached notes.[50]

The excised sentences make fascinating reading. Some of them are set out below:

Para 43: Limavady District: A majority of the Secondary Principals are strongly in favour of integrated provision for pupils in the age range 16 plus–18 plus and have suggested that this be made in Limavady Technical College. But this College is already full … There would appear to be a balance of advantage in changing the existing Grammar School, which has a considerable degree of integration already, into an integrated 6th-Form College …

Para 44: Londonderry District: A parent–teacher group has suggested that an integrated 6th-Form College be provided in the vicinity of the Technical College …

Para 49: Southern Board: There is ample 6th-Form accommodation in the Voluntary Secondary Schools under Roman Catholic management in Dungannon. Alternatively, this amalgamated school could, with considerable mutual benefit, share 6th-Form facilities with the amalgamated Controlled School … Every effort should be made to co-operate at 6th-Form level with St. Patrick's …

Paras 51, 52, 53: Belfast: re. Princess Gardens. It is clear that in a non-selective system this school could operate in the full 11 plus–18 plus range only with great difficulty. In view of its close proximity to and excellent relationship with Rathmore Convent School, it may be possible for the two schools to evolve a common 6th-Form provision …

Para 102: North-Eastern Board: for many years the Rainey School was the sole Secondary School in the area and to a significant extent it continues to provide for both Protestant and Roman Catholic pupils … [It could be] an integrated 6th-Form College … [Catholic schools] in Magherafelt, Maghera, etc. [could] contribute at 16 plus to an integrated 6th-Form College in Rainey Endowed School.[51]

Carvill's paper continued:

> Shared Schools: Note for the Record:
>
> In the discussion with Mr. Moyle yesterday the following points were established:
> 1   The Minister does not want major consultations on this topic to be initiated until after the consultation stage of the Consultative Document, i.e. into the New Year.
> 2   In the interim, soundings will be taken with the most important bodies (the only opinions taken so far were from the Cardinal, Lady Fisher and Mr. Garrett) on the extent and nature of wider consultation in the New Year, e.g. the Conference.
> 4   A paper will be prepared by the Minister suggesting the bodies with whom he might take preliminary soundings.
> ACTION Mr. McAllister and Mr. Jennings[52]

The 'integrated education complication'

Clearly, ministers and civil servants in the Department of Education were greatly exercised by the need to keep separate the issues of comprehensive and integrated education. They were anxious that there should be no accusations of foot-dragging on their part; at the same time they were concerned that there was not enough support for shared schools to warrant a conference. Arthur Brooke drafted a confidential paper headed 'Confidential/secretary of state/shared schools' over the summer. In it he observed:

> I think we must avoid a situation where a conference is held which turns out to be little more than an opportunity for interested groups such as All Children Together to air their views and at which major interests such as the Roman Catholic Church are unrepresented.[53]

In a long document, Brooke wrote that his thinking was greatly influenced by three considerations:

1   the need to ensure that the newly expressed interest is sufficiently broadly based to provide a foundation on which to build a constructive conference;
2   the importance of keeping the integrated education issue separate from that of comprehensive education and ensuring that consideration of the former does not inhibit the latter; and

3   the desirability of not giving a public impression that Government is
    stifling discussion or dragging its feet on the issue of shared schools in
    the face of a public desire for them.[54]

Brooke was firmly of the opinion that the issues of integrated education
and comprehensive education must be kept separate:

> some groups who would be favourably disposed to shared schools might
> well be unfavourably disposed towards comprehensive education. The
> reverse is also obviously possible. It is essential to avoid a situation where
> those who may be opposed to comprehensive education are able to use
> the integrated education complication as a delaying tactic.[55]

Brooke suggested sending out a widely circulated letter asking for
written views and posing questions about the most appropriate form for
a proposed conference and who should sponsor it. He concluded:

> The letter would also offer the more directly concerned recipients a
> meeting at which the possibilities and desirability of a conference could
> be discussed. These would as it were be talks about talks ... and the
> publicity which I have suggested would provide an effective answer to
> any who wish to suggest that government was doing nothing.[56]

This paper could hardly be regarded as a call to action, particularly when
it was read by Roland Moyle, whose interest in shared schools could at best
be described as tepid. But Moyle was about to leave the Northern Ireland
Office and later in that month of September Roy Mason arrived as the
new secretary of state and Lord Peter Melchett as the minister of state
with responsibility for education. Melchett also had charge of health and
social services and community relations; such a busy man, burdened with
much responsibility, was forced to rely heavily on the advice of civil
servants in the Department of Education, men (and they were all men)
keen to pursue the line adopted by Moyle and maintain continuity.

Meanwhile the debate on shared schools continued in public. At a
meeting in September 1976 Brian Garrett sparred with Andrew Boyd,
author of the best-selling *Holy war in Belfast*. The discussion was fully
reported next day by the *Irish News*:

> 'There is nothing whatever wrong with shared schools or with
> integrated education in principle', said Mr. Andrew Boyd, author and
> lecturer in the Belfast College of Business Studies ... But there was
> much wrong with the theory that segregated education was the main

cause of political conflict in Northern Ireland and that integration of schools would consequently create communal harmony ... There were denominational schools in other countries, besides Northern Ireland, and they did not cause conflict.[57]

Garrett said that only a fool would suggest that the school system was the cause of the Troubles – Cardinal Conway 'made that point very strongly in his booklet on Catholic Schools'. The real issue, he continued, was whether reform and movement to bring children together could help lay a foundation for resolving the conflict. He argued that even if there could not be an early widespread interchange of pupils, could one not have interchange of teachers? There could be much more sharing of facilities in teacher training and more attempts to organise joint projects for the children. He referred to the argument on the Catholic side that Catholic schools were a necessary part or extension of the Catholic faith; but 'serious doubts about how fundamental this idea was were underlined by the recent words of Cardinal Hume when he said there was a very strong case for integrated primary schooling in Northern Ireland'. He concluded, as reported by the *Irish News*:

> He had the suspicion that many people who stated practical objections to the idea of integration were at heart either cynics or, at worst, fundamentally against the whole idea of community reconciliation.[58]

Two years on – still no decision

Lord Melchett, who had succeeded Roland Moyle as minister of state with responsibility for education in Northern Ireland in 1976, now had to decide where he was going to go with the shared-schools issue. On 21 October, in some haste, he called together three officials in the Department of Education (McAllister, Carvill and Jennings). He had in his hands a 'background note' prepared for him by his private secretary, John Pitt-Brooke. The urgency of the meeting was that 'matters had come to a head with the receipt in the morning of an Oral PQ [parliamentary question] which was required by NIO [the Northern Ireland Office] (London) the next day. Some sort of a decision/statement was required immediately.' The question in the Commons was to be put by the redoubtable Sir Nigel Fisher, as follows:

> To ask the Secretary of State for Northern Ireland whether he proposes

to convene a conference on the subject of shared schools in Northern Ireland as his predecessor undertook to do; and if so when.[59]

Roy Mason, the new secretary of state, when visiting the Department of Education the previous week, 'had expressed his personal interest in this matter and had said no decisions were to be taken without his having been consulted'. In this 'Résumé of discussions with Lord Melchett' – marked 'Confidential', as was usual – this paragraph appeared under the heading 'Action taken':

> The Minister could not see himself at this stage saying either YES or NO to holding a Conference. It seemed to him that the safest and most sensible action was to undertake a round of public and private talks initiated by Mr. Moyle. Only after this fact-finding exercise could he gauge whether a Conference would be appropriate.
> The reply to the PQ would take this line.[60]

The minister of state indicated that he would take the opportunity to discuss the issue with teachers' unions over the next few weeks 'so as to reduce the number of "arranged" meetings'. He felt that he would postpone talking to the churches 'until towards the end of the exercise'.

> He also thought he might wish to discuss this with the Roman Catholic hierarchy in Great Britain, but accepted that if he did so it would be done very informally and certainly without publicity.[61]

The reply to the parliamentary question was duly written and passed on to Mason and the Northern Ireland Office the following day. The reply, given in the House of Commons on Thursday, 28 October, was as follows:

> The Minister of State intends to continue with the consultations which his predecessor had initiated on this subject. He does not intend to make any decision on the holding of a conference until he has had the opportunity of informing himself of the views of the wide range of interests involved.[62]

Arthur Brooke, the permanent secretary, summarised the situation on shared schools and provided further advice in a memorandum in November:

> Mr. Moyle had already had preliminary discussions with Lady Fisher, Mr. Garrett and Mr. Quigley who could be described as generally in favour of a conference and with Cardinal Conway and the Bishops who were firmly opposed to the idea. The subject was also mentioned during

discussions with Protestant Church leaders about the Consultative Document on Reorganisation of Secondary Education, who tended to show rather more sympathy with the idea of shared schools than did the Roman Catholic hierarchy.

Other bodies who have been suggested for consultation include a) Teachers' unions b) Northern Ireland political parties c) Northern Ireland Members of Parliament d) Parents Organisations:

1   Northern Ireland Parents' Organisation

2   ACT, the All Children Together movement which is the main supporter of the whole concept.

In the light of your discussions with the bodies suggested above you might then consider it appropriate to consult Church leaders – both Protestant and Roman Catholic – before taking any decision on the merits or otherwise of holding a conference …

It had been suggested that the invited organisations might be given the opportunity to submit their views in advance in writing and that, if they wished, a press statement incorporating those views might be issued after the meeting. This could have the advantage of letting the public at large see that the Government was actively following up the new initiative and, hopefully also let the public see how little or how much support there was for the holding of a conference. The disadvantage would be that some interests would be slow to produce written statements of views, especially those who might be hostile to the idea.

The alternative would be to treat the discussions as private and confidential. Discussions could then be held informally with little publicity until the full round had been completed, and a final decision about the holding of a conference could be announced.[63]

This much was clear: there would be no movement on shared schools until the new year at the very earliest. Merlyn Rees and Roland Moyle had succeeded in getting their way.

'Integrated education … hardly an issue worth worrying about'

As soon as he was appointed minister of state for education, Lord Melchett made it plain that he intended to bring Northern Ireland into line with the rest of the United Kingdom and introduce comprehensive education. This aim he pursued with an almost fiery zeal. The opposition he faced was formidable and included much from members of the Catholic hierarchy. ACT supported the drive to get rid of the '11 plus' and to introduce comprehensive secondary schools – but would the minister include provision for integrated schools in his scheme?

There is little doubt that Melchett was instinctively in favour of integrated schooling but he appears to have concluded that the difficulty of gaining support for the Cowan report's recommendations on secondary reorganisation, published in August 1976, was so great that seeking backing for integrated schools in addition would have to be regarded as a luxurious optional extra. A senior Department of Education official, D.K. Middleton, and a colleague, called on Bishop Edward Daly of the Derry diocese on 9 December 1976. Middleton reported:

1 Mr. Leahy and I called on Bishop Daly yesterday. He told us he had set up a diocesan working party to consider the Cowan Report. He wholeheartedly welcomed the Department of Education's efforts to encourage a public debate on the issue of secondary education.

2 The Bishop rehearsed a number of well-known themes – the entrenched attitude towards grammar schools; the special problems of rural areas ... he very much hoped that legislation which radically affected the pattern of secondary education in the Province would not be enacted during direct rule ...

3 If there were an opportunity for the Minister of State to call on Bishop Daly for an informal talk on the Cowan report, I think, it would be helpful. As you know, the Bishop is a young man with progressive ideas, and he is especially interested in education. He carries a great deal of weight in the diocese and exercises his not inconsiderable influence widely and generally in the Government's interest.[64]

A handwritten note, possibly from Roger Darlington, was attached to this minute:

Peter: This would be a v. good idea – Daly is far and away the most liberal of the 'Armagh Three' – it may be useful to get him away from Conway on shared schools.

Any expectation that the bishop would be flexible on the issue of comprehensive schools or differ from Cardinal Conway on shared schools was dashed on 24 January 1977. On that occasion Melchett travelled to Derry to meet Bishop Daly together with the headmaster of St Columb's College, Msgr Coulter, and Msgr Kielt of the Western Education and Library Board (WELB). According to the 'Note for the record', the bishop:

> gave his own views, which were strongly against reorganisation along comprehensive lines. He said that Northern Ireland was a conservative society ('with a small 'C' if not a large one') and that he felt both communities would resent major social innovation of this nature; the big grammar schools were justifiably famous and should not be changed. Monsignor Coulter quoted Durkheim, saying that it would be wrong to impose an alien educational system on a society which was not structured for it. They both particularly feared that comprehensive reorganisation would be forced on the country by the present government and then abandoned by some future Tory government …
>
> It was generally accepted that the 11 plus as presently arranged would have to go, and Monsignor Coulter proposed that it be replaced by a system of 'Election' by which parents chose which schools – grammar or secondary – their children attended. Lord Melchett commented that this was unrealistic as more parents would opt for grammar schools than there were grammar school places; it was also socially retrogressive, since all middle class parents would opt for grammar schools and most working class parents for secondary schools …[65]

Under the heading 'Integrated education' the 'Note for the record' continued:

> In a general discussion on integrated education Bishop Daly and Monsignor Coulter said that there were so few parents who wished their children to be educated at an integrated school that it was hardly an issue worth worrying about. Certainly hardly any of their own community wanted their children educated in other than Roman Catholic schools. Bishop Daly said that he continued to put the greatest importance on a close link between the home and the school environment, and so children brought up in the Roman Catholic faith ought to be educated in schools of that faith; schools had proved a rare stabilising influence over the last seven years, and it would be divisive to force integration on the community – 'the playground would become a battle ground'.
>
> Lord Melchett said that there was no intention of forcing integrated education on anyone, although he did point out that religion was the only field in which parents had this freedom of choice[;] they did not, for example, have any say whether their children attended a grammar or a secondary school. He asked for Bishop Daly's reaction to the holding of a conference on shared schools which had been suggested by the previous Secretary of State – if there really was no public support for the idea such a conference would demonstrate that fact. Bishop

Daly's reaction could not be described as enthusiastic. He said that it would merely be a gimmick designed for its media impact and would not reflect any real public interest. He advised Lord Melchett to tell any supporters of secondary reorganisation whom he might meet to 'come and have a word with me'.

It was generally felt that the views of the Protestant church on this matter would be exactly the same.[66]

In view of the argument Catholic clergy frequently put forward that shared schools would add to the costs of transporting children, the final discussion is of interest:

Bussing

Finally Lord Melchett referred to the difficulties which had arisen in Londonderry and in Fivemiletown where individual Catholic families who had sent their children to a state school on grounds of principle had not been granted free transport as the rules said that they were only allowed free transport to the nearest RC school. (Lord Melchett said that the case of the Londonderry family had been raised with him by William Ross at which Bishop Daly said that he had never met Mr Ross!).[67]

Bishop Daly replied that the general issue was one of how the instructions about bussing were interpreted and that this was a matter for the department although he did not wish to see the rules so amended in a way that Catholic families would have the choice between Catholic schools of the same type. Lord Melchett said that this was not a possibility, but that he hoped to be able to amend the rules to allow more flexibility on this matter.[68]

'So little thought for the scholars'

Brian Garrett did his best to urge the Westminster government to be less cautious. On 9 June 1977 *The Times* published his article entitled 'The growing urgency for shared schools in Ulster'. He began by reminding readers that Rees had assured an audience at the Oxford Union that 'he was willing, indeed anxious, to convene a conference to consider proposals for integrated schools in Northern Ireland'. In addition, he continued, Jim Callaghan, in a speech at the 1970 Labour Party conference, had given public support for the idea of shared schools. 'The assurance had been given at the end of an indignant, impassioned speech. One wondered what weight could be placed upon it. The answer is now clear: absolutely none.'

Garrett continued:

> Northern Ireland ministers have engaged in some half-hearted,
> perfunctory discussions on the subject. The message is that Labour
> ministers in Northern Ireland regard Mr Rees's assurance as a distinct
> embarrassment, and not an opportunity for the creative development of
> the present system of direct rule.
>
> Direct rule is likely to last for some time. It is widely accepted, though
> not enthusiastically supported. It is a tragedy, therefore, that in this
> period the opportunity to create a basis for radical social change is
> neither appreciated nor grasped.
>
> No one who knows the attitudes prevalent today among young
> children, as well as the hardened teenagers of Belfast and Londonderry,
> will be satisfied by the list of arguments put up by nervous government
> ministers or ultramontane Roman Catholic prelates against the case for
> even the most modest experiment in integrated schooling in Northern
> Ireland. Why should this approach be accepted? There is clearly
> substantial support within both communities for the *principle* of shared
> schools.[69]

Garrett pointed out that teachers within both systems 'are questioning
the situation' and that recently the Ulster Teachers' Union had made
renewed demands for integration. He continued:

> In the past such demands have often seemed token, but they are now
> displaying a new urgency. The inspired example of Mr John Burrell of
> Fivemiletown High School in Co Tyrone, who has over a period of years
> successfully demonstrated that integrated schooling can work in
> practice, has become a focus of attention ... Opinion polls conducted
> during the past 10 years have consistently shown a high degree of
> support for the idea of integration.[70]

Garrett did feel that in some of the worst-affected areas divided by frail
peace lines 'an integrated school is not a practical immediate alternative
but might well be a battle-ground'. Hostility mounted by fundamentalist
Protestants could be expected but 'the opinion polls suggest that only a
minority would actively support such opposition'. In any case the 'most
potent weapon against the idea of integrated schooling remains the
reaction of the Irish Catholic hierarchy'. This opposition, however, was not
as monolithic or absolute as it earlier seemed:

> Cardinal Hume's support for integrated schooling in Northern Ireland,
> voiced this year in a television interview with Ludovic Kennedy, has

opened up gaps. Many devout Catholics question the relevance of the Canon Law argument to Northern Ireland today. Certainly any new integrated schools in Northern Ireland would need to be pioneered against a clear acceptance that the right to existence of the Catholic schools as such will not be threatened.[71]

He pointed out that increasing numbers of Catholic parents – 'admittedly mainly middle-class living in the Belfast and North Down area' – were sending their children to state schools. 'It is clear,' he continued, 'they would prefer to send their children to a new type of shared school.' After referring to Bishop Philbin's refusal to confirm children not attending Catholic schools, Garrett concluded:

> The late Cardinal Conway consistently argued that the separate school system did not cause the Northern Ireland troubles and divisions. He was undoubtedly correct. But his argument sidestepped the real question. It is not any answer to the question whether a shared integrated school system would help in some measure to heal community divisions to reply that the schools did not cause those divisions. The true question has simply been avoided. It is a pity that in this land supposedly of saints and scholars there seems to be so little thought for the scholars.[72]

Less than a week after the publication of Garrett's article, on 14 June 1977, Melchett announced that the '11-plus' examination would be scrapped and that secondary education in the region would be reorganised on comprehensive lines. No provision was made for government-supported shared schools.

5

All Children Together challenges the status quo

The issue is not whether any particular schools are divisive in Northern Ireland, it is that our educational system IS entirely divided, echoing and reinforcing the divisions which already exist in the province along political, religious, historical, social and cultural lines.

CECIL LINEHAN, 1977[1]

Large majority of Catholics and Protestants favour shared schools

ACT members soon recognised the limitations of a loosely formed organisation. The fairly widely reported debate on the possibility of a conference on shared schools being held had brought at least one fact to the fore: the Catholic Church made it clear that it did not negotiate with informal groupings. This situation was quickly remedied. At an inaugural meeting on 29 January 1977 in the Presbyterian Community Centre, Queen's University, Belfast, ACT adopted a formal constitution.[2]

The movement immediately began to argue vigorously that there were strong indications that the people of Northern Ireland wanted the opportunity to send their children to integrated schools. In 1967 and 1968 two surveys carried out by National Opinion Poll found that 64 per cent of adults, 65 per cent of youths and 69 per cent of Catholics favoured integrated schools. A further poll, carried out for the *Sunday Times* and *Fortnight*, found these figures in response to the following question:

How would you feel about your children, or children you know, going to a school attended by pupils and taught by teachers some of whom were Catholic and some Protestant?[3]

Of the respondents 31 per cent were 'strongly in favour'; another 31 per cent were 'in favour'; 24 per cent were in the 'don't mind/willing to accept' category; 10 per cent were 'against' and only 3 per cent were 'strongly against'.[4] In short, a large majority of people in both sections of the community wanted shared schools. Yet an analysis of the school population showed approximately 99.5 per cent of Protestant children in state schools and 98 per cent of Catholic children in Catholic schools (see Appendix 9).

The Cowan report

The Cowan report on the future reorganisation of secondary education in Northern Ireland, published in August 1976, had caught the attention of ACT members. Cecil Linehan, then ACT chairman, drew attention to its failure to discuss the possibility of providing for shared Christian schools. Roland Moyle, the former minister with responsibility for education, had written on 8 July 1976 to the honorary secretary of ACT, saying, 'I think I should add that current thinking on the re-organisation of secondary education has not been taking into account the integration aspect.'[5] Yet the government had declared, by way of Moyle's address to the Association of Education and Library Boards in September 1975, and again in response to a parliamentary question by Sir Nigel Fisher on 22 January 1976, that its policy was 'to encourage those who provide schools to share when the opportunity arises'.[6] And three weeks before the publication of the report it had announced its intention of holding a conference of all interested parties on the shared-schools debate.

The ACT response to the Cowan report was submitted to Lord Melchett, Moyle's successor in the Department of Education on 21 March 1977. The response stated:

> The movement regrets that in its definition of a comprehensive school … the Consultative Document ignores the religious and cultural groupings in society in Northern Ireland … it will be impossible for this community to solve these problems without introducing integrated education where it is possible and in accordance with parental wishes.

We recognise, as the Consultative Document does, that there are effectively two school sectors in Northern Ireland 'the Roman Catholic and the non-Roman Catholic sector' … The proposals in the Consultative Document appear not only to accept this dual system but would, if implemented, destroy the hopeful amount of integration actually taken place.

The statement went on:

ACT regrets the cursory dismissal of the idea of new sixteen plus institutions, both 6th Form Colleges and Further Education Colleges. We believe that further education should be involved in any re-organisation, yet the Consultative Document avoids this issue … Everyone in the province, it would seem, is keen to see our sixteen to eighteen year olds being educated together. We have the shining example of the technical colleges with us to show the way.

Lord Dunleath was an early member of ACT. He steered the 1977 Education Bill through the House of Lords with great skill and patience. The Education (Northern Ireland) Act 1978 received the royal assent on 25 May 1978 and soon became known as the Dunleath Act. Lord Dunleath was president of Lagan College and also chairman of its first appeal. His untimely death in 1993 robbed Northern Ireland of a great and much respected public servant. ACT inaugurated a memorial lecture to commemorate his outstanding contribution to reconciliation through education.

Finally, ACT expressed its concern that:

Re-organisation of secondary education as proposed in the Consultative Document would not, as we had hoped, look forward to the next century and to encouraging a spirit of community in Northern Ireland's education scene concordant with the growing interest in Europe, but would, if anything, put the clock back and condemn our children to further generations of segregation and sectarianism.[7]

Challenge taken to Westminster

In addition to responding to the Cowan report and four other Department of Education working parties established to examine various administrative and legal changes to school structures, the ACT executive was taking a new direction. At the inaugural meeting in 1977, Dr John Burrell, then headmaster of the High School in Fivemiletown, County Tyrone, raised a matter that became an important issue, leading the ACT movement into frenzied action. Dr Burrell pointed out that approximately 30 per cent of the student body at his school, which was a state school, were Catholic. However, there was no administrative structure to protect such a situation at management level and he had no Catholic teachers on his staff. He felt the new proposed developments in secondary education could threaten the significant sharing in a school like his. The ACT executive began to prepare the ground for a parliamentary bill to enable integrated schools to come about in areas where sufficient numbers of parents wanted them. The Queen's University senior lecturer in sociology, Tony Spencer, with his administrative and legal experience, had a big impact in getting a draft bill together. Many long tiring hours (frequently over weekends, as most of the executive had full-time jobs), were spent refining and finalising the text.

As Stormont, the local Northern Ireland parliament, had been prorogued in 1972 owing to the levels of violence in the province, the only way to get a private member's bill onto the statute book (and the ACT bill would definitely have to be a private member's bill) was to have it introduced through the House of Lords. ACT member and Alliance peer, Lord Dunleath, offered to present the bill in the Lords. He also joined the ACT executive on many working sessions to familiarise himself fully with the thinking behind the bill's provisions. Basil McIvor, minister of education in the ill-fated power-sharing executive of 1974, took the draft bill to Fred Martin, the parliamentary draftsman at Stormont. He and his staff knocked it into shape so expertly that the draftsmen in the House of Lords could find no fault in the drafting.[8] On 28 April 1977 the bill 'to facilitate the establishment in Northern Ireland of schools to be attended by pupils of different religious affiliations or cultural traditions' received its first formal reading. It was due to have its second reading on 23 June (see Appendix 7).

The day after its introduction into the House of Lords, the ACT executive held a press conference in Belfast to explain the bill's main provisions. In brief, the bill, a simple enabling measure, would allow a majority of either the transferors (the representatives of the Protestant churches that had transferred their schools to state control in the 1930s) or the trustees (the Catholic bishops or their representatives) to opt for a new scheme of school management. This would allow the churches *together* to share power with parents, thus developing integrated schools from existing state (controlled) or Catholic (maintained) schools. In other words, there could be no forcing of church representatives or parents to develop integrated schools unless 75 per cent of church representatives on school boards of management took the initiative to allow the legislation to be invoked. In addition, 75 per cent of parents with children at a school had to be in favour before it could become integrated.

The bill went out of its way to 'safeguard existing developments' as well as to facilitate new developments in integration. Its two guiding principles were parental consultation and goodwill between the main churches – sufficient goodwill to allow children to be suitably instructed *in school* in the tenets of their particular faith. The ACT chairman, Cecil Linehan, emphasised that:

> the shared schools envisaged in the Bill will come from the people; NO ONE will be forced to ACT against his will. This is very important, and, as ACT members, I think you have a duty to point this out whenever you can. There is no doubt that several people see us as a threat to church schools. We cannot emphasise often enough that in claiming shared schools for our children as a right ourselves, we respect equally the right of parents and churches to denominational schools.[9]

The bill was reintroduced in the new session of parliament as there had not been enough time to get it through before the summer recess. In his speech in the second-reading debate in the Lords on 24 November 1977, the minister of state, Lord Melchett, said:

> The Government believes in the value of integrated education. We believe that increased contact between the two communities in Northern Ireland can and does improve community relations, and any increased contact among young people clearly has particular scope for altering or softening attitudes received from parents or the community at large … this is not something that can be imposed on unwilling or hostile communities, parents or children. To some extent we have to recognise that developments like integrated education, which we hope will change attitudes, are themselves only going to be possible when attitudes have altered.[10]

He did, however, say that he had grave reservations regarding the clause in the bill 'which would allow redundant school premises to be kept open as integrated schools rather than being closed down'. Lord Dunleath believed 'that this matter is cardinal to the whole principle of the Bill'. However, to facilitate the passage of the bill he agreed to an amended wording saying that:

> where any school either State controlled or voluntary is proposed for closure, the views of parents with children at the school, the views of parents with children of pre-school age in the area, shall be ascertained to find out whether they would prefer the school to continue as a controlled integrated school instead of closing.[11]

Lord Melchett also expressed his determination to investigate the possibility of creating integrated sixth-form colleges and integrated nursery provision.

Pressure on ACT members to drop the bill

Members of the ACT executive attending the debate in the House of Lords had been directly lobbied to drop the bill by senior Northern Ireland civil servants from the Department of Education, Northern Ireland. These civil servants were also doing all they could to persuade Lord Melchett to drop his support. Their anxiety seemed to be to preserve the status quo. Bill Brown recalled:

> The department didn't want to change anything. It appeared that the permanent secretary went up to Melchett at the bar in Westminster and he was still lobbying him at the last moment, trying to get him to change something.[12]

The civil servants did not succeed. The bill passed the committee stage in the Lords on 19 January 1978; it was passed by the Lords on 9 February; it was introduced into the Commons by Peter Hardy, vice-chairman of the Labour Northern Ireland Committee on 16 February; and the Education Bill (Northern Ireland) 1978 (eventually to become known as the Dunleath Act) completed its passage through the Commons on 12 May, receiving the royal assent on 25 May.

Immediately afterwards, in a widely covered press statement, ACT issued an appeal to the churches to ask them to use their initiative under the terms of the act to bring about shared schools where parents so wished. In particular ACT looked to Protestant church representatives to take a lead: the three main Protestant churches had all, over the years, passed resolutions in favour of integrated education at their assemblies and synods.

'The bill, on its own, will achieve little, unless acted upon,' Cecil Linehan correctly observed. She continued in a further article:

> legislative change alone will achieve little without a change of heart, and it is in this area that one looks to the influence that can be exerted on public opinion through speaking at meetings, writing newspaper articles and personal contact.[13]

Front cover of House of Lords Hansard of 16 Feb 1978 and copy of Education (Northern Ireland) Act 1978.

The ACT-sponsored Education Bill makes its way through the House of Lords, becoming law on 25 May 1978.

Lobbying the ministers responsible for education

A meeting with Lord Melchett took place in June 1978. It was a positive meeting in which he confirmed that the education and library boards would be contacted and instructed to set out the main provisions of the act and that model schemes for consulting parents would be prepared by the following October.

As the 1979 election had seen the return of a Conservative government, maintaining pressure on government became a paramount activity for ACT. Members of the ACT executive – Bettie Benton, Cecil Linehan, Sr Anna Hoare, Bill Brown and Liam Mallaghan – met Lord Elton, the new under-secretary of state for education, in February 1979. They reported:

> On the designation of a school as 'integrated' after widespread sounding of public opinion in an area [in accordance with the provisions of the Dunleath Act], the Minister was extremely hesitant. He made it clear that the Government would never impose integration. They would respond to requests to facilitate integration but would not initiate anything that might be seen as enforcing integration.[14]

It was necessary to assure him that ACT was completely opposed to forced integration. The minister seemed reluctant to support further changes to legislation to allow parents to bring about change.

Lobbying the churches

In February 1979 meetings took place with the churches' boards of education. ACT was anxious to find out the attitude of the various churches to the new act, since the legislation left the initiative very strongly with them.

- The Presbyterians felt that pilot schemes should come first and admitted that Presbyterian support for sharing had regressed since the onset of the Troubles. The ACT representatives, Bettie Benton, Liam Mallaghan and Kathleen Lindsay, did not agree with the argument that without a high representation by churches a good ethos could not be maintained. 'The Presbyterians kept trying to claim that our [state] schools are open to all,' Bill Brown recalled. 'They supported integration but not at the expense of rocking any ecumenical boat or raft.' Rev. John Dunlop, a highly regarded former

Presbyterian moderator dedicated to improving community relations, explained to Brown the dilemma of those clergy who had given their support to resolutions in favour of integrated education. Many were members of governing bodies of controlled (that is, state) schools with shrinking intakes, likely to be threatened by the opening of new integrated schools – 'when they go up to the school, which is so scared of losing staff and losing pupils, what are they to do?'[15]

• The Church of Ireland was even more anxious to avoid action which might threaten ecumenical relations; it was concerned about the diminishing Protestant community in the Republic; and it was also concerned that, in areas west of the Bann, Catholic representatives on area boards were virtually controlling all schools. This had implications for any move by the church to give up control. It was clear that the Church of Ireland would be seeking considerable action on the part of Catholic parents before any initiative would be taken. Fellow Anglicans, Margaret Kennedy and Sr Anna, had a meeting with Archbishop Robin Eames. Kennedy recalled hearing that his predecessor as Church of Ireland primate, Archbishop George Simms, had stated that, since the Church of Ireland lay somewhere between the Catholic Church and other Protestant churches in beliefs and forms of worship, it was in a good position to interpret one church to another. Eames smiled and said, 'It was I who said that.'[16]

The meeting was extremely cordial but, beyond some encouragement, there was little in the way of practical support. The most sympathetic was Rev. William Arlow, assistant secretary of the Irish Council of Churches and one of the Protestant clergy who had met republicans in secret talks in Feakle, County Clare in December 1974. A 'lovely man', Arlow ended a meeting with ACT members with the words, 'I'll arrange a meeting.' This was to be a meeting with representatives of the four main churches in Ireland, but he did not get the backing he needed and that meeting never took place.

Strong opposition was voiced by Rev. Houston McKelvey, representing the Church of Ireland. Some years later, when the Catholic Council for Maintained Schools was formed as a governing body for Catholic schools, McKelvey argued that 'we [the transferors

– the representatives of the Protestant churches] need a council for controlled schools'. Margaret Kennedy retorted, 'You've got one – the education and library boards.' After one of the meetings with Dr McKelvey, subsequently dean of Belfast, she 'felt as if [she] had been sandpapered all over'.[17]

- Since they formed only five per cent of the community, the Methodists concluded that a lowering of church representatives on boards would all but eliminate their representation. However, they strongly supported the 1978 act and let the ACT representatives know that they had vigorously backed the McIvor proposals.

In brief, all the Protestant churches felt that, unless the Catholic Church changed its rules and practice on matters such as mixed marriages, it would be difficult to persuade their adherents to accept substantial change.

An ever-widening debate

Despite the fact that the 1970s were the most violent in the whole 30 years of the Troubles (a total of 2,261 violent deaths took place between 1969 and the end of 1979), several factors meant that the debate on integrated education was rarely out of the public arena. Among these were:

- Attempts by direct-rule ministers to avoid organising the public conference on shared schools, promised by government in July 1976.

- ACT's persistence in ensuring that in its responses to the four government working parties established by the Northern Ireland Department of Education on the reorganisation of secondary education, the importance of integrated education was constantly highlighted. This was in marked contrast to the government's efforts to reorganise secondary education in Northern Ireland without taking account of the issue of integration.

- The publicity accompanying the introduction of the Dunleath Bill into the House of Lords in 1977, and its continued progress through both houses of parliament, highlighted in ACT press releases and conferences throughout 1977 and 1978.

- A debate on integrated schools held in Derry City Council in 1977 and a resolution in favour passed by a majority of the councillors.

- A widely publicised seminar held by ACT in March 1979 entitled 'Cooperation in education', which focused on the ecumenical developments that had led to the establishment of the Roehampton Institute in London, a federation formed by the amalgamation of four colleges of education: Anglican, Methodist, Catholic and Froebel.

- The furore caused by the reaction to the interim Chilver report on teacher education in Northern Ireland.

Alarm in the Catholic hierarchy

The Catholic hierarchy displayed some alarm at all this activity. On Easter Sunday, 11 April 1977, Dr Edward Daly, bishop of Derry, preached a sermon which seemed to cause an ever-widening ripple of disappointment. Clearly he was reacting to the vote in favour of integrated education passed by Derry City Council. He expressed fears that schools might become forcibly integrated: 'Closing down Catholic schools and introducing an integrated school system will only succeed in creating new and added problems.' He also expressed grave concern about religious education in state integrated schools and dismissed the idea that Catholic schools were divisive. These views Daly expressed again in an interview a week later in an RTÉ news programme. ACT responded that Catholic parents had a right to Catholic schools and that it did 'not believe that shared or integrated schools would have to be God-less schools', saying, 'our movement is totally against any idea of forced integration'.[18] It should be pointed out, however, that Bishop Daly was perfectly cordial when meeting ACT members face to face, and, after all, it was he who had confirmed the Catholic children from the diocese of Down and Connor who had been refused the sacrament. The elevation of Dr Tomás Ó Fiaich to the College of Cardinals, necessitating his absence from Armagh for long periods, led to a postponement of a meeting with him at that time. (When he did meet ACT representatives, Cardinal Ó Fiaich was equally charming and said privately to ACT members that it might take something as radical as integrated education to change things for the better in the region.)

While the Catholic Church continued to be the most overtly opposed

Notice to parents from Belfast Education and Library Board announcing it had received an application from Throne Primary School in north Belfast to invoke the 1978 Education Act – known popularly as the Dunleath Act. It was the view of ACT that the Belfast Education and Library Board had done little to promote the image of integration. BELB, however, did agree to convert Throne Primary School in north Belfast into a controlled integrated school on 1 January 1982 – Catholic children could take up places left vacant by the fall in the enrolment of Protestant pupils. The experiment was not a success.

to integrated education, all in all, ACT felt that there was much hypocrisy in the attitude of all the churches to what it was trying to achieve – the education together in school of Catholic and Protestant children in Northern Ireland. As Margaret Kennedy observed, 'The churches were preaching reconciliation. We were preaching the most radical form of reconciliation – yet all the churches were often against us.'[19]

Supporting schools seeking to use the 1978 act

A school in north Belfast, Throne Primary, had invoked the 1978 act in late June 1979 and ACT naturally was most anxious to ascertain what support the school, both management and teaching staff, would receive from the Department of Education and the Belfast Education and Library Board (BELB) – particularly in light of the positive meeting with the minister of education in June 1978. The minister had assured ACT that explanatory schemes for education and library boards and support for schools would definitely be ready by October 1978.

'To our surprise we discovered that the schemes and statutory instruments necessary for the implementation of the Act were not ready, despite assurances given to us by the previous minister', it reported. The minister was reluctant to admit that the Department of Education had responsibility for informing the public of new legislation.[20]

Despite this lack of support, Throne Primary School went ahead, invoked the Dunleath Act and opened as a controlled integrated school on 1 January 1982 – but it was not a success. BELB had done little to promote the image of integration; the school's management committee represented the Protestant community only, as places reserved for Catholics had not been taken up and no Catholic teacher had been appointed. In short, Throne Primary was constantly threatened with closure as Protestants moved out of a bitterly fractured and run-down district, frequently convulsed by intercommunal violence. After two years

BELB decided to close the school. Bettie Benton, then chairman of ACT, concluded from this outcome that an integrated school must clearly be seen a) to have an integrated management committee, b) to have an integrated teaching staff, c) to have an integrated ancillary staff, and d) to offer an integrated curriculum, if it was to attract pupils from all religious affiliations and cultural traditions. She added:

> No school with the threat of closure hanging over it will attract pupils. Parents will not enrol their children and some will take their children away. We deplore the way this school appears to have been treated.[21]

Another school threatened with closure, Park Parade Secondary School on the Ormeau Embankment in east Belfast, was also seeking integrated status. An emergency resolution was passed at ACT's 1984 AGM, declaring that:

> ACT welcomes the decision … and expresses its willingness to offer assistance and support particularly with problems related to integration of the Management Committee, staff and student body and the teaching of sensitive areas of the curriculum.[22]

The decline of Park Parade had gone too far, however, and as the school flanked a loyalist enclave there were no prospects of attracting Catholic pupils. Further-education students of the Belfast College of Business Studies, temporarily left homeless after the bombing of their shared premises in Ormeau Avenue, were housed for a year in vacant mobile classrooms at Park Parade (with the present author as the senior lecturer in charge). In time, the whole site was turned over to the further-education sector – which, of course, was and remains integrated.

In early 1984 a third school, Malone Primary on

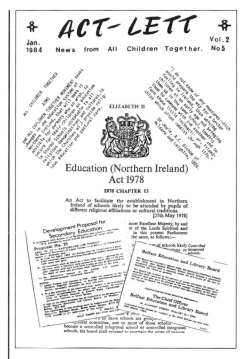

Front cover of *ACT-LETT*, January 1984. Work continues as the critical development proposal seeking recognition for Lagan College as a maintained school is sent to the South Eastern Education and Library Board (grant-maintained integrated status did not come in to the legislation until Dr Brian Mawhinney brought in the Education Reform (Northern Ireland) Order in 1989); and a further public notice from the Belfast Education and Library Board announcing that Malone Primary School in south Belfast was also seeking to invoke the Dunleath Act. Lagan College was successfully grant-aided in March 1984. Without the support required from the churches, the education and library boards and the Department of Education in Northern Ireland, Malone's bid to use the 1978 act failed. It later opened as an independent integrated primary school.

Balmoral Avenue, also within BELB's area, also tried to invoke the Dunleath Act. Its attempts were also rejected by the department but, with ACT support, it opened in 1985 as an independent integrated primary school known as Forge.

ACT's disillusionment with the churches

The question foremost in the mind of ACT members was whether or not the churches would take up the new opportunities offered by the Dunleath Act. The three main Protestant churches had given their support to integrated schools – but did that mean that they would take the initiative to set them up? It soon became clear that they would only respond to pressure from parents. In her last report before handing over the ACT chair to Bettie Benton, Cecil Linehan concluded:

> I feel strongly that we must strengthen our resolve; that while retaining good relations with the churches we may have to move forwards on our own – not because we do not wish to retain the cooperation of the churches but because each church in turn seems to be waiting for parents to take the initiative … How long can our children wait? For their sake we must make a start.[23]

This was to prove sound advice. In the ensuing years members of ACT were to be bitterly disappointed that none of the churches, for all their expressed support for integrated education, were prepared take risks by using the powers granted to them by the 1978 act.

Sr Anna, now ACT's vice-chairman, called on parents to take the initiative:

> If your child goes to a school which is already partly mixed, and if you believe that a majority of parents in your area would welcome integration, form a local group – it can be quite informal – drawing in as many other enthusiastic parents as possible, and approach the church representatives on the management of the school your child attends … one school can have the honour of getting the ball moving. We must be prepared to make haste slowly, but not go to sleep. The Government has expressed its intention to help any authority which wishes to introduce voluntary integration.[24]

In a very well-worked-out piece in *Fortnight* in May 1980, Tony Spencer, then treasurer of ACT, set out the deep disillusionment felt by parents and all those in Northern Ireland who supported integrated education at the total lack of action by the churches. More than that, Spencer, an influential member of BELB, was able to record:

> very hostile comments from individual church representatives on the Area Board who did not see themselves as morally bound by the successive resolutions at synods, assemblies and conferences, nor by supportive comments made by the churches' spokesmen after the passage of the '78 Act.[25]

In addition, Tony Spencer tellingly pointed out that the churches were not following their own advice as laid out in their report entitled 'Violence in Ireland', where they said:

> total religious segregation is by no means a necessary nor a desirable consequence of legitimate denominational difference … [and] the Churches have not adequately faced up to to the fact and the consequences of this religious segregation.[26]

Spencer went on to comment that for the umpteenth time in history, when faced with concrete situations where basic Christian values point one way and the protection and/or enhancement of institutional powers point the other way, church representatives put power first and values second:

The lack of support for the 1978 Education Act was highlighted in a pithy article in *Fortnight* by ACT member, Tony Spencer, entitled: 'All children apart: the thwarting of integrated education'.

> In so doing, they illustrate the way the historic link between religion and politics in Ireland makes religion into an apparently insuperable obstacle to problem solving in the Northern Ireland conflict … and they underline the validity of the very cause they notionally accept and really oppose, [that] **one** of the conditions of an ultimate solution is the creation of a third [integrated] sector in the N. Ireland education system where Church power is replaced by Christian values.[27]

In June 1980 the chairman, Bettie Benton, issued a direct appeal to the churches. It took the form of an open appeal on behalf of the members of ACT and made their disappointment plain:

> This letter is addressed to the Churches on behalf of our members.

We have had many months of intense educational debate on school management and now on teacher education.

We have been disappointed with the attitude of the Churches to sharing equally in school management with teachers and parents.

We have been disappointed at the lack of initiative from those churches committed to voluntary integrated education.

We have been disappointed at the reluctance of the Roman Catholic Church to take account of the developments in other countries where sharing in school and colleges with others is becoming more and more common, to the benefit of all.

WE APPEAL TO ALL THE CHURCHES TO SET UP A WORKING PARTY TO STUDY THESE DEVELOPMENTS IN OTHER COUNTRIES.

At a time when all the Churches are encouraging their laity to engage in bridge-building, let us see evidence that the churchmen are prepared to set an example.[28]

Benton was able to get a wider audience for her appeal in an interview published in the Northern Ireland edition of the *Sunday Independent* on 13 July 1980. She noted that the reformed churches had declared their commitment to integrated education and that Cardinal Tómas Ó Fiaich had expressed support for bridge-building between the communities. Then she observed:

the fact that the appeal has so far been ignored must cast doubts on the sincerity of the churchmen … The Education (Northern Ireland) Act 1978 (The Dunleath Act), which depends almost totally on the Churches to initiate it, sits unused on the Statute Books (except for one case of a school threatened with closure). In our innocence we in All Children Together (and others of the general public judging by letters to the Press) believed that in some mixed areas the churches would take the opportunity offered by the new Act to demonstrate their goodwill and desire for reconciliation amongst those already one in Christ. Alas, how naïve we have been! Yes, we are disappointed. Yes, we are disillusioned … It is not my wish to appear to be 'getting at' the Churches but sometimes it behoves a lay person to give a bit of a nudge.[29]

6
Lagan College

The reality, on September 1 this year, will be a small group of eleven-year-olds and a tiny band of teachers, in temporary premises, with the most basic of resources. Can this tiny seed grow into a college of more than 500 pupils in its own school building? Will Catholics, Protestants and Agnostics live and learn peacefully together? Shall we build a school that is trusted by parents and which children will enjoy attending?

SHEILA GREENFIELD, FIRST PRINCIPAL OF LAGAN COLLEGE, 1981[1]

First day of Northern Ireland's first planned integrated school: Lagan College principal, Sheila Greenfield with five eleven-year-old pupils, September 1981.

The birth of Lagan College took place at a time of bitter intercommunal conflict and a fresh increase in violence. The year had opened with the serious wounding of Bernadette McAliskey and her husband. Five days later, in revenge, the Provisional IRA killed Sir Norman Stronge, aged 86, and his son James by burning down their home at Tynan Abbey. Following the removal of political status, republican prisoners in the Maze prison had embarked on blanket and dirty protests. Then, on 1 March 1981, Bobby Sands began his hunger strike. Sands, who was elected MP for Fermanagh/south Tyrone on 9 April, died on 5 May. On the day of the funeral at least 100,000 people – nearly one fifth of the entire Catholic population of Northern Ireland – crowded the route to Milltown cemetery. In all ten republican prisoners in the Maze had died on hunger strike by 20 August. Riots reminiscent of those that had taken place a decade earlier erupted after every death. Amongst those who died were Carol-Anne Kelly, aged 11, and 14-year-old Julie Livingstone, both killed by plastic bullets; and a milkman and his 15-year-old son, fatally injured when their float was pelted by bricks in Belfast. Meanwhile, the Provisionals stepped up their relentless war on the security forces. In the worst incident five soldiers were killed by a landmine near Bessbrook on 19 May. The violence continued after the hunger strike had ended in September. Five Provisionals shot dead Rev. Robert Bradford MP and a caretaker who tried to stop them on 14 November. Altogether 118 people (18 Protestant and 34 Catholic civilians, 45 members of the security forces, 16 republican and three loyalist paramilitaries, and two others) met with violent deaths in 1981. The following year the death toll was 112,

Sheila Greenfield with the first 28 pupils and first staff members – 1981.

almost as high. The bravery of the 28 pupils who enlisted in Northern Ireland's first integrated school has to be set in the context of a city with a fractured community daily convulsed by rioting and killing.

Scout-hall beginnings

The failure of the churches to take the initiative to set up even one pilot integrated school led directly to parents taking the matter into their own hands, which ultimately resulted in the setting up of Lagan College in 1981. Its origins could be traced back to the 1974 ACT open seminar entitled 'Interdenominational schools – why? how? and the way ahead'. In the years that followed, ACT gave a commitment to hold further seminars on religious education and cultural heritage in shared schools. This it did, and it gradually became clear that a change in legislation was needed to protect schools that already had a significant degree of mixing between Catholic and Protestant pupils and to permit the establishment of integrated schools where desired. This resulted in the drafting of the bill which became law in 1978, as outlined in the previous chapter.[2]

In the years 1978 to 1980, just after the Dunleath Act was passed, hopes ran high among ACT members and other interested groups that integrated schools would now develop though the action of church representatives invoking the new enabling legislation – after all, most of the Protestant churches had reacted reasonably positively to the McIvor shared-schools plan of 1974. While it was very unlikely that the Catholic hierarchy would show any interest in sharing power with Protestant representatives on integrated school boards, this would not invalidate the invocation of the Dunleath Act. The Protestant representatives could have given up some of their places on school boards to parents. In fact, the initial vocal backing did not convert itself into practical initiatives and support from the Protestant churches melted away. ACT was particularly disappointed at the lack of recognition and understanding by the churches of its ecumenical and reconciliatory vision. What could be more conducive to community understanding, members argued, than bringing Protestant and Catholic children together in school? ACT believed this would be an application of the basic principles of Christianity.

Disappointment and frustration mounted throughout 1980, with the churches' refusal to use the legislative powers they now had, and on 2

March 1981, parents – some of whom were long-standing members of ACT (especially Tony Spencer from south Belfast and Maeve Mulholland from Lisburn, County Antrim) – approached the ACT executive and trustees to seek ACT's support for the opening of an integrated all-ability coeducational school in their area, starting with first-form children transferring from primary seven. The ACT executive acted promptly, met on 10 March 1981 and, following lengthy discussion, agreed that a proposal 'to open an all-ability post-primary college for Catholic and Protestant boys and girls in south Belfast'[3] should be brought to the annual general meeting on 3 April 1981.

At the ACT AGM the proposal was endorsed. It has to be made clear that, despite what has been written elsewhere, the only dissenting views expressed at that 1981 AGM were by those who felt the timescale was just too impractical and that the proposal should be amended to allow the opening of the school to be postponed until the following September. But, as the proposal was endorsed by the majority at the AGM, work began immediately. Aware that not a moment was to be lost if a school was to be up and running by the following September, ACT called a public meeting in south Belfast to ascertain parental support for the proposal. The ACT trustees were asked to establish a governing body, appoint a principal and seek financial aid. ACT, of course, then had no money to speak of: at the 1981 AGM the accounts showed that the movement had a paltry £36.11 in its current account and absolutely no capital. This was clearly a leap of faith – some might say, Cecil Linehan reflected later, that it was almost irresponsible to be taking such risks with the education of post-primary pupils.

A public meeting was called on 23 March 1981 to discuss the possibility of opening an integrated, all-ability post-primary college for Catholic and Protestant boys and girls.

The 15 parents who had enrolled on 23 March provisionally accepted 'Lagan College' as the school's name on 27 April. Tony Spencer's expertise guiding them along the way, they also agreed that a limited company should run the school through a board of governors and that a dummy-run self-assessment for parental contributions should be carried out. A draft prospectus was drawn up on 7 May. The ACT trustees placed advertisements to seek a principal and short-listing took place on 12 May.

Sheila Greenfield was duly appointed. A 43-year-old Englishwoman, educated in St Albans, a graduate of history from Leeds University, she had been head of English in a large comprehensive in Sheffield, where much of her work involved providing programmes to assist the integration of children of Caribbean and Asian origin. In 1974 she had been appointed deputy head of Wisewood School in Sheffield, a coeducational comprehensive school, where she had special responsibility for pastoral and social welfare, discipline, careers and the sixth form. Greenfield had come to Northern Ireland because her husband Tony had been appointed professor of medical statistics at Queen's University in 1980. Clearly, Lagan College was fortunate to obtain a principal of such experience and standing with no inappropriate cultural baggage. She had been chairman of the Sheffield branch of the National Childbirth Trust, chairman of the BBC Radio Sheffield Local Advisory Council and a member of the BBC Northern Ireland Advisory Council.[4]

Soon after her appointment, Sheila Greenfield wrote an article explaining why she had applied for the post and saying that when she first saw the advertisement, she 'knew nothing of the long history and background efforts of the All Children Together Movement in their struggle to establish integrated education in Northern Ireland'. She continued:

Mrs Sheila Greenfield, principal 1981–6.

> Three aspects of the college attracted me. First, it seemed both logical and right to bring together children of school age of all religious denominations since they were going to spend the rest of their lives living together in Belfast. I have worked all my professional life in schools catering for many faiths and many races, so perhaps I underestimated how novel, indeed controversial, was this concept in Northern Ireland. I am now a little wiser at the magnitude of my undertaking, but remain unshaken in my belief as to the rightness of what we are attempting to do.
>
> Secondly, the establishment of a college for children of all abilities accords precisely with my fundamental belief that *all* children are entitled to equal opportunities in education. In our struggle for an equal and just society, schools must be used to reduce, not actively perpetuate, the many divisions that already exist. Little is heard in Ulster of the many hundreds of excellent schools which are quietly providing opportunities for children of all abilities in other parts of the United Kingdom ...

The third factor which will distinguish Lagan College is its high degree of parental involvement. It is a salutary lesson, in times of falling rolls, to remember that without children there would be no schools and no teachers. The raising of children is a responsibility which must be shared between home and school. This partnership is strengthened and enriched if both sides have the same objective and trust can be established through continuing dialogue.[5]

Greenfield was well aware that Northern Ireland then had no true comprehensive school on the British model – Lagan College would be the first – and that parents of prospective pupils might fear that standards might not be maintained in a part of Belfast noted for its flagship grammar schools. So, to reassure those parents who were considering sending their children to Lagan College, she added:

I do understand the anxiety many parents and educators feel about all ability schools, which they see as a threat to academic standards. After 12 years experience of working in all such schools, I have been convinced that when they are well managed, the opposite is the case. The able do not suffer and the advantages for the average and below average children have been clearly demonstrated and acknowledged …

Whatever the distinctive character of the school, it will be judged according to the academic standards it sets and achieves for its pupils. We shall aim for academic excellence from those capable of achieving it. We shall also seek excellence in sport, in practical skills, and in relationships. All pupils must have hope of achieving success and due recognition of their worth.[6]

Lagan College's first prospectus.

Much care and work by the newly appointed staff was clearly required before the curriculum could be claimed to represent fully both Catholic and Protestant cultures. The first programme offered mathematics, English, science, French, history, geography, religious education, swimming, art, craft and drama. The school had the use of a minibus five days a week and was promised the use of science laboratories and a gymnasium at Stranmillis College and of the swimming pool at Queen's University. Finding a site in a safe and positively neutral area proved to be an enormous and time-consuming hurdle which ACT members worked arduously and strenuously to overcome. In the end it was agreed to rent temporary premises at Ardnavalley Scout Centre, near Shaw's Bridge (appropriately close to the River Lagan).

However, even this simple step was fraught with serious problems, as the district council of Castlereagh, within whose boundary the premises lay, was strongly opposed. At the council's May 1981 meeting councillors argued against the use of the scout hall for this purpose – only, they said, out of concern for the safety of the children as the adjacent road had such heavy traffic. ACT members had no doubt that this was a clear case of veiled Protestant obstruction to the concept of Catholic and Protestant pupils going to school

together in such a venue. After all, the scout hall and its surrounding grounds were frequently used by large numbers of boys for various scouting activities during the year and every so often hosted an immense gathering of boys for scout jamborees. However, a majority of the councillors on Castlereagh District Council, led by Peter Robinson, deputy leader of the Democratic Unionist Party, persisted in its opposition. Castlereagh Council voted against granting temporary planning permission to permit the scout hall to be used as an integrated school. At that stage, the ACT trustees and executive had no choice but to ask Basil McIvor to ask his contacts in parliament to use their influence to have the decision reversed. As a result the decision was indeed reversed and the school opened in September 1981 as planned. Sheila Greenfield observed:

Ardnavalley Scout Centre, close to Shaw's Bridge and almost on the banks of the River Lagan, became the first home of Lagan College. ACT had to apply for temporary planning permission to the District Council of Castlereagh, within which the scout premises lay. During a council meeting in May 1981, a majority of the councillors, led by Peter Robinson, deputy leader of the Democratic Unionist Party, voiced strong views against this temporary change of use and voted against the proposal. The decision was later overturned. ACT had always been deeply grateful to the scout movement in Northern Ireland 'for coming forward and offering hospitality to the school'.

> The reality, on September 1st this year, will be a small group of eleven-year-olds and a tiny band of teachers, in temporary premises, with the most basic of resources. Can this tiny seed grow into a college of more than 500 pupils in its own school building? Will Catholics, Protestants and Agnostics live and learn peacefully together? Shall we build a school that is trusted by parents and which children will enjoy attending?[7]

The resources certainly were basic. School life in the scout hall for those first few months seemed to resemble that of the most remote national school in the previous century. In addition, every desk, every book and every piece of chalk had to be cleared away at 4 p.m. to allow scout use to continue as normal; then every piece of equipment had to be brought out again the next morning for the pupils. During the first couple of weeks, as they made their way into the school, the first 28 boys and girls who had enrolled had to run the gauntlet of hostile DUP supporters.

The first staff appointed also took risks. There was no guarantee that Lagan College would survive and certainly no prospect of promotion at that stage. From the very beginning teachers came from schools where they had posts of special responsibility and/or were heads of department, yet they were prepared to give up their extra emoluments to come to Lagan College. Bill Brown recalled:

> Early on in the life of Lagan College, it was agreed that a teacher was needed for the pastoral care and religious education of the Catholic children. The Board of Governors met to interview up to five candidates for the post. We found to our delight that two very competent staff with posts of responsibility as heads of department in RE had applied. But the governors were in a very difficult position – the school did not have the resources to offer even one scale post.
>
> In the middle of the opening discussion about this, the door opened and Dr Brian Lambkin asked if he could have a word with the committee. He said that he and the RE teacher had spoken with most of the candidates. Some they felt were outstanding but he knew the school could not offer any post money. He was also aware that at least two of the candidates were on fairly senior posts. Dr Lambkin informed the board that if they felt they wished to appoint a candidate already holding a post of responsibility, he was willing to surrender his own post allowance to enable the board to offer such an incentive to the candidate of their choice!
>
> It does not end there. The board that night offered the head of department post to a candidate who was already on a scale-four salary. The candidate was told they could offer a lesser post to him, but not a scale four. The successful candidate as it happened replied that he and his wife had already decided that this was the right job for him despite a much lower salary. No wonder Lagan College has gone from strength to strength![8]

Enter the Rowntree Trust

Although Lagan College had been receiving muted voices of approval from government quarters, it did not get any financial support from them until four years after it was up and running. It was entirely dependent on contributions from private sources. Here the backing of the Joseph Rowntree Charitable Trust, an organisation that gives financial support to projects promoting political equality and social justice, was crucial. It offered to pay the salaries of the teaching staff to be drawn for the purpose from a total grant of almost £45,000. Cecil Linehan wrote to over a hundred charitable trusts for assistance but Rowntree was the only one to take the plunge.

Wallis Johnson, assistant secretary of the Rowntree Trust, is an Englishman with Ulster connections – his father was from a Quaker family living in Richhill, County Armagh. During the worst years of violence in the 1970s, the social scientist Robin Hughes Jones persuaded officers of the Rowntree Trust that Northern Ireland was a legitimate field of interest. South Africa was then the trust's principal concern but Johnson, after meeting voluntary organisations in Northern Ireland, persuaded his organisation to set up a subcommittee to discuss ways of providing help there. Projects which attracted Rowntree financial support included the Upper Springfield Trust, Schools Cultural Studies, the Divis Education Project and the Northern Ireland Community Trust.

In the early 1970s, at a meeting of the British Irish Association in Belfast, Johnson met Cecil Linehan and later Bettie Benton and they talked intensely about hopes and plans. On his next visit he dined with the Linehans, where discussion centred on the possibility of setting up an integrated primary school. Johnson was appalled to find that Bettie Benton and Cecil Linehan were 'in effect excommunicated by the bishop of Down and Connor' and that the 'enabling legislation of the Dunleath Act had not been taken up'.[9] They were not in fact excommunicated. Johnson may have thought that the bishop's refusal to confirm Catholic children not attending Catholic schools meant that they and their families had been officially excluded by the church. This misconception can arise easily as Church of Ireland children receive communion following confirmation at age 13–14, whereas Catholic children make their first communion at age 7–8 and are confirmed later, at 11–12 years of age.

Johnson had attended several ACT annual meetings and had been instrumental in obtaining grants for ACT to run its seminars during the

THE
**ALL
CHILDREN
TOGETHER**
CHARITABLE
TRUST

SHARING SCHOOLDAYS

FOR THE ADVANCEMENT OF
INTEGRATED EDUCATION
BY CONSENT IN
NORTHERN IRELAND

C.I. (CLAIMS) Ref. No. 441/79

ACT set up the All Children Together Charitable Trust in 1979, the International Year of the Child.

1970s. Thus he was very well acquainted with the work of ACT, with the commitment of the people involved and the detailed study they were undertaking of all aspects of integrated schools around the world. In due course he expressed the view that it was looking more and more likely that ACT and parents were going to have to set up a school of their own if the mould of ongoing total educational apartheid was ever to be broken. His most immediate advice was that ACT should become a charitable trust or at least acquire a charitable arm. This ACT did, establishing the All Children Together Charitable Trust in 1979, the International Year of the Child.

When Lagan College was set up, Rowntree was one of the trusts that ACT approached. Johnson's knowledge of ACT was invaluable. It enabled him to say to his trustees that he was 'very struck by their enterprise, the degree of commitment' and that he hoped 'they could be given their chance'. A crucial meeting of the Rowntree Trust followed and Johnson prepared the notes for his case with care. 'After a longish discussion,' Johnson recalled, 'the trustees agreed to commit £15,000 a year for three years to cover staff costs at Lagan College.'[10]

The secretary of the ACT Trust at the time, Cecil Linehan, was overjoyed when she received this news. It seemed like a very large grant in comparison to anything the movement had received before. Above all, she felt that it would enable the ACT Trust to honour a decision (already taken by the trustees and the founding parents) that the teachers in Lagan College would always be paid at the proper rate. Little did the ACT trustees, the teachers and the parents know then that it would take some £750,000, acquired over four hard years from private benefactors, church groups, parents and large foundations, before Lagan College received grant aid of any kind from the Northern Ireland Department of Education.

Other costs had still to be met. The only option was to charge fees of around £600 per annum to parents – the going rate for annual fees for a child who had not passed the '11-plus' examination but was still given a place in the first form of a voluntary grammar school. These schools were allowed to offer between 10 and 15 per cent of their places in this manner in those years. At an early meeting of Lagan College governors-elect with the Department of Education in June 1981, Tony Spencer, Sheila Greenfield and Cecil Linehan were dismayed to hear that the true cost of educating a child in a grammar school was £1,250 – in other words, the governors of Lagan College were going to have to reckon on each place in the school costing over £1,000 but knew they could not ask parents enrolling children in the new college more than the going rate of £600.

To make it possible for a full range of pupils to attend it was agreed to provide bursaries averaging £450 per annum or £150 per term. Linehan reported that a group of people in Britain was raising funds to help any family wishing to send their child to Lagan College but unable to afford £600 a year – 'in fact over half the families already enrolled have applied to have their income assessed and some will be paying as little as £25.00'.[11]

It must be explained that Northern Ireland is not a region that contains public schools like those in England, Scotland and Wales. Parents of children attending the most prestigious grammar schools paid modest top-up fees but, at that time, nothing close to the fees Lagan College felt compelled to charge to those who were able to pay. 'Lagan College is open to all and money is not a barrier,' Linehan said, but this policy would test the energy and ability of ACT members to the limit. She declared:

> Yours truly has been writing daily to all parts of the universe for Money! Money! Money! ... So let us know about everything – from coffee mornings to children's sales – small is beautiful in fund-raising and even the smallest amount raised by members or parents or governors strengthens our hand when we write to trusts or foundations.[12]

On 6 September BBC Radio Ulster allocated its appeal slot for charitable causes to ACT and Lagan College and this was presented by Margaret Percy.

Moving site

Lagan College had moved from the Ardnavalley Scout Centre after Christmas to the former Castlereagh Special School, now redundant premises managed by SEELB. ACT expressed their 'deep indebtedness to the Scout movement for coming forward and offering hospitality to the school'. These premises would be too confined when the next cohort of 11 year olds arrived in September 1982. The chairman was 'overjoyed by the way the school is going ... the art and music [are] exciting. The unity

The former Castlereagh Special School, on Church Road, Castlereagh, then redundant premises managed by the South-Eastern Education Area and Library Board, became the second home of Lagan College.

First pupils to attend the
Church Road site.

and dedication of the staff and enthusiasm of the parents, as well as the happiness of the children, makes every effort on their behalf, for me at least, 100 per cent worthwhile.' ACT members and parents voluntarily helped out with transport and one regularly travelled 12 miles to vacuum clean the school floors. Sr Anna's energetic commitment became legendary – she hitch-hiked, for example, in France 'on a shoe-string budget' on a fund-raising visit and addressed countless groups in London and elsewhere.[13]

ACT still had no offers of financial help from government and had to direct much of its energy into fund-raising. It was decided to employ a professional fund-raiser, Butcher Gayle of Sheffield. A target of £500,000 was set to finance Lagan College until it could be taken into the system, as well as a primary school should parents demand it and a rapid-response fund in case pressure should occur elsewhere in the region. The appeal was launched on 6 May 1982 in the House of Lords with Lord Dunleath as president. Forty-two prominent individuals gave their names as patrons. Four Lagan-College pupils went over for the launch. Around a fifth of the target had been received or promised before the launch and in the following months some 500 grant-making trusts were approached. A gala evening was organised on 27 May in Monte Carlo, under the patronage of Princess Grace and attended by Princess Antoinette and her daughter.[14] A particularly interesting donation was a grant of £3,000 to Lagan College made by the priorities fund of the Church of Ireland. As the *Church of Ireland Gazette* put it, this grant to the college was 'to encourage its interdenominational educational experiment in Northern Ireland. This is in keeping with the 1970 resolution of the General Synod stating that it would welcome experiments in integrated education.' The Church of Ireland's synod standing committee regarded the college as 'an ambitious project towards furthering reconciliation in Northern Ireland'.[15]

Lagan principal and deputy – lead speakers
at 1982 ACT seminar on 'Planned shared schools'

Sheila Greenfield was given the opportunity to make a detailed progress report in her paper *Lagan College: the first six months*, given at the ACT seminar, 'Planned shared schools', on 6 March 1982. What distinguished the college from all others, she said, was that it was the first school in the region where integration was deliberately planned and where the 'principle of balance is crucial to the maintenance of confidence for all parties involved … from the outset steps have been taken to ensure an equal balance amongst our Governors, teaching staff, ancillary helpers and pupils.' The college had no academic selection and 'admits pupils of all abilities, apart from those with severe educational, physical or emotional handicaps who could be more appropriately catered for elsewhere'. She continued:

> In our first intake the spread of ability is reasonably wide, although the College is at present disadvantaged in its bid to attract the most able pupils, since these are guaranteed free places in grammar school under the existing system of selection for secondary education.
>
> Classes within the College are planned to reflect the full range of ability, boys and girls, Protestants and Catholics and non believers, since we believe that the individual talents of pupils are best fostered when there is no labelling or division of pupils by ability. We believe all pupils to be of equal worth and thus to deserve equal opportunities. Although the basic unit of instruction is an unstreamed class, it is seen as essential for pupils at both ends of the ability range to be offered special teaching in small groups, on a withdrawal basis. In our first six months there has been an intensive programme of special help to provide less able pupils with the basic skills of literacy and numeracy to enable them to benefit from teaching in the class group.[16]

Much work was being devoted to rethinking the entire teaching programme 'in terms of its relevance to a rapidly changing society and in terms of a commitment to reflect the cultural values and traditions of the two major communities in Northern Ireland'. For this reason 'we are grateful for the wise decision to admit one intake at a time, starting with eleven year olds and building gradually upwards'. The generous provision of advice from the department was acknowledged and two inspectors had visited the school in October 1981. Advisers from SEELB and BELB had also been helpful and had assisted with staff appointments. Greenfield said that the college 'has been fortunate to recruit teachers of the highest calibre in their specialisms, as well as in their commitment to the philosophy and aims on which the College is founded'. This was crucial since parents, in addition to supporting the principle of shared schooling, 'also expect, and quite rightly, that this must not be achieved at the expense of academic excellence'. She continued:

> Thus we aim for the very highest standards of which our pupils are capable and realise that if the school is to compete on equal terms with many existing excellent schools within the Province, it will be judged, and ultimately succeed or fail, on the quality of the teaching it provides.[17]

She commented on the very high level of parental involvement, particularly through the Parents' Council, which was 'a positive contribution to our growth and, equally importantly, a means of extending our work for reconciliation and understanding beyond our pupils and out into the wider community'. The pupils had their own council, 'both as a training ground for democracy and as a step towards their involvement in a shared responsibility for the welfare of the school community'. No pupil had left so far and relationships between pupils are:

> friendly and normal with no hint of religious subdivisions or factions, but plenty of evidence that friendships are forming across the religious divide. Our Catholics cross themselves without self consciousness and although debate is lively and our differences expressed and acknowledged, no insuperable problems have so far arisen in our teaching programme.[18]

The religious-education programme

Although pupils of parents of other religions and of no religion were welcomed at Lagan College, the decision was made at its foundation that it should be a Christian school. The aim of the college was, the prospectus stated, 'to provide a programme that meets the requirements not only of parents belonging to the main Christian churches but also to those of other faiths or none'.[19] As Brian Lambkin, in charge of Lagan College's religious-education department, explained at the same seminar:

> This might seem to be an impossible aim: to develop a Christian ethos and at the same time hold open the door to all comers. But 'ethos', after

all, simply means 'the characteristic spirit or tone of a community' and a Christian community is surely one which both welcomes all comers and provides for them.[20]

Entering the caveat that the religious-education programme was in its infancy, Lambkin outlined its three main elements: the phenomenon of religion (which dealt with the history and ideas of the major religious and philosophical traditions of the world); the common Christian tradition (which dealt with doctrine and practice held in common by Christian denominations); and the denominational tradition (which dealt with doctrine, moral and ethical traditions and sacramental practice specific to particular denominations). He explained further:

> These three elements combine to form the Christian view of religion inspired by the prayer of Jesus which the College has taken as its motto, 'ut sint unum' – that they may be one. The programme is, thus, Christian but open as far as possible to non Christians. It is hoped that all pupils could participate in the first element. Since the College is established to serve a predominantly 'Christian' community it would seem reasonable to anticipate that most pupils would participate in the second element. Parents are free to choose the combination of elements which best suits their needs. They may opt their children out of elements of the R.E. programme, in which case alternative provisions will be made, or opt their children into particular denominational teaching.

Topics covered in the common Christian tradition element included baptism, eucharist, advent, Christmas, epiphany, the week of prayer for Christian unity and the gospel of Mark. Lambkin expanded on how baptism, mutually recognised by the Christian churches, was dealt with in the classroom:

> The essential elements of Baptism – the pouring of water and the formula 'I baptise you in the name of the Father, the Son and the Holy Spirit' – can be identified. Children can be encouraged to discuss their own experiences of Baptism. With a number of different denominations represented in the class, divergences in practice will become apparent; for instance the Catholic will realise that other denominations do not all have a lighted candle or white garment as part of the ceremony of Baptism. Differences can be discussed in common, thereby giving children understanding of other denominations, while what is held in common remains clear.

One period a week was reserved for the use of chaplains for the denominational traditions element, to be used by each chaplain at least twice a term. The approach of each chaplain was to be pastoral rather than pedagogical, to provide a 'linked denominational back-up' to the main programme.

> His presence in the school symbolises the interest which his own Church takes in its members who are pupils at the College and the encouragement which the College aims to give to pupils to grow in membership of their own particular church. The Chaplains safeguard the denominational identity of the pupils.

Lagan College adopted the policy of providing a chaplain for every denomination represented by children in the school, partly to avoid the over-simplistic Protestant/Catholic split. Yet what was ground-breaking was that Protestant and Catholic pupils in Northern Ireland were being given a comprehensive religious-education programme designed to give due weight to both traditions. Certainly in the most prominent grammar schools Catholics often attended religious-education classes in Protestant schools and in the few Catholic schools where some Protestants attended, such as the Dominican College at Portstewart, they too were prepared to receive religious instruction. In neither type of school, however, had conscientious attempts been made to give anything like equal weight to both religious traditions.

This novel approach threw up some unexpected problems. For example, Catholics did not add to the Lord's prayer the words provided by Martin Luther, 'For thine is the kingdom, the power and the glory, for ever and ever' (the doxology). After initial embarrassment, discussion followed on the origins of the doxology and on other aspects of differing Christian traditions and henceforth the Lord's prayer was said with and without the doxology on alternate weeks. Brian Lambkin concluded his address to the seminar by referring to the 1965 Second Vatican Council document on education, *Gravissimum educationis*, which stated that it was 'the special function of the Catholic School to develop in the school community an atmosphere animated by a spirit of liberty and charity based on the Gospel'. Substitute 'Christian' for 'Catholic', he suggested, and 'you have a statement which expresses well the aim of Religious Education in Lagan College'.[21]

Seeking maintained status

It was Dr John Benn (a distinguished former permanent secretary of the Department of Education and Northern Ireland's first ombudsman) who suggested that the governors of Lagan College should apply to the local area board – in this case SEELB – for maintained status. The governors agreed and the application was sent on 29 June 1983. It was passed by SEELB's Educational Services Committee on 14 July, then by the full board on 2 August. During September and October 1983 prolonged discussion took place between the board and the Department of Education on the wording of the development proposal the board then had to publish on behalf of Lagan College. The wording was finally agreed in October and the proposal was published on 31 October 1983. Allowing for the statutory two-month period during which other educational institutions could lodge objections with the board in regard to the proposal, the earliest date on which the minister could have made a decision regarding admitting Lagan College to the maintained system was 31 January 1984.

No signs of significant movement could be found in official quarters, however. By the beginning of 1984 Lagan College had 164 pupils in forms one to three and good numbers had enrolled for September without waiting for the '11-plus' results. The governors of Lagan College and ACT members waited anxiously for the government's response to the school's request for maintained status. They were aware of all of the demands of the legislation but the fact was that by this time, having run for almost three years on private and charitable donations, governors were faced with unavoidable expenses of £20,000 per month and the coffers were becoming emptier and emptier. The strain of trying to keep up a confident exterior, to organise open days in the spring as all second-level schools did, and to hold to their commitment always to pay teachers at the proper rate and to keep up their pension contributions and other expenses, was increasingly taking its toll on all associated with the school.

Then on 1 April 1984 Lagan College was granted maintained status. This lifted a huge financial burden from ACT and vindicated the courageous action of the Rowntree Trust in funding salaries until now. The need for funds was still urgent to cover capital expenditure and, in particular, the additional accommodation required for September's intake, which would bring the school's enrolment to around 300. The seventh annual general meeting of ACT took place on Saturday, 7 April 1984 in Lagan College. The secretary, Yvonne Gilmour, described the scene:

> Coffee was served before the meeting and members sipped appreciatively while taking in the breathtaking view across the city to Divis on what was a bright clear sunny morning. Some slipped away for a quick look around the campus. An air of suppressed excitement permeated the atmosphere as the business meeting commenced. All were conscious that it was a historic occasion to be treasured and remembered.[22]

In her address as chairman of ACT in 1984, Bettie Benton declared:

> The break-through that we have all longed for [for] so long has come. It has come in the recognition of Lagan College as a grant-aided voluntary maintained school providing interdenominational all ability secondary education for boys and girls.

She continued:

> With that approval must come official recognition that there is a demand for planned shared schools of this particular character and that where a demand can be shown Government will respond and even welcome it. Mr Nicholas Scott, Under Secretary of State appearing on the UTV programme *Counterpoint*, stated that he hoped to see other instances of demand for integrated education.
>
> The other thing we must take immense heart from is that it proves that determined parents can bring about change and that is good and bodes well for the future.[23]

Harsh financial realities

Euphoria accompanying the recognition of Lagan College as a maintained school was quickly followed by a realisation that fund-raising had to remain a top priority. As Bettie Benton pointed out in January 1985:

> our experiences in setting up Lagan College necessitated circa £500,000 to be raised to totally fund the school until Government decided the school had a right to exist and was a legitimate choice for parents [and have] brought home sharply to us that progress towards the development of further integrated schools appears to rest on our ability to raise massive sums of money – a daunting task and prospect indeed.[24]

Mr Terence Flanagan, principal
1987–93

Dr Brian Lambkin, principal
1993–7

Mrs Helen McHugh, principal
1998–2009

A second appeal was launched with the dual aim of consolidating the work at Lagan College and of giving financial support to a group of parents in south Belfast 'who have expressed a wish to open an integrated school at primary level in September 1985'.[25]

As secretary of the Board of Governors, in her report to the school's annual general meeting in 1984, Cecil Linehan observed that SEELB had been as generous as it could be but that 'Lagan College cannot expect and does not receive special treatment'. The Department of Education had approved in principle £140,000 for new mobile buildings, £10,000 for a new car park and £33,000 for the purchase of the existing school site. However, a total of £187,000 would have to be paid by the college up front before the 85 per cent of that sum would be repaid as grant aid by the department. At the same time, the ACT Trust had to raise £60,000 to enable the school to acquire enough land to provide a car park, a turning circle for buses and improved access for vehicles. The Department of Education would not fund any of the expense incurred in the car park, bus-turning circle etc, yet these were all essential requirements for the planners before they could grant permission for the additional mobile classrooms. Linehan concluded:

> It has only slowly become clear exactly what our continued financial requirements are:
>
> 1 [Learning] to live with the reality of providing 15% of all capital expenditure and waiting for grant-in-aid to be paid.
>
> 2 Supplying the essential equipment and books which our local and most helpful Education Board just cannot supply.
>
> 3 Building up in three short years a repository of new school equipment which long-standing schools have been able to acquire over several years.[26]

Fund-raising – an ongoing headache

ACT had by now obtained office accommodation closer to the city centre by renting a room in a warehouse overlooking the Castlereagh Road. Lagan College, too, was seeking bigger premises. In September 1984 there were 296 children attending the school (from 47 different primary schools) and a total of around 400 was expected for September 1985. Then eyes fell on a severely dilapidated eighteenth-century mansion, Lisnabreeny House, in the Castlereagh Hills. Owned by the National Trust, the building had long been used by the Youth Hostel Association until it had become too decayed to continue in that role. Less than a mile from its site on Church Road there was ample room for expansion and, since the house was surrounded by 18 acres, playing fields could also be developed. A 99-year lease was negotiated but a great deal would have to be done before the entire college could move there. For a time Lagan College would have to become a split site, with September's first-year intake being taught in mobile classrooms at Lisnabreeny. Hopes that the portico of Lisnabreeny House could be preserved were unfounded.

In the four financial years ending on 31 March 1985, the total sum raised was £561,000 and – after meeting expenses of around £28,000 – all of this had been disbursed. The main cost had been the purchase of an established school building in south Belfast and the erection of sectional wooden classrooms nearby, which had come to approximately £337,000. The sum of £48,000 was allocated to help meet the costs of Forge, the first integrated primary school, and a further £65,000 was given to the ACT Trust to be used in supporting other groups endeavouring to establish integrated schools in Northern Ireland. Most of the remaining balance was spent in supporting the financial needs of Lagan College, particularly in the period before it gained maintained status. Here the main items of expenditure included salaries, school books and equipment, stationery, postage, telephones and transport.

'Not one of my journeys has cost Lagan College 1p'
– Sr Anna

Sr Anna was indefatigable in her fund-raising. On a shoestring she hitch-hiked and journeyed on long-distance coaches and trains, sometimes changing at three o'clock in the morning. 'Not one of my journeys has cost Lagan College 1p,' she wrote, and continued:

> You've also got to be prepared to venture into the unknown, to thrust yourself, for the sake of Lagan College, onto likely and unlikely people (well heeled Irish abroad, people with a special concern for Northern Ireland etc); to sleep anywhere, such as in someone's summer house …
> In fact you have to be robust, like an ox.
>
> Of course it's only a minority who are interested in far distant Northern Ireland, but some in Europe have a real sense of our interdependence and suffer with us. Little Holland and bigger Germany especially are amazing in the many different ways they have rallied round to help … I find people are so happy that we are DOING something, that it's not just all talk, that we have taken the initiative and sacrificed to do so …
>
> That is the joy of it. The financial side is but an external, concrete expression of something far deeper: one can only call it love: a deep, inner, concern and identification and a costly willingness to get alongside.[27]

Sr Anna had been to France four times and referred in particular to the constant support of Anglican chaplaincies there, Princess Antoinette and the Monte Carlo Lagan College gala which she had arranged, and the widow of the racing driver Eddie Hall, 'who asked for no flowers at the funeral and opened instead an Eddie Hall Memorial Fund for Lagan College'. In Germany, where she had been three times, students in Munich had raised £16,465:

Sr Anna came to Belfast in 1981 with Mother Teresa of Calcutta. Mother Teresa left but Sr Anna remained for 31 years.

> It has been a joy to join them in a beautifully organised sponsored walk, beginning with an ecumenical service and ending with a disco, or in various projects bringing Lagan College into the Katholicentag – the gathering of Catholics from every part of Germany and beyond. There is also the extremely hard working Stuttgart group: one of Northern

Ireland's greatest friends there really worked herself into the ground. She was already ill, but paid no heed, and then died; or of the Hamburg group, so enthusiastic, who recently collected to get out two minibuses plus insurance, electric cooker and two other valuable pieces of equipment.

I also remember a friend in her seventies, who loves Northern Ireland. Her family collected to cover a return air fare here and she gave the total sum for Lagan College as circumstances had blocked a speedy return, saying, 'If Providence wants me to visit later, the money will come.'[28]

In the Netherlands and Belgium, Sr Anna encountered 'wonderful enthusiasm, friendship and help'. She had been gathering peace-education materials for schools from various sources in the United Kingdom and the Republic of Ireland since 1976 and in 1984 she was invited to the United States to create an exhibition of these, naturally placing Lagan College to the fore. Church Women United, 'a vital, active, ecumenical movement throughout the States', took her to many venues in Wisconsin; the American Presbyterian Church took her to a centre in New Mexico; and her tour included the eastern seaboard and Chicago. 'Such kindness, such warmth, such generosity, can never be forgotten,' she reported to ACT members, and she concluded:

> Without all these friends, Lagan College could never have overcome all the hurdles and continually expanded. We would have been sunk long ago. Have we, parents, ACT members, trustees and local supporters done as much as these friends so far away? Sometimes I think many of our nearest do not grasp our present, on-going urgent need. We are still very much in the wood.[29]

Margaret Kennedy recalled that Sr Anna burst into the middle of a Lagan College meeting with large bundles wrapped in newspaper. When the newspaper had been stripped away, seven quarter-size violins were revealed on the table. How did she get them? It turned out that she had visited the prestigious Yehudi Menuhin School and boldly asked if there were any 'spare' instruments which could be used to instruct Lagan College pupils. Her friends could only speculate what devious charm she employed to cajole the director into handing over the instruments. Another one of Sr Anna's ploys on her many travels was to enter a café

Sr Anna's fund-raising for Lagan College – Mrs Helen McHugh thanks Sr Anna on behalf of all involved in Lagan College. Sr Anna Hoare came to Belfast in 1972. A religious sister of the Anglican Community of the Sisters of the Love of God from Oxford, England, Sr Anna laboured for over 31 years for the young people of Northern Ireland and was dedicated totally to the work of reconciliation through education. From 1982 to 1994, Sr Anna made 28 overseas trips, listed below, raising funds for Lagan College. In 2003 at the age of 86 Sr Anna Hoare returned to live in her convent in Oxford. Her residence there could not be more different from the small house situated in the middle of the conflict zone in the Ardoyne in north Belfast.

in her nun's habit with an old kettle and ask for some hot water to make some tea. Inevitably she would be asked what her mission was and, more often than not, both the proprietor and the customers would find themselves dipping into their pockets to contribute to fund-raising for Lagan College.

'We still wait in vain'

The years 1981 to 1984 had been tumultuous. The enrolment of the new integrated college had grown from 28 pupils in 1981 to 296 in 1984; the sacrifices made by pupils, teachers and parents were at times formidable. In addition, all of this was taking place during one of the most violent periods of Northern Ireland's 30 years of Troubles, with the extreme tensions accompanying the H-block hunger strikes of 1981. Yet, through it all, support for the concept of educating Catholic and Protestant children together in Northern Ireland continued to pour in. By the time the two Lagan College appeals were finally closed, £750,000 had been raised. That is what it had cost parents and ACT to bring the first planned integrated school in Northern Ireland into existence – and it must be noted that 95 per cent of the monies raised came from outside Northern Ireland and much of the fund-raising on the continent and in the USA was done by Sr Anna.

As chairman of ACT in 1982, Sr Anna observed that meetings with *individual* clergy were 'most supportive and encouraging', but, she continued:

> we still wait in vain for those churches committed to voluntary integration in education, or at least to pilot schemes, in our search towards unity. As we are constantly reminded we are the church, the people of God. However, acting corporately, we seem so often to be guided by caution, as a paramount evangelical virtue: to be fighting various rearguard actions in society. In the sphere of education it seems at times for lack of bold, imaginative, forward looking action, the whole future of Christian education could be at stake.[30]

The Education Act of 1978 had been:

> an attempt to give to others the power to initiate. As you know, nothing happened. It was no good waiting indefinitely for someone else to start. Sheer parental pressure has driven ACT to act and to put into practice

what we have been preaching. So Lagan College was born in South
Belfast on 1 September 1981.[31]

Over 1,000 pupils and all staff at the millennium 2000.

7

St Bede's School, Lagan College and shared religious-education syllabi

Joint Church Schools are in no way second best to single denominational schools ... Most children who attend these schools grow as Christians, rooted in their own tradition, but also develop a full appreciation of the richness of other Christian traditions. The experience is one of immense enrichment.

ENGLISH ANGLICAN-ROMAN CATHOLIC COMMITTEE, 2000[1]

'Divisions among Christians are a scandal to the young people of today'

All Children Together were attempting to facilitate the joint education of children of all denominations in a manner that had not been attempted before – in the twentieth century, at any rate – in any part of Ireland. It therefore made sense to look further beyond the island's shores to discover whether or not similar experiments had been made. St Bede's School in Surrey, England, provided an inspirational model which very closely matched that envisaged by the founders of Lagan College.

Two schools in Redhill, Surrey, a Catholic coeducational school and a nearby Anglican school, were threatened by the local education authority with the loss of their sixth forms. The governors of the two schools met in March 1972 to discuss cooperation to create a viable sixth-form provision. Two proposals were considered: one to create a sixth-form centre to be run as a joint enterprise; and another, which would lead to the 'gradual merging of the two schools in a coeducational comprehensive school'.[2]

The second proposal was the one that found favour and in November 1972 it received full approval from both the Anglican and Catholic diocesan authorities – an unlikely happening at that time in any part of Ireland. The 'Manifesto' published by the headteachers made it clear that the joint school was to have an uncompromising Christian ethos and a commitment to Christian unity:

1 The condition of society at present calls for a clear and convincing witness of Christian solidarity in face of the challenge from humanists, the general indifference towards moral issues, and the apathy of nominal Christians who are uncommitted to the Christian way of life.

2 Divisions among Christians are a scandal to the young people of today. Their reasoning is that if we are sincerely following Christ, minor differences become petty and irrelevant.

3 Not only is specifically Christian teaching in the form of school assemblies and religious education under fire but the Christian values of honesty and truth are also very much at risk. We believe that they can only be taught in a convincing way in the Christian context …

6 Between the ages of 14 and 16 young people go through a period of revolt against every established standard and authority. With the understanding and tactful handling of a community of faith, they come frequently in the Sixth Form to see the values of what they have been tempted to reject. They are, at this stage, prepared to accept a more mature approach and a more personal commitment to the content of the whole Christian message …

8 One of the encouraging aspects of this whole idea is that the project of a united Christian school is unique in the whole of the country. It could well blaze a trail for further collaboration in other areas.[3]

To reflect the Catholic population in the catchment area and a reasonable balance of boys in the new intake, it was agreed that the ratio of Catholics to Anglicans should be 2:3. The difficulties usually accompanying amalgamations had to be addressed – in particular, that of achieving a balance of staff to match the pupil intake ratio. However, the expected difficulties emerging from the amalgamation of staff were, if anything, eased by a feeling that 'we are all Christians together'. One teacher observed in 1981, 'I have never met so much goodwill in any staff. The emphasis is on resolving problems. There are no factions, and things here do not get out of proportion.'[4]

The Second Vatican Council's decree on ecumenism certainly helped to smooth the way for the founders of this amalgamated school, which was to be named St Bede's. In addition, Pope Paul VI had issued a statement that the Anglican Communion was to be treated by Rome as a 'sister'. The main remaining difficulty was that the Catholic Church could not acknowledge the sacramental authenticity in an Anglican eucharist. The national Catholic secondary-schools adviser wrote, 'I do plead that people do not rush into this kind of venture – it requires years of discussion and consultation.'[5]

But the governors were not to be deterred. The new school, which was to open in September 1976, was to have 18 governors – six representing the Anglican diocese, six the Catholic diocese and six the local education authority.

Religious education in St Bede's: plans and problems

The first chairman of the new school, Canon John Montague, later described his task as 'the most creative activity in which I have ever engaged in over 40 years'.[6] Such a positive approach was vital in resolving how best religious education could be provided. The governors' statement of intent included these words:

> We recognise that in Worship and in Religious Education there is much that at the present time must take place separately, for conscience's sake, and because of church discipline. It is our hope, however, that at least some worship and religious education can take place together, and that this area of what can be done together will be allowed to increase and expand naturally as the staff feel it right.[7]

It was widely understood that if assurance could not be given that both Anglican and Catholic interests would be safeguarded, the new school would not succeed. It was vital to make certain that both parties were satisfied that the religious-education programme met their needs and, to this purpose, a working party on religious education was established by St

Bede's, holding its first meetings in 1975. Because of the pioneering nature of the work, this committee was high powered: it included the two headteachers, the two heads of religious education, diocesan religious-education advisers and representatives of the hierarchies. Priscilla Chadwick, later head of religious education at St Bede's, found that the minutes of the first meeting indicated extreme caution:

> There may well have been an underlying dread that the idealistic atmosphere in which everything had been discussed hitherto might be quickly shattered if the more obvious sources of mutual discomfort were dealt with. Some of the distinguished national figures serving on the working party acknowledged at interview that they felt the initial sessions were unstructured and desultory ... there seemed to be a fatal propensity to take off into abstract discussions of religious education and the theoretical principles and theology underlying it.[8]

A particularly significant difference to emerge was how the Anglican and Catholic churches understood the role of church authority in defining Christian truth. One Anglican observed:

> The Christian life is an interaction between tradition and the experience of the individual. The individual then arrives at his own personal faith. The school can at best put them on the right path on which they will, hopefully, continue and grow.[9]

This contrasted with the comment of the Catholic headteacher that 'the Catholic school exists for the purpose of teaching religious doctrine – our concepts of the Church school are totally different'.[10]

Separate or shared religious education?

In February 1973 the governors had made it clear that separation for general religious education was not desirable. Now, nearly three years later, it was becoming equally clear from the deliberations of the working party that this could not be agreed – general religious education would be provided to Anglican and Catholic children together *only* because it would be supplemented by separate denominational teaching.

The governors received the working party's report in June 1976, just two months before the school was due to open. It could be said that the recommendations, duly adopted, were somewhat timid for a school which was declaring itself to be ecumenical in a part of the United Kingdom where regular participation in Christian worship had become very much a minority activity.

The 1978 ACT seminar: 'Shared schools in action'

Some two years later, ACT decided it was time its members heard of the St Bede's experience at first hand and invited Angela Lawrence, a Roman Catholic lecturer in religious studies and a governor of St Bede's, to address the 1978 ACT seminar entitled 'Shared schools in action'. Canon Eric Elliott, a distinguished Church of Ireland member of the Central Committee of the World Council of Churches, agreed to be the second speaker. He was to talk on interdenominational agreed religious syllabi and the joint syllabus for CSE and GCE religious-education examinations in Northern Ireland.

In her address, Angela Lawrence, who had been involved with St Bede's since its inception, declared, 'I have, as a Catholic involved in the field of education, come to share in the creativity, the joy and the whole adventurous spirit which St Bede's engenders.' She then spoke on the establishment of St Bede's in 1976 and on the development of its curriculum. This mixed comprehensive now had 70 teaching staff and 1,100 students between the ages of 12 and 18 (one third of the staff and pupils were Catholic). It had *not* been originally envisaged that a united church school would eventually be born out of a common-sense sharing of resources at sixth-form level in 1970. 'That it did happen,' she said, 'is attributed to the creative power of the holy spirit ... All those working together on the emerging plan for a united school grew, in a spirit of sincerity and charity, to have a better understanding of each other's beliefs.'[11]

Since religious education was a central theme of the seminar, Lawrence had much to say on that subject. A commission (the working party) with representatives from both the Anglican and Catholic churches met on a number of occasions to work out the basis of a joint religious-education syllabus. It was eventually decided that all students would have three periods of religious education a week; during two of the sessions they

---

ALL CHILDREN TOGETHER

invite you to an afternoon Seminar

Shared Schools in Action

Speakers:
Angela Lawrence on
    St Bede's Shared Sch., Redhill, Surrey
Canon Eric Elliott on
    Inter-denominational Agreed Syllabi

Saturday, 15th April, 1978
    2·15 p.m.
BELFAST Teachers' Centre
Tea: 5·30 p.m. Panel Discussion: 6·30–7·30 p.m.
Seminar fee: £1·50

ACT looked beyond Ireland's shores to discover what other countries were doing in the field of educating children together. In this 1978 seminar, St Bede's School in Surrey, England, a coming together of an Anglican and a Catholic school, provided an inspirational model which very closely matched that envisaged by the founders of Lagan College. Shared religious-education syllabi in Africa were also studied.

would follow the common syllabus together, taught by members of the religious-education department; and, during the third session, they would separate into their denominational groups. Catholics would be taught by a Catholic member of staff and Anglicans by an Anglican teacher. The third period would focus on the doctrine and practice of that particular denomination. 'The teachers of R.E.,' Lawrence observed, 'have remarked that their doctrinal teaching has been enriched because it has been rooted in the seed bed of a common study of fundamental Christian principles.' Experience of working together in the early years of St Bede's had elicited the following comments from members of staff:

> Sharing does not necessarily imply a 'watering down' of the faith, but can result in a particular enrichment difficult to achieve in isolation. Unity in the Spirit does not diminish, but serves to endorse what each holds dear. One can only share with others that which one first possesses.[12]

Shared religious-education syllabi – worldwide and in Northern Ireland

Canon Elliott, appointed education officer of the Church of Ireland in 1950, spent 21 years as rector of parishes, at the same time acting as chief inspector of religious education in the dioceses of Connor and Down and Dromore. He stated:

> At first my visits to schools were concerned with denominational teaching and inspecting the agreed syllabus. More and more, as the years passed and circumstances changed in terms of the religious situation, the needs of the pupils and my understanding of the faith, I have found myself placing more and more emphasis on the agreed syllabus. One has to see this shift as a reflection of the growing irrelevance of much that was seen as denominational in a situation in which there is a growing loss of the spiritual dimension. Increasingly Christian witness in society has to be on an interdenominational basis or not at all, and this is true in universities, schools and industry.
>
> The truth is that we live in a society which is becoming much more complex, open and pluralistic, and in such a society one of the most important contributions of religious education is to lay a foundation for tolerance, openness and sympathy.[13]

In such a situation, Canon Elliott believed, there was an overwhelming case for experiments in agreed syllabuses. He referred to the common catechism prepared by Swiss, German and French theologians and a new joint syllabus in east Africa. 'In the end,' he asked, 'is it largely … non-theological pressures which compel the Churches to re-examine their theological positions?'[14] Canon Elliott's comments would be remembered vividly by ACT some 12 years later, when they had great difficulty bringing the churches in Northern Ireland together to develop a core religious-education syllabus for pupils in all schools in Northern Ireland.

Having listened to Lawrence's accounts of the positive developments in St Bede's, Cecil Linehan, then chairman of ACT, commented:

> What is unique to me, when I read of St Bede's shared school, is that it came about by the positive action of two churches who said: 'Let's form a united church school' … [and] what must strike all of us here in Northern Ireland is the open and honest way in which the venture was approached. St Bede's united church school … exists today because two groups of people in two different churches took a positive decision to pool their resources.[15]

And with regard to Canon Elliott's comments on the actual existence of common R.E. examination syllabi in Northern Ireland as well as in Switzerland, Germany, France and east Africa, Linehan said that the fact that common syllabi in religious education had been in existence for some time in Northern Ireland had prompted her to ask the simple question, 'Why cannot our children, with the blessing of the churches, do equally well together what they do now, identically, but apart?' The kernel of the whole problem was the phrase 'with the blessing of the churches'. 'To wish to integrate one's children in school,' she continued, 'does not mean one wishes to abdicate from church membership.'[16]

The 1979 seminar: 'Cooperation in higher education'

Through a very timely seminar held in the Servite Priory, Benburb, County Tyrone, in March 1979, ACT members learnt at first hand of the development of the Roehampton Institute in London, a federation of four colleges of education: Anglican, Methodist, Catholic and Froebel. One year later, there would be a furore in Northern Ireland when the interim report of the Higher Education Review Group, known popularly as the

CO-OPERATION
in
EDUCATION

A ONE-DAY COURSE
on
SATURDAY, MARCH 31st 1979
in the
**SERVITE PRIORY,
BENBURB, CO. TYRONE**

Programme for seminar on 'Cooperation in higher education' held in Benburb, County Tyrone, 1979.

AIMS

The aims of the course will be:

(i) to study in depth a federation of four colleges of education and the implications of shared resources for teachers and the classroom.

(ii) to examine the separate/closed systems of education here and the effects of a closed system on culture and values.

(iii) to examine the case for a shared curriculum and cultural studies.

★ ★ ★ ★ ★

For directions to Benburb please see back cover.

This seminar was planned just as the Chilver report, *The future of higher education in Northern Ireland*, was about to be delivered.

Chilver report, suggested amalgamating on one campus the three colleges of education in Belfast, namely St Joseph's for Catholic men students, St Mary's for Catholic women students and Stranmillis College, a coeducational Protestant college.[17]

The opening address of the 1979 seminar was given by Mary Bradbury, dean of studies and principal lecturer in history at the Catholic Digby Stuart College. She explained that the James Committee (appointed in 1970) had recommended a radical reduction in teacher-training provision – recommendations accepted by the government the following year. Many colleges were closed and the remaining had to find ways of pooling their resources. She said, 'There is nothing so capable of focusing the mind and energies of those who want to survive as the threat of imminent destruction.' Four colleges – Digby Stuart (Catholic), Southlands (Methodist), Whitelands (Anglican) and Froebel ('undenominational') – all situated within two miles of each other in the Roehampton/Wimbledon district of south-west London, began to work together. 'Hitherto,' she said, 'they had been virtually isolated from each other, though physically so near.' Fortunately, the ground had been prepared because 'the spirit of ecumenism was already having an influence in the Christian communities'. She explained the outcome:

> The students from all four colleges attend lectures, seminars and tutorials together and are taught by whichever member of the subject department (or syndicate) is responsible for that particular course. This means that students in teacher training who are following the bachelor of education degree course mix freely with students on other degree courses and are part of a much wider spectrum of learning experience than was ever possible before ... We have found that it had been of great advantage *educationally* for teachers in training to be part and parcel of classes which comprise arts, humanities and science students as well as education students.[18]

On the question of religious education Bradbury explained that 'this is a denominational course and each college runs its own and has its own pattern'. In the much broader sense of religious education, however, 'there is active collaboration between members of staff and students right across the colleges'. Attendance at courses in religion had been 'gratifying' and, she concluded:

> All this helps to break down barriers, to dispel misconceptions and to make a positive contribution to a better understanding of each other's point of view. The more we know of our own and of other Christian traditions, the more we find to love and respect in them … This sharing of their insights is further helped by regular occasions of worshipping together.[19]

Mary Bradbury ended her talk by observing that it was also an exciting venture from an ecumenical point of view. Her account of the close collaboration of the four colleges was of particular interest to ACT members because of their long-held conviction that all teachers in Northern Ireland should be trained together – and could be, without in consequence undermining the denominational element of education.

The Chilver report

The Chilver report had suggested amalgamating on one campus the three colleges of education in Belfast. The report made it clear that both the Catholic and the Protestant authorities would have autonomy within a federated system – a development which was taking place all over the UK at the time, as it was seen to have clear educational and financial advantages. Despite these assurances and a guarantee given by the Department of Education to the Catholic authorities that they would have complete control over the manner in which religious education would be taught in their own institutions in particular, the report resulted in uproar, with petitions to 'protect our schools' being circulated after mass in many Catholic churches.

The account of the close collaboration of the four colleges in the Roehampton federation increased the conviction of ACT members that all teachers in Northern Ireland should – and could – be trained together. ACT warmly welcomed the Chilver report, saying that the movement was confident 'that a merging of the various colleges with safeguards as suggested, was not only realistic but absolutely feasible'. ACT re-emphasised that:

RC clergy rapped for 'whipping up unnecessary fear'

SOME ROMAN Catholic leaders have been accused of whipping up fear over the proposals to re-structure teacher training in the Province.

Their accuser was a founder member of the All Children Together movement. Mrs Cecilia Linehan, who said: "I believe some of the statements made by Catholic spokesmen, and comments from pulpits have clouded the main issues on occasions and caused unnecessary fear."

The Holywood housewife, who has spearheaded voluntary moves to bring together at school level children from differing religions, was pinpointing criticism of the recommendations made by the teacher training study team chaired by Sir Henry Chilver.

Critics

Mrs Linehan said Roman Catholics in the Down and Connor diocese had been "spoken to once, in some instances twice, from the pulpit concerning the report of the Higher Education Review Group for Northern Ireland, generally referrred to as the Chilver Report."

The Catholic clergy were criticised for 'whipping up unnecessary fears' following the publication of the Chilver report, *The future of higher education in Northern Ireland*, 1980.

at present the Colleges of Education are the only areas of Higher Education which are still segregated and we deplore this because student teachers are segregated in school years, go back after training to segregated schools and miss the only opportunity, during Higher Education, for intermingling with those of different traditions and academic disciplines. Although there is some claimed co-operation at present between the colleges, we see this as rather contrived and very exaggerated.[20]

ACT continues to draw inspiration from St Bede's

As the 1980s approached, there was no indication that ACT's ongoing study of developments of ecumenical education projects and shared religious education would lead to the movement blazing a trail in a part of the United Kingdom then being torn apart by sectarian violence. ACT had, after all, been successful in getting the 1978 act through parliament and was very hopeful that the churches, especially the Protestant churches, would move to invoke the act, thus ensuring that a gradual development of a third sector of integrated schools, paid for out of state funds, would develop in Northern Ireland. It was to be another year before members of the ACT executive would put pen to paper to set down their thoughts on the most suitable areas of the education system where integrated pilot schemes might develop, and another three years before Lagan College would be opened. The close association that developed between ACT and St Bede's and the in-depth study of the development of their religious-education curriculum, allied to the work on shared cultural heritage initiated by Bill Brown at the first ACT seminar in 1974 and continued through the 1970s, would prove invaluable when parents and ACT finally opened Lagan College in 1981.

After the first year in which St Bede's had been in operation as an ecumenical school it was reported that fourth- and fifth-year pupils, including those from Christian homes, showed considerable resistance to religious education. Appointed head of religious education in 1979, Priscilla Chadwick had the challenging opportunity to streamline and improve religious-education provision. In particular, she proposed that denominational teaching be integrated into the examination courses for fourth- and fifth-year pupils. By this time, St Bede's also had two full-time chaplains, one Catholic and one Anglican, and they were invited to discuss doctrinal and other differences with the mixed group of pupils in seminars. In addition, staff and chaplains were to accompany these senior pupils to places of religious significance. All in all, the St Bede's model would have a major influence on the way religious education would be taught at Lagan College. That school later went on to adopt the St Bede's model of common general religious education for all pupils completed by denominational religious education.

'The declared backing of the hierarchy is crucial'

Dr Philomena Dineen, headmistress of St Bede's, writing for the ACT newsletter in June 1984, observed:

> Although many factors contribute to making a joint-Church school thrive, experience shows that the declared backing of the hierarchy is crucial. In areas where the decision has been made to establish such schools, our Bishops and priests must be seen to give support equal to and as positive as that traditionally given to Catholic schools.[21]

This was just the kind of support that the founders of Lagan College and Forge Integrated Primary did not have. *Violence in Ireland*, a report produced jointly by the Irish Council of Churches and the Roman Catholic Church Joint Group on Social Questions in 1976, stated:

> Lack of contact, lack of dialogue, breed an environment of fear, suspicion, ignorance and prejudice, which can rightly be termed sectarian. It is to the elimination of this whole frame of mind that the combined efforts of the Churches need to be directed. Ireland needs a programme to combat sectarianism wherever it is found.[22]

Recognising that lack of contact and dialogue breed an environment of fear and suspicion, the report's concrete proposals to combat sectarianism included bringing Catholic and Protestant pupils together where possible in joint debates, shared sixth-form colleges and common nursery schools (so that parents of different religions might meet). Even teacher exchanges were mentioned, but there was no discussion on the 'question of an *integrated* system of education currently being canvassed' because 'members of the Working Party were not in agreement on that issue'.[23]

The Catholic hierarchy in Ireland, it could be argued, had not kept pace with advances in other parts of the Catholic world in ecumenism, interdenominational education and the development of shared religious education. For example, the *Universe*, the English Catholic weekly paper, had made this report on 15 April 1983:

> VATICAN CITY: Cardinal Jan Willibands, President of the Vatican Secretariat for Promoting Christian Unity, will take part in celebrations in Leipzig's Church of St Thomas ... on November 11 to mark the fifth centenary of Martin Luther's birth.[24]

In the same year Pope John Paul II responded to a statement by Archbishop Runcie of Canterbury, when he appealed to all Christians to:

> accept the commitment to which Archbishop Runcie and I pledge ourselves anew before you today. This commitment is that of praying and working for reconciliation and ecclesiastical unity according to the mind and heart of our Saviour Jesus Christ.[25]

Sadly, this vision of shared enterprise did not appear to penetrate the thinking of the Irish hierarchy.

'I do not see integrated education as the way forward'[26]

In Ireland in 1976, the Catholic hierarchy, in its *Directory on ecumenism in Ireland*, had argued:

> The replacement of Catholic by interdenominational schools in Ireland would not contribute to overcoming the divisions in our midst ... we must point out that in such schools the full Catholic witness is inevitably diluted.[27]

Not all Irish Catholic clergy agreed with this point of view. Fr John Brady, the Jesuit director of the College of Industrial Relations in Dublin, wrote in 1978, 'There are no insuperable difficulties about educating Catholic and Protestant children in the same school.' If the Catholic Church was 'prepared to pursue its legitimate interests in education through participative structures, at least in some instances and on an experimental basis' it would be stating 'in deeds rather than words that [it does] not wish to perpetuate the divisive social structures of Northern Ireland'.[28]

By 1982 Cardinal Ó Fiaich had conceded that integrated schools could be regarded as 'experimental'. Indeed, having some contact with ACT, the cardinal invited some representatives of the movement to visit him at his home in Armagh. This visit included Bettie Benton, Bill Brown and at least two other members of the ACT committee. Bill Brown recalled:

> We had a most pleasant and easy welcome and spent well over one and a half hours in discussion with the cardinal, ranging from general educational issues to the philosophy and aims of ACT. He was a very patient and attentive listener and did not react to what we said in the ... way ... we were most often responded to by the hierarchy of the Catholic Church. He did, of course, explain the worry that many had on the Roman Catholic side that faith schools would be seriously threatened, but we could not have had a more pleasant time. All of us felt he behaved graciously and interestedly. Going out, as I searched for my raincoat in the hall, the cardinal spoke to me in quietness, saying, 'You will not be quoting me on this in your publications but I often think it will take something as radical as you people are proposing to really change things here for the better.' My impression was that this comment was genuine and from a reflective attitude. I for one came away with a much enhanced and warm view of Cardinal Ó Fiaich.[29]

Nevertheless, Catholic parents of Lagan College pupils were becoming increasingly frustrated at lack of support from their parish clergy. Bishop Cahal Daly continued to argue that integrated schools had practical disadvantages, such as the 'bussing' of children out of their communities. He could have added that great numbers of Catholic children were already being 'bussed' to ensure that they were educated in their segregated schools. Members of ACT often commented that children seemed to be 'bussed' everywhere to ensure segregated education continued, yet to 'bus' children to allow them to be educated together according to their parents' wishes was, in the bishop's words, 'more impractical'. Bishop Daly argued, in addition, that single-denominational schools were more representative of neighbourhood communities, providing pupils with a stronger sense of identity and security and promoting the partnership of school, home and parish – an argument which might hold water for districts such as

This was the first time the Department of Education had publicly espoused, unequivocally, 'the inescapable duty ... on every teacher, every school manager, Board member and trustee, and every educational administrator, to ensure that children do not grow up in ignorance, fear or even hatred of those for whom they are educationally segregated'.

Department of Education
Londonderry House
21/27 Chichester Street
BELFAST
BT1 4RL

1 June 1982

To: Education and Library Boards,
       Governing Bodies,
       Managers and Principals of all
       Primary and Secondary Schools

THE IMPROVEMENT OF COMMUNITY RELATIONS: THE CONTRIBUTION OF SCHOOLS

1. Under the Northern Ireland Community Relations Order 1975, the Department of Education has a statutory responsibility for -

"formulating and sponsoring policies for the improvement of community relations".

2. Our educational system has clearly a vital role to play in the task of fostering improved relationships between the two communities in Northern Ireland. Every teacher, every school manager, Board member and trustee, and every educational administrator within the system has a responsibility for helping children to learn to understand and respect each other, and their differing customs and traditions, and of preparing them to live together in harmony in adult life

3. The Department wishes to emphasise that it is not questioning the right to insist on forms of education in schools which amount to segregation. It considers, however, that this right is coupled with an inescapable duty to ensure that effective measures are taken to ensure that children do not grow up in ignorance, fear or even hatred of those from whom they are educationally segregated.

4. While it is aware that positive work to this end is already going on in schools, the Department of Education is also conscious of the need for continuing and greater effort. It wishes, therefore, to stress the need for all concerned in the education of children to keep this duty constantly in mind.

5. The Department will be promoting discussions on this aspect of the role of the education service in the Department's Summer Schools and the Schools Inspectorate is being asked to concentrate on promoting and encouraging ways of improving community relations in the course of their duties.

6. The Department would also welcome any ideas and/or suggestions for initiatives which you consider might assist in the promotion of improved community relations. Administrative responsibility for community affairs within the Department lies with the

Sport and Community Division
Londonderry House
21/27 Chichester Street
BELFAST
BT1 4RL

Telephone: Belfast 32253

the Falls and the Shankill in Belfast, but not for more mixed urban residential and rural areas.

In May 1984 Msgr Colm McCaughan, shortly to become director of the Council for Catholic Maintained Schools, said to a reporter of *Newsweek*, 'Integrated education is a facile solution to an extremely complex problem. I cannot give encouragement or approve of it.'[30]

That this view – provided to a worldwide reading public – was representative of the hierarchy is demonstrated by responses to questions during the sessions of the New Ireland Forum. This forum had been set up in 1983 by Taoiseach Garret FitzGerald to seek solutions to the Northern Ireland problem in the wake of the upsurge in violence and bitterness during and following the H-block hunger strikes and deaths of IRA prisoners at the Maze prison. It met for a year, generally in Dublin Castle. Representatives of all constitutional political parties from the whole island had been invited and the main sessions were televised. Bishop Daly was questioned closely, in a manner that in former times would have been regarded as impertinent. Senator Mary Robinson, later president of the Republic of Ireland, posed a question on integrated education. Bishop Daly's response was that the church did nothing to oppose the efforts of people to promote integrated education but that he did not think this development was of value because it affected very few people and left unaffected those who needed this kind of mixing most. He was more direct in response to a question given to him in a radio phone-in programme in February 1984: 'I do not see integrated education as the way forward.' Indeed, this could be regarded as a step back from Cardinal Ó Fiaich's position that 'experimental' schools were to be welcomed.

Catholic parents of Lagan College pupils continued to request help from their church. Their letters asking for regular meetings and a celebration of mass in a city-centre church were met by refusal. In Catholic schools a class mass was usually held once a term, but the church would not facilitate such celebrations in Lagan College. The Catholic head of religious education in Lagan College produced extracts from church documents to support the parents, including the following:

> Acknowledging its grave obligation to see to the moral and religious education of all its children, the Church should give special attention and help to the great number of them who are being taught in non-Catholic schools.[31]

The fact that in their own individual ways all members of the school community share this Christian vision makes the school 'Catholic'.[32]

In situations where, for one reason or another, Catholics and members of other churches are educated together, every attempt should be made to diminish the inherent disadvantages for religious formation. It is to be hoped that whatever Church is in charge of such schools would agree to arrangements by which children of other denominations could receive a religious education in accordance with the requirements of their own churches.[33]

Only one detectable step forward was achieved: in December 1985, around a thousand pupils, staff, governors and parents (including the author) attended Lagan College's carol service in a Catholic church on the Falls Road – the by now well-known Redemptorist monastery, so involved over the years with the most difficult and often the most dangerous parts of the peace process. One important piece remained missing from the Catholic Church's desired triangular relationship between home, school and parish – the church itself.

How the Catholic parents with children in integrated schools would have welcomed the same level of support from diocesan clergy as that proffered by the Redemptorist order – which, while under the jurisdiction of the local bishop, enjoy a degree of freedom not afforded to diocesan clergy.

ACT's response to Department of Education Circular 1982/21: an essay competition for second-level pupils. The winning essays were subsequently published in full in *ACT-LETT.*

8
Strains of growth

In over twenty years of working in various ways at
cross-community relations within this City, the
setting up of Oakgrove Integrated Primary School
and the work towards an integrated college here have
proved, in terms of intercommunity relationships and
coming together, the most positive, the most fruitful,
the most hopeful, the most forward-looking, the
most heart-warming, and at times, the most moving
work of reconciliation we have ever been involved in.

FOYLE TRUST FOR INTEGRATED EDUCATION, DECEMBER 1991[1]

Expansion or consolidation?

Tony Spencer had been a much-valued and central member of All
Children Together since 1974. He was key speaker at ACT'S first public
seminar in 1974, a signatory to the interim ACT constitution drawn up
in 1976, a member of the ACT executive from 1976 to 1979, ACT
treasurer from 1979 to 1981 and one of the first six ACT trustees elected
in 1980, serving until 1982. A devout English Catholic, not afraid to be
outspoken on ecclesiastical matters, Tony taught sociology at Queen's
University and had directed much of his academic energy towards
searching for explanations for the bitter divisions in Ulster society.
Protestants in Northern Ireland rarely sent their children to Catholic
schools, he found, but Catholics (particularly from middle-class families)
did attend the more prestigious Protestant grammar schools such as Belfast
Royal Academy and Methodist College in Belfast. Spencer found that,
though these grammar schools were a clear route to academic and career
success, their ethos was Protestant – Catholic pupils there felt the need not

to advertise their religious affiliation. When his daughter Jane was due to transfer from primary to secondary education, Tony became a prime mover behind ACT's drive to set up Lagan College in 1981 and became a key figure in all parts of its development, working at all times with the greatest enthusiasm and commitment.

From 1981 to 1984, much of ACT's energy was absorbed in seeking adequate funding for the college and in campaigning to get maintained status for it. When this was obtained in 1984, ACT devoted much of its time into the task of creating Forge, an independent integrated primary school, which opened in 1985. At the same time ACT continued to campaign for parental and government backing for integrated education across the region. While it is clear now that during 1983 Spencer was coming to the conclusion that the movement ought to be moving more swiftly and taking greater risks, at no time during that year did he share his feelings of frustration with fellow executive members. In fact, it was the autumn of 1984 when he informed the ACT executive that he had been working for approximately 18 months on a plan of very rapid expansion of integrated schools within the area covered by BELB. He also told the ACT executive they had *four days* to consider this vastly ambitious plan and, if they did not support it, he fully intended going ahead with other supporters.

Demanding 'support and immediate implementation of proposals'

In 1984, Bettie Benton was honorary treasurer/secretary of the ACT Charitable Trust and on 7 September she contacted Tony Spencer, then honorary treasurer of Lagan College, to deal with routine financial matters relating to the school. He made no mention of the proposals he was about to submit to ACT. Yet, on the same day, he was in the process of inviting three members of the ACT executive committee, one ACT trustee and a few Lagan College parents to a meeting in his home on the evening of 9 September. At that meeting, Spencer gave each person there a copy of his study, entitled 'The development of integrated education in Belfast: a planning study'. It was a substantial document of around 90 typed foolscap pages. During this meeting Cecil Linehan (then honorary secretary of Lagan College and also a trustee of the ACT Trust, who had not been invited) had occasion to ring Tony Spencer on ongoing Lagan College business; he said *nothing* to her about the meeting then taking place in his home.

When Yvonne Gilmour, another founding Lagan College parent who had been invited, later told Bettie Benton about the meeting, she 'declared that T. Spencer's action had been most improper and unnecessary'. The ACT executive met on 11 September, as the minutes record:

> Y. Gilmour, M. Blair and D. Haughey gave further details of meeting at T. Spencer's. The general impression had been that T. Spencer intended demanding support and immediate implementation of proposals for new integrated schools to be opened very rapidly in redundant school premises vacated by the Belfast Education and Library Board (BELB) and also for a Development Officer to be appointed. The 30th September was the deadline set by T. Spencer for his objectives to be adopted …
>
> No explanation had been given by T. Spencer as to why he had decided to take this course of action when we were all still heavily involved in raising essential funds for Lagan College and providing necessary accommodation and large equipment.[2]

On Wednesday, 26 September 1984 Spencer was invited to address a joint meeting of the ACT executive and trustees at a meeting in Lagan College. For the first time he presented his colleagues of ten years with a copy of his planning study. On the cover he had added these words: 'Not to be communicated to the Press, or quoted without the author's permission in writing, prior to formal publication.' He presented his paper on Wednesday, 26 September and asked for a definite commitment from ACT by the beginning of the following week, Sunday, 30 September. The minutes record:

> In answer to questions of clarification T. Spencer said he was the director of the Pastoral Research Centre and no-body else other than himself was involved with it. He had written the document during the month of August [1984].
>
> T. Spencer was then invited to begin his address. This he did with the aid of maps of Belfast. He spoke for 40–45 minutes without interruption during which time he revealed detailed plans to open four primary and two comprehensive integrated independent schools in the city of Belfast by September 1988, in school premises still in use by the BELB and yet to be declared surplus to their requirements. Three of

these schools to open in September 1985. A Development Officer to be appointed and be in post by the 30th September 1984 to commence immediately the week by week plan of action outlined in the document. T. Spencer made it clear that if ACT did not accept his plans in their entirety and appoint a Development Officer immediately he would go ahead and set up his own charitable trust and appoint his own Development Officer to carry out his plans. He demanded a response by 30th September 1984.[3]

An hour of discussion and questions followed. The ACT executive members and trustees were worried that the 'principle of integrated education by consent advocated by ACT' would be damaged and that confusion would be caused 'if yet another charitable trust was set up duplicating the ACT Charitable Trust'. Members then drafted a response to Tony Spencer, the wording being finalised on 28 September and posted on the same day. Signed by Bettie Benton on behalf of ACT, the response stated:

> We did not feel we wished to dwell on what some of us considered to be inaccuracies, but rather to take the proposals by the horns and look at them with you.
>
> During discussion it became apparent that there were many grave concerns particularly about the time scale e.g. Chapter Five Suggested Timetable which dealt with 'the three schools suggested for opening in September 1985'.
>
> I have to tell you that while the All Children Together Executive Committee and Trustees naturally were at one with you regarding the advancement of integrated education by consent the view on the Belfast proposals was as follows.
>
> 1 The time table was unrealistic.
> 2 There was considerable doubt about the availability of the redundant school premises named.
> 3 There was serious doubt about the assumption of attaining maintained status for each proposed school by the time projected.
> 4 The opening of 6 new integrated schools in Belfast with all 6 seeking maintained status within 4 years (Chapter Six Suggested Budgets (d) Legal Status p. 55) at a time of acute financial stringency might provoke antagonism and hostility from other schools and particularly from parents and teachers whose own schools had been closed (and whose premises we might even be occupying).

5 All Children Together is committed to responding to an identifiable demand from a sufficient number of parents for a school at a particular level. There is no evidence of such a demand at this time.

6 When such a demand is identified it will be given serious consideration.

7 The uncertain financial situation of the All Children Together Charitable Trust makes it impossible to pledge support for the proposals by the date demanded i.e. Sunday 30th September 1984.

8 The continuing responsibility to support and meet the needs of Lagan College must have priority. We would be concerned if our scarce energies and resources were dissipated while this need remains.[4]

Benton thanked Tony Spencer for sharing 'your paper with us' and concluded that ACT was happy to continue discussions on the proposals but 'stress that developments could not take place at the speed you propose … we cannot commit ourselves by the date set by you i.e. Sunday 30th September 1984'.[5]

BELTIE: a new charitable trust

Spencer clearly became extremely impatient with the ACT executive and criticised it for its failure to appoint a development officer in 1983 and early 1984. This was an initiative with which the ACT executive was very keen to proceed but it had decided that it 'would be very poor politics to have an advertisement for a Development Officer appearing in the public Press at the same time as Lagan College's application for maintained status was under critical examination'.[6] In addition, ACT remained seriously concerned about the constant drain on its funds. During the summer of 1984, ACT had purchased 63 Church Road for Lagan College for £33,000, and, on the insistence of planners, it was given no choice but to buy a field beside the college to provide for a car park at the exorbitant cost of £60,000. Even though the college had been accepted for grant aid in March 1984, ACT had to be very sure it had the funds to pay for a development officer and had calculated the costs of such an appointment, counting salary and insurance, at between £17,000 and £20,000 per annum. For these reasons, ACT deferred the placing of the advertisement for the development officer's post until August 1984.

Cecil Linehan drafted a paper for fellow members of the ACT executive entitled 'Inaccuracies in Mr. Spencer's paper relating to All Children Together's "failure" to appoint a development officer'. She made 21 points and the penultimate one was:

> 20 At no time did Mr. Spencer come and consult with Trustees or Executive Committee from the ACT/AGM in April and ask **why** they had not appointed a Development Officer.
> Nor did he inform them that he was researching in North Belfast.
> Nor did he offer his plan to them.[7]

Meanwhile, Spencer wasted no time in activating his plan to set up an alternative organisation, the Belfast Charitable Trust for Integrated Education – soon known as BELTIE – and appointed his chosen candidate, Mr Jo Mulvenna, as development officer. Then, when Wallis Johnson of the Rowntree Trust was visiting Belfast on 9 and 10 October, he met Tony Spencer to discuss his proposals. A letter from Spencer on 16 October confirmed that BELTIE had been set up.

'The All Children Together movement and proposed school closures in Northern Ireland'

'The development of integrated education in Belfast: a planning study' had been presented to the ACT executive and trustees in the autumn of 1984. Only much later did it emerge that Tony Spencer had written a similar paper, calling for the same kind of action, a year earlier. This was entitled 'The All Children Together movement and proposed school closures in Northern Ireland', dated 21 September 1983. This was sent to the Rowntree Trust, but (with one exception) it became clear over 20 years later that no other member of the 1983/1984 ACT executive had been aware that this paper existed.

Wallis Johnson, then development officer of the Rowntree Trust, had met Tony Spencer in Belfast in 1983. The two men agreed that a document should be drafted detailing ways in which the integrated movement could move forward. In short, it was Johnson who had suggested that Tony Spencer write a development plan. Interviewed in May 2002, Wallis Johnson recalled:

> I remember thinking that, looking from a distance, we want to see where this is going, what they have in mind, what are the goals in their

sights and I thought it would be useful from our point of view … to see if there was a basic outline development plan.[8]

Spencer 'immediately responded so maybe his thoughts were going the same direction'. The result was, Johnson concluded, 'a very comprehensive development plan'.[9] This plan, however, was not submitted to the ACT executive or trustees for discussion.

The principal assumption made by Spencer in his 1983 paper was that a considerable number of schools would be closed as a result of falling rolls. This was not an unreasonable assumption: Belfast had been an exceptionally compact city (before the German air attacks in the spring of 1941 the area just north of the city centre had been judged the most densely populated district in the United Kingdom) and now, like so many other cities in the western world, the population was moving to the periphery. Improved transport, rising housing standards and slum clearance were largely responsible for population decline within the city boundaries but the Troubles provided an added impetus. Protestants in particular moved to areas such as Monkstown and Glengormley in north Belfast, Ballybeen in east Belfast and beyond.

Spencer began by stating that the purpose of the paper was to consider the ACT strategy 'in the light of its objectives and of the demographic trends in the child population that have created a crisis of over-capacity within N. Ireland'. He quoted a statement from ACT's founding principles as laid down in 1974, and later incorporated into the 1977 constitution:

> The All Children Together Movement seeks changes in the education system of Northern Ireland that will make it possible for parents who so wish to secure for their children an education in Shared Schools acceptable to all religious denominations and cultures, in which the Churches will provide religious education and pastoral care.[10]

Spencer drew four points from this declaration of aims. 'First, the aim is to change the education system of N. Ireland – a system of some 1500 schools – not the education system of a few localities.' Second, shared schools were voluntary, not compulsory, for parents who wanted integrated education for their children. Third, education in shared schools was 'to be acceptable to all religious denominations and cultures. In the context of N. Ireland that means an equality of status between Catholics and Protestants and their respective cultural traditions.' Fourth, the shared schools were to be Christian, 'so much so that the Christian Churches as institutions are offered pride of place in religious education and pastoral care'.[11]

Spencer identified four successive strategies adopted by ACT since its foundation in 1974.

1 The state must take the initiative

This lasted from late 1974 to late 1976:

> The Movement pointed to the United Nations Declaration on Human Rights, to the European Convention on Human Rights, to the second Vatican Council's Declaration on Christian Education, to Art. 34 of the Education & Libraries (N.I.) Order, 1972, and to a string of public opinion polls, and demanded that Area Education and Library Boards and the Department of Education should take the initiative and carry out the elementary duty of a Western democracy of providing a sub-system of schools that would be acceptable to the majority of the citizens.[12]

The problem was that the area boards lacked the necessary legal power to create integrated schools and that the Department of Education would not take any initiative in the matter.

2 The churches must take the initiative

The leaders of ACT, Spencer particularly, impressed by the fact that Protestant churches insisted that they supported integrated education, sought to draft legislation that would allow the churches to take the initiative (it was Spencer who brought the first draft for the 1978 Education Act to the ACT executive). This – which Spencer classed as 'Strategy 2: "The Churches must take the initiative"' – led to the Dunleath Act of 1978.

3 The movement must take the initiative

Since the invitation to the churches to use the enabling powers provided by the 1978 act fell on deaf ears, ACT adopted a third strategy: 'The movement must take the initiative.' As ACT's officers waited in vain for the churches to make a move, in 1979 they drafted proposals for possible future initiatives in integrated-school projects at nursery, sixth-form and post-primary levels. This was done on the advice of Prof. Teunissen, a professor of peace studies at Nijmegen University in Holland and a frequent visitor to Belfast in the 1970s as part of the Dutch–Northern Irish Advisory Committee. Another indication that ACT was moving on to this third strategy was that in 1979, on the advice of Wallis Johnson of the Rowntree Trust, the ACT Charitable Trust was set up. This progressed naturally to the fourth strategy.

4 The movement must support parents' initiatives

This was the decisive step taken to establish Lagan College in 1981.

Spencer's paper then focused on the opportunities presented by Northern Ireland's declining enrolments in primary and secondary schools. Tables were extracted from the Department of Education's 1981 report, *Schools and demographic trends: a backcloth to planning*. They gave actual enrolments from 1970/1 to 1979/80 and projected enrolments between 1980/1 and 1994/5. These figures showed that primary-sector enrolments would continue falling until they bottomed out in 1985/6, and that secondary enrolments would bottom out in 1991. These statistics applied to Northern Ireland as a whole: they took no account of the different trends in Catholic and Protestant schools and in different areas. BELB, for example, was being put under considerable pressure to rationalise provision in the city by amalgamations and closures. This led Tony Spencer to arrive at the following conclusion:

> My own view is that there will be a lot of closures and amalgamations, especially in Belfast, though not as many as the DENI would like. If this proves the case we can expect two consequences:
>
> i   An acceleration of closures and amalgamations in the mid-1980s, tailing off in the primary sector in the later 1980s, and in the secondary in the early 1990s, and
>
> ii The carry forward in both sectors of considerable over-capacity, which would gradually be absorbed in the 1990s.[13]

Spencer argued that structural change was easiest when enrolment and the whole system were expanding. In the contracting situation he was describing 'the creation of new institutions is opposed and impeded by existing institutions which feel threatened by them'. The demand for shared schools was at present an 'outsider movement' and Spencer felt that in the circumstances, because new purpose-built schools were costly:

an outsider movement would find it exceedingly difficult to secure grant-aided status at the planning stage … Why should Government commit costly resources to developments proposed by an outsider movement which might encounter little effective demand when eventually opened?[14]

In short, what he described as 'an integrated education sub-system' could succeed only if it 'can acquire insider status in the mid-1980s'. In addition, 'falling rolls create unique opportunities for an outsider movement trying to break in'. He continued:

> The first of these is the sudden closing or amalgamation of purpose-built schools that come onto the market at a price that is a fraction of the cost of new building. An alert and nimble outsider movement can organise and open integrated schools as suitable properties are identified.
> The second consequence of falling rolls is the creation among governing bodies, staffs and parent clienteles of some existing schools of a readiness to embrace radical change in the shape of real ethno-religious integration. (It has to be added that others will prefer 'tokenism' as a method of self-defence). We can therefore expect a renewed interest in the enabling provisions of the Education (NI) Act of 1978 in the mid- and late-1980s.[15]

Crucially, Spencer reached the conclusion that the time had come to broaden out the campaign to encompass the entire region – 'to use the period of declining enrolment to lay the foundations of a sub-system of integrated education, not just in a few favoured localities but throughout N. Ireland'. He suggested two strategies. 'The first is to monitor all school closures and amalgamations in the hope of identifying premises where the creation of a new integrated school would satisfy a latent demand from parents for an alternative to the existing Protestant and Catholic schools'. The second strategy, 'which should be run in parallel with the first, is to facilitate all suitable cases where the 1978 Act is invoked'.

Spencer concluded his paper with an urgent call to action:

> Are we going to go on talking about integrated education, and writing memoranda for departmental committees, or are we going to commit ourselves, without reservation, to using the unique opportunities of the declining enrolments of the 1980s to lay the foundations of a system of integrated education throughout N. Ireland?

> It does not take long to betray an ideal. The ideal of integration in the National School system was betrayed in the eight years after 1831. The similar ideal enshrined in the 1923 Act had been betrayed by 1930. The ideal enshrined in the McIvor initiative of 1974 was betrayed by the U.K. Government within two years. We in the All Children Together Movement can betray that same ideal once more within the next few years by dithering, disunity, discord, or a simple failure of nerve. Or we can achieve the objective I have suggested, and lay the foundations of a system of integrated education throughout N. Ireland.[16]

This call to action might suggest that the ACT executive had been discussing with Spencer for a long period his plans to 'lay the foundations of a system of integrated education throughout N. Ireland'. The situation was quite the reverse: the ACT executive had never seen the initial 1983 paper, nor his 1984 plan to open six more integrated schools by 1988, nor had he informed them that he had been working and planning the opening of two more integrated schools in north Belfast, even before Lagan College obtained maintained status, nor had they been aware that he had been laying plans to establish another charitable trust for integrated education.

In his penultimate sentence, Spencer referred to 'disunity' and 'discord'. Over the next year the integrated movement was to suffer from both conditions as a result of disagreements over strategy. ACT and the ACT Trust were not divided by Tony Spencer's paper – all stood firm in their belief that Lagan College as the flagship of integrated education had to be made secure. Collectively, they regretted Spencer's decision to move away from them, his colleagues for more than ten years, and set up BELTIE.

An ever-widening chasm

When Malone Primary School in south Belfast was closed in 1984 by BELB because of falling enrolments, parents in the area made an attempt to use the 1978 Education Act to transform the school to a controlled integrated school. When this was turned down by the Department of Education the parent group stayed together and eventually opened the school as an independent integrated school, eventually known as Forge Integrated Primary School (FIPS). ACT had been involved with the parents of Malone Primary for some two years, looking on this development as their opportunity to help establish an integrated primary school, for which it had sought funds in the first appeal launched for Lagan College in 1982.

Then, in October 1984, when the ACT executive's monthly meeting took place, members were informed that Jo Mulvenna, now the development officer of BELTIE, had visited Malone Primary with the purpose of informing parents that more integrated schools were being planned. Bettie Benton reported that she had spoken with 'someone high up in government' who had made it clear that 'they could not wear a sudden surge in the number of new integrated schools, all asking for grant aid'.[17] It was agreed to inform the principal of Malone Primary School and the Department of Education that ACT had no connection with BELTIE.

On 22 October 1984 Tony Spencer asked to see Mary Connolly, an ACT trustee who had been at the meeting in his home on 9 September, to 'bring her up to date with developments'. He said that Lagan College should be capable of 'standing on its own feet now' and that another project should be taken on and plans made for others, 'so as one was set up, another was started and so on'.[18] His priority would be to set up one primary school and one secondary school in north Belfast. He felt that there 'would be no confusion with our benefactors' between ACT and BELTIE. Spencer had won the support of some prominent Northern Irish people including Lord Blease, Judge John McKee, Councillor John Carson, Councillor Muriel Pritchard, Fionnuala Cook and Ann Teague. Mary Connolly reported that 'specific questions regarding finance, where the parents who wanted all these schools were, attitude of Dept., manpower to work on these plans and raise funds, needs of Lagan College, were not answered'.[19]

ACT held interviews for the post of development officer on 23 October 1984. Jo Mulvenna, one of the candidates, said that he was already employed by BELTIE and clearly hoped to work for both organisations. In the event, he was not appointed.

Malone Primary School parents

The Malone Primary School Parents' Association met on 6 November 1984 to discuss the implications of opening an independent integrated primary school. ACT vice-chairman, Yvonne Gilmour, and Pauline Perry, both founder parents of Lagan College, were there. So, too, were Tony Spencer and Jo Mulvenna. Yvonne Gilmour spoke on:

- the considerable funding which would be required to finance the 'independent' period before grant aid would be approved;
- the necessity of obtaining 'a reasonable balance between Roman Catholic and Protestant children';
- and the great commitment required from parents.

She reported back to ACT afterwards that the picture painted by Spencer and Mulvenna 'was one of supreme certainty that the scheme outlined in the Pastoral Research Centre document [the paper presented by Spencer to ACT on 26 September 1984] would succeed' and that they implied that 'the approach of ACT was too slow'. She continued:

> The real financial commitment was not discussed in any depth: how to make a school viable so that it might be taken into the maintained school system was not put to the meeting – in general, there did not seem to be an understanding by the parents (most of whom were probably Protestant) of the commitment they might be taking on if they were going to proceed with an independent or even maintained integrated school.[20]

At the ACT committee meeting in November 1984, what the minutes describe as 'a long and exhaustive debate' ensued. The general view of the ACT executive was that Tony Spencer had set up a competing organisation while still a member of ACT and that he was in the process of implementing plans 'which he knew ACT could not support for very valid reasons'. The following were the principal anxieties voiced:

> Fears that the principle of integrated education by consent would be damaged by a new and very aggressive thrust as envisaged by T. Spencer and J. Mulvenna to set up some six schools in four years all seeking maintained status one year from opening.
>
> Fears in regard to any harm to Lagan College from possible reduced recruitment of children for the college.
>
> Future possible difficulties in obtaining co-operation from the Dept. of Education, who had been most helpful to date regarding Lagan College.[21]

Should Tony Spencer be expelled from ACT? Some felt he would love to be. However, it was agreed that membership of ACT should not be withdrawn from him.

Disagreements over strategy, and more particularly between ACT and Tony Spencer, surfaced on 4 December 1984 during a joint meeting of the directors of Lagan College and trustees of the ACT Trust. The trust was due to receive £65,000 from the joint appeal for a quick-response fund, but this was not yet available – Lagan College still needed all the funds ACT could provide it with. Basil McIvor reported that the possibility of the National Trust site at Lisnabreeny becoming Lagan College's permanent home was becoming ever more likely. Indeed, the Department of Education was 'anxious to get us off the Castlereagh site'. In short, many of those present were worried about the ongoing funding of the college, and with very good reason.

Tony Spencer declared that he was confident a new appeal would raise '£500,000, if not more'. Cecil Linehan said 'we were down to £7,000' and that a request for help had come from Malone Primary School. Malone's request was confirmed by George Hewitt, an ACT executive member, and he said that Lagan College needed a library and a chapel, which would not be grant aided. Bettie Benton reminded those present that money for a primary school had been requested in the first appeal, and added:

> We were morally bound to help the Malone parents; the trust still had liabilities of £21,675; the trust had not received any money due to it as yet though it had paid £187,500 for the Sectional mobiles in 1983–'84; until these were valued by the District Valuer and approved for purchase by DENI, the trust would have cash-flow problems – hence the necessity to raise the bank loan for the adjoining field.[22]

A subcommittee to launch a new appeal was established; it was asked to consider engaging professional assistance. This brought Tony Spencer to his feet. He 'objected to the launching of a joint appeal; he would prefer two appeals to go; he objected to Lagan College handing over its finances to another body'. Bill Brown asked if Spencer's trust intended to do similar work, as it was 'important that it should be known if he was also appealing for funds'. When Spencer said that his trust would be launching a public appeal in the autumn of 1985, Bill Brown said that 'this disturbed him'. Bettie Benton asked whether 'Mr Spencer's trust were appealing at the moment to our benefactors'. Spencer responded that he needed to pay his development officer but Benton felt that his reply was evasive. Basil

McIvor intervened to say that he did not wish to pre-empt ACT's reply to Spencer, 'but that ACT trust was concerned with integrated education in the whole of N. Ireland and another trust was not necessary'. Stung by this observation, Spencer 'said that this was the sixth roasting he had had'. The strength of the opposition to his approach now became apparent. Maeve Mulholland, who with Tony Spencer and Yvonne Gilmour had been the first three parents to enrol their children in Lagan College in 1981, declared that:

> Mr. Spencer has pre-empted any decisions made by ACT and gone along a course of his own; he had presented the paper and made the time scale such that ACT could not possibly have responded in the time he had allowed; he had jumped the gun and she had already told him several times that the real danger was that it would appear publicly that integrated education did not work.[23]

George Hewitt added his opinion. He said:

> The children in Lagan College will suffer; the way had always been open for Mr Spencer to use the democratic system and call an extraordinary General Meeting; there was no one knew the constitution better.[24]

Cecil Linehan, appointed convenor of the subcommittee to plan the launching of another appeal, said that:

> She felt uneasy and found it difficult to see how the plans could proceed unless Mr Spencer came clean on what he [was] doing. She said she would have thought that people he had worked with for over 10 years were as much his colleagues as those he had been with since October this year and had a right to know what he was doing.[25]

Clearly the fissure dividing Tony Spencer from the ACT executive, the ACT trustees and the directors of Lagan College was fast becoming a chasm. Finally, on 10 December 1984, and despite all the difficulties, ACT and Lagan College launched a joint appeal for funds. The press release explained that the money was required to fulfil two aims:

- to consolidate the work at Lagan College which still requires substantial funds for capital expenditure despite Government recognition as a grant-aided school in April 1984.
- to seek financial support for a group of parents in the South Belfast area who have expressed a wish to open an integrated school at primary level in September 1985.[26]

The parting of the ways

Movements concerned with defending the status quo tend to find it easier to maintain unity than those committing themselves to instituting change. By the end of 1984 campaigners for integrated education in Northern Ireland were dividing into two camps. The majority in ACT believed that their organisation should concentrate on ensuring Lagan College's success and financial security. Executive members argued that Lagan College had to succeed: if it failed then the whole cause of integrated education in the region would be imperilled. Lagan College still needed a great deal of money and, while obtaining maintained status for the school had been a primary aim of its founders, there was a very marked decrease in charitable donations since it had begun to receive grant aid. This decrease in donations was stressed by then treasurer of Lagan College, Bob Crawford, who was aware of the enormous financial requirements needed to try to establish a sixth form. Without this provision the college was losing many able students, especially those expected to achieve a level of academic success that would enable them to gain admission to higher education. In addition, the first form had to be extended and accommodated. ACT was also committed to set up an integrated primary school in south Belfast and they wanted to continue intensive lobbying for government and public support for integrated education – without causing unnecessary alienation.

Those who followed Tony Spencer's lead sought to establish integrated schools over a wider area and at much greater speed than ACT thought wise. Members of ACT were proved right when they predicted that Spencer had overestimated the number of school premises that would become available as a result of closures. In part this was due to BELB's extreme unwillingness to provoke the ire of Protestant citizens by pushing through amalgamations and closures. Belfast City Council, with its unionist majority, proved extremely reluctant to alienate a diminishing electorate by closing neighbourhood schools. ACT-executive members had been right to urge caution about making assumptions about future closures.

Spencer, however, was proved right in his argument that the time had come to take greater risks. He was successful in convincing charitable trusts – notably the Nuffield Foundation and the Rowntree Trust – that they should back a more expansionist approach. Spencer also persuaded public figures, not notably active in the movement previously, to support his campaign. In addition, parents in north Belfast, eager to see both an integrated primary school and an integrated secondary college in their area, gave wholehearted backing to BELTIE.

ACT seeks to establish collaboration in organisations and joint applications for funding

At the same time, despite the frequent exposure of raw nerves, ACT executive officers constantly looked for ways to re-establish harmony and close collaboration. ACT took the initiative to seek the coordination of all those seeking to promote integration by inviting representatives to a residential weekend conference at Corrymeela, Ballycastle, in May 1985. The weekend was jointly organised by Joanne McKenna, the ACT development officer, and Jo Mulvenna, the BELTIE development officer.

The financial risks taken between 1985 and 1989 were very great and new integrated schools were almost completely dependent on the generous support of charitable trusts. Soon afterwards other 'trustlets' were established in other education and library boards. Parents' groups were able to secure bank loans and financial support from charitable foundations to permit the starting of new integrated schools. There were three in 1985 – Forge Primary, Hazelwood Primary and Hazelwood Post-Primary College, all in Belfast; there was one in 1986 – All Children's Primary, Newcastle, County Down; there were two in 1987 – Millstrand Primary, Portrush, County Antrim and Bridge Primary, Banbridge, County Down. In 1988 one integrated school opened – Windmill Primary, Dungannon, County Tyrone – and two followed in 1989 – Braidside Primary, Ballymena, County Antrim and Enniskillen Primary, County Fermanagh.

In February 1986 Basil McIvor had sent a memorandum to government asking for some degree of government guidance and involvement in the growing movement for integrated education. Meanwhile, in February 1987, ACT called the first joint meeting of treasurers of all integrated schools and 'trustlets' to prioritise and apply in a coordinated way for assistance from the International Fund for Ireland. The Nuffield Foundation, ACT's most generous benefactor, had expressed a particular interest in such a coordinated approach. Des Haughey, then ACT secretary, later explained that the movement continued this work during 1987 and also organised joint treasurers' meetings with representatives from the Nuffield and Wates Foundations. In June 1987 ACT formally adopted the McIvor policy of petitioning government to establish a commission for integrated education, a type of umbrella organisation to oversee the burgeoning integrated-schools movement, consisting of representatives of all interested parties.

However, BELTIE also had ideas, and very strong ideas at that, on the need to set up a 'central group' with a tight legal framework, doing far more than simply coordinating applications to the major trusts for funding. ACT became more and more uneasy as the days went by and they were pressurised to join this group, which BELTIE had decided to name the Northern Ireland Council for Integrated Education (NICIE), and which was also being directed by BELTIE to follow the five-year rapid-expansion plan Spencer had outlined to ACT in 1984. ACT secretary Des Haughey explained:

> Whilst ALL CHILDREN TOGETHER are happy to continue meeting in an informal way for funding, we feel the Central Group is now moving too fast in other areas, which have not been agreed to by all schools and supporting bodies, and which are outside the original agreed remit of this group, namely, co-ordinated approaches to Trusts in an informal way.
>
> There is growing pressure from some representatives for the Central Body to adopt a legal constitution which would represent integrated education in Northern Ireland, to government, DENI, ELBS, the Churches and the mass media. An interim name, the 'Northern Ireland Council for Integrated Education' (NICIE), has been given to the group, although ACT and some of our schools have not agreed to this. We are worried that the administrative costs required to service such a representative body would drain already meagre resources available for integrated schools.
>
> ACT and our schools have worked hard over the past years, and we hope to have built good relationships with government, DENI, local Boards, Trusts, the Churches and the Media. We are concerned that an aggressive approach could perhaps jeopardise these valued relationships.
>
> We realise that any new grouping will inevitably gather momentum and regret that in being unable to accept all developments within the Central Group, we may be seen to be unco-operative.

> A conference has been organised by the Central Group to draw up a Charter for Integrated Education on 27 February 1988. Representatives from ACT, Lagan College, and Forge Integrated Primary School will not be present at the forthcoming conference for the reasons as outline above.
>
> ACT are happy to meet and co-operate with this new group in areas of mutual benefit and in an ad hoc way, but at this time, feel that we can contribute more as an independent body supporting our schools and servicing new parent groups.[27]

ACT founder members, all previous chairmen and the incumbent executive of ACT decided on 4 February 1988 not to join NICIE but left the door open for continued cooperation on applications for funding and amicable discussion. During the summer of 1988, for example, ACT voted to ask its development officer and two part-time workers to devote 90 per cent of their time to NICIE. The decision not to join was definite and was communicated on 8 February 1988. ACT felt obliged to inform the Department of Education about its decision shortly afterwards.

Sr Anna, in a 'Historical résumé' compiled in September 1988, commented that since the time ACT had decided against joining the 'central group':

> relentless pressure has been brought to bear on it, and any hesitant bodies, to join in the plan and an ever more controlled, centralised and legalised group. Naturally new schools, in process of formation, are delighted to hear 'Go ahead, inexperience and finance no problem', and to receive funding through the Central Group.[28]

She observed that ACT executive members had become 'totally exhausted by meetings of the Central group, quantities of paper work, debates as to what attitude to take to the steam rolling process'. In short members of ACT felt that movement was too rapid to ensure secure foundations and financial viability. Sr Anna attempted to explain that differences were primarily about speed of development and prioritisation. In particular she felt that the needs of Lagan College were being underestimated:

> Personally I do not believe there are differences in aims, nor that 'personality' is of importance. The issue is one of POLICY. We are all committed to every child in an integrated school, and every staff member, also to every existing school. We belong together. The failure

of one would be to the detriment of all. It is NOT true that ACT, Lagan and Forge are only concerned about themselves, want to rule the roosts and impede sound developments …

All Children Together is as committed as BELTIE/NICIE to develop[ing] integrated education. Let me repeat: the difference is mainly one of PACE. ACT believes in a sound base and some degree of consolidation before too many schools are on line. (It does NOT wish to confine the scene to two or three ONLY and no more at all!)

I work for Lagan College because, being the largest school, having 40% plus of all the children in integrated education, being forced to build, its needs are by far the greatest of all the schools (far, far more than in the days when it only had 28, 90, 175 or 280 pupils even though it was then independent). It is BY NO MEANS secure or established: quite the contrary. **When its buildings are completed**, it should be able continue under its own steam and I will turn my energies to helping Hazelwood II or some other school.[29]

Joanne McKenna, the ACT development officer, sending out an agenda for the next meeting of the ACT executive in March 1988, wrote to Cecil Linehan on 24 February. She was about to send out letters explaining to Jo Mulvenna of BELTIE that ACT would not be joining the 'central group' and would not be attending the forthcoming NICIE conference:

I spoke personally to Jo Mulvenna before sending the official letter from ACT. He was saddened by our decision but thought that a 'three tier' structure might be possible, where there could be (a) fully fledged members, (b) 'advocacy' staus (for ACT and those of a similar persuasion) and observer status for DENI etc., on the Council.

On Friday 19 February, Mr Tomei phoned me to ask if ACT would like to meet him when he visited N.I. on 25–27 February. Jo Mulvenna had spoken to Anthony Tomei but I gather had not been given the whole picture. I explained that we were quite happy to continue with the original agreed purpose of the Central Group but that other aspects emanating from the group had not been agreed by ACT. Mr Tomei was unaware that the Paul Getty Trust had decided to underwrite Hazelwood College. (This Trust had been interested in a co-ordinated approach.) Mr Tomei was also unaware that ACT, Lagan College and Forge would not be attending the 'NICIE' conference.

He asked me how I felt about recent developments. I said that for the past year 90% of my time had been taken up with the Central Group and its sub-committee. I had done little for our schools and was a little weary of countless meetings where more often than not very little progress was made. I explained that I wanted ACT to get back to its job, as an independent body supporting new parent groups.[30]

Lagan College, too, resisted the centrifugal tendencies of the movement for some time. Donal McFerran, honorary secretary of the Board of Directors of the college, wrote to Jo Mulvenna of BELTIE on 19 February 1988 to explain that 'I have been instructed by my directors not to attend any further planning meetings of NICIE'. He added:

> We are not closing the door on future co-operation with NICIE but until such times as everyone has decided what they are doing in the future, my directors have asked me to refrain from attendance of any meetings and we can then consider any proposals the remaining groups have to make concerning the composition and function of any group known as NICIE.[31]

He enclosed a statement which he asked to be read out:

> The Directors of Lagan College have watched with interest the development of the group known as NICIE. As we explained at the last meeting of this group we consider that any move towards formalising such a group into a legal body is premature before we have decided what the nature and function of such a group is to be. We indicated at that time our intention to co-operate as may prove to be necessary in fund raising and we would reiterate our intention of rendering any assistance or giving any advice to new schools, schools in formation or schools in transformation. At the present time we consider any move towards legal formality and expounding of a charter or defining the function and ambit of an integrated school is premature and we would like to reserve our own position at the present time and certainly at least until someone can explain the necessity of such a group as NICIE.[32]

Continued growth despite differences concerning strategy – south Down

The disagreements over strategy did not undermine the growth of the movement and it would be quite wrong to conclude that ACT was opposed to expansion. Indeed, a group of people from south Down approached ACT in September 1985 with a plan to open an integrated primary school, with a nursery unit, in September 1986. Joanne McKenna attended regular meetings in Newcastle and ACT provided 'pump-priming' finance and approached benefactors on their behalf. By the early summer of 1986 more than 50 pupils had been registered – for a school which had yet to agree on a name – and there was a sizeable waiting list for the coming years. Anxieties that the religious balance of the intake would be lopsided proved unfounded. By that date the parent group had received a total of £5,310. The Ford of Britain Trust promised at least £1,000 and the Nuffield Foundation was giving parents practical advice and support. Fundraising included a sponsored runner in the Belfast marathon, a series of discos for under-18s, a jumble sale and a teddy bears' picnic in Castlewellan forest park. A Christmas fair, with broadcaster Sean Rafferty and singer Linda Nolan as guest celebrities, raised over £1,500. Joseph Rodgers, with 27 years' teaching experience, was appointed principal. One parent, Anne Carr, who became a governor, wrote the following:

> As a mother of three, I had felt for a long time that my children and others would benefit greatly from being educated together. I watched my three year old daughter making little friends at playschool and thought it a real shame that, due to the dual system of education in Northern Ireland today, once these children were primary school age, they would go their separate ways and there would be little chance of those special friendships flourishing.
>
> So a notice in Newcastle Library in January this year attracted my immediate attention:
>
> AN INTEGRATED NURSERY/PRIMARY SCHOOL FOR SOUTH DOWN – INTERESTED?
>
> I surely was! I went along to a public meeting and was introduced to a very determined and hard working group of Protestant and Catholic parents with one main aim – to educate their children together.
>
> I got very involved in the discussion that night and there was no lack of enthusiastic volunteers when the election of the steering committee took place later. I left, elected to be Publicity Officer with the prospect of a hectic few months ahead. We wanted to open our new planned integrated primary school in September 1986. We had eight months and a lot of hard work ahead of us!
>
> Committee meetings have been held practically every week with many going on into the wee hours. Public Meetings and Coffee Mornings have been organised, Newsletters and reams of paperwork – trust applications, leaflets, information sheets, posters etc. prepared and

an incredible amount of 'house-hunting' has been done in our efforts to find suitable school premises.

But it has all been worth while as we approach September with over 60 children enrolled for the school, a Principal appointed, over half our total expenditure for the first year to hand, equipment ordered and the leasing of a school site in the final stages.

Our school **will** open in September this year and the lives of my children and [of many] others will be enriched greatly through learning with, from and about one another.

It might be just a 'baby' step towards solving the problems which exist in our strife-torn community but I believe it's a 'giant' step in the right direction.[33]

Seventy children walked through the school gates in September, by which time the parent group had raised almost all of the £100,000 needed to run the school, All Children's Integrated Primary School, for the first year. The site was a temporary one and parents had to put in a great deal of work, painting, cleaning and doing DIY work over weekends.

Graph showing growth of pupil numbers in integrated schools from 1981 to 2008.

GROWTH IN INTEGRATED SCHOOLS

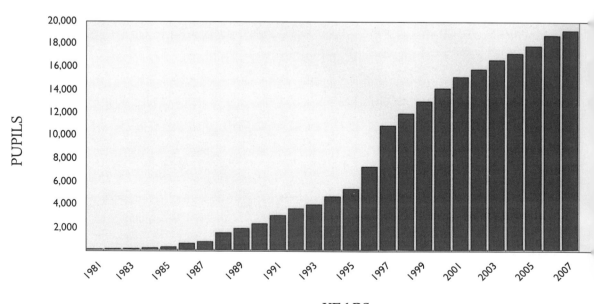

PUPILS

YEARS

North Belfast

Meanwhile, Hazelwood Primary School was officially opened by the 1985 sports personality of the year, Barry McGuigan. It had 117 children from nursery to primary-seven level on the site of the former Throne Primary School. Grant aided status was achieved in October 1986. The school had begun life in premises in York Lane, which had now become the temporary home of the second-level school, Hazelwood College. The number of pupils attending integrated schools in the Belfast area was now over 600.

North Antrim

By the beginning of 1987 the integrated-education movement had acquired greater momentum. On the initiative of Alan and Elaine Smith a group of eight couples had met in October 1986 to consider setting up an integrated school in the triangle area of Coleraine, Portstewart and Portrush. 'Ordinary living stopped from that date!' Dorothy Wilson recalled. By early 1987 the growing group was at the stage of signing contracts for premises in Portrush – a large house, since there were no redundant schools in the area. Like other groups, they had 'working groups busy on premises, Trust applications, transport, fundraising, publicity, religious education and nursery provision'. Dorothy Wilson continued:

> I suppose the most hair raising feature of starting a new school, is wondering whether you are just a few freaks, or 'trendy intellectuals', or whether there are others out there with you. Our first public meeting was well attended and did ease our qualms … On the whole, individually we have all felt supported in this venture, and do not sense much opposition in the local community, except in the teaching profession, where there is naturally unease about losing children and therefore teachers. We have written to all the schools, offering to come to talk with us.[34]

Mid-Down

The Banbridge Area for Integrated Education, yet another parent group, held its first meeting in October 1986 and since the editor of the local newspaper was there it was given front-page coverage. The chairman of the

Southern Education and Library Board (SELB) invited two parent representatives and members of ACT to meet their senior education officer, Miss McClenaghan – the first time that such a meeting had taken place at such an early stage in the development of an integrated school. A trust was formed with the acronym SUTIE – the South Ulster Trust for Integrated Education. A notable feature of this development was the close cooperation of both ACT and BELTIE, and the advice and encouragement provided by those who had recently been through the many processes involved. As Agnes McConville reported:

> In many ways, Banbridge is having it fairly easy, as they are benefiting from the experiences and agonies of those who have gone before. Without their expertise and support, each step would have been so much more difficult, and the group intend to utilise these valuable skills in the future.[35]

She explained the motivation behind establishing this integrated school:

> The desire to set up an integrated school in Banbridge stemmed from a number of reasons. This town is one of the fastest growing in Northern Ireland and generally community relations between different traditions [have] been comfortable. It is upon this base that the group wish to expand and develop the existing good relations through promoting shared education of our young children. The two local nursery schools are already operating on a mixed basis – why should this early start not be carried through into the primary school sector?[36]

In September 1987 75 children began their first term at suitably named Bridge Integrated Primary School. 'Teething troubles were inevitable,' it was reported, 'and as classes continued inside, renovation and reconstruction [were] effected outside to provide, among other things, a play area to allow the children to stretch their legs and let off steam.'[37] In short, the first year of Bridge was similar to that to be experienced by the growing number of integrated primaries across the region. Teachers returned after the Hallowe'en half-term break to prepare a curriculum document based on their perception of the meaning of integrated education, and this was subsequently discussed and accepted by the school governors. Open evenings were arranged to allow parents (along with teachers from neighbouring schools) to discuss the use of the 'Ginn Reading 360' and 'Letterland' systems and other approaches unfamiliar to many parents. Following the horror of the Remembrance Sunday bomb in Enniskillen, class three was taken to the memorial service in Banbridge town centre. There were parents' evenings and two open evenings, a nativity performance for senior citizens and school visits to the Ulster Folk and Transport Museum at Cultra and to Ardress House.

Bridge's school hymn included the words, 'We are one in the Spirit. We are one in the Lord.' Throughout the academic year Presbyterian, Church of Ireland and Methodist clergy attended class assemblies, to which parents were also invited. Lord Flowers of the Nuffield Foundation attended one of these ecumenical occasions of worship, but no Catholic priest accepted the invitation to be there. However, sacramental preparation for Catholic pupils was provided at the parochial house by Fr O'Hare and by parents at the school. The pupils, staff and parents subsequently attended the service in St Teresa's for the seven communicants.

Dungannon and beyond

In June 1987 the first steps were taken in Jean and Pearse Kelly's house in Dungannon to set up Windmill Integrated Primary. The movement was now reaching deep into the heart of the province. Clare Dolan, secretary of the Dungannon Integrated School Association, reported that 'setting up a school in this way is a gruelling and rather awe-inspiring task for any group of parents'. The growing number of schools, however, ensured that they could draw on the experience of the increasing number of people who had already gone down this path. They were able to visit schools that were already up and running, and they were assisted by Joanne McKenna and Adree Novotny, who:

> warned us of the problems and immense workload ahead – but we all had children approaching school age, and we could see no other way for them than by trying to set up a school ourselves in Dungannon. Newcastle had already shown that it could be done outside Belfast, and Bridge and Mill Strand were about to open that September – why should our children be deprived just because they lived 'west of the Bann'?[38]

The school was to be in mobile units on a greenfield site in Dungannon town. Eighty children had already been signed up. As with almost all integrated schools, success could only be guaranteed if appropriate transport could be laid on. A minibus was to take children from

Cookstown and other areas outside Dungannon town.

In short, the parents of Northern Ireland were acquiring integrated primary schools which, if not always close by, were for the most part within a reasonable driving distance from every part of the region. One parent from Derry was prompted to write:

> In over twenty years of working in various ways at cross-community relations within this City, the setting up of Oakgrove Integrated Primary School and the work towards an integrated college here, have proved, in terms of intercommunity relationships and coming together, the most positive, the most fruitful, the most hopeful, the most forward-looking, the most heart-warming, and at times, the most moving work of reconciliation we have ever been involved in.[39]

By the spring of 1994 the integrated primary schools were: Hazelwood, Belfast (1985); All Children's, Newcastle, County Down (1986); Bridge, Banbridge, County Down (1987); Millstrand, Portrush, County Antrim (1987); Windmill, Dungannon, County Tyrone (1988); Braidside, Ballymena, County Antrim (1989); Enniskillen, County Fermanagh (1989); Portadown, County Armagh (1990); Carhill, Garvagh, County Londonderry (1991); Corran, Larne, County Antrim (1991); Oakgrove, Derry (1991); Cranmore, Belfast (1993); Loughview, Belfast (1993); and Saints and Scholars, Armagh (1993). There were six integrated secondary schools: Lagan, Belfast (1981); Hazelwood, Belfast (1985); Brownlow,

Map of Northern Ireland showing location of all 60 schools.

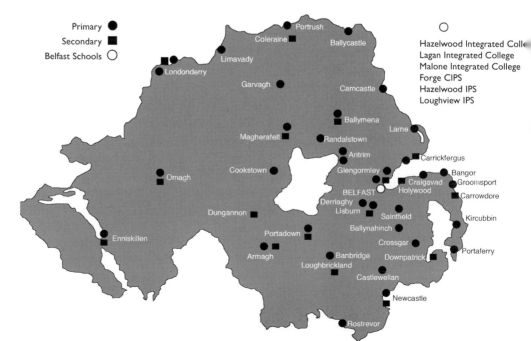

Craigavon (1991); Oakgrove, Derry (1992); and Erne Integrated College, Enniskillen and Shimna, Newcastle, County Down, due to open in September 1994.

Impressive though that list is, the total number of pupils in Northern Ireland was then around 330,000 and, of that number, only 3,300 were attending integrated schools – that is, about one per cent of the school population. In his *Belfast Telegraph* review on 16 October 1993 of the book entitled *Education together for a change: integrated education and community relations in Northern Ireland*, edited by Chris Moffat, Eric Waugh concluded:

> The dissenters are those parents who have opted out; and as Colm Cavanagh of the Foyle Trust makes clear, the movement, first and last, has been what he calls a superb example of parent power. His own Oakgrove College, opened last year, was the 18th integrated school and there are already three more in the making. The aim is to have at least one in each of our 26 district council areas, so widening the options for more parents.
>
> The tragedy is that the trailblazers in this most Christian enterprise are having to force their way through the bush without help either from churches or parties, with the single exception of Alliance. The rest are satisfied, as Mr. Cavanagh found in Derry, that there are no votes in it. Nor does he expect much help from the pulpit either. Strange it is: the schools can have their imprimatur in England, all right – where they do not really need them. But, no, sorry – it's not on theologically here, where we do. Joint Anglican–Roman Catholic schools have existed in England since the early 1980s with the full approval of both sets of bishops. Three merciless spokeswomen for All Children Together as good as accuse them of valuing ecclesiastical power politics above possibilities of reconciliation. Why church leaders leave themselves open to this damning charge we are all well aware. Each of us is part of the problem. But then it is they who have been called to lead.[40]

The percentage of pupils in integrated schools would quadruple in the following years despite the lack of support from political parties and church leaders. Sufficiently determined parent groups generally found that they could establish an integrated primary school in around two or three years. There was, however, one very notable exception: this was Forge Integrated Primary School in south Belfast, which occasioned a struggle which for several years threatened ACT with financial ruin.

9
The saga of Forge

As the sapling bends so will the tree grow.[1]

Brian Garrett, ACT's lawyer. A deputy county-court judge and arbitrator, Brian is also Chairman of the Northern Ireland Teachers' Salaries and Conditions of Service Committee; a former visiting fellow at Harvard; and a former president of the Irish Association. Brian is currently chairman of the board of Annaghmakerrig, the Tyrone Guthrie Centre for creative artists in Newbliss, County Monaghan, founded in 1981.

Instead of taking perhaps two to three years to accomplish, the setting up of Forge Integrated Primary School (FIPS), one of the first integrated primary schools in Northern Ireland, lasted over 12 years. Before the thriving primary school was secure, some six different voluntary and statutory bodies became involved and ACT itself was very nearly rendered bankrupt.

The various bodies involved in the saga were: the Forge Board of Directors; the Forge Board of Governors; the Nuffield Foundation; the ACT Board of Directors; BELB; and the Department of Education, Northern Ireland. Of all of these bodies, the one that caused ACT the most distress and almost led to its bankruptcy was BELB.

The story begins

When Malone Primary School, at number 4 Balmoral Avenue, close to the Lisburn Road in Belfast, was closed in 1984 by BELB because of falling enrolments, parents saw the opportunity to establish an integrated primary school there. As noted earlier, an attempt by parents in 1984 to use the 1978 Education Act to transform the school to a controlled integrated school was turned down by the Department of Education. The school eventually opened as an independent integrated primary school in 1985 with the support of ACT and other trust funds. Looked on as the primary school for which funds were sought in the second Lagan College/ACT appeal in 1985, it was known as Forge Integrated Primary School and housed in the original Malone Primary School premises. Then, in August 1986, having obtained a one-year interest-free loan from the Nuffield Foundation, ACT purchased the site and premises from BELB on behalf of the parents at the full asking price of £110,000 and drew up a two-year lease with Forge at a peppercorn rate to run from 1986 to 1988. (At this stage, an ever-expanding Lagan College was occupying the property through a lease taken out with BELB. After ACT bought the property, the college continued to share the site until 1987. ACT arranged separate leases for both schools at a beneficial rent each paying £3,500 per annum. When Lagan moved out at the end of the 1987 school year, FIPS was liable for the full rent of £6,100 per annum.)

Almost from the very beginning FIPS was a thriving plant and, after only two years, much to the delight of parents, teachers, directors of FIPS, ACT and Nuffield, the school was given maintained status in 1987. This meant it would be financed by the Department of Education, as Lagan College had been, at the rate of 100 per cent of recurrent expenditure and 85 per cent of approved capital costs. Under the 1986 legislation, receiving maintained status also meant that FIPS now had to establish a board of governors. It was the Board of Governors which was then responsible, with the principal, for the day-to-day running of the school, the curriculum and appointing teachers. This body was separate from the directors of the Forge Company Limited, which had run the school since it was established in 1985. However, the limited company and the FIPS directors remained in situ. They had a very similar relationship with the school as the Catholic bishops who had acted as trustees for the Catholic maintained schools in Northern Ireland since the state was formed.

Since the school had been granted maintained status, the FIPS directors had to own the Balmoral Avenue premises before they could apply for a government grant. They were therefore very keen to purchase the premises from ACT. All round, the timing seemed

Front cover of newsletter from Forge Integrated Primary School.

ideal. ACT was aware from the experience of Lagan College that government grants were paid retrospectively, often with a delay of several months. Yet ACT still felt confident that it would be in a position to repay the loan to Nuffield before the interest-free period had elapsed in 1987. Unfortunately that was not to be, for a variety of reasons.

FIPS governors seek to double the school's annual intake

For a start, FIPS was becoming more and more oversubscribed and the governors wanted to explore the possibilities of doubling the enrolment numbers from 200 to 400. The Department of Education did not consider the site suitable for such an expansion because the building was old and becoming unsafe in parts. The department informed the FIPS governors that if the school was to expand they would have to undertake a feasibility study and look at four other sites. As the government was going to have to pay 85 per cent of the capital costs of whatever site and/or buildings the school would eventually be housed in, it was obvious that the department would not approve the sale of the premises to FIPS directors while there was any doubt about the school remaining there.

All of this took months; the months became years and by 1990, three years after the date on which the interest-free loan should have been repaid to Nuffield, ACT was left in the invidious position of having to pay compound interest on the original loan of £110,000, which by then was £57.26 per day. And the FIPS directors could not proceed with the purchase of the premises from ACT: a purchase unapproved by government would not subsequently be grant aided.

Good news?

Eventually, and to the great relief of all concerned, the feasibility study was completed and the decision was taken by the FIPS governors to stay on the Balmoral Avenue premises, even though it meant they would have to keep to an enrolment of 200. In the meantime, in the years 1989–90, the district valuer determined that the premises had development potential; instead of the original value of £110,000 the site was deemed to be worth £325,000. FIPS directors received a letter from the the Department of Education on 25 July 1990 approving the sale of the premises to ACT at this new increased value. With capital grant at 85 per cent, ACT hoped that, allowing for the loan repayment, accrued interest and other expenses, it might eventually be left with a surplus of £175,000–£200,000 from the sale. It seemed almost too good to be true to all concerned.

The necessary steps to transfer the premises from ACT to the FIPS directors began in August 1990, but the sale was delayed by legal difficulties which the directors were to sort out. On behalf of ACT, Bettie Benton, then ACT treasurer, wrote to the secretary of the FIPS Board of Directors on 28 November 1990. Two days previously, the directors had signed 'the sale contract for the premises, subject to certain conditions'. In effect Benton was clarifying what those conditions were:

> You will recall that ACT agreed to permit completion [of the sale] to be effected on the basis that as soon as the DENI make funds available, they will be paid to Brian Garrett's firm of solicitors[ii] and he will immediately repay the Nuffield loan plus interest accrued (currently c £19,000). You undertook to furnish Brian Garrett with an irrevocable authority to submit to the DENI to enable this to happen. After that the final settlement between ACT and Forge could be made ...
>
> We were pleased to attend the meeting and sign the sale contract at last. We realise that you have had a lot of difficulties to overcome and we hope now that all will proceed without further delay. We are very conscious that each day is costing £57.26 in interest thus depleting the surplus remaining when everything has been settled ... It is a very exciting time for you all and we wish you every blessing in the days to come. Please let us know if there is anything more you want us to do.[3]

The Education Reform (Northern Ireland) Order 1989 – a watershed for the development of integrated education

In 1990 a momentous piece of education legislation came into force in Northern Ireland: the Education Reform (Northern Ireland) Order 1989.

> [This] was something of a watershed for the development of integrated education as it introduced statutory support for integrated education, and also provided for existing controlled or maintained schools to 'transform' into integrated schools following a ballot among parents of pupils in attendance at the schools.[4]

In addition, the order stated that:

> all rights and liabilities subsisting immediately before that date which were acquired or incurred by the trustees for the purposes of the school shall be transferred to the relevant [education and library] board.[5]

FIPS governors drop a bombshell

Taking advantage of this new legislation, in December 1990, just days after the FIPS directors had agreed to purchase the premises from ACT, the FIPS governors decided that they would prefer to opt for controlled integrated status rather than continue as a maintained school. If the Board of Governors was successful in its bid to transform the school, all financial responsibilities, both capital and recurrent, would become the sole responsibility of BELB.

The FIPS governors duly applied to have the school recognised as a controlled integrated school (abbreviated as CIS in correspondence) and the balloting of parents and other procedures followed. Parents approved the proposal to transform the school to controlled integrated status in March 1991. Was this a wise decision?

Given that one of the main thrusts of the 1989 Education Reform (Northern Ireland) Order was to make it easier for parents to opt for integrated schools without suffering financial penalties as a result, it is easy to understand why the FIPS governors sought to go down the controlled-integrated-status route. Indeed, another integrated primary school, All Children's in Newcastle, County Down, which opened in 1986, also decided in 1991 to go for the controlled-integrated option and, in November of that year, the South-Eastern Education and Library Board (SEELB) gave the All Children's trustees a cheque for approximately £27,800 in partial settlement of liabilities incurred on behalf of the school. Then, in 1992, SEELB paid all outstanding debts that the All Children's School had (over £100,000) and, to fund the payment of these debts, the Department of Education gave SEELB an additional earmarked grant.[6]

Was the decision to choose controlled integrated status a wise one?

The FIPS directors remained uneasy with the timing of the governors' decision to pursue controlled integrated status just as the procedure to transfer the Balmoral Avenue premises from ACT to the FIPS company was reaching its final stages. Simon Lee, chair of the FIPS directors (and professor of law at Queen's University), decided to consult Basil McIvor, not only as an ACT member but also as a distinguished and experienced lawyer. He wrote on 30 April 1991:

> Thank you for your patience re the transfer of the school premises. As you know, the position has become more complex since you and I met

over lunch in December 1990. Our Board of Governors decided to proceed with a ballot of parents on CIS (controlled integrated status), despite the worries expressed by [the FIPS] directors. You are probably aware that the parents approved that proposal in the March ballot … our transaction was in train before the governors initiated the ballot and I am given to understand that DENI would in any event approve our arrangement … Finally, the directors appreciate that any surplus from the transfer of premises will be held by ACT.[7]

Bettie Benton, treasurer of ACT, wrote to Lee on 17 May 1991:

We are of course aware that Forge [Board of Governors] has opted for controlled integrated status and that the process is well advanced … We believe that the climate of support for integrated education is not as favourable as it was when Brian Mawhinney was Minister and that this must be taken account of.[8]

Benton regretted that the school's directors had not been able to complete the purchase of the premises while the school still had maintained status and went on to say that the accumulated interest on the loan to Nuffield was now almost £30,000. She also quoted from a letter she had received from Nuffield on 28 January 1991 in which Nuffield indicated that 'they would welcome urgent repayment' and pointed out that the loan 'has been considerably extended beyond the original provision in the deed which was for one year, interest free'. They also said that they would welcome a contribution out of the surplus 'to enable us now to deal with the consequences on other [integrated] schools of the extended time during which the Forge loan was outstanding on an interest free basis'. Benton wrote:

However, we [ACT] feel that the settling up can be done in an amiable way between ACT, Forge and Nuffield. A fourth predicament, i.e. the Belfast Board, could create major complications. We hope this advice is of some use to you. We will help in any way we can – just ask.[9]

The minds of the Forge governors were firmly made up, however, despite these prophetic warnings. And indeed, in July 1991, the Department of Education advised the FIPS directors that grant aid for the purchase of the premises would not now be forthcoming in view of the uncertain status of the school. Also in July 1991, the department announced that controlled integrated status had been given to FIPS and, in March 1992, BELB wrote to ACT informing it that controlled integrated status would be effective from 1 April 1992.

It is worth emphasising two points here: firstly, in July 1990, the department had earmarked £276,250 in grant aid for the FIPS directors had their purchase of the Balmoral Avenue premises from ACT gone through; and secondly, the department had made BELB aware in July 1991 that FIPS was becoming a CIS school and that it (BELB) would be required to provide premises for the school. Yet eight months later, in March 1992, BELB wrote to ACT, making it known that it was undecided about purchasing the premises and that it was only at the stage of planning to carry out an 'investment appraisal' in order to investigate possible options for the future provision of premises.

ACT'S financial problems deepen

This was crippling news for ACT. Two years previously, in July 1990, it had come close to selling the Balmoral Avenue premises, which would have enabled it to repay the loan plus interest to Nuffield and, above all, get on with helping other emerging integrated schools – something it had been totally unable to do since the whole complicated Forge story began to develop. Now, with the sale of the property deferred, ACT's financial problems were deepening alarmingly. At the 1992 AGM, ACT's auditor stressed the extreme urgency of finding a purchaser for the property. 'The situation,' he said, 'can not be allowed to continue.'[10] By now, ACT owed £156,704 to Nuffield (the loan of £110,000 plus £46,704 in accumulated interest). Nuffield could put in a receiver, the auditor said, adding that ACT could lose its charitable status. He ended by saying that it was the ACT directors' responsibility to find a buyer for the property on the open market within a period of six weeks, even if the school had to move out. ACT was, he concluded, facing insolvency. And, in fact, during the summer of 1992, ACT had to cease operations because of its precarious financial situation.

The ACT directors once again offered the Balmoral Avenue premises for sale to BELB but the board was not interested in buying. So in July 1992 ACT instructed its agent to place the premises on the open market with a closure date of 30 October 1992. The possible disruption to the school was certainly not making ACT any friends and, as the founding movement for integrated education in Northern Ireland, the last thing it wanted to do was to upset a thriving integrated primary school. It was an agonising decision for the ACT directors, made all the more painful by the knowledge that all the stress could have been avoided had BELB begun to plan for suitable premises when notified in July 1991 that FIPS was to become its responsibility. The simple fact of the matter was that ACT was constrained by the short-term loan that had to be repaid urgently to Nuffield as interest was accumulating at such an alarming rate. And there were further financial constraints on ACT as a result of BELB's intransigence – BELB had refused to pay a rent grant to FIPS directors to enable it in turn to pay the rent due to ACT, which from September 1986 to April 1992 had risen to the huge sum of £31,966.

The battle to obtain a proper rent from BELB

When BELB wrote to ACT in March 1992, it requested a one-year lease, from April 1992 to April 1993, and made it clear that it was seeking an option to renew this lease while it carried out its investigations into possible options for future premises. BELB also stated quite baldly that it would pay rent to ACT from April 1992 to 1993 at the same favourable rate that ACT had given to Forge since 1986. This was totally unacceptable to ACT, which believed that BELB as a statutory body had a responsibility to pay rent at the proper market rate from the time the school became BELB's responsibility. Thus began a battle with BELB which would not be fully and finally settled for years – until the payment to ACT of: the arrears of the rent grant to cover the period July 1987 to end of March 1992; rent *at market value* for the period April 1992–April 1993, when FIPS was a controlled integrated school and therefore BELB's responsibility; and a sum to cover the enormous amounts ACT was losing daily in the compound interest it had to pay to on its loan to Nuffield because of BELB's ongoing and illegal occupancy of its premises.

At one stage in 1992, Gerry Moag, chief officer of BELB, asked Bettie Benton, ACT treasurer, to meet him at his offices. She was requested to come alone and presented with a cheque to cover the rent arrears. The sum offered was £35,150, an amount BELB had calculated by applying the annual fee of £6,100 for all years from 1987 to 1993. As no account had been taken of ACT's demand for a proper market rate for rent from

March 1992, Benton felt obliged to refuse the cheque. Later, in February 1993, following legal advice, ACT agreed to accept 'without prejudice' the sum Moag had offered.

A very reluctant eviction of squatters

Since the Balmoral Avenue premises had been recognised by the district valuer as having development potential, it was clear that it was in fact a prime site and it was not long before ACT was approached by a developer with an offer to purchase at the asking price of £325,000. ACT could have completed the sale in 1992, subject to the developer's success in obtaining planning permission. But it would be 1 January 1994 before BELB provided new premises for the school and it was only because of the extremely accommodating nature of the developer, who put the completion date off three times to accommodate the school and BELB, that the latter was able to stay on the premises.

ACT had given BELB permission to stay on the premises from April 1992 to April 1993, having had the cost of renting such a property for a year determined by a professional surveyor and having insisted that BELB would have to take financial responsibility for the continued interest on its loan to Nuffield. As there was no sign of BELB having made any arrangements to accommodate the school elsewhere after 1 May 1993, nor to compensate ACT for its continued occupancy, ACT had to instruct its surveyor to inform BELB that it had to vacate the premises before midnight on 30 June 1993, thus ensuring that the school year could be completed. ACT also informed its legal adviser of these steps.

Was BELB squatting?

A meeting of the ACT Board of Directors on 25 August 1993 indicated how desperate the situation was becoming. ACT's legal adviser sought opinion of counsel and, as a result, a construction summons was served to BELB on 27 August 1993 to get the school to move out when the sale went through at the end of that month. In a letter to Brian Garrett dated 4 September 1993, counsel commented that:

> a spokesman for BELB stated categorically that children should turn up as usual to the premises at 4, Balmoral Avenue to commence [the school year at] Forge Integrated School. To date the planned site at Annadale Embankment has not even been started and while as it is

hoped to have buildings ready by Christmas it strikes me as hugely over optimistic given that building work has not even begun. On the same radio and TV programme a spokesman for ACT intimated that the BELB had not been in any contact whatsoever with them. He made it clear that they had sold the premises and the completion date was the end of August. I await developments.[11]

Finally there was a response from BELB and, without going to court, it agreed to vacate the premises by 31 December 1993 – a whole eight months after it should have done so. Having previously contended that it had to abide by the figure of £12,500 per annum set by the district valuer's rental valuation of the property, a spokesperson for BELB's legal department then conceded that this was an unreasonable figure bearing in mind the interest ACT could have earned on the purchase price payable by the developer. The BELB spokesperson:

> then proposed that if ACT would allow it to stay on 'the premises' until December 31st 1993, the BELB would pay a special licence fee of £500 per week for the period May to December 1993 and that ACT and its legal adviser could impose any penalty we wished in the Agreement to ensure the property is vacated on that date [31/12/'93].[12]

During the period May–December 1993, BELB could have been said to have been squatting on ACT's property as it only had permission to remain there until 30 April 1993. ACT's legal adviser worked on the agreement with BELB's senior legal adviser and the result was that penalties were imposed on BELB as follows: it had to pay ACT a total of £17,004 to cover the £500 weekly licence fee for the months April to December 1993, when it had been squatting and it also had to send a statement to the media, the school's staff, the parents and the governors acknowledging all the help it had received from ACT while new premises were sought for the school. The statement included the words:

> The Belfast Education and Library Board appreciates the help and co-operation of All Children Together in delaying the completion date of the proposed sale and in allowing the school to remain in occupation of Balmoral Avenue premises until 31 December 1993. By permitting the children to remain at Balmoral Avenue, All Children Together has assisted the board in achieving its objective of minimising the potential disruption to the school, children, staff and parents, associated with the move to the new accommodation.[13]

But it would still be a long time before BELB compensated ACT for the enormous sums it had had to pay out in compound interest on its loan to Nuffield owing to BELB's ongoing occupancy of its premises. (A figure of £21,228.42 was finally paid to ACT in 1997 to cover the interest paid on the Nuffield loan, which by 31 December 1993 had risen to £151,251.79.)

The episode placed great strain on the ACT movement. It had been the subject of some very uncomplimentary coverage in the press and relations between ACT and the FIPS governors were stretched almost to breaking point, with ACT being accused of not making proper provision for the children. This was both unfortunate and unfair – ACT was doing all it could to help the school at a time when the movement itself was almost in liquidation and had had to cease operations temporarily.

BELB only moved finally to pay ACT its due costs when ACT's legal advisers served it with a writ. This was in marked contrast with the supportive approach adopted by SEELB to All Children's Integrated Primary School in Newcastle. Not only did that board move in to help the All Children's trustees with a partial grant in November 1991, it also subsequently settled all the school's liabilities in 1992. And if ACT and its supporters were shocked at the intransigence of BELB, there was even worse to come. The FIPS directors would wait another four years before receiving a final settlement for all liabilities incurred on behalf of the school, again following the institution of legal proceedings.

FIPS directors in serious financial trouble

When FIPS became a controlled integrated school on 1 April 1992, its directors had been incurring costs in the establishing and running of the school since its opening in 1985. A minute of the FIPS directors' meeting in July 1990 reads:

> Company's balance at end of May '90, £546.10; local fund-raising for the period £2323.25; staff costs £6199.62; transport costs £5857.56 of which £3496.70 had been collected from parents; £1694.56 had been spent on essential items of educational equipment.[14]

In common with other integrated schools, FIPS held several fund-raising events, organised by a fund-raising subcommittee of the Board of Directors. In July 1990, the subcommittee had prepared appeal packs which were being distributed to over 60 trusts during the summer in an attempt to raise further funds to help defray constant ongoing expenses. Despite its hard work, by 1 April 1992, when FIPS became a controlled integrated school, the directors had liabilities of almost £29,300, all incurred on behalf of the school. This sum was made up of:

a bank overdraft (salaries, insurance, accountancy, transport, architect's fees): £15,000;
b Flexibus: £3,000;
c outstanding audit and survey fees: approximately £2,000; and
d ACT expenses (solicitor's fees, insurance, salaries): £9,300.

The FIPS honorary treasurer, Sam Frizzell, contacted BELB's finance officer in mid-April 1992 to open discussion with him regarding the settlement of the FIPS directors' liabilities. Cecil Linehan, FIPS director at the time, commented:

> From the Forge Primary Board of Directors' point of view, the Belfast Education and Library Board has a statutory duty to the school as a controlled integrated school since 1st April '92, under Article 95 of the ER (NI) 89 to assume the liabilities of the trustees [directors] for expenditure in the provision of property for the use of the school. These have been with the BELB since 25/4/'92.[15]

Many letters were exchanged between BELB's finance officer and Frizzell during 1992 and 1993, with Frizzell continuing to press the case for the FIPS directors to have their claims settled as trustees of a CIS under the 1989 legislation. All in vain. Brian Garrett, legal adviser to the FIPS directors, sent a stiff note to the education and library boards' senior legal adviser on 2 June 1993, saying that 'there are a number of items claimed which have not yet been admitted and settled as the responsibility of BELB'. He concluded, 'surely my clients are entitled to have the liabilities incurred exclusively in relation to the School reimbursed by BELB under Article 95 (1) (b) of the 1989 Order'.[16]

The smooth setting up in 1991 of All Children's Integrated Primary School in Newcastle, County Down, also a controlled integrated school, was again referred to and the sharp contrast between that and the Forge situation was highlighted. As early as 17 February 1992, Ken Brown, the chief finance officer of SEELB, had informed the Department of Education that:

[the] 1989 Order Article 95 1 (b) states that all 'liabilities shall be transferred to the relevant Board'. This Board (the SEELB), being the relevant Board for Newcastle Integrated School, has paid the outstnding liabilities of the trustees. To date it has cost this board £116,302.94.[17]

However, the senior legal adviser for the education and library boards wrote to the FIPS solicitors Elliott Duffy Garrett on 7 June 1993, giving his views:

at all times the Belfast Education and Library Board provided to the Forge Maintained Integrated Primary School all necessary support and assistance in terms of ancillary staff, transport and general administrative expenses. If the school decided, of its own volition, to employ ancillary staff over and above the normal and reasonable requirement of any school, I do not think it is reasonable that the Belfast Education and Library Board should simply be saddled with the bill. I do not believe that the legislation ever intended that governors and trustees could avoid the consequences of excessive expenditure, simply by passing the bill on to the Education and Library Board ... If the school decided to incur expenditure on transport for the benefit of the pupils over and above the provision made by the Board (that is, free transport to all children living more than two miles from the school), that seems to me to be a matter for which the school should accept responsibility.

My view on the Board's liability towards the governors of Forge remains unchanged.[18]

The senior legal adviser's negative comments on both the ancillary workers and the transport that the FIPS directors had provided for the school shows little understanding of the difficulties of setting up a new integrated primary. As one of the first integrated primary schools, FIPS was involved in original curriculum work. The ancillary workers were classroom assistants who provided essential support to the teaching staff in the delivery of a fully integrated curriculum. FIPS was neither a local nor a parish primary school. It was a flourishing integrated school with an unusually wide catchment area, so the provision of safe and supervised transport was an absolute necessity for many of the FIPS pupils, given their young age and the fact that they lived more than two miles from the school. FIPS directors made these points clearly in letters to their own legal adviser.

It became increasingly clear that the FIPS directors were now in serious financial trouble. Several times during 1992 and 1993, the bank manager wrote to Sam Frizzell, honorary treasurer of the FIPS directors, pointing out that the agreed overdraft of £9,000 was exceeded and, by 27 April 1993, the bank was clearly anxious as the account was £15,747 overdrawn and accumulating interest daily. Sam Frizzell warned Bettie Benton, honorary treasurer of ACT, on 25 August 1993 that:

> [the] fact that BELB have so far refused to sanction and pay the full claim of the Company has meant that our main creditor, the Bank of Ireland, will institute legal proceedings for the recovery of the monies owed to them if we cannot settle by 1 September 1993.[19]

ACT's financial position had improved greatly with the sale of the Balmoral Avenue premises and the settlement with BELB, so in January 1994 ACT advanced a loan to the FIPS directors to settle their account with their bank, thus avoiding the threatened litigation.

Another summons served on BELB

In the autumn of 1993, the Balmoral Avenue premises had been sold, Nuffield's loan plus interest had finally been repaid and, as a result of the writ issued by ACT's legal adviser, BELB had paid ACT all costs and rent arrears plus interest due. BELB finally had plans to house Forge on a new

site in the grounds of a grammar school by the banks of the river Lagan known as Wellington College. It might reasonably have been assumed that in the following months BELB would have attempted to settle the problems with FIPS directors amicably. That did not happen. For another four years, BELB flatly refused to settle the liabilities incurred by the Forge directors. Once

> ### NEW HOME FOR FORGE
> We were delighted when the new school premises were completed, enabling Forge to move after Christmas to its modern well equipped, well heated accommodation on the Wellington College campus. Naturally everyone felt rather sad after nine years, to be leaving Balmoral Avenue with all its memories. ACT was pleased that it was able to facilitate staff and pupils by delaying the sale of its Balmoral property until the new school was ready and appreciated the public acknowledgement of the help given by ACT, made by Gerry Moag Chief Executive BELB. We wish Forge continued success and every blessing in its new home.

again, the only course seemed to be to go to court. Christopher Duffy of Elliott Duffy Garrett warned Cecil Linehan in his letter of 4 December 1995 that this involved considerable financial risk:

ACT announces that the decision regarding a permanent home for Forge Integrated Primary School has finally been taken by the Belfast Education and Library Board, January 1994.

> If proceedings are to be issued, it is likely that the costs of those proceedings would be very high and certainly, if a trial is required, could amount to a sum in the region of **£20,000**. Of course if your claim

succeeds then most, if not all of your costs would be met by the BELB. Should you lose, however, you will be responsible for **both** parties' costs.[20]

Elliott Duffy Garrett sought the opinion of Peter Smith QC, who gave his response on 2 May 1996. He felt BELB was hiding under its interpretation of 'rights and responsibilities' in the Education Reform (Northern Ireland) Order 1989. Peter Smith ended his opinion by saying:

> For my part, I consider that the trustees' argument is to be preferred to that of BELB. Turning to procedure, I am satisfied that this matter can be dealt with by way of Originating Summons.[21]

ACT supported the FIPS directors in every way and at its annual general meeting on 15 May 1996 the following resolution was passed unanimously:

> That All Children Together will support the Directors of Forge Integrated Primary School in their legal bid to recover from the Belfast Education and Library Board, under Article 95(b) of the Education Reform (Northern Ireland) Order 1989 and other relevant legislation, their legitimately incurred liabilities in the running of the school, by means of a Construction Summons (or Originating Summons).[22]

ACT was fully aware of the historic significance of the case and, while it was also aware that the legal advisers were rather uneasy at the possible outcome given the untried nature of the legislation, ACT felt it had to support the FIPS directors as many other schools could have been adversely affected in the future if this claim was lost. A construction summons on behalf of the FIPS directors was duly issued in October 1996.

Establishing that the FIPS directors were the school's trustees

During 1994 and early 1995, when the affidavit for the construction summons was being prepared, FIPS directors and members of the ACT executive spent a great deal of time in discussion of the complexity of the legislation with ACT's solicitors, Elliott Duffy Garrett, and with counsel. BELB wanted to claim that the FIPS directors were *not* actually acting as trustees for the school. If this point was accepted, BELB could avoid taking on the liabilities the FIPS directors incurred on behalf of the school, both while it was an independent school and when it was a maintained one, Earlier, in 1993, Cecil Linchan had sent this note to Brian Garrett:

> we feel it is essential NOW to establish that once the school became a maintained school in 1987 the Board of Directors continued as trustees for the school. As trustees, in June 1987, the Forge Directors nominated 6 members to the first Board of Governors of the school established in accordance with 1986 legislation for school governance. They also assisted the Governors financially.[23]

She concluded by saying:

> We contend therefore through all that is said here that we, the Board of Directors of the Forge Company Ltd, are the trustees of the school.
> **We contend that we are fully entitled to have the liabilities which we incurred on behalf of the school paid for by the Belfast Education and Library Board under Article 95 (1) (b) of the Education Reform (NI) Order 1989.** We can see no reason why we should be treated differently to ALL CHILDREN'S INTEGRATED PRIMARY SCHOOL, NEWCASTLE, CO. DOWN. On the granting of controlled integrated status by the Department of Education to that school, the Board of Directors of its Limited Company had its liabilities settled IN FULL by the South Eastern Ed and Lib Board.[24]

The FIPS directors had assumed the following financial responsibilities:

1 Assuming responsibility for the premises and any essential repairs to the building.

2 Meeting the needs of the school in regard to essential equipment when, due to its rapid increase in size, the Area Board's grant was inadequate.

3 Paying the salary of a classroom assistant, thus giving staff members the necessary time to develop the integrated curriculum. As FIPS was one of the first integrated primary schools, no work had been previously done in this field. Both the principal and the Board of Governors recognised that it was an essential part of the trustees' responsibility to provide for this salary while the school was maintained.

4 Paying for daily bus transport for pupils, essential given the wide catchment area of the school and the children's very young ages.

Help from Nuffield

Cecil Linehan reported developments to the Nuffield Foundation on 24 June 1996. She reiterated the facts surrounding All Children's School in Newcastle and the benign manner in which its trustees had been dealt with by SEELB. She went on to say:

> Our Solicitor has sought the opinion of Senior Counsel. Counsel's advice is that he believes we have a case against the BELB, and that we should proceed by means of a Construction Summons. Given that there is precedent involved here with the numbers of integrated schools growing all the time, and with increased impetus from Government for integrated schools to 'grow', where possible, from existing schools, this could become a very important claim.[25]

She concluded with a request for documentary evidence that Nuffield's loan to Newcastle was repaid with monies from SEELB. This was sent and, in a letter dated 20 July 1996, Linehan thanked Richard Marshall, the finance officer of the Nuffield Foundation, for 'chasing up old files' in preparation for the court case. One file, he had pointed out, showed that:

> in November 1991 SEELB repaid us [Nuffield] the balance of the loan for the purchase and construction of the school. This balance was the remaining amount of the loan after repayment in October 1989 of the major part of the loan when DENI grants for purchase were paid to the Trustees of the school.[26]

Linehan observed:

> Certainly, from where we stand, the SEELB seems to have interpreted the spirit of the '89 legislation correctly, and been supported in their actions by DENI. Obviously, we have an interest! However, we were involved in the drafting of the '89 legislation where it impinged on the future of integrated schools. What is difficult to understand is the reverse treatment of the Forge Trustees by the BELB, given that all the Education and Library Boards have a joint legal service and the same legal advisers. The Affidavit is being lodged before the end of this month.[27]

The case was set out in the High Court of Justice in Northern Ireland, Chancery Division, on 7 February 1997 and, as a result, BELB had to pay a total of £36,648.31 to the FIPS directors. This was paid in March and May 1997.

Two education and library boards, two completely different responses

The question remains: why did BELB delay payment? It had been aware of its responsibilities since 1 July 1991 and it had taken over its controlled responsibility from 1 April 1992. Was it hostile to the development of integrated education? Certainly there was little evidence that Gerry Moag, the chief executive, his staff and the board members had made adequate preparations for the assumption of responsibilities agreed by the Department of Education. By contrast, SEELB placed no such difficulties in the way of All Children's Integrated Primary School in Newcastle, County Down when it became a controlled integrated school. Had BELB ever approached the department and asked for financial help with the FIPS liabilities as SEELB had done for All Children's? After all, in 1990, the department had earmarked some £275,000 in grant aid to be awarded to the FIPS directors if the sale of the Balmoral Avenue premises went through that year. It is impossible to believe that some of that money could not have been made available to BELB.

Thus it was that it took 12 years to resolve the FIPS affair, which consumed vast amounts of the energies of ACT members. In the end the Balmoral Avenue premises sold for much more than originally estimated and this gave ACT an invaluable fund to assist in the establishment of new integrated schools in the 1990s.

10
The Mawhinney breakthrough

As a Christian and as a Minister I was always unimpressed by the perversity of thought that viewed an integrated school as more divisive to a community than the existing polarised system. And the ethos of integrated schools was accommodatingly Christian.
I found it hard to understand other Christians' antagonism to them.

BRIAN MAWHINNEY AND RONALD WELLS, 1975[1]

Dr Brian Mawhinney: born in Belfast, educated at Royal Belfast Academical Institution, a graduate of Queen's University Belfast and MP for Peterborough, 1979–97. He was under-secretary at the Northern Ireland Office (with responsibility for education and information 1986–90, and finance and security, 1990–2); minister of state, Health Department, Whitehall, 1992–4; Privy councillor, 1994–5; and minister without Portfolio and Conservative Party chairman, 1995–97.
He was given a knighthood for political service and was raised to the peerage in 2005.

A new minister

Born, brought up and educated in Belfast, Dr Brian Mawhinney was appointed under-secretary with responsibility for education and information at the Northern Ireland Office in 1986. He was the first Northern Ireland-born minister under direct rule and was to be one of the longest-serving ministers there. He held very strong Christian beliefs and brought to the Department of Education carefully thought-out views on schooling in Northern Ireland. 'I did not come to the Northern Ireland Education Department without any policy baggage,' he wrote subsequently. In 1975 – four years before being elected a Conservative MP for Cambridgeshire – he had written, with Ronald Wells, *Conflict and Christianity in Northern Ireland*. This book included these words: 'How bright the prospects for peaceful coexistence in Ulster can be while children are educated separately is a matter of considerable doubt.'[2] In his memoirs he explained further:

> As a Christian and a Conservative I supported the principle of parental choice. Catholic parents clearly valued the Christian ethos associated with Catholic schools. Protestant parents chose state schools. But I

asked myself, what of those parents whose choice could not be accommodated by either system? Did they not have the right to choose as well? I believed they did and that we needed to cater for their choices too.

Some parents did not want their children educated within a system which was as divided as this one was. Even if the teaching was non-divisive, which could not always be guaranteed in either part of the system, the whole education system relayed a powerfully symbolic message of division to young minds.[3]

Mawhinney was deeply impressed by the determination of the parents who had founded Lagan College, particularly as its 'ethos was Christian and its educational practice and appeal were non-denominational'. He saw that the school faced formidable opposition:

The Education Department would not recognize it. Initially civil servants did not believe in its long-term viability – not least because of its unique genesis – so would not give it taxpayers' money. Officials simply ignored the paradox that while parents wanted the school, the absence of tax money reduced its chances of survival. Parents and charitable trusts maintained the rudimentary buildings, bought the books and paid the teachers. They were radical pioneers with a commitment to their children's welfare which was quite remarkable. They were amongst the first genuine 'peace people'.[4]

He disapproved of the way the churches did not approve of this innovation – 'They interpreted it as undermining their authoritative Christian teaching. In reality, what they did not like was a lay initiative challenging their status quo.' Mawhinney saw that there were powerful interests pressing the government not to supply the school with necessary resources. 'They recognized,' he continued, 'that as resources followed pupils, money for Lagan College meant less money for "their" schools. To his credit my predecessor, Nick Scott, started the initial funding.'[5]

Mawhinney's arrival as a minister created quite a stir in Rathgael House. Civil servants used to explaining why things could not be done, or at least why they could not be done as rapidly as expected, found their objections brusquely swept aside. They found the new minister's certainties unnerving. On occasion it was necessary for Mawhinney to arrive at the Stormont estate by helicopter; when it touched down, they joked to each other that 'the Ego has landed'. However, there were some civil servants

– particularly in the inspectorate – who warmly (if quietly) welcomed changes they considered long overdue. Mawhinney certainly shook up the department and pushed through the most striking educational changes Northern Ireland had witnessed since the implementation of the Education Act in 1947. His first concern was to secure the future of Lagan College:

> When I arrived in 1986, Lagan College's survival was still precarious. Demand to attend the school far outstripped its ability to cope. Parents wanted it to expand, but to do so it needed new buildings and more teachers. In other words, it needed large amounts of money. Considerable pressure was quickly put on me to support existing schools and not to divert resources to this 'friendless experiment'. But I too had beliefs. I twice increased the school's pupil capacity and provided a considerable amount of new money for new buildings. Today Lagan College is thriving.[6]

Mawhinney was doing much more than this: he was preparing the way for a major increase in integrated-education provision across Northern Ireland.

Mawhinney's White Paper 1988:
Education in Northern Ireland: proposals for reform

The plight of Hazelwood College in north Belfast was soon brought to the minister's attention. He met the school's trustees at Stormont Castle:

> They were very low. They made it clear, without aggression, that the school's survival was in my hands … the stakes were even higher than the immediate education of just over 200 pupils. If Hazelwood failed in a high-profile way, other parents would be discouraged from trying to start other integrated schools.[7]

What became starkly clear to Mawhinney at this meeting was that Hazelwood could only survive if he eased 'the criteria for deciding when a school was educationally viable and therefore eligible to receive taxpayer funding'.[8] The minister was fast coming to decisions about how best integrated education could be advanced across Northern Ireland.

First, Mawhinney had to overcome resistance within his own department. 'Officials told me I had a responsibility to use taxpayers' money wisely,' he recalled, 'and advised me not to change the rules.' It was explained to him that other local schools could easily accommodate Hazelwood's pupils. He was told, questionably, that while some parents admirably supported the integrated college, greater numbers of parents were concerned by the 'damage' that funding Hazelwood would do to the funding of *their* schools. Mawhinney continued:

> I spent time reflecting on the decision and its importance and on what I personally believed as a Christian. The decision was mine and I would have to defend it and live with its consequences. I also thought about the damage that might occur to the Christian faith I shared with others if I funded the school and it still collapsed due to community antagonism …
>
> Finally, the issue facing me was not just the funding of this one school. If I eased the central funding criteria, we were likely to face a continuing series of funding crises as parents started other schools and then demanded that the State support them financially.[9]

'My reflections and prayers gave me a clarity of purpose which I knew was right,' Mawhinney wrote. He altered the funding rules and Hazelwood not only survived but flourished.[10]

Across the Irish Sea Margaret Thatcher's Conservative government was putting Britain's education system through a major overhaul. A key feature of this reform was the introduction of the national curriculum, which very specifically laid down what would be studied in the classroom all the way through primary and secondary education until the age of 16. Mawhinney was expected to extend these changes to Northern Ireland, with appropriate adaptations to suit the region. The result was the publication in March 1988 of his White Paper, *Education in Northern Ireland: proposals for reform*.

Paragraph six stated:

> It is also crucial to acknowledge that the task of raising standards in education in Northern Ireland is being tackled in a community with deep divisions which are reflected in the education system. Children from the two traditions in Northern Ireland are – for the most part – educated separately. There is, of course, room for debate over how far this separation contributes to the continuation of the divisions in the Northern Ireland community. But even those who would question the significance of that contribution would probably acknowledge that segregation in education, as in housing, does little or nothing to reduce community divisions.[11]

The government undertook to back parental choice, to continue to support programmes fostering greater tolerance and mutual understanding, and 'to act positively to facilitate the development of integrated education where there is sufficient parental demand to support a viable school'.[12]

ACT was naturally excited by this prospect and, since comments were invited, members were soon busy drafting submissions. There was much warm support for the White Paper in ACT and its response included advice that religious education should be regarded as a foundation subject (though it was admitted that it did not lend itself easily to assessment).

The proposal to allow parents of existing schools to opt to transform a school to maintained integrated status was, of course, welcomed. However, ACT regretted that no provision appeared to be made for new schools to opt for this status from day one. This was in stark contrast to the situation which obtained in the Catholic maintained sector.

Mawhinney moved swiftly; the draft order in council was ready in June and the government's decisions on the education-reform proposals were announced on 5 October 1988.

'Against all the odds': the Education Reform Order 1989

In his press statement launching a second White Paper, *Education reform in Northern Ireland: the way forward*, the education minister stressed that all the responses to the first White Paper 'were considered very carefully and have informed our thinking'. Section 6 of the document dealt with integrated education. This included:

a Provision of financial help for newly established integrated schools at an early stage in their development.

b 'priority to be given to capital projects for the provision of additional pupil places in integrated schools'.

c Provision for existing schools to opt for grant-maintained integrated status (GMIS).

d The retention of legislation for establishing controlled integrated schools.

e The introduction into legislation of a statutory responsibility on the

STATUTORY INSTRUMENTS

1989 No. 2406 (N.I. 20)

NORTHERN IRELAND

The Education Reform (Northern Ireland) Order 1989

BELFAST
HER MAJESTY'S STATIONERY OFFICE
£10.50 net

Department of Education to encourage and facilitate integrated education 'which may be achieved in part through an independent body assisted by public funding'.[13]

The legislation was placed on the statute book as the Education Reform (Northern Ireland) Order 1989.

Though many questions still needed to be answered, this reform was clearly a decisive step forward for integrated education. Looking back in April 1991, Basil McIvor, as chairman of ACT, paid this tribute to the minister:

> PART VI
>
> INTEGRATED EDUCATION
>
> CHAPTER 1
>
> GENERAL FUNCTIONS OF DEPARTMENT AND BOARDS
>
> *General functions of Department and boards in relation to integrated education*
>
> 64.—(1) It shall be the duty of the Department to encourage and facilitate the development of integrated education, that is to say the education together at school of Protestant and Roman Catholic pupils.

Had it not been for Dr Brian Mawhinney's courageous, single-minded and enthusiastic support for integrated schooling, we would not now be enjoying the tremendous advantages which the 1989 E.R.O. offers the integrated sector. Despite his critics and detractors, and against all the odds, he finally managed to legislate integrated education on to the Statute Book. I know that he did this because he *really believed* that children of both traditions in Northern Ireland should be educated under the same roof.[14]

A statutory duty is placed on Department of Education to encourage and support the education together at school of Protestant and Roman Catholic pupils.

ACT BLAZED TRAIL IN 70 s
FOR EMU, CULTURAL HERITAGE AND COMMON CORE R.E.
—————— PART OF EDUCATION REFORM IN 90 s ——————
ACT ON SHARED SCHOOLS
Policy Document 1976
~~ACT ON SHARED SCHOOLS~~

The cross-cultural themes of the Education Reform (Northern Ireland) Order 1989, were undoubtedly influenced by ACT's 1976 policy document, 'ACT on shared schools'.

An early indication that integrated schools would be high up the list for capital funding (as stated in the legislation) was the grant of £3.3 million given to Lagan College in 1989. Yvonne Gilmour, ACT acting secretary, described this as 'a wonderful boost to their finances [which] will enable them to undertake permanent capital works'.[15] 'I recall one incident,' Mawhinney wrote later, 'when I was cutting the first sod of the new building project at Lagan College.' He continued:

In Northern Ireland some refer to Catholics as 'left footers' or those who 'dig with the left foot'. So when the time came for the ceremony, I put the spade into the ground twice for the television cameras – first using my right foot and then my left. The images and their explanation reinforced the message of integrated education in tens of thousands of homes that evening.[16]

Mawhinney recalled that 'one consequence of pushing ahead with this policy was that I came in for a good deal of personal public criticism'. Church leaders were critical and said so. Education and library boards sought to ignore the reality of these developments because these integrated schools were not within their control. Opposition from the churches to the increased provision for integrated education was considerable, he remembered:

There is still pressure on parents not to choose integrated schools. Neither the Catholic Church's hierarchy nor many Protestant ministers approve of this coming together in the classroom. They have a sense that it undermines their authority and makes 'defending their corner' more difficult. I respect their views. I simply think they are wrong. In Northern Ireland the strength of the Christian faith sometimes appears to depend too much on uniformity. But strength can also be found in diversity …

The two Cardinals who held office while I was a Northern Ireland Minister, along with their Bishops, felt particularly strongly that integrated education was a direct attack on Catholic teaching about the importance of Catholic education. I pointed out to them repeatedly that the choice on offer was optional. If 'good' Catholics adhered to the Church's teaching, then there would be few, if any, new integrated schools. No Minister – certainly not this one – was going to try to persuade Catholic parents to abandon Catholic schools just to bolster integrated schools. But equally, if good Catholic parents, knowing how much importance the Church attached to educating their young people in Catholic schools, nevertheless felt strongly that their own children should be educated with children from other but non-Catholic families, then as parents they should have the right to make that choice.

The Bishops were unmoved. They insisted on a meeting with the Secretary of State to demand that the legislative proposal be dropped. They were joined by Protestant Church leaders. The Secretary of State gave me his full support. Parliament passed the measure into law in 1989.[17]

Even then, in 1990, the Catholic hierarchy took action in the courts to challenge the legality of the previous year's Education Reform Order in

---

ALL CHILDREN TOGETHER

SEMINAR

SATURDAY, 31st March 1990
FRIENDS MEETING HOUSE
MARLBOROUGH PARK SOUTH, BT9
COFFEE / REGISTRATION ~ 09.45 / START ~ 10.15
CLOSE : 4.00 p.m. approx

CHANGES AND CHALLENGES!

- **EDUCATION REFORM (N.I) ORDER 1989**
- **CULTURAL HERITAGE**
- **EDUCATION FOR MUTUAL UNDERSTANDING**
- **ROLE OF THE CHURCHES IN EDUCATION**

TO BOOK CONTACT JOANNE McKENNA ~ ALL CHILDREN TOGETHER
13 UNIVERSITY STREET BELFAST
Telephone : Belfast (0232) 327335
ADMISSION FREE   LUNCHES AVAILABLE

ACT members and all interested parties were invited to discuss the wide implications for the integrated section of the Education Reform (Northern Ireland) Order 1989. In Basil McIvor's words, 'had it not been for Dr Brian Mawhinney's courageous, single-minded and enthusiastic support for integrated schooling, we would not now be enjoying the tremendous advantages which the 1989 E.R.O. offers the integrated sector'.

respect of provision for integrated schools. The legal challenge failed.

Soon afterwards, the implementation of another element in the legislation would arouse much distress in the ranks of ACT.

New impetus to develop a central body for integrated education

In 1986, Basil McIvor, on behalf of ACT, was the first person to submit to the Department of Education a memorandum on the need for an integrated schools advisory commission. He began by observing that up until now 'growth has depended on the convictions of individual parents' but that if 'growth is set to assume dramatic proportions over the next ten years there is a clear need for some directional activity, which would best come from outside the public service'. In that case it 'would be the height of folly to allow integrated education to propel itself forward uncontrolled and in a haphazard way' without the advice of a professional body. He continued:

> Careful consideration must be given to the viability of new integrated schools, for the failure of one could seriously damage the whole sector, especially given the hostility in the Province from powerful vested interests in schools in other sectors. Such hostility, which will continue for a long time to come, will inevitably mean very strong resistance to the danger of a challenge to the 'integrity' and 'probity' of existing schools from this quarter … No integrated schools should be established which is likely to be less advantageous to its pupils than the best schools in the other sectors.[18]

McIvor argued that integrated education must have the benefit of the professional advice and guidance of a central body to: assess and evaluate proposals for new integrated schools; advise on the formation, planning and curriculum of such schools; and act as a focus for integrated schools, becoming 'a representative voice in this sector'. The commission should include 'people with outstanding credentials' and funding would be needed for the necessary office, professional and secretarial backup facilities. He wanted ACT and BELTIE to work together to identify areas where parents desired integrated schools and provide counselling, encouragement and financial assistance for them. ACT saw the eminent good sense of this approach and, in June 1987, formally adopted the McIvor plan as policy. ACT *never* envisaged itself being the sole constituent of the commission but definitely believed that, with its collective experience of almost 20 years working for the development of integrated education, it would be strongly represented on it.

There was little by way of government response over the ensuing two years. The arrival of Brian Mawhinney as minister of state with responsibility for education immediately provided a more proactive approach by government, especially as Section 6.2 of *Education reform in Northern Ireland: the way forward* set out a range of measures to support integrated education, including the possibility that a statutory duty to encourage it might be placed on the Department of Education and that this duty might be achieved in part through an independent body assisted by public funding. Thus it was with high hopes that ACT corresponded with the minister, putting forward and elaborating on the same points that had been made in McIvor's memorandum two years before. The submission included the following:

> We believe that there is now an urgency for the establishment by government of an interim standing committee on integrated education. If you do not wish to go as far as an Integrated Schools Council, could there not at least be some kind of integrated schools committee, comprising the Department of Education, the Area Board, teachers and voluntary representatives?
>
> We envisage this committee becoming the main line of communication with large charitable foundations, not as a funding, but as an advisory, body.[19]

As previously explained, the ACT executive decided in 1988 not to join the Northern Ireland Council for Integrated Education (NICIE), which they felt did not allow the various constituencies freedom to retain differences in strategy and which was, in fact, advocating the same policies as those put forward by BELTIE in 1984. To recapitulate, for ACT the main problem areas of the BELTIE/NICIE approach were:

- A rapid pace and continued proliferation of new integrated schools.
- A parallel proliferation of small 'trustlets' supporting and funding the new integrated schools, the whole edifice resting on an unapproved bank-loan system.
- An extremely aggressive approach to existing providers, which was alienating education and library boards, churches and others.

- The diverting of too much finance into administration.
- The danger of an integrated school, dependent on a large bank loan, failing.
- The lack of professional expertise.
- A total lack of time for consultation or democratic decision-making – the council was to decide all funding priorities.

The very success of the pioneers of integrated education was creating new problems. For a long time energies had been channelled into getting the movement off the ground and setting up Lagan College and Forge Integrated Primary School. Now parent groups were busy right across Northern Ireland, from north Belfast south to Banbridge and Newcastle, west to Omagh and beyond to Derry. To a very considerable degree these parent groups, and the schools they subsequently founded, depended on trusts across the Irish Sea for survival. Those trusts were being inundated with requests for money from many quarters. In addition, Brian Mawhinney's White Paper proposed 100-per-cent capital funding for integrated schools proving viability. How would that prospect alter the attitudes of the funders?

Certainly the directors of Lagan College were anxious. Donal McFerran, their chairman, expressed his concerns in a letter to Cecil Linehan on 19 September 1988. He referred to Mawhinney's White Paper and observed that:

> the one proposal that seems to have got wide publicity is for 100% Capital Funding for Integrated Education … Funding from the Trusts in England has … dried up. The Trusts that have supported us in the past are now considering requests from eight different schools in Northern Ireland. They quite simply do not know how to manage all these requests and they either make no donation to anyone or make donations to newer schools that are not yet maintained …
>
> Our fund raising campaign locally could hardly be called a success … Both the Trusts and the local businesses as I said are aware of the proposals for 100% Capital Funding and it makes it very difficult to explain that we also need nearly £3000 per week to keep the College going during term time.[20]

In short, there was very good reason why ACT was becoming increasingly anxious about the future of its first offspring, Lagan College.

If that school was to go under, what hope remained for the integrated-education movement elsewhere in Northern Ireland? In addition, Donal McFerran was not pleased by the manner in which NICIE was putting pressure on Lagan College directors and governors alike. However, he warned:

> we are not in a strong financial position and we are in no position to throw our weight about when it comes to negotiating with NICIE. Through the work of Anthony Tomei in Nuffield all the English Trusts are now channelling their money through NICIE. Almost £400,000 has been channelled through NICIE this year and not one penny has come to Lagan. The explanation for this is that the priorities decided by NICIE are:
>
> 1 Non-maintained schools
> 2 Nursery and Primary Schools.[21]

McFerran, who had had a meeting with the DENI assistant secretary, Stephen Quinn, at the Department of Education in June 1988, reported that:

> Lagan's abstentionist attitude from NICIE was a matter for some comment in the Department, and in essence it could be said that their view was our attitude did not reflect well on the Integrated Education Movement.[22]

McFerran later called a joint meeting of directors and governors. 'All of us,' he wrote, 'resented the pressure we felt was being put on Lagan College for whatever reason to join NICIE.' Nevertheless, he continued:

> in view of the difficult financial position we found ourselves in and the possible split in the Integrated Education movement that would be caused if we failed to co-operate further with them, I was directed along with one other director to continue to negotiate with NICIE concerning their constitution and aims. I have had one informal meeting with Alan Smith, the acting Chairman of NICIE, and with Chris Moffatt concerning the constitution.[23]

He concluded with the observation that the best approach was to persuade 'everyone' that NICIE did not need to be any more than 'an unincorporated association' (in other words, there was no reason why the loose cooperation enjoyed by the treasurers at their 1987 meeting, leading to joint applications to funding, could not have continued without a tightly controlled central body) and 'we might be able to use our influence to temper some of the worst excesses of the Spencer/Mulvenna connection' (that is, the BELTIE approach of 1984 which led to the formation of NICIE.[24]

The recognition of NICIE

Donal McFerran's hope that NICIE would be no more than an 'unincorporated association' was not to be realised. The trusts had strong reasons to back a central body with some muscle in order to simplify the distribution of monies they were providing and the opinion that NICIE was that body rapidly gained ground. In addition, that view was also being accepted in Rathgael House. ACT was being drawn into a long and exhausting struggle which it would comprehensively lose.

Mawhinney called together representatives of ACT (Basil McIvor and Yvonne Gilmour), BELTIE (Muriel Pritchard) and NICIE (Fiona Stelfox) on 8 May 1990. The minister opened by asking the representatives to show him why he should fund all three organisations. Muriel Pritchard explained that BELTIE was winding up with the belief that NICIE was the vehicle for integrated education now. Fiona Stelfox spoke about NICIE being representative of all interests in integrated education and developments on the ground. Basil McIvor said that NICIE was not representative of all interests and went on to say that ACT had been involved in this field for 17 years – there had been no need for the formation of another group.

Mawhinney put forward various options and observed that it had been a pity that NICIE was set up before the new legislation 'as it would have been better for all of us to have worked on the creation of a new body now'. He then tried to ascertain 'how much "good will" existed between ACT and NICIE in order for these groups to work together in the creation of an overviewing body'. The minutes of the meeting record:

> NICIE and BELTIE gave the impression that all supporting organisations could work together very well; there was in fact no problem in us co-operating and working together.
>
> Mrs Gilmour said that this was not so. She had attended NICIE meetings for over a year and [said] that we had been unable to work together ... The Minister agreed that 'birth pangs' and 'clashes' were inevitable in such an emotive area.

Mrs Gilmour further endorsed Mr McIvor's suggestion for a 'commission' where in this new forum ACT and NICIE could be represented with Government in monitoring developments and controlling the 'purse strings'.[25]

At the bottom of this minute was this 'Note':

The Minister was not aware that new integrated schools had to find all their capital costs. New schools are planned for Omagh and Portadown this September but banks are refusing to give loans as they believe if Government is committed to integrated education that it should underwrite the costs of these new schools.[26]

On behalf of ACT Bettie Benton wrote to the minister on 14 June 1990, again recommending McIvor's proposed commission. She suggested a working party of '11–12 people representative of the Department of Education, the Education & Library Boards, All Children Together, BELTIE and NICIE'.[27] However, the legal challenge mounted by the Catholic bishops resulted in delay. On behalf of the Department of Education, Stephen Peover wrote to the ACT secretary, Sr Anna, on 17 July:

In June the Northern Roman Catholic Bishops challenged the constitutionality of the provisions of the 1989 Education Reform Order dealing with integrated education. Specific reference was made in that challenge to the duties and powers under Article 64, which is the one empowering the department to pay grants to bodies supporting integrated education. Judgement in the case was reserved and is not expected to be given until September. In these circumstances the Minister has deferred a decision on assistance for bodies involved in integrated education until the outcome of the judicial review is known.[28]

Judgement was given in September 1990: the case was dismissed and there was no appeal. Six months later, in March 1991, as there was still no response from the department, Bettie Benton wrote again. By now Lord Belstead was minister of education. Writing for the minister on 9 April 1991, M.T. Donnelly assured Benton that the matter 'is currently under active consideration' and added:

The minister appreciates that, as representations from ACT and others were made some time ago, it is desirable that the issues be resolved as soon as possible, and we are seeking to do this.[29]

ACT had also raised the broader question of how the government proposed to meet its obligations under Article 64 (1) and (2) of the Education Reform Order 1989. In response Donnelly replied:

> As you know, the Order provides opportunities for both the creation of new integrated schools and the integration of existing schools, and these have been underpinned with financial arrangements which, inter alia, provide for 100% grants on approved capital expenditure. These provisions reflect the spirit of Article 64 (1), though policy in this context will be kept under review to ensure that all appropriate encouragement is given to integrated education. Article 64 (2) is, of course, a discretionary provision which does not impose specific obligations on Government. I hope this clarifies the position for you.[30]

No more was heard from the Department of Education until Benton received a phonecall on 23 May 1991, during a bank-holiday weekend, with a request for ACT to contact the department urgently to arrange a meeting. Bettie Benton, Cecil Linehan and Basil McIvor met Department of Education officials on 30 May 1991. This was almost one full year since Benton had written to the department asking for a meeting. To ACT's surprise, Stephen Quinn, assistant secretary, said that the department had received a number of submissions from bodies seeking government funding to promote integrated education. In considering those applications, he said, the department had two important considerations in mind:

- The department was looking to maximise impact on the ground, in terms of services delivered to schools and parents.
- The department's objective, which was shared by the Department of Finance and Personnel, was that administration costs should be kept to a minimum.

And then came the decision:

> Consideration of these factors had led the Department to conclude that financial assistance should be routed to/channelled through NICIE. In particular, the department had taken note that
>
> 1 NICIE is a widely representative group, with many schools and support bodies affiliated to it, covering all of Northern Ireland; and
> 2 it is already providing some central services to schools;
> 3 it has an administrative structure which has the potential to be built upon;

4 it appears to have access to other sources of finance. This point is important because the Department will not be providing 100% funding [for integrated schools].[31]

Quinn said he realised the decision would be a disappointment to ACT although he hoped that ACT would recognise that it was a conscientious attempt 'to act on the Article 64 duty'. He recognised the key role which ACT had played in the development of integrated education but it would, however, 'be the responsibility of NICIE and ACT to collaborate in planning activities likely to attract funding'.[32]

Clearly, this was a severe disappointment for ACT. McIvor, speaking in his capacity as chairman of Lagan College, said that the school 'had no confidence in NICIE and that other schools might feel the same'. When he drew attention to the role that ACT and its members had played in the origins and development of integrated education, Quinn acknowledged this. Cecil Linehan felt that the department had shown discourtesy to ACT through its failure to consult with them at every stage of the process. Bettie Benton felt that it would be 'demeaning' for ACT to have to go to NICIE for funds and pointed out that it was ACT that had initiated the concept of NICIE – the ACT executive had first instituted the idea of joint applications to the large trusts in the UK. She explained that there were major differences of opinion between the two organisations and that ACT had no confidence in NICIE's financial ability. Quinn responded that most of the other integrated schools seemed to have confidence in NICIE and said that this was evident in the way in which they called upon its services.[33]

ACT's first action following the meeting with the Department of Education was to send a message of goodwill to the newly funded NICIE. The ACT executive then met to consider its reaction to this disappointing rejection by the department after almost 20 years of work and very cordial relations with department officials. They had organised a seminar, for example, on 9 April 1991 on the Education Reform Order 1989 at which the main speakers were two senior Department of Education officers, Stephen Peover and David McCormack.

Next day the directors of ACT wrote to Stephen Quinn to express their concern at the decision. They argued that this decision 'pre-empted … what [were] to have been discussions between yourselves and ourselves as per your letter of 9th April '91' and that 'no objective grounds were given nor criteria established as the basis for this decision'.[34] They were in the process of consulting their solicitor. ACT also wrote to Peter Brooke, the secretary of state, and to Brian Mawhinney in his capacity as minister of community relations, informing them that there was 'no discussion' and that its representatives had been presented with 'a *fait accompli*'.

Lord Belstead attempts to mollify

On 3 June Lord Belstead issued a press release announcing that the Department of Education, Northern Ireland had decided 'to provide financial assistance to the Northern Ireland Council for Integrated Education to support its work in the promotion of integrated education'.[35] The minister met Bettie Benton, Cecil Linehan and Bill Brown at Rathgael House on 28 June 1991. Belstead was at pains to show courtesy throughout but it proved a long and difficult meeting. Benton said that ACT never saw itself as the central body but that it appeared that 'a narrow body is to be funded not having the representation of credible professionals or expertise'. The minister responded that it was he who had made the decision: NICIE were employing four people and 'they did seem to be representative of most of the schools and support bodies'. Bill Brown assured Belstead that ACT representatives intended:

> not to carp at NICIE as it is today, contributing well to the development of integrated education, not to be spiteful and bitter … let us ensure that you understand that we are not opposed to NICIE – our first action prior to the public announcement was to send a message of goodwill.[36]

Then he asked:

> Why has your Department chosen NICIE and only NICIE as the vehicle to promote integrated education and support it by finance? Why has the experience of ACT for almost 20 years been totally ignored? Why has the hard work of three people who have been honoured for their work in integrated education by other significant figures in government been now demeaned virtually? They are still dedicated despite this.
>
> Minister, the two companions with me today have had between them 17 years of service in Education Boards. Mr McIvor was the originator of ideas for integrated education. Sister Anna had made the issue world-

wide. And these are only 5 of a large group of deeply concerned and dedicated people. I do not recall your Department ever being embarrassed by our work.[37]

Bill Brown then moved on to what for many in ACT was a key point:

Minister, I have a personal view as to why this has all happened as it did. I have seen for 25 years how fearful or hostile the Department in Northern Ireland is to anything to do with RE in schools – totally unlike Great Britain. My conclusion is that your civil servants saw us in ACT as taking too much interest in religious issues and culture. So they opted for a group that would be totally value free and free from religion.

That is our dismay. After working with the Humanist association and others with no religious convictions for many months, we come to the decision that integration in Northern Ireland would only progress if parents saw something of a Christian ethos in the schools. It would have been much easier for us early on to have ignored religion as NICIE appears to do. But the facts on the ground forced us otherwise to move. We have to integrate Protestants and Catholics so religion is central. It is in the legislation too. We were [not] interested in proselytising but in EDUCATION. We have had to withstand the criticism of the churches but it has been tempered because our schools were to be ecumenical schools. If one set up integrated schools with no Christian ethos, all that will happen is that schools will develop for disaffected Catholics or Protestants or those of no religion at all.[38]

Brown asked why, in choosing four department representatives for NICIE, was all the work of ACT ignored:

By appointing two people from ACT what a harmony could have been achieved and how much useful and broader experience could have been tapped … Integration means harmony. We are not here to complain but to build bridges … as it stands your department's decision is critically bad for harmony.[39]

The minister said that the government could not fund two bodies:

no matter what way it was worked out there would have been duplication of administration … there is no reason ACT cannot work in partnership with NICIE and I do hope that this will be done.[40]

Cecil Linehan explained that ACT had received no government grant whatsoever until 1986 and that it was with the help of the Rowntree Trust that funding had been found for a development officer. She read out extracts from the letter sent by Donal McFerran to her on 19 September 1988, quoted above. Linehan said that ACT had been put under the same pressure. She then pointed out that ACT was represented on the administrative structures of Lagan College, Forge Primary and Bridge Primary, Banbridge and had been involved with integrated schools further afield in matters pertaining to parental involvement, religious education, academic standards and legal and financial matters.

It was clear that the minister was not shifting his ground; he repeated his statement that the Department of Education was giving £250,000 directly to NICIE; that approved integrated schools would be given 100 per cent of their capital costs; and that 'efforts will continue to ensure the involvement of the major trusts in additional sources of income'.[41]

Lord Belstead wrote to Bettie Benton about the meeting on 28 July 1991. He explained why he had chosen NICIE as the means of channelling money for the promotion of integrated education, saying that 'This decision was taken essentially on the basis of NICIE's widely representative nature, its extant administrative base and its relationship with other potential funders.' He added that he had taken the opportunity to inform ACT that the department's Community Relations Division 'will be making a grant of £6,000 grant to ACT, for the 1991/92 financial year only'. He noted 'with gratitude' that the suggestion had been made that the department 'might consider appointing ACT people as Directors of NICIE' and ended with the hope 'that ACT will continue to make its unique contribution'.[42]

Appealing to the ombudsman

The directors of ACT felt that they had no choice but to lodge a complaint of maladministration against the Department of Education to the parliamentary commissioner for complaints. The ombudsman, Jill McIvor, replied in February 1992 and explained:

> I am not empowered to question the **merits** of a discretionary decision unless maladministration was present in the decision-making process. Similarly, it is not open to me to question a Department's policy unless it also appears to have been affected by maladministration or to have been made without consideration of all the relevant facts.[43]

ACT decided they had sufficient evidence to go ahead. The formidable task of gathering together the necessary documentation and putting together the submission largely fell to Bettie Benton and Cecil Linehan, and they did it on 28 November 1991. In their statement of complaint the last three points were at the core:

(12) ACT was not given the same opportunity as NICIE had to discuss with DENI its proposals for an Overviewing Body and the necessary financing;

(13) ACT's role in development of integrated education, through seminars, lectures etc., (complementing NICIE's promotional activities) was just as deserving of funding under Article 64 of the Educational Reform (NI) Order 1989; and

(14) the Department and Minister in arriving at the decision not to fund ACT and to fund only NICIE did not give proper weight to all the relevant facts.[44]

Sir James Kilfedder MP sponsored the complaint. The complaint was not upheld.

11
The closing years

Sir, I have only been here over two days but I am not surprised that you have community problems in Northern Ireland. You segregate your children by ability, by sex and by religion – Is it any wonder you have hostility here?'

AMERICAN VISITOR TO A NORTHERN IRELAND GRAMMAR SCHOOL[1]

Through their achievements All Children Together and Lagan College have successfully redefined the meaning of peace building through education in deeply divided societies like Northern Ireland and have set a standard against which education for tolerance can be judged throughout the world. This accomplishment has required 20 years of persistent and dedicated work on the part of the founders of this movement.

DR COLIN IRWIN, 1995[2]

ACT regroups

All Children Together, the organisation which had launched the movement for integrated education and sustained it alone for almost two decades, now had to reconsider its position. Had it made serious miscalculations? Certainly ACT had good reason to believe that its executive had been kept in the dark for almost 18 months between April 1983 and September 1984 while BELTIE was being formed. A more open and diplomatic approach over many matters by Tony Spencer and others who were eager to move forward rapidly could well have kept the movement united. Many of the anxieties and fears expressed by ACT in 1984 were to be dissolved by the changed circumstances brought about by the statutory financial assistance for integrated schools that obtained as a result of Brian Mawhinney's courage in pushing through the Education Reform (Northern Ireland) Order 1989. BELTIE did succeed in setting up Hazelwood College and Hazelwood Integrated Primary and thus met the needs of parents in north Belfast much in the way that Lagan College and Forge Primary served south and east Belfast. BELTIE, however, did not succeed with its plan to set up another six integrated schools within Belfast, based on the idea that redundant school buildings would rapidly become available. No disused school buildings became available and even at the time of writing there are only three post-primary integrated schools in Belfast and none in disused schools.

When BELTIE emerged in 1984, ACT had warned that parent groups forming all over the region were dangerously dependent on very large bank loans and lacked experience and professional advice. To their credit, seasoned ACT members went out of their way to help these new groups and gave their time freely to them on many a dark night. There is no doubt that by the middle of the 1980s many integrated schools found themselves in serious financial difficulties. Indeed, the principal of Hazelwood Primary School later wrote a telling article saying just how difficult the situation had been for teachers in his school, a school which was set up with almost no funding and with little consultation with teachers for its future.[3]

ACT had first interested the large UK trusts in integrated education in Northern Ireland through the meeting between Cecil Linehan and Wallis Johnson at a meeting of the British-Irish Association in Belfast in the early 1970s. Johnson later met Bettie Benton and then for several years attended ACT's annual general meetings. However, and to BELTIE's credit, Anthony Tomei of the Nuffield Foundation and professionals in other trusts came on board with significant funds for integrated schools in the 1980s. Moreover, these professionals calculated that their trusts and foundations alone could not be expected to sustain the growth of integrated education for long – the government would eventually step in. They calculated correctly. Nicholas Scott was the first education minister to begin to make provision. But it was Brian Mawhinney who not only saved the integrated-education movement but also provided the legislative muscle and finance to enable it to surge ahead. Had someone else been education minister during those crucial years, the movement might well have been faced with the embarrassing collapse of a new integrated school and of the whole movement.

It was also Mawhinney who faced down the Catholic hierarchy and those Protestant clergy who were hostile to integrated education. ACT was anxious about the ongoing financial needs of Lagan College and, in the late 1980s, when the trusts moved on to support other integrated projects, the financial plight of the school was for a time severe. Again, it was Mawhinney who saved the day by assigning £3.3 million towards the development of Lagan College on the Lisnabreeny site.

ACT kept its disagreements with BELTIE and NICIE behind closed doors as much as possible. Its regular publication, *ACT-LETT*, applauded the formation of new parent groups and the schools they founded and provided generous space to providing news about those schools, often getting principals to report on progress made.

ACT's concern about the religious-education core curriculum

The formation of NICIE notwithstanding, members of ACT remained convinced that there was much they could do to sustain integrated education. As the new Northern Ireland curriculum took shape, ACT continued to make submissions to the Department of Education to ensure that it took account of the needs of children of all religions and of no religion being educated together. ACT's strong Christian ethos ensured that members devoted a great deal of time to advising on religious education as a subject on the curriculum. The knowledge ACT had gathered over the years from speakers at several of its seminars, detailing the widespread use of shared religious-education syllabi in integrated schools in several parts of the world, became highly significant. Some of this information, viewed as fairly radical in some circles in Northern Ireland, was included in a detailed submission ACT made to the Churches' Religious-Education Core-Curriculum-Drafting Group set up by Brian Mawhinney in 1990.

ACT was alarmed that the group contained not one religious-education teacher from an integrated school. This was surprising since there had been almost a decade of valuable interdenominational experience in teaching this subject in integrated schools. There was dismay also that world religions were not included in the syllabus and that the proposed syllabus was based very much on the Old Testament. Bill Brown and Margaret Kennedy had a meeting with the Department of Education to put their views. While the department said that the common core curriculum was not at that time set in stone, ACT felt that opportunities to highlight the Christian message of reconciliation were missed.

In the conclusion of its submission to the group ACT stated:

> For too long, responsibility for the interpretation of the Gospel of Jesus Christ has been left in the hands of people presenting their own denominational or individual slant, however hard they try not to. With the widely differing religious attitudes in Northern Ireland and the political situation in which we live, this is understandable but not justifiable. Religious education can only be justified on the curriculum of Northern Ireland's schools if it is being effective as a reconciling influence rather than a divisive one.[4]

Little did ACT know at the time that the very existence of this group, and the final emergence of a possible shared religious-education syllabus, was due once again to Brian Mawhinney's persistence. He brought church leaders together to insist that such a step was taken. Mawhinney wrote:

> In Northern Ireland it was thought the height of absurdity to believe that a common RE curriculum might be devised, never mind taught. No one even raised the possibility with me at an official level ... it was just 'not on', a step too far.
>
> Eventually, after many meetings which got us nowhere, I met with all the church leaders and their educational advisers. They took it in turn to tell me, in no uncertain terms, why I was wrong. They spoke with one voice, and for a long time. There was total immobility, a lot of tension and, I thought, much defensiveness in what they said. We had stalemate.
>
> After well over an hour of covering the same ground without making any progress, I decided it was time to bring the meeting to a conclusion in the way I had planned beforehand. Rather theatrically, I fear, I told them that maybe we had different understandings of why we had come together ... I had the impression that they thought the meeting had been called to decide whether or not we should develop a common RE syllabus for use in all our schools. For my part, I saw the meeting as an opportunity for them to tell me whether they wanted to form an inter-

Church committee, aided by officials, to draw up the new syllabus, or whether they just wanted to leave me to get on with it.[5]

Eventually, faced with that somewhat outrageous suggestion, the church leaders said it would be 'unthinkable' for the minister of education to have to undertake such a task and so they agreed to work together on a draft common religious-education syllabus – much to the surprise of Mawhinney's officials. 'Finally,' Mawhinney continued, 'a totally acceptable syllabus emerged and was implemented and the church leaders in the province took great pride in it.'[6]

ACT outreach work post-1991

ACT continued to organise seminars, including a two-part colloquium held in Queen's University in 1991 entitled 'Children, churches and culture'. The first part dealt with 'Religious education and chaplaincy in inter-denominational schools' in April of that year. The second part was a study of 'Our common cultural heritage', held in October, just four months after ACT had been excluded by the Department of Education from playing any role in the body to promote the development work the burgeoning integrated-education movement so badly needed. Moreover, ACT had to fund this seminar from several sources as by now it had been informed that its modest grant of £6,000 was to cease.

The directors of ACT were invited to meet President Mary Robinson on 3 December 1991 at Áras an Uachtaráin in Dublin, the first anniversary of her election as president. ACT was pleased to have the opportunity to

Three former ACT Directors renew acquaintance with Mary Robinson, former President of Ireland, when she gave the 2008 Amnesty International Lecture during the Queen's University Festival.
From left: Bill Brown, Mary Robinson, Thelma Sheil and Cecil Linehan.

thank her for the help and support she had given them in the past. The Dalkey School Project had launched the integrated movement in the Republic almost at the same time as ACT had been formed. By 1993 there were ten Educate Together schools in the south, with four more in the pipeline. In January of that year, Cecil Linehan helped to maintain links with the integrated movement in the Republic when she attended the launch at the North Dublin National-School Project of an information pack entitled 'Starting an integrated school', produced by Educate Together. President Robinson was the guest of honour at the launch and she said she remembered with affection the day she had welcomed ACT to Áras an Uachtaráin and paid tribute to the work they had done in Northern Ireland since the early 1970s.

1992: the citizens' inquiry – Initiative '92

In 1992, a project headed by Professor Torkel Opsahl of Norway listened to what the people of Northern Ireland had to say about the conflict that had raged in their midst for over 20 years. The report of this independent commission, entitled Initiative '92, was published in 1993, the result of a series of public hearings and written and oral submissions from over 3,000 contributors.[7] Margaret Kennedy, on behalf of ACT, made a written submission that included ACT's basic philosophy on parental freedom in the choice of schools, an appeal to the churches to share power with parents on boards of integrated schools, and ACT's firmly held belief that integrated education was a very radical form of reconciliation, affecting not only school pupils but also parents, grandparents, staff and governors. To these central tenets Kennedy also added much of what ACT had written in the submission on the need for a common religious-education syllabus to the Churches' Religious-Education Core-Curriculum-Drafting Group. The ACT submission was widely quoted in the report's section on education and community relations.

The Warrington Project 1993

On a Saturday afternoon in March 1993 IRA litter-bin bombs in Warrington killed two young boys, Tim Parry and Jonathan Ball. Out of this atrocity emerged the Warrington Project, with John Donlan, uncle of Jonathan Ball, as coordinator. Three ACT directors, Margaret Kennedy,

Mary Connolly and Bill Brown, attended the launch of the project in October 1993. A spin-off of historic significance was that John Donlan was able to arrange for Prince Charles and President Mary Robinson to meet for the first time. This he achieved by staying up almost all night, speaking to advisers on protocol and altering plans. Originally the prince and the president were to have attended the launch at separate times and would not have met. Many feel this meeting was influential in prompting later meetings between the queen and the presidents of Ireland.

Bill Brown gave a presentation to the conference that followed the launch, outlining the origins of the division in Northern Ireland, the emergence of a segregated education system, the formation of ACT and its work and in particular why, though there were now 23 integrated schools in the region, opposition to integrated education remained so strong. He recalled the time when he escorted exchange teachers around a prestigious grammar school in Northern Ireland. When the headmaster finished speaking and asked for questions, one American responded:

> Sir, I have only been here over two days but I am not surprised that you have community problems in Northern Ireland. You segregate your children by ability, by sex and by religion – is it any wonder you have hostility here?[8]

The project, in which Colin Parry, Tim's father, is still deeply involved, has developed a programme entitled Ireland in Schools in conjunction with the Institute of Irish Studies at the University of Liverpool. As the project literature explained, the key to understanding its work is that:

> 'Ireland in Schools' does not attempt to add another subject to a crowded curriculum. Rather it encourages teachers to draw, where appropriate, on Irish examples in their teaching of the main subject areas within the National Curriculum and of existing GCSE and Advanced Level syllabuses.
>
> In Ireland it supports programmes that create better understanding. In both countries it encourages student and teacher exchanges and in-service training.[9]

1994: ACT celebrates the twentieth anniversary of its first seminar

The 1994 seminar celebrating ACT's twentieth anniversary was entitled 'Schools of reconciliation' and involved two key speakers: Dr Priscilla

Chadwick, formerly head of religious education in St Bede's School in Redhill, Surrey (the school that had become a virtual template for Lagan College). Chadwick completed her doctorate in a joint study of St Bede's and Lagan College and her subsequent book, also entitled *Schools of reconciliation*, was published in 1994.[10] By then she had become dean of educational development at South Bank University, London.

The second speaker was Dr Colin Irwin, then a research fellow in the Institute of Irish Studies at Queen's University, Belfast. Dr Irwin worked on the human-rights cases of children and young people in education. He took these cases to the UN Committee on the Rights of the Child and the UN Committee on Economic, Social and Cultural Rights to establish the rights of children to attend integrated schools in Northern Ireland. ACT was pleased to support him in some of this work.[11]

In 1995 Dr Irwin nominated ACT for the 1995 UNESCO prize for peace education. Though unsuccessful, ACT is still proud of the application Dr Irwin submitted on its behalf and on behalf of the young people in Northern Ireland, some of whom are still deprived of a place at an integrated school. Dr Irwin stated:

> Successive governments have believed that integrated education could improve inter-community relations and promote peace in Ireland and Northern Ireland. The first national system of education established in Dublin in 1831 was intentionally created to be non-denominational with the expressed 'hope that by learning to live together as children they would at least tolerate each other as adults'. Unfortunately, in the face of objections from the Churches, the schools became segregated within twenty years of their foundation. Similar interests also prevented the formation of an integrated school system in the Province of Ulster in 1922 when Ireland was divided into North and South. After the resumption of the 'Troubles' in the early 1970s the All Children Together movement (ACT) was formed by a group of Catholic parents seeking religious instruction for their children outside the Catholic school system. Within two years they were joined by Protestant parents after which they dedicated themselves to seek[ing] 'changes in the educational system of Northern Ireland that will make it possible for parents who so wish to secure for their children an education in shared schools acceptable to all religious denominations and cultures'. In the absence of effective government initiatives on these objectives ACT actively stimulated public debate and founded the first integrated

school, Lagan College, in 1981, in a scout hut, with an initial 28 students … During its first three years the College received no government funding and with ACT had to raise over 1.5 million pounds from the international community to cover its building and operating costs. Twelve years later, in 1994, Lagan College has a student population of nearly 1000 & another 23 integrated schools have been established in the province.

Through their achievements All Children Together and Lagan College have successfully redefined the meaning of peace building through education in deeply divided societies like Northern Ireland and, arguably, have set a standard against which education for tolerance can be judged throughout the world. This accomplishment has required twenty years of persistent and dedicated work on the part of the founders of this movement.[12]

1995: ACT twenty-first-anniversary exhibition in Linen Hall Library

The 1994 seminar had been combined with an exhibition showing the work of ACT since 1972 through a display of letters, artefacts, posters for meetings etc. Such was the interest in the exhibition that the directors were persuaded to remount the display one year later in the Linen Hall Library, where it ran for over two weeks to much acclaim.

Some of the items displayed included:

- A copy of the programme for the first seminar held in 1974: 'Interdenominational schools: why? how? and the way ahead'.

- An account of the 'pray-in' outside the church in Newtownards in 1977.

- The dates from Hansard of the debates relating to the passage through the House of Lords of the Education (Northern Ireland) Act 1978.

- Reports of the libel case taken by the bishop of Down and Connor against the *Irish Times* in 1981.

- A collection of individual ACT directors' proposals for various models of integrated schools written in the Christmas holidays of 1979 at the behest of Professor Teunisson of Holland, who at that stage was visiting Northern Ireland regularly as part of the Dutch–Northern Irish Advisory Committee.

- ACT's perilous financial situation in 1979, 18 months before Lagan College was opened – the organisation was 'in the red' to the tune of £189.95.

- ACT's response to the 1980 interim Chilver report[13] which, as has been seen, became the subject of wide and, at times, extremely acrimonious debate.

ACT invited to give an oral submission to the Forum for Peace and Reconciliation

In March 1995 ACT joined with NICIE, speakers from St Mary's University College in Belfast, a spokesman from the education and library boards in Northern Ireland and the chairman of Educate Together, the movement for interdenominational schools in the Republic of Ireland, to give an oral submission to the Forum for Peace and Reconciliation in Dublin Castle. The ACT delegation included Margaret Kennedy and Bill Brown, who addressed the forum on behalf of the movement. After the oral presentations the political parties had the opportunity to put questions to the panel, and many were raised about the role of schools in reconciliation in Northern Ireland and the obstacles to integrated education. There was laughter when the speaker from St Mary's, in answer to a question about church power in education, said that the bishops, of course, were not interested in power. At the reception that followed the reaction of forum delegates to the ACT and NICIE spokespersons was very warm, many commenting that it had been one of the best sessions at the forum. ACT felt that the case for integrated education had received a wide and influential hearing.[14]

ACT director Bill Brown addressing the Forum for Peace and Reconciliation, Dublin Castle, April 1995.

1996–7: three new integrated schools – and no government support

While all these headline issues took up much time and energy, ACT and new integrated schools were still struggling desperately for funds. ACT directors had spent nearly a decade

ALL CHILDREN TOGETHER
The pioneering movement for integrated education by consent
INVITES PARENTS, TEACHERS AND OTHERS INTERESTED
to a
PUBLIC MEETING
at
NEWTOWNARDS MONDAY 20 NOVEMBER, QUAKER MEETING HALL, KILTONGA LEISURE CENTRE and
BANGOR MONDAY 27 NOVEMBER, HAMILTON HOUSE (ROOM 2), HAMILTON ROAD.
at 7.45 p.m.
TO ASSESS THE SUPPORT FOR AN
INTEGRATED
ALL-ABILITY POST-PRIMARY COLLEGE FOR BOYS AND GIRLS
to serve Ards and North Down District Council areas
and other surrounding areas
SPEAKERS FROM : ACT, LAGAN COLLEGE, HAZELWOOD COLLEGE, NICIE
ALL WELCOME

in a state of anxiety about Forge Integrated Primary School. Bankruptcy seemed just around the corner. As chronicled in Chapter 9, this was due to what they justifiably regarded as intransigence on the part of BELB as regards the payment of large sums of money they owed ACT. Until BELB finally capitulated, ACT had virtually no funds to assist other projects.

When BELB finally settled, ACT could begin a debate on how best to use its newfound resources. The Education Reform (Northern Ireland) Order 1989 had laid down conditions to be met before the Department of Education could provide funding for new schools. Michael Ancram, who been appointed minister of state with responsibility for education in 1994, sent shockwaves through the integrated-education movement in 1996 when he refused grant aid to an existing integrated primary school and refused to approve development proposals for two new integrated post-primary colleges, even though all three fully satisfied the criteria then laid down by the department. The school was Oakwood Integrated Primary School near Dunmurry in south Belfast, and the proposed second-level schools were Ulidia College in Whitehead, County Antrim and Strangford College in Carrowdore, County Down.

Critics of the integrated-education movement had often applied the term 'middle class' pejoratively to it. This certainly did not apply to Oakwood, situated on the interface between loyalist and nationalist housing estates, an area frequently in the news for violent disorder. Indeed, many of the school's parents and governors were unemployed. Whitehead was also in an area that had witnessed economic decline. North Down had long sought integrated post-primary provision and, in response to much leafleting and other publicity by ACT during the period 1994–5,

ACT directors at a public meeting called to assess support for an integrated college in north Down and Ards, November 1996. Left to right: Seamus Leonard, vice principal of Hazelwood Integrated College, Belfast; ACT directors, Cecil Linehan, Bettie Benton and Margaret Kennedy; at the back, Dr Brian Lambkin, principal of Lagan College; and Ronnie Brittan, ACT director. ACT in 1990 had assisted a parent group in Bangor known as the Campaign for Education Together in its attempts to have a new state a co-educational secondary school opened as a 'controlled integrated' school. Despite impressive parental support, the campaign failed as a result, ACT believed, of pressure by politicians and other vested interests. Eventually, Strangford College in the County Down town of Carrowdore opened in 1997 and now has over 500 pupils in a new permanent building.

a group of parents formed a steering committee to set up a new integrated school for the area, Strangford College.

In 1992 the Integrated Education Fund (IEF) had been set up as a kind of war chest filled by substantial lump sums provided by the Nuffield Foundation and the Rowntree Trust (as a parting gift to Northern Ireland) and by money given by the Department of Education. The plan was to use the interest (and in very special circumstances) some of the capital to help parent groups get projects off the ground and set up schools until they met the criteria for funding laid down by the Department of Education. The IEF trustees (chaired at first by the author) also set out to raise further sums from other foundations and likely donors. With so many integrated schools attempting to get started, the demands on the IEF were soon more than they could possibly meet.

When Lord Ancram turned down the three schools for government support in 1996, ACT, NICIE and the IEF joined forces to form a coordinating committee. The committee set out to publicise the plight of the three schools and focus the government's attention on them. Meanwhile, parents of these independent integrated schools had to run jumble sales, treasure hunts and dances, coffee mornings and all manner of fund-raising events (reminiscent of the early days of Lagan College) to attempt to keep the schools going.

Then Labour returned to power in the spring of 1997. Tony Worthington was appointed minister with responsibility for education. Newspapers and interviews gave the impression that Worthington would move integrated education higher up the agenda and that he would be as successful as Mawhinney at 'managing' officials in Rathgael House.

ACT's loans bail out Ulidia and Strangford Colleges

At first this optimism was reinforced by the arrival of additional funds from the European Union to assist the peace process in Northern Ireland. The Department of Education, Northern Ireland, was appointed one of the bodies responsible for deciding how a considerable proportion of this 'peace and reconciliation' money should be spent. The integrated-education movement was shocked when it learned that the department had turned down applications by the three independent schools for financial support. During the approach to Christmas 1997 children from integrated schools produced hundreds of hand-made greeting cards exhorting Tony Worthington to release funds for the three independent schools; the minister was reported to be 'not amused' when these piled up on the mat of the department's headquarters at Rathgael House.

The IEF had exhausted all of its funds in supporting other new integrated schools and turned to ACT to see if it could help. ACT was anxious to preserve its funds to continue its own activities – in particular, to meet the emergency needs of future schools. After much discussion ACT decided not to give outright grants but to provide interest-free loans of £75,000 each to Ulidia and Strangford. ACT, however, did not want to release money without security.

The day was fast approaching that protective redundancy notices would have to be issued to the staff of Ulidia College. A fax sent to ACT, marked 'Totally confidential' and entitled 'Update on funding situation as of May 1999', outlined Ulidia's plight. The college had to enlist a minimum of 80 new pupils to obtain any hope of recognition and to do this it had to move to a new site that would appeal to parents. The fax stated that: the IEF would provide £200,000 if the school achieved 80 enrolments by 31 May 1999; an application to the Department of Education for peace and reconciliation money had been turned down; and an application to the Lottery Board had yet to produce a reply. The college anticipated expenses of £654,063 for the next academic year and the cost of moving site would be around £200,000. It continued:

> Permission has been given to stay in Whitehead if we need to; this option will only be taken as a last stand as it will affect enrolments. It is imperative that we have 80 pupils in September … If we do not move to our new site, it is unlikely that we will have 80 pupils.
>
> Redundancies: At this time the Governors of Ulidia will have to issue protective notices to the teaching staff on 31 May 1999, as we do not have sufficient funds to remain open to Christmas … For the first time the College is looking closure in the face; we will be the first Integrated College to fail. We have no more time to negotiate loans …
>
> The Governors of Ulidia request that ACT will offer us a grant of £100,000 … 130 children will be without a school in September and a further 80 will be frantically searching for a school.[15]

ACT could not stand by and see this happen. At this stage, therefore, it declared that it was willing to provide funding against a 'chattels

Northern Ireland secretary of state, Dr Mo Mowlam, with the principal, Eugene Martin, in Ulidia Integrated College, 1999, with the good news that the school was finally to be funded following its *eighth* development proposal.

mortgage', using as security school equipment, demountable buildings, computers and the like held in the school's name. This kind of security was hardly satisfactory as such assets had a value that dropped rapidly. Nevertheless, the immediate future of the schools was secured.

Another three years would pass and several more development proposals would be submitted before the schools would eventually be recognised by the Department of Education. Though Ulidia College had 17 staff and 240 students enrolled, with religious balance, it was again refused government grant aid for the school year 1999/2000. But the end of the terrible difficulties surrounding Ulidia's insecure future was in sight and with its *eighth* development proposal, submitted in December 1999 to the then-new secretary of state, Dr Mo Mowlam, the Department of Education finally capitulated and granted Ulidia Integrated College full funding, effective from September 2000.

Transformation

ACT always believed that integrated schools should be completely financed through public funds and through the education and library boards, and stated this quite clearly in its 1976 policy document, 'ACT on shared schools', saying, 'we do not believe it would be necessary or practical to build new schools in order to provide parents with this choice'.[16] It was only when there was no move from church or state to allow parents to bring their children together in school that parental frustrations led to the opening of Lagan College, paid for with independent charitable funds. Subsequent attempts to use the 1978 Education Act by Malone Primary School (the predecessor of Forge Integrated Primary School) and Throne Primary School failed in 1979 – the former because of very low enrolment figures, the latter because no work had been done either by the Department of Education or by BELB to circulate guidelines on the provisions of the 1978 act or to support the school in any way. This was unfortunate, because the governors of Throne had made a truly genuine attempt to use the legislation, having obtained the support of some of the Protestant clergy to make the act effective. The

1978 act remained unused and when the Education (Northern Ireland) Order was being amended in 1986 the Department of Education intended to drop the 1978 act from the new legislation completely. At the time, Bettie Benton, co-founder of ACT, was president of the Association of Education and Library Boards of Northern Ireland. She succeeded in getting support from all five boards to retain the act and to have it included in the Education Order. But for Benton's action and her standing in the education field at the time, the 1978 act would have been lost forever. Two years later, in 1988, a very thorough attempt was made by a state secondary school in County Armagh to 'transform' to an integrated college. It would become known as Brownlow High School.

Brownlow High School –
the flagship of transforming schools

Brownlow High School was opened in 1973 as a junior high school for boys and girls aged between 11 and 14 years in the central Craigavon area of County Armagh, as part of SELB's Dickson comprehensive plan. With inadequate enrolments it was modified to cater for pupils up to the age of 16. For a time it took in considerable numbers of children whose parents were in the army, billeted at nearby Westacres, and some Vietnamese children from refugee families settled in Craigavon. 'Even at that,' the principal, G.F. Loan, pointed out to Margaret Kennedy of ACT in April 1991, 'maximum enrolments never exceeded 350, and half the building was given over to the Craigavon Teachers' Centre.'[17]

Then, in 1987, the North Armagh Group for Integrated Education (NAGIE) was formed, arising from parental demand for integrated education in the Portadown, Brownlow and Lurgan areas of County Armagh. The parents' original intention had been to open a new integrated college along the same lines as Lagan College but, having been approached by Frank Loan, who expressed the view that as his school already had Catholic pupils and pupils from other minority religions, they believed that the Board of Governors and staff of Brownlow and NAGIE could work together to try to transform Brownlow High School into an integrated college using the 1978 act, now the 1986 Education Order.

Loan claimed that 'since discussions about integration started, an increasing number of children have travelled from Lurgan and Portadown, and further afield, and these currently make up over 10% of the current enrolment'. Though he did not mention it specifically, clearly some of this wider intake was made up of Catholic children. The principal was upbeat about overcoming any difficulties which might arise by opting for transformed integrated status:

> The integration of pupils at the moment is not an issue. Catholics and Protestants (and others) have very good relationships and school policy has been to avoid upsetting these through the avoidance of potentially divisive issues ...
>
> Policy has not inhibited pupils making explicit their allegiance to, for example, either Rangers or Celtic, or to varying musical traditions. In fact, a couple of years ago we had a number of very keen fluters who belonged variously to Orange and Green bands, but who practised together and played for each other, at lunchtime.[18]

He added:

> The main problem so far has been the opposition from some local politicians and parents sympathetic to their views who see integration as Protestants giving ground to Catholics. Brought up as I was in a totally segregated area, and attending totally segregated schools, I can understand this gut reaction very well indeed. Nevertheless blind obstinacy and refusal to face facts can be very frustrating.
>
> On the other hand, the extent of support, both for the school, and also for the principle of integration, which has become evident amongst parents, has been extremely encouraging, and does great credit to the absence of bigotry in the outlook of, I believe, the majority of local people.[19]

Loan's optimism notwithstanding, the tolerance of the community in this part of Ulster was soon afterwards, particularly in 1996, put to a severe test during bitter and violent confrontations associated with the traditional Orange march in July from Drumcree Church to Portadown.

The rest of this long letter made it clear that the principal understood the main implications of opting for integration in matters such as staffing, religious education and school assemblies. In 1985 he had introduced the Irish language into the curriculum. The school provided religious education in line with the Northern Ireland statutory requirements. A number of pupils, specifically Muslims and Jehovah's Witnesses, had exercised their right to opt out of these classes. No Catholic pupils had done so. Muslim pupils were allowed time out of class on Fridays to attend prayers at the local mosque and a member of the Jehovah's Witnesses' community came in each morning to take a separate assembly. He had obtained the services of four Protestant clergy as chaplains but had not so far succeeded in finding anyone to minister to his Muslim pupils within the school. Approaches had been made to the local Catholic clergy without success.

Despite this outstanding commitment from the principal and his staff, and the ongoing enthusiasm and continued hard work from the parents in NAGIE, two attempts to use the 1986 order to transform the school were thwarted owing in the main to opposition from local unionist politicians, some of whom alleged that this was an attempt to 'de-Protestantise' the school and turn it into a 'semi-Roman Catholic one'.[20] But the Department of Education also dragged its feet and, much as was the case with Throne Primary School in 1979, it gave little support to the school and parents by delaying for one whole year permission for a parental ballot (to determine the numbers in favour or against the school becoming integrated) to be organised as set out in the provisions of the 1986 Education Order. Two ballots were eventually held in February and June 1989. The first, though receiving the 75-per-cent majority in favour of integration was declared 'void on technical grounds' in the heat of a fierce political storm amongst local politicians; the second received a healthy 63 per cent in favour but was short of the 75 per cent required.

To their credit, neither the school nor NAGIE gave up on their vision of transforming Brownlow into an integrated college. The 1989 Education Order altered the rules governing transformation in two very significant ways. First, a straight majority of parents voting in favour of integration would now be sufficient for a school to start the process of being transformed; and second, the request for the transformation process to commence could be initiated by parents as well as by the church representatives on school boards. It would take two further votes and more acrimonious political debate before a successful ballot gave a return of 60.5 per cent of parents voting in favour of integration in 1990. So it was that by 1991 Brownlow High School was granted integrated status and became the flagship for the integrated schools that would develop through the transformation route.

In 1995, in *ACT-LETT*, the ACT leaders noted with great pleasure that there were now five controlled integrated schools and commented:

> Has the slim enabling Bill introduced by All Children Together through
> the good offices of the late Lord Dunleath come full circle to provide
> government with the most suitable route for the development of
> integrated education into the next millennium? Are those who sought
> to persuade ACT to drop this gentle measure in 1977 glad we resisted?
> One thing is absolutely sure; there can be [no] greater testimonial to
> the late Lord Dunleath, whose life was dedicated to reconciliation than
> to see this successor to his legislation playing such a central role in
> developing greater opportunities for ALL parents to choose integrated
> schools for their children.[21]

A new minister – and some alarming changes to the rules for transformation

Yet, two years later, ACT would be expressing very serious concerns about
the numbers of schools opting to transform, some maybe for the wrong
reasons. There could be no doubting the genuine commitment of Frank
Loan (as the author, a former colleague, can testify) to carry through all
the changes in staffing, curriculum and ethos that transformation
required. Loan's successor as principal, Errol Lemon, wrote in 1992 of the
vexed question of religious balance in Brownlow, saying:

> Brownlow started off with an 85 : 15 imbalance of Protestant pupils
> and with only one Catholic member of staff. Clearly if the school is to
> be successfully integrated, many more Catholic than Protestant pupils
> will have to be recruited over a number of years … and if [pupil]
> numbers increased new staff would have to be recruited and this would
> give an opportunity of recruiting more Catholics onto the staff,
> notwithstanding the difficulties inherent in policies of positive
> discrimination.[22]

Thus Brownlow continued to grapple with the reality of trying to reach
a 70 : 30 Protestant–Catholic ratio, the guidelines laid down by NICIE
for the majority–minority balance in all integrated schools. All in the
integrated education movement felt the transforming schools should keep
to these guidelines, while accepting the fact that it would take time for
some schools to reach the 70 : 30 ratio, especially where the makeup of the
feeder communities was unevenly balanced. The question ACT was now
asking was: would other principals and governors, worried about falling

enrolments, opting for transformed integrated status, possess the energy and understanding to create genuine integrated schools? Members of ACT were beginning to doubt if the regulations laid down by the Department of Education for transformation were rigorous enough.

The Education Reform (Northern Ireland) Order 1989 not only enabled the Department of Education to fund grant-maintained integrated schools deemed to be viable but also, as has been seen in the case of Brownlow, made it much easier for existing schools to transform to integrated status. Over the years, as few established schools appeared willing to transform, parent groups much preferred to set up new schools embracing the full integrated ethos which had been honed, particularly by ACT, for more than two decades. This caused mounting alarm in Rathgael House as new schools, especially second-level schools, dug deeply into the department's limited budget. It was becoming clear that the Department of Education's favoured route towards honouring the 1989 order was by the transformation of existing schools to controlled integrated status. Only state – that is, controlled – schools were showing any interest in being so transformed and, to date, no Catholic maintained school has opted to transform.

In July 1996, when Michael Ancram was minister with responsibility for education, the department issued a consultative paper entitled *Integrated education: a framework for transformation*. In essence, the government proposed that 'the creation of any integrated school should reflect the freely expressed wishes of parents for that form of education'; the impetus for transformation could come from the board of governors, the headteacher and the parents with balloting to follow; close consultation with NICIE should take place before a decision was made; and the board should provide:

> evidence that the school has been able to attract enrolments from the relevant minority religion by September of the school year in which the school proposes to acquire integrated status. For the latter, evidence that at least 5% of the annual intake are drawn from the minority religion will be required (with the objective that over time this would increase to no less than 30%).[23]

It was this last point that caused most anxiety in the ranks of ACT. The misgivings of ACT's directors about transformation were on the increase.

There was no doubt that there were successful examples of controlled schools transforming out of a sincere desire to embrace the difficulties of turning an all-Protestant school into one that also catered for Catholic pupils in its staffing, curriculum and governance. However, other controlled schools showing willingness to be transformed were generally afflicted by falling rolls and ACT felt that these schools' interest in becoming integrated was, at best, skin deep. Would the governors of such schools be able to attract more than just a token number of Catholic pupils? The very lax Protestant–Catholic pupil ratio that the department was willing to accept did not appear to offer a firm base for building up a numerically balanced integrated school. How realistic was it to expect a school staff already used to the ethos of a Protestant school suddenly fully to embrace the totally different concept of a religiously integrated school? No programme for the induction of teachers was suggested. With falling rolls, would there be any vacancies to enable governors to recruit any Catholic teachers? Would the governing bodies of transforming schools be willing or able to adopt and implement a genuinely integrated educational philosophy? If a transforming school failed through lack of preparation, the whole integrated movement could be brought into disrepute.

Before July 1996 was out, ACT issued a press release beginning, 'Integrated education could be in danger.' It continued:

> While ALL CHILDREN TOGETHER would welcome the expansion of integrated education by means of the AUTHENTIC transformation of controlled schools we submit that the motivation for transformation must be genuine, that successful transformation can only be built on an already existing ethos of integration and that the unique characteristics of integrated education must be fully maintained.
>
> ALL CHILDREN TOGETHER are concerned that some schools might be tempted to transform merely to increase their enrolments and we would view with grave concern a transformed school which was integrated in name only. There should, in a transforming school, be a suitable religious balance amongst pupils, staff and governors, an appropriately planned curriculum and respect for religious and cultural diversity.[24]

ACT set out its objections and concerns in a submission to the Department of Education on 24 August 1996. It welcomed the department's 'continuing support for the development of integrated education in Northern Ireland' but added:

> The foundations from which an existing school could be transformed into a controlled integrated school must be solid ... Where this ethos of integration is absent, parents realise that transformation could be fraught with difficulties and be unlikely to fulfil their expectations of a GENUINE integrated school.
>
> ACT, as the pioneer for integration by consent, totally agrees that no school should be 'compelled in any way to transform into an integrated school'. The acceptance of a 51% vote of approval by parents, however, leaves the possibility of 49% disapproving. This would be totally against the spirit of existing integrated schools, and could be most distressing and unfair to parents ...
>
> Schools with an uncertain existing viability and not having previously attracted pupils from the minority community should not be considered genuine candidates for integrated status, unless the initiative is coming strongly from the minority community. ACT appreciates that every situation is different and would like DENI to be more prescriptive ...
>
> If DENI wishes transforming schools to achieve an eventual balance of 30 : 70%, ACT feels that an initial intake of 5% is much too low and would not ensure the process of transformation being well grounded. In a school with an intake of 100 pupils, this means only 5 pupils need be from the minority community ... It would be difficult to ensure that this small number of pupils felt 'comfortable and valued'. It is unlikely to inspire confidence among parents belonging to the minority community ...
>
> We agree that NICIE, with all their experience, should be involved in the vetting procedure ... [25]

Further detailed submissions followed but the government stuck to its initial formula of only a minimum of five per cent of the intake being from the minority religion. Frances Donnelly, senior education officer at NICIE, carried out rigorous research on transformation as a dissertation for a master of education (professional development) degree. Submitted in 1998 and entitled 'Transforming integrated education: an historical and contemporary analysis of developments in integrated education', her findings were not reassuring. Principals of transformed schools had as their main anxiety how they could recruit sufficient numbers of 'minority' pupils to reach the Department of Education's requirement. The issue of staffing had proved a sensitive one. 'The concerns and expectations amongst the majority of teachers in integrated schools are mainly related to job security,' she remarked. She quoted an extract from the Department of Education draft document of September 1997, which, in its guidance to transforming schools, stated that:

> over time, it would be expected that the religious composition of staff may need to reflect more closely the changing make-up of the pupils and schools will wish to examine what steps may be taken to achieve this.[26]

Frances Donnelly's analysis of questionnaire returns led her to come to these conclusions:

> Such a statement inevitably causes concern amongst teachers who may see their own positions put in jeopardy in order to accommodate minority staff … there is a need to reassure permanent teachers that they will not be ousted from their jobs as a result of transformation. While additional funding from DENI has made it possible for some transforming schools to appoint supernumerary teachers from the minority community, these 'token' positions may not be tenable after the two year funding limit set by the Department.
>
> It is unlikely that a balance amongst staff will ever be achieved in some of the larger schools that are currently proposing to transform. While it may change naturally over time … the necessity of appointing the 'best person for the job' may inevitably conflict with the need to incorporate a member from the minority community into the staff.[27]

She observed that the government's support for integration through transformation would 'continue to make it more difficult for new planned GMI schools to be opened'. 'The opening of a transformed integrated school,' she continued, 'has the potential to dramatically increase the number of children attending "integrated" schools' but it had to be borne in mind 'that many of these schools will not achieve an accepted religious balance amongst pupils for up to ten years'. If schools were to transform successfully, they had to acknowledge that it was a long-term process requiring change, 'often at a fundamental level'. 'Anything less,' she concluded, 'will result in an increase in the number of *mixed* schools in Northern Ireland but not in the number of *integrated* schools.'[28]

She outlined her findings in a lecture she gave to ACT in 2000 and they seemed fully to justify the fears ACT had expressed in relation to a significant number of schools proposing to proceed with transformation.

Nevertheless, it has to be acknowledged that, in the ensuing years, transformation did spread both the ethos and practice of integrated education to a greater extent than ACT had dared to hope.

ACT 1997–2001

In the mid-1990s, meetings were held to consider a wide range of suggestions about the organisation's future. One suggestion was to cease mainstream activities and form a trust. The most drastic suggestion was to close down completely and give away the organisation's funds. At the 1997 AGM, Cecil Linehan and Bettie Benton put forward proposals that included closing the office at 13 University Street and 'seeking regular meetings on a bi-annual basis, or at intervals suitable, with the Trustees of the Integrated Education Fund, to determine which projects/schools are most needy and worthy of financial support'.[29] This was not agreed. In the end, what was agreed was that ACT's main role, as an independent body, was that of watchdog and lobbyist and of generally raising public awareness. A close eye needed to be kept on the transformation process. NICIE, with its funding coming almost entirely from the Department of Education, had never been allowed to do any promotional work across Northern Ireland. This was work which ACT, as an independent organisation, could continue to do and the reason why it always felt it needed the services of a development officer. There remained the anxiety that if devolved government returned to Northern Ireland the work of IEF and NICIE might be endangered by a local administration hostile to integrated education. These all seemed strong arguments as to why ACT should remain as an independent voice. The principal hands on the ACT tiller now were those of Margaret Kennedy, chairman; Thelma Sheil, honorary secretary; and T.J. Kennedy, who, though not a board member, had taken over from Bettie Benton as treasurer. He would have a great deal of work to do over the next seven years.

At a planning meeting in October 1997, the directors agreed that ACT 'should not duplicate NICIE's work' and came to the 'collective view … that we were lobbyists, information givers/adult educators and encouragers, event organisers, catalysts for change and responders'. A new mission statement was adopted for use in ACT publicity material:

> To protect the integrity of integrated education and to encourage the

extended provision of genuine planned integrated schools of all kinds.
To continue to advocate widely the benefits of integrated education
and its potential for reconciliation in Northern Ireland.[30]

Raising public awareness

While the energies of ACT were still absorbed in fund-raising for the three
independent schools, this was combined with the important work of
raising public awareness. ACT was able to present the Northern Ireland
premier of the film *Mrs Dalloway*, based on the novel by Virginia Wolff.
In the spring of 1998 the screening took place in the Queen's Film Theatre
and was followed by a reception in the university's great hall. This took the
message to a new and wider audience and brought about both an increase
in membership and more money for the schools. A further appeal to
ACT's members helped to raise a total of £5,000 for the purchase of new
equipment.

The Dunleath lectures

Lord Henry Dunleath had died in January 1993. A great strength to the
integrated-education movement, as an Alliance peer he had introduced
the private member's bill which became the Education Act 1978, generally
known as the Dunleath Act. He served as president of Lagan College for
many years and was long remembered for his involvement in a wide range
of Northern Ireland's charities and for his wonderful sense of humour.
ACT decided to institute the Dunleath memorial lecture to mark his
contribution to the organisation and to the integrated-education

Raising public Awareness
about integrated
education, ACT shows
the film *Mrs.Dalloway* at
Queen's University
Belfast, 1998
From left; Inez Bleakeley,
who organised the
evening; ACT director,
Margaret Kennedy; and
Marion Campbell, who as
education officer of the
Queen's Film Theatre
obtained permission for
ACT to show the film.

movement in general. Dr Brian Lambkin, a teacher at Lagan College from the outset and later its principal, gave the first lecture, entitled 'Integrated education in Northern Ireland into the new millennium' on 26 February 1997 in the prestigious Canada room in Queen's University's Lanyon building. On 30 September, the second lecture, entitled 'Thy people shall be my people', was delivered by Colm Cavanagh, chairman of NICIE, who with his wife had done so much to advance integrated education in the city of Derry.

Still trying to involve the clergy

Colm Cavanagh's lecture was the first event organised by ACT that had attracted a significant number of representatives of the churches. Encouraged by this, the ACT executive decided to run a conference exclusively for the clergy in 1999. To encourage free discussion this was *in camera*, with no photographers or journalists and no press statements given afterwards. With talks given by Dr Brian Lambkin and Charles Graham (principal of Bridge Integrated Primary School), participants were made aware – in some cases for the first time – what actually went on in integrated schools. A video was also shown of an integrated church school, namely St Cuthbert Mayne School, Torquay. Actually seeing a flourishing integrated school in action appeared to dispel some myths and a very useful discussion ensued.

Raising the awareness of the clergy to what ACT members strongly believed to be the reconciling role of integrated education in Northern Ireland had always been an important concern for the organisation. Where there was approval from the clergy, it was seldom expressed in public. ACT's first aim – to bring forward new enabling legislation – had been achieved; the second aim of involving the institutional churches had not. And so ACT continued to lobby the clergy.

The final windfall

Lagan College had been born in a scout hall and was then transferred to a disused special school on Church Road in the Castlereagh Hills. The Church Road premises lay empty for a time after the college moved to its permanent site further west at Lisnabreeny. This then became the home of Loughview Integrated Primary School   a school that was highly successful in attracting pupils. Loughview governors were later successful in acquiring a new building on the site.

It soon became clear that, owing to the narrow width of the access road and the volume of school traffic, a second entrance was needed at Loughview to allow buses to drive straight through the school grounds, exiting again onto the main road. Back in the 1980s, while Lagan College was still located at Church Road, ACT had found that it had no choice but to buy a sizeable piece of land – 11 acres – behind the school. In fact, all that had been used was a strip of frontage of only half an acre, but it had been urgently needed – the Roads Authority had insisted it was the only way a safe turning circle for the school buses could be provided. The ten and a half acres remaining had then been let to a local farmer for grazing.

This piece of poor agricultural land had magnificent views over the city and Belfast Lough, but was not zoned for development. Then a speculator made ACT an offer for this land and thus established a much higher value than could be expected for land confined to agricultural use. Meanwhile, Loughview was growing rapidly and the first year's intake had to be doubled. To meet this need, the Department of Education realised the area covered by the school would have to be increased. The district valuer recommended a price of £285,000 and this was the sum the department had to pay. Thus, for a second time, and a result of rising land values, ACT fortuitously gained a substantial sum of money as a consequence of helping an integrated school.

ACT was now able to turn its loans to Ulidia and Strangford Colleges into grants. Then Mo Mowlam, the secretary of state, declared that the two schools had proved their long-term viability and brought a happy end to their precarious independent existence by the allocation of state

ACT directors support Strangford College: ACT directors Thelma Sheil and Margaret Kennedy with Strangford College principal Anne Rowe, Strangford Governors and Lembit Opik MP, 1997.

funding. The Good Friday Agreement of 1998 in time led to the restoration of devolution and the appearance of Martin McGuinness as minister of education. ACT's anxiety concerning the possibility of a local minister of education opposed to integrated education was eased with McGuinness's appointment: he was well disposed to both Irish-language and integrated schools and directed more of the taxpayers' money their way.

Winding up

Relations between ACT and NICIE steadily eased. In 1994, Cecil Linehan was appointed to the NICIE board and was followed a few years later by Bill Brown and then Margaret Kennedy. By the beginning of the new millennium relationships between the two bodies had strengthened and, indeed, become cordial.

NICIE, meanwhile, was widening the scope of its own activities to engage in promotional and outreach work, which ACT had for so long considered vital. The IEF gave NICIE a grant to create a communications team of six or seven, made up of a manager, lobbyists and three outreach workers. In addition, the IEF, previously housed with NICIE, acquired its own staff and premises. While previously it had subsisted solely on the interest generated from the nest egg provided by the Department of Education, the European Union and the trusts, now it was raising funds in a highly professional manner to give further assistance to the expanding integrated-education sector. In short, the time seemed to have arrived to wind up ACT.

Cecil Linehan joins the board of the Northern Ireland Council for Integrated Education (NICIE, 1994)

NICIE Board members 1995:
Front row, from left: Cecil Linehan, Ken Dunn, Colm Cavanagh, David McAughey, Gerti Campbell.
Back row, from left: Bert Montgomery, Barney Evans, Helen Honeyman, John Unsworth and Bernard Farrell.

War weariness

Reflecting back, Margaret Kennedy wrote:

> After over 30 years of intense activity, much burning of the midnight oil and being constantly watchful, on top of establishing Lagan College, a hugely demanding and uncharted enterprise, activists were a tad weary.[31]

The membership of ACT, which was wide and interdenominational, consisted of parents, teachers, lecturers, lawyers and well-wishers in Northern Ireland, on the continent and in north America. While this continued to grow in the 1990s, fewer real activists were coming forward since so many members were very involved in the integrated schools their children were attending.

In January 2001, Margaret Kennedy issued a 'directors' letter' to ACT members, suggesting it was time for the movement to take stock and, when she addressed the twenty-sixth ACT AGM on 8 February 2001, she said:

> It is hard to believe that it is 30 years since this movement had its beginnings with a small band of hopefuls – Cecil, Bettie, Thelma, Bill and myself included, to be joined by Sr Anna, Basil McIvor and others. At that time we had very few friends – in the education and library boards, in DENI, in the churches, amongst political parties. Now we have 45 integrated schools and legislation which has worked. I have the greatest pride in this movement. It is the activity in my life of which I have most pride …
>
> I have pride in the fact that the very existence of the integrated schools has nudged the other sectors and DENI into looking closely at their stance on community relations and the curriculum:
>
> • Pride in the ripple effect which has moved out from the child in the integrated desk to siblings, grandparents, friends, neighbours, ancillary workers, etc;
>
> • Pride when I consider that parents of all persuasions move into an area near a good integrated school thus beginning to desegregate that area;
>
> • Pride that honours have been bestowed on our members in the form of MBEs for Sister Anna and Cecil and OBEs for Bettie and Basil McIvor.
>
> I have pleasure in the friendships that have resulted from it all. It has been an honour to have been part of All Children Together. How many

ordinary people in life can look back and say that they were part of a group that changed structures, frameworks, systems? We can. You can.

This is an appropriate time to close this chapter. We are now part of Northern Ireland's recent history. Northern Ireland is the better place for us having been here.[32]

In short this was 'an appropriate time to begin to wind down our activities', but this took longer than expected.

At the twenty-eighth AGM on 15 January 2003 Margaret Kennedy reported that the '12 months intervening have been burdensome'. The plan had been to set up a trust to provide long-term security for the salaries of the chaplains at Lagan College by amalgamating the ACT money with that already collected by Sr Anna solely for the purpose. The plan to donate money to the Chaplaincy Fund in Lagan College came to nothing because of legal and other difficulties, some of which were related to the winding up of ACT. Between December 2002 and mid-January 2003, ACT 'had to consider … whether the money might not be better used in supporting and securing an expansion in the number of overall places in integrated education'.[33]

This was agreed. On 22 January 2003, money was advanced to NICIE to continue the activity of its communications team, which was considered to be doing very valuable work. Kennedy wrote to Michael Wardlow, the NICIE chief executive:

> I am pleased to inform the Council that ACT will be awarding a grant to extend the life of part of the Communications Team. This is to include the Outreach workers, project manager and Public Relations Officer. The Outreach people, we know, are encouraging a sizeable number of parent groups. We hope that this grant will enable them through these groups to significantly increase the number of integrated places …
>
> We will be making £200,000 available in the first instance for the above purpose. We understand that this will be augmented by £100,000 from the IEF, thus extending the life of the reduced team by some 22 to 24 months.[34]

She added that if NICIE would take responsibility for the annual Dunleath lecture for ACT, using income from ground rents in Belfast amounting to some £600 a year, this 'would amply cover the cost'.[35]

'We had this passionate conviction'

At a closing celebration which was also a farewell dinner for Sr Anna in the Canada Room at Queen's University, Belfast in 2003, Margaret Kennedy was at last able to make a final speech as chair of ACT. First she paid tribute to Sr Anna:

Invitation to celebration dinner for ACT's 30 Years' work – and an opportunity to honour Sr Anna who was returning to her religious order in England, June 2003.

> This quite unique lady has worked endlessly and tirelessly for the cause of reconciliation in this war-torn province and, in particular, for Lagan College and its chaplaincy. She has raised an enormous amount of money for that cause through speaking tours across the water, on the continent and in North America. She was able to squeeze money out of anyone who heard her speak with passion about how wonderful it would be if Northern Ireland's children could attend school together. Her energy and enthusiasm often put the rest of us to shame, for one of such diminutive size and advancing years. She has been quite unique in this movement and she will be remembered with love and gratitude.[36]

She continued:

> It is difficult to encompass over 30 years of activity and striving in the cause of integrated education in a few minutes. We had this passionate conviction that it would help to free our young of the burden of ignorance and intolerance which they inherited from a segregated and sectarian society and, if it were established and nourished, that it would help to make Northern Ireland a better and more peaceful place for all.
>
> For a long time we were quite alone. Some of us remember all the rather clandestine excitement felt during those early, isolated years. There were endless phone calls, lengthy meetings and much burning of the midnight oil. On collating our archives recently I have been amazed at the sheer volume of what we had written – and the quality of it. I sometimes think I couldn't write that today.
>
> I needn't remind you that for roughly two decades we had no official friends at institutional level in the Department of Education, the education and library boards, the political parties by and large and, of course, in the main churches. The mainstream schools came to be fearful of the movement as well. During this last decade, opposition has receded and we even have a few champions amongst officialdom, among them Dr Brian Mawhinney, Mo Mowlam and, lately, Martin McGuinness. Alas, the institutional churches have yet to give us their warm-hearted blessing, or, in some cases, any blessing at all. They remain by and large unconvinced by our vision of shared Christian

schools and our belief in this radical form of reconciliation.

That early vision has been embodied in our first and greatest success – Lagan College … the establishment of the school, its success in so many areas and activities, its great heads … *alone* would have made *all* our endeavours worthwhile. But now there are 49 other integrated schools and at least eight more in the pipeline. All Children Together has established a whole new framework of which we can be rightly proud …

My view is that there will evolve a whole spectrum of integrated schools with a variety of ethos and approach to R.E. Some may even become more secular than the ACT founders would like. But the mere existence of integrated schools has forced the mainstream ones to look more closely at their community relations and at their curriculum. Can't be bad.

This is the activity in *my* life (excluding family) of which I am most proud.

The story of the integrated movement has been one of the empowerment of ordinary people. We were just a bunch of housewives at the start, with one or two exceptions and apologies to Bill Brown and, I suppose, Sr Anna. Two of the bunch of housewives were exceptional people – our two founders, Cecil Linehan and Bettie Benton – in their vision, energy and determination in the face of daunting opposition … And I keep saying that all the people involved in the integrated schools – the founding parents who took up our torch, the dedicated teachers, the governors, all involved in having to overcome almost insurmountable difficulties in finding sites, buildings, finance – these people are all heroes to me …

We have entered into an arrangement with NICIE and the IEF which has turned out to be far more beneficial than we could have imagined. In ACT's winding up, we hope that these two organisations will carry our banner and our vision of what might be in Northern Ireland's schools.[37]

ACT presents the Rowel Friers cartoons to Helen McHugh, principal of Lagan College, June 2003. From left: ACT directors, Marion Campbell, Margaret Kennedy, Charles Graham and Iris Nesbitt with Lagan College principal, Helen McHugh, third from left.

Epilogue
The long view

1

Once in a great while, the historian has the pleasure of looking at things that were all askew in the past and observing them begin to come right in the present. That is one of the satisfactions provided by reading Jonathan Bardon's insightful history of All Children Together. Another is the innocent joy in watching ordinary decent people behave in a manner that transforms them into ordinary decent local heroes, something quite different and infinitely rarer. What makes this narrative convincing is that Bardon and his subjects have not tried to lacquer over the ugly spots and miscues in the whole business. Mistakes were made and friends sometimes fell out, and that is chronicled honestly. One can watch good, smart people learn and move forward. And the narrative is all the more believable because the principals of ACT knew when the time had come to sign the ledger for the last time. Thus, we know how the story of ACT turned out, while naturally having to ponder how the longer-term story of integrated education in Northern Ireland will evolve. Along which of several possible paths future progress will be made is anyone's guess, but my own faith is that integration will continue to expand. There is no going back.

To be able to say that gives me enormous pleasure, because it was not always thus. I spent a fair bit of time in the 1960s writing the history of Irish primary education in the nineteenth century.[1] Mostly this was the story of the old national schools and of their depressingly ambiguous success. Undeniably, the Irish national system of education was the vehicle by which a generally impoverished population was transformed from illiteracy to functional literacy and numeracy. The schools provided a kitbag of knowledge that was useful not only in dealing with the Irish economy as it modernised after the Great Famine, but also enabled them to adapt to life in Britain, Canada, the United States and Australasia. This latter characteristic was important for, to take the year 1890 for example, four out of every ten Irish-born persons then alive were spending their lives outside of Ireland. A successful educational system in the narrow sense, then, but a complete failure in terms of implicit social content for, as is summarised in the first chapter of the present study, the national-school system's original intention of mixing Catholic and Protestant children together took a terrible kicking – from the churches, from lay religious enthusiasts and from simple demography (in lots of places there were just not enough Protestants to go round). Thus, by 1860, segregation in state-provided and state-governed schools was the normal social configuration, and thus the latent social lesson, of the schools. This lesson – 'don't get near the other side' – was greatly reinforced by the aggressive stance of the Catholic Church internationally in the early 1870s and by the politically aggressive posture of the unionist population in the north of Ireland from the mid-1880s onward. It was a perfect feedback system, a swirl of misunderstanding, divisiveness and ultimately hatred, and its impact on education seemed destined to be a perpetual mortmain on the nation. Having seen this work out in depressing detail, I swore never to write anything more about the history of education in Ireland.

So it took a good deal of pleading by Prof. T.W. Moody before I looked again into that abyss. Moody was the godfather of the Irish historical establishment of his era and, more directly relevantly, he was trying to herd the geese of the Irish historical trade into little boxes so that each would contribute to his great vision – *A new history of Ireland*. This would be completed by the mid-1970s at the latest and would seal the revolution in historical method that he had begun in the 1930s as the engineer of a new traction engine, *Irish Historical Studies*. The trouble was that poor Theo was driven nearly spare by his Irish colleagues in the history profession, who were quite happy to sign on to the venture, stake out topics, attend conferences and luncheon meetings bankrolled by various government and private benefactions, and then blithely ignore their briefs altogether. On the topic of education in the nineteenth and twentieth centuries – in both Northern Ireland and in the Irish Free State and its successors – Moody was stuck because the contributor who had signed on to do those essays in the collective history never got them done because of other responsibilities. Reluctantly, and in the spirit of paying one's non-economic dues to the historical profession, I agreed to take over.[2]

In practical terms, this meant writing two complete books in order to produce a rather small essay on education in post-partition Ireland, since at that time there was very little scholarly work in the field and certainly not enough to synthesise into a satisfactory summary. One of the resulting books, *A mirror to Kathleen's face: education in independent Ireland, 1922–60*[3] was greeted at the time (1975) by the clerically controlled educational establishment in the Republic of Ireland as an instance of *lèse majesté*. Since then it has become fashionable in training colleges and, rather alarmingly, it is still cutting edge. Much more rewardingly, the other volume, *Education and enmity: the control of schooling in Northern Ireland, 1920–50*[4] (1973) fell into a conversation that was beginning to form on how to blunt, and ultimately erase, Northern Ireland's cultural fissures.[5]

This amount of backfill is necessary to give credence to one simple assertion: when I put forward the judgement that ACT and its various allies have begun to overcome one of the most perduring and seemingly intractable problems in the history of Irish society, I have done my homework. And I am absolutely confident that this skein of private and practical people, following idealistic goals, will be seen in the telescope of history as a band of revolutionaries – gentle, collectively generous, modest and ultimately victorious.

2

If one grants my assumption that integration will almost inevitably move forward in the future, it is now time for everyone involved to take a deep breath and ask what could distort or impede progress. To do this is not suddenly to introduce a negative tone into what has been an impressively hopeful, and at heart optimistic, movement. It is merely to suggest that the safest and most efficient way across country is to pay attention to the social and cultural geography ahead and to avoid certain rugged patches of terrain.

Two sociocultural moraines that might look like trouble are not – the Irish language and the falling birth rate. In Northern Ireland, the Irish language is either a low-intensity cultural talisman among the Catholic population or, for a few, the lynchpin of an entire belief system. In the former case, the integrated schools (especially the secondary schools) have already shown that they can provide Irish-language instruction at a level satisfactory to Catholic parents – and of interest to a surprising number of Protestant students. Since most parents of children in integrated schools understand the benefit of pupils' acquiring one or more of the major modern European languages, the old danger of Irish and Latin shouldering aside modern languages has disappeared. As for the tiny proportion of the Catholic population that wants total-immersion schools for Irish-language acquisition, the Department of Education in 1998 wisely created an Irish-medium category of educational institution. There is no chance of Irish-medium education becoming meaningfully integrated as it is based on a set of cultural, political, and historical beliefs that are anathema to almost the entire non-Catholic population. So, let it be; there is no big issue here.

The drop in Northern Ireland's birth rate, which is occurring in common with that of all of the most economically advanced parts of the European Union, might augur trouble: when school enrolments decline, local authorities are apt to cling to practices that keep their pupil numbers above the threshold for viability. In general that would inhibit increased integration. But this is a matter of swings and roundabouts. I suspect that integration indeed will be baulked somewhat by declining enrolments in many urban catchments, especially in Belfast – mostly because there are relatively cheap ways of keeping the existing schools' numbers up: urban transport of children is relatively cheap. However, Northern Ireland is highly rural by European standards and it is in the countryside where most of the viability-threatening enrolment decline in future will occur. Distances in rural areas are considerable and the purpose-created transport links needed to stretch catchment zones are very expensive. Thus in many rural areas the choice for both Protestant and Catholic primary-school governors will be whether to keep the children local by joining in with an integrated school or to maintain denominational affiliation by putting them on buses for two or three hours daily. Here a concerted strategy of speaking directly to the needs of the rural primary-school parents and governing agencies about the advantages of integration could be very productive.

Those, then, are not real obstacles. Apt to be encountered, I would guess, will be limitations and occasionally dangers based either in the social physics of education in Northern Ireland or in deep and legitimate variations in democratic political philosophies.

First, some matters of social physics. The Department of Education will almost certainly become more and more committed to integrated education and will place pressure upon local educational administrations (whatever their particular form) to contemplate integration. The mode that integrated schooling has taken at the secondary level – coeducational, mixed ability – is not only the educational fashion among this generation of educational bureaucrats, it is also the easiest to administer and the cheapest to underwrite (assuming, of course, that size is equivalent in any comparisons). And, as indicated above, at the primary-school level, integration is the least costly answer to declining enrolments in overlapping segregated rural schools.

What, then, is the danger? It is that a Northern Ireland movement that has been defined and energised by citizens will be hijacked by apparatchiks and its entire purpose turned upside down? The reason I know this to be a possibility is because of the case of New Zealand. There, in the 1970s, two segregated school systems – fully funded state schools and mostly funded Catholic schools – were brought under the same umbrella of full state funding, much to the electoral benefit of the Labour Party and the satisfaction of the central government's educational administrators, who now had a larger cheque book to write in. Thus was segregated education made structurally permanent. But notice the trick. The claim was that the Catholic schools were being 'integrated' into New Zealand's national system. In an Orwellian moment, 'segregation' had been renamed 'integration'.[6] The lesson here is: police the vocabulary of discussion and never lose control of your brand. In the immediate future this implies the need to apply a tight metric to the so-called 'transforming' schools.

Related to the integrated-schools movement's necessarily policing the vocabulary of the endeavour, there will, I hope, be a built-in modesty and patience. *Integrated education is a means to an end and not an end in itself.* Assuming that the overarching goal is to increase social amity and cultural tolerance in Northern Ireland, there will inevitably be spots on the map where pressing for integration will cause more harm than good, and therefore long-term patience will be demanded. The sharp resegregation of Northern Ireland during the Troubles means that in many areas integrated education will have to wait for a generation. In particular, the limits on transporting primary-school children are considerable. Thus, instead of there being any benchmark of final success on the integration front, it would be better to see each decade or so as having its own level of desirable, but necessarily temporary, equilibrium.

I would guess that the most yeasty matter the integrated-schools movement will face in future in the realm of social physics has to do with the definition of the schools as 'Christian'. This label is absolutely necessary in Northern Ireland: no Christian ethos, no integration. 'The integrated school is essentially Christian in character' is the mission definition of the Northern Ireland Council for Integrated Education. The future problem is that the focus on Christianity may be scrutinised very sharply by the European Union. Thus far, the EU has given Northern Ireland a free pass on a large variety of issues because of the jurisdiction's special history. However, at some point a challenge is likely to be launched against several of the province's educational practices. Vulnerability in this regard is increased because educational planners and upper-level administrators have taken to employing a vocabulary developed elsewhere in the English-speaking world to deal with situations that do not have real counterparts in Northern Ireland. One worries when one reads in the Bain report that one of the principles of successful schools are that they 'reflect the pluralist nature of Northern Ireland'.[7] Actually, Northern Ireland is one of the least pluralist jurisdictions in Europe. Bilateralist, certainly; pluralist, not even in fantasy. Similarly, words such as 'multicultural' and 'inclusive', which have real meaning in, say, London or Toronto or Sydney, do not apply. However, their usage sets up grammar and a set of norms which induce outsiders to apply a set of criteria to Northern Ireland that are potentially destructive of the strenuous efforts of people of goodwill to create and manage a set of institutions that fit the unique contours of this society.

Now, to turn to issues of democratic philosophy. There is no doubt that in recent years successive governments of Northern Ireland have failed to respect the wishes of a large number of parents in Northern Ireland to have their children educated in integrated schools. The sequence of polls conducted by Millward Brown Ulster for NICIE have established this beyond question. So, for the moment, the integrated-schools movement is on firm ground in arguing on the unambiguous basis of democratic rights for the provision of more integrated schooling. But consider a future when, say, a full third of Ulster schools at all levels are integrated. What if the parents of the remaining two-thirds do not favour integration? What is the democratic response? It would be useful to have that discussion early, the more so as it is possible that the central educational bureaucracy, realising the money-saving potential of integration, could take the bit in its teeth and press integration on those that do not want it. Does the democratic right to integrated education not also imply a democratic right to segregated schooling? And where should the movement stand?

Finally, the elephant in the room. The integrated-schools movement from its very beginning has operated on a fiction – a necessary one, but a fiction nonetheless. This is that the interests of parents and the interests of the churches are at heart one; and that the purpose of increasing social harmony in Ulster is a goal shared equally between the churches and the movement – and why, why cannot the churches see this and join the cause? The harsh fact is that the core values of the churches and those of the movement are incompatible. In part this is because in ideology the various denominations are operating in the spiritual realm, the schools' movement in the social realm. Paradoxically, in pursuit of their goals in the realm of the invisible, the churches must survive in the everyday, nastily Darwinian world of economic and social competition. Any specific social goal is secondary to the need for the churches to survive organisationally. Thus, the welfare of children and the cause of social peace in Northern Ireland are at best of tertiary importance and the churches would be self-destructive if they acted otherwise. This is especially true of the Catholic Church since, through its control of a segregated school network, it gains patronage over more resources than it acquires from any other source. In the larger collective perspective, the cause of integrated education and the larger goal of breaking apart the denominational clots in the heart of Ulster society are indirect, but potentially devastating attacks upon the institutional configuration of the major Northern Ireland denominations. Of course the integrated-schools movement must continually state that it is pushing for 'Christian' ends, and indeed it is. However, the leaders of the major denominations know exactly where that is leading.

But then, no man, having put his hand to the plough, and looking back, is worthy of the kingdom of heaven (Luke 9:62).

DONALD H. AKENSON, D.LITT.
DOUGLAS PROFESSOR OF HISTORY
QUEEN'S UNIVERSITY
KINGSTON, ONTARIO

APPENDICES

APPENDIX 1

Some milestones before the conflict

1801   Act of Union

1806   Act empowering Lord Lieutenant to appoint commissioners to inquire into the state of education in Ireland (14 reports, 1809–13)

1811   Kildare Place Society founded

1829   Catholic emancipation

1831   Board of Commissioners for National Education set up National Schools

1845   Act setting up Queen's colleges in Belfast, Cork and Galway

1845–9   Great Famine

1868   Powis Commission appointed to review national schools

1869   Disestablishment of the church in Ireland

1878   Act to set up intermediate schools

1899   Department of Agriculture and Technical Instruction

1900   Intermediate Education Act

1908   Irish Universities Act sets up Queen's University, Belfast, and the National University of Ireland

1912   Third Home Rule Bill

1920   Government of Ireland Act establishes Northern Ireland

1921   Anglo-Irish Treaty

1922   Lynn Committee reviews elementary education in Northern Ireland

1923   Education Act (Londonderry Act)

1925   Amendments to 1923 Education Act

1930   Education Act (50 per cent capital grants to Catholic schools and 'Bible instruction' in state schools)

1947   Education Act (50 per cent capital grants to Catholic schools and Bible instruction in state schools)

1949   Ireland Act (Westminster)

1962   IRA 'border campaign' called off

1964   Intercommunal conflict in Divis Street, Belfast

1965   Lockwood report recommends Coleraine as the site for a second university in Northern Ireland

1966   Free post-primary education promised in the Republic of Ireland; UVF members imprisoned for sectarian murders in Belfast

Timeline Northern Ireland 1967–2009

A chronology of the conflict	Significant developments in integrated education in Northern Ireland (NI)
1967 Northern Ireland Civil Rights Association (NICRA) is formed in Belfast to demand fairness in housing, voting and employment, January. Terence O'Neill, prime minister of Northern Ireland, meets Jack Lynch, taoiseach of the Irish Republic, at Stormont, December. Ian Paisley mounts protest to the meeting, December.	Schools of all kinds in Northern Ireland are segregated, in practice if not always in theory. Some schools do have a 'mixed' intake (some isolated rural primary schools and a few of the more prestigious grammar schools) but none can claim to be integrated.
1968 Austin Currie squats in a council house in Caledon, County Tyrone, June. 2,500 people take part in NICRA march from Coalisland to Dungannon, August. RUC baton civil-rights marchers and visiting MPs in Derry, October. O'Neill agrees package of reforms, November. O'Neill's 'Ulster at the crossroads' speech, December.	Some Catholic parents in the north-Down area sending their children to state-controlled schools and other voluntary non-Catholic schools have difficulty obtaining help from the church as they strive to instruct their children in the tenets of the Catholic faith. A small group of Catholic parents in Bangor come together to form a Sunday school and take turns to instruct their children.
1969 Burntollet Bridge is attacked during a People's Democracy march from Belfast to Derry, January. Stormont elections, February. O'Neill resigns; James Chichester-Clark is the new prime minister of Northern Ireland, April/May. 'Battle of the Bogside' and intense conflict in Belfast, August. British troops arrive in Northern Ireland on active service, August. Provisional IRA formed, December.	Policy on the administration of confirmation in the diocese of Down and Connor changes: cards are given to children prior to acceptance for confirmation but only if they attend the local Catholic school or if the bishop considers a child's attendance at a 'non-Catholic' school a special case and therefore acceptable to him.
1970 Ulster Defence Regiment (UDR) comes into existence, January. Ulster Special Constabulary disbanded, April. Alliance Party founded, April. Lower Falls curfew, July. SDLP founded, August. Macrory proposals on local government reform accepted, December.	Parent-run catechism classes continue following the syllabus prescribed at the time by the Catholic Education Advisers in Ireland.
1971 Prime Minister Chichester-Clark declares that 'Northern Ireland is at war with the IRA provisionals', February. Chichester-Clark resigns and is replaced by Brian Faulkner, March. First meeting of the Northern Ireland Housing Executive, May. Imposition of internment followed by the worst violence since 1922, August. UVF bombing of McGurk's bar in north Belfast leaves 15 people dead, December.	Parent-run catechism classes continue.

1972	14 are killed on Bloody Sunday in Derry, January. Direct rule is introduced, March. PIRA ceasefire, begun in June, breaks down in July. Bloody Friday: 22 PIRA bomb blasts in Belfast kill nine people, July. 467 are killed in the Troubles in this year.	Letter from Cecil Linehan to the press suggests integrated schools might help children of those intending to 'stick it out' in Northern Ireland. Letter leads to meeting between Bettie Benton and Cecil Linehan, co-founders of All Children Together.
1973	First elections for new district councils, May. Elections for 78-member assembly, June. Sunningdale Agreement is signed, December. Power-sharing executive is established with Brian Faulkner as chief executive and Gerry Fitt as deputy chief executive, New Year's Eve.	All Children Together is formed; it issues its first publication, 'Guidance for parents'. Numbers of parents involved in the Sunday classes and children attending them grow so that most parts of north Down and parts of east Belfast are covered.
1974	Power-sharing executive takes office, January. Westminster general election – 11 of 12 Northern Ireland MPs are against the Sunningdale Agreement, February. Ulster Workers' Council strike of 15 days paralyses the region and brings down the executive, May. Loyalist bombs during UWC strike kill 22 in Dublin and 5 in Monaghan. Guildford and Birmingham pub bombs: 5 are killed and 65 are injured in Guildford, October; 21 are killed and 182 are injured in Birmingham, November. IRA truce, December 1974–January 1975.	Basil McIvor, minister for education in the power-sharing executive, announces his shared-schools plan. ACT is formally constituted. ACT becomes interdenominational: a meeting to discuss proposal that ACT should become interdenominational is postponed from May to September owing to violence during the UWC strike. ACT holds its first public conference, entitled 'Interdenominational schools: how? why? and the way ahead'. A written appeal on behalf of Catholic parents in Down and Connor is forwarded to the Vatican.
1975	There are four IRA bombs in London, January. IRA ceasefire, February–September. Election and first meeting of the Northern Ireland Constitutional Convention, May. Miami Showband is killed by the UVF, July. The last detainees are released, December.	ACT is asked by the BBC to make two programmes: one a *Platform* programme for Radio Ulster, the second an *Open door* programme for BBC2.
1976	Special-category status is removed for paramilitary prisoners, March. Final sitting of the convention ends in uproar, March. British ambassador to Ireland, Christopher Ewart-Biggs, is killed in Dublin, July. Death of three Maguire children leads to the Peace People movement, August. Blanket/dirty protest begins in the Maze prison.	'ACT on shared schools', ACT's first policy document, is produced. Department of Education, Northern Ireland publishes the Cowan report, containing firm proposals to abolish selection at the age of 11. ACT's second public conference is cancelled as the main speakers are not allowed to attend the conference in Down and Connor.
1977	Seven IRA bombs explode in London's West End, January. 26 UVF members are jailed for more than 600 years, March.	Education Bill (the first piece of legislation in Northern Ireland to enable schools to transform to integrated status) is drafted by ACT and introduced into the House of Lords by Lord Dunleath.

1977   Loyalist 'stoppage', May.
       Lord Melchett, education minister, announces the
       scrapping of the '11-plus' and the introduction of
       comprehensive education, June.
       Queen Elizabeth II visits Northern Ireland, August.
       Two Peace People founders, Mairead Corrigan and
       Betty Williams, are awarded the Nobel Peace Prize,
       October.

A small group of Catholic parents in ACT travel
to Dublin to see the papal nuncio to discuss the
church's lack of help with religious education
and the withholding of the sacrament of
confirmation.
First issue of *ACT-LETT*, the bi-annual ACT
newsletter (1977–97).

1978   12 people are killed by the PIRA bombing of La
       Mon House hotel, February.
       Mason announces £56-million subsidy for planned
       DeLorean car factory in south Belfast, August.
       Northern Ireland gets five more MPs at Westminster,
       November.
       IRA bombs 11 towns in Northern Ireland and
       announces that it is 'preparing for a long war',
       December.
       IRA bombs explode in Liverpool, Manchester,
       Coventry, Southampton and Bristol, December.

Education (Northern Ireland) Act 1978 passed –
first breakthrough in legislation.
Interim transfer arrangements put in place.
Bishop Philbin of Down and Connor holds a
'special Confirmation ceremony'; among those
confirmed are a large number of children from
whom the sacrament had been withheld because
of their attendance at non-Catholic schools.
ACT's third and fourth public conferences:
'Shared schools in action' and 'Agreed syllabi in
religious education'.

1979   Conviction of 11 loyalist 'Shankill Butchers',
       February.
       Airey Neave, Conservative MP, is killed by Irish
       National Liberation Army (INLA) bomb blast,
       Westminster, March.
       18 soldiers are killed by PIRA bomb blasts at
       Warrenpoint, County Down, 27 August; Lord
       Mountbatten, his 14-year-old grandson and two
       others are killed by a bomb outside Mullaghmore
       Harbour, County Sligo.
       Pope John Paul visits Ireland and appeals for peace,
       September.

International Year of the Child; All Children
Together Charitable Trust is established. ACT's
fifth public conference: 'Cooperation in higher
education (teacher training). ACT's sixth public
conference: 'The case for a shared curriculum'.

1980   Three RUC members killed in a 1,000 lb bomb,
       January.
       Meeting between Prime Minister Margaret Thatcher
       and Taoiseach C.J. Haughey in London, May.
       First IRA hunger strike begins in October; it is called
       off after 53 days, November.
       Thatcher meets Haughey in Dublin, December.

First plans are drawn up for the opening of new
integrated schools: nursery, post-primary and
sixth-form.
Rowntree Trust offers financial assistance.
ACT's seventh public conference: 'Sharing and
integration: English, Welsh and Scottish models
and practice'.

1981   Second hunger strike begins at the Maze prison
       when PIRA prisoner, Bobby Sands, refuses food,
       March.
       Sands elected MP for Fermanagh/south Tyrone,
       April.
       Sands dies on hunger strike, May.
       Hunger strike ends after ten deaths, October.
       Sinn Féin 'armalite and ballot box' policy announced
       at *Ard Fheis* in Dublin.

First integrated school, Lagan College, opens
with no government support or funding with 28
pupils in a scout hall.
Sheila Greenfield becomes first integrated-school
principal.

1982   DeLorean plant in Dunmurray closes, May.
        38 IRA prisoners escape from the Maze prison,
        September.
        First sitting of the Northern Ireland assembly
        without any nationalist presence, November.
        INLA bomb at the Dropping Well pub in Ballykelly
        kills 11 soldiers and 6 civilians, December.

        ACT's eighth public conference: 'Planned shared
        schools'.

1983   Taoiseach Garret FitzGerald opens New Ireland
        Forum at Dublin Castle, May.
        Gerry Adams of Sinn Féin is voted MP for west
        Belfast, beating Gerry Fitt of SDLP in Westminster.
        General election: one SDLP candidate and 15
        unionists are elected, June.
        Catholic Reactionary Force kills three church elders
        and wounds 11 others in Pentecostal Church,
        Darkley, County Armagh, November.

        Lagan College grows to 120 pupils.
        Lagan College governors apply to SEELB for
        maintained status.
        ACT's ninth public conference: 'Education
        acrossthe religious and academic divide'.

1984   New Ireland Forum report is published, Dublin,
        May.
        IRA bombs Conservative Party conference, Brighton,
        killing 5 and wounding 34 others, October.

        Lagan College grows to 164 pupils and is finally
        recognised by the government with the first
        grant aid to an integrated school.

1985   Nine RUC officers are killed by IRA mortar attack,
        Newry, County Down, February.
        Anglo-Irish Agreement signed by Prime Minister
        Margaret Thatcher and Taoiseach Garret FitzGerald.
        Irish government has an advisory role in Northern
        Ireland's affairs but confirms no change in the
        constitutional position of Northern Ireland unless a
        majority agrees, November.
        Unionist rally in Belfast starts 'Ulster says no'
        campaign, November.

        Belfast Charitable Trust for Integrated Education
        (BELTIE) is established and opens Hazelwood
        Integrated College in north Belfast.
        Forge Integrated and Hazelwood Integrated
        Primary Schools – the first integrated primary
        schools – open in Belfast.

1986   Unionist 'day of action' against the Anglo-Irish
        Agreement closes much of Belfast, March.
        Banned Apprentice Boys' march causes clashes
        between the RUC and loyalists in Portadown,
        March.
        Peter Robinson of the DUP arrested when he led
        some 500 loyalists to Clontibret, County Monaghan,
        August.
        200,000 unionists attend a rally at the City Hall,
        Belfast on the first anniversary of the signing of the
        Anglo-Irish Agreement, accompanied by disorder
        and the destruction of shops, November.

        All Childrens' Integrated Primary School (IPS),
        Newcastle, County Down – the first integrated
        primary school outside Belfast – opens.
        The Dunleath Act is incorporated into the
        Education (Northern Ireland) Order 1986.
        Basil McIvor publishes a discussion paper
        outlining the need for an overviewing body for
        future developments in integrated education.
        Ulster-born Dr Brian Mawhinney, MP for
        Peterborough, is appointed minister in the
        Northern Ireland Office.
        ACT's tenth public conference: 'Into the future:
        the role of integrated education'.

1987   IRA bomb British army base, Germany, March.
Eight IRA members shot dead by SAS at Loughgall,
County Armagh, May.
150 tons of arms for PIRA seized on board the
coaster *Eksund*, November.
Remembrance-Day IRA bomb kills 11 Protestants
and injures 63 others in Enniskillen, November.

ACT takes the first steps to encourage
coordination in funding applications to major
trust funds.
Northern Ireland Council for Integrated
Education is informally established.
Two more integrated primary schools open:
Bridge IPS, Banbridge, County Down, and
Millstrand IPS, Portrush, County Antrim.

1988   Hume–Adams dialogue begins, January.
Three IRA members are killed by SAS, Gibraltar,
March.
Michael Stone attacks mourners at the funerals of
IRA members shot dead in Gibraltar in Milltown
Cemetery, Belfast, killing 3 and injuring over 60,
March.
Broadcasting ban on Sinn Féin and other
paramilitary groups is introduced, October.

Windmill IPS, Dungannon, County Tyrone,
opens.

1989   Pat Finucane, solicitor, is shot dead, February.
Michael Stone is jailed for 30 years for Milltown
Cemetery killings, March.
IRA bomb at Deal, Kent, kills 11 bandsmen,
September.
Guildford Four are released, October.
Peter Brooke, Northern Ireland secretary of state,
suggests talks with republicans, November.

NICIE is formally established.
Education Reform (Northern Ireland) Order
1989 represents a major breakthrough in
legislation, placing a statutory duty on the
Department of Education 'to encourage and
facilitate the development of integrated
education – that is the education at school of
Protestant and Roman Catholic pupils'.
Two integrated primary schools open:
Enniskillen IPS, Co. Fermanagh, and Braidside
IPS, Ballymena, County Antrim.

1990   Brooke's talks initiative is launched, January.
Community Relations Council is established,
January.
London stock exchange bomb, July.
Ian Gow, Conservative MP, is killed by an IRA
booby-trap bomb, July.

Foyle Trust for Integrated Education is set up in
Derry.
Two new integrated primary schools open:
Omagh IPS, County Tyrone, and Portadown
IPS, County Armagh.
ACT's eleventh public conference: 'Changes and
challenges: a study of the new Education Reform
(Northern Ireland) Order 1989'.

1991   PIRA launches three mortars on Downing Street,
February.
Peter Brooke outlines 'three strands' for future talks,
March.
Convictions of the Maguire Seven for the Guildford
and Woolwich bombings are quashed, June.
Brooke talks are wound up without agreement, July.
Gerry Adams of Sinn Féin writes to the British and
Irish governments seeking 'open-ended discussions'.
Prime Minister John Major meets Taoiseach C.J.
Haughey in Dublin, December.

NICIE is grant-aided by the Department of
Education.
Brownlow Integrated College, Craigavon,
County Armagh, becomes the first post-primary
to transform to integrated status.
Two new integrated primary schools open:
Corran IPS in Larne, County Antrim, and
Oakgrove IPS in County Londonderry.
Carhill IPS in Garvagh, County Londonderry,
becomes the first primary school to transform to
integrated status.

NICIE statement of principles is agreed. ACT's twelfth public conference: 'Children, churches and culture' takes place. Part 1: 'Religious education and chaplaincy in interdenominational schools', April; Part 2: 'Our common cultural heritage: saints, scholars and scrolls', October. NICIE 'Statement of Principles' agreed.

1992   Eight Protestant workers returning from a British army base are blown up by an IRA bomb in Teebane, County Tyrone, January.
Albert Reynolds becomes leader of Fianna Fáil and declares the Northern Ireland problem his first priority, February.
Sinn Féin publishes a paper setting out its political strategy, February.
Five Catholics are killed by loyalists in Ormeau Road bookmakers, Belfast, February.
IRA bomb in the Baltic Exchange, London, kills three people and inflicts damage estimated at hundreds of millions of pounds, April.
2,000 lb bomb wrecks Northern Ireland Forensic Centre in Belfast and damages about 1,000 homes, September.

Integrated Education Fund (IEF) is established. One integrated post-primary college, Oakgrove Integrated College, opens in Derry. One integrated primary, Acorn IPS, opens in Carrickfergus, County Antrim.
ACT's thirteenth public conference: 'Shared religious education: proposals from the churches in Northern Ireland'.

1993   IRA bombs kill two young boys in Warrington, March.
IRA bomb in Shankill Road fish shop kills nine civilians and one bomber, October.
UFF kills eight civilians in the Rising Sun bar in Greysteel, County Londonderry, October.
Secret talks between Major government and IRA are revealed, November.
Downing Street Declaration is signed by Prime Minister John Major and Taoiseach Albert Reynolds, offering talks to paramilitaries if they cease action and arguing for self-determination on the basis of consensus for all the people of Ireland, December.

Education (NI) Order 1993, dealing with capital grants to voluntary schools.
Three integrated primary schools open: Cranmore IPS and Loughview IPS in Belfast and Saints and Scholars IPS in Armagh.

1994   President Bill Clinton grants visa to Gerry Adams, January.
UVF kill six and wound five in Loughinisland bar, June.
Sectarian and tit-for-tat murders increase, January–August.
PIRA ceasefire is declared, 31 August.
Combined Loyalist Military Command ceasefire is declared, 13 October.
First official meeting between British government representatives and Sinn Féin, December.

Two integrated post-primary colleges open: Erne in Enniskillen and Shimna in Newcastle.
Cecil Linehan, co-founder of ACT, is appointed to the board of NICIE.
ACT's fourteenth public conference: 'Schools of reconciliation: education, peace-building and human rights – a twentieth-anniversary celebration of the first All Children Together public seminar'.

1995 Peace process begins with 'Joint Framework Documents', February.
First 'siege of Drumcree' begins when Catholics near Portadown refuse to allow the annual Orange Parade to pass along the Garvaghy Road; David Trimble becomes UUP leader, September. President Clinton visits Northern Ireland, November.

Three integrated post-primary colleges open: Drumragh in Omagh, New-Bridge in Loughbrickland, County Down, and the Integrated College in Dungannon, County Tyrone.
One integrated primary school, Cedar, opens in Crossgar in the outskirts of Belfast.
One primary school transforms to integrated status – Portaferry Primary School.
ACT mounts an exhibition in the Linen Hall Library, Belfast, celebrating its twenty-first anniversary of work for the development of integrated education.

1996 Mitchell Commission recommends that talks and weapons decommissioning should occur in parallel, January.
IRA ceasefire ends with Canary Wharf bombing in London, February.
Northern Ireland Forum elections are held, May.
Second Drumcree stand-off leads to the murder of Catholic taxidriver Michael McGoldrick and widespread riots and destruction across Northern Ireland, July.
In its first bomb attack in Northern Ireland since 1994, IRA strikes army HQ in Lisburn, fatally injuring a soldier, October.
Protests begin outside the Catholic church in Harryville, Ballymena, County Antrim, November.

Education (NI) Order 1996 deals with special-needs education.
Increased viability criteria make approval for state funding for new integrated schools more difficult.
Two integrated post-primary colleges open: North Coast College in Coleraine, County Londonderry and Slemish College in Ballymena, County Antrim.
Two primary schools transform to integrated status: Hilden in Lisburn and Rathenraw in County Antrim.
One integrated primary school opens: Oakwood IPS, Derriaghy, County Antrim.

1997 Bombardier Stephen Restorick is killed by IRA sniper in Bessbrook, February.
Dr Mo Mowlam is appointed secretary of state for Northern Ireland, May.
IRA restores the ceasefire, July.
Further rioting and violence follow third Drumcree stand-off, July.
UUP and Sinn Féin sit together for talks for the first time, September.
Prime Minister Tony Blair meets Gerry Adams and Martin McGuinness of Sinn Féin at Downing Street, December.
Leader of the Loyalist Volunteer Force, Billy Wright, is shot dead by the INLA in the Maze prison, December.

Three integrated post-primary colleges open: Ulidia in Carrickfergus, Strangford in Carrowdore, County Down, and Malone College in south Belfast.
One primary school transforms to integrated status: Annsborough, Castlewellan, County Down.
Bettie Benton, co-founder of ACT, is appointed first chair of the governors of Strangford College.
ACT holds two Dunleath Lectures: Dr Brian Lambkin, a founding Lagan College teacher and later principal speaks on 'Integrated education in Northern Ireland into the new millennium'; Colm Cavanagh, chair of NICIE and a founder of the Foyle Trust for Integrated Education speaks on the theme 'Thy people shall be my people'.

1998 Good Friday Agreement is signed at Stormont, April.
Agreement is endorsed by the Northern Ireland

ACT gives interest-free loans of £75,000 to Ulidia and Strangford Colleges. Three post-primary schools and three primary schools electorate in a referendum, May.

Three Quinn children – Richard, Mark and Jason – die in a sectarian attack on their home in Ballymoney during the fourth Drumcree stand-off, July.

Bomb in Omagh, planted by the Real IRA, kills 31 people (including unborn twins) – the largest loss of life of any single incident in Northern Ireland during the Troubles, August.

The Northern Ireland Act establishes the assembly, the Human Rights Commission, the Equality Commission and north–south bodies, November.

transform to integrated status: Down Academy, Downpatrick; Priory College, Holywood, County Down; Forthill College, Lisburn, County Antrim; Bangor Central PS, Bangor; and Kilbroney IPS and Kircubbin IPS in County Down.

1999
Announcement of major army base closures, January.

RUC reports that punishment beatings have ceased, February.

Murder of prominent Lurgan solicitor, Rosemary Nelson, March.

Patten report recommends 175 changes to RUC, September.

David Trimble, UUP, is appointed first minister, and Seamus Mallon, SDLP, deputy first minister of new Northern Ireland assembly, November.

The Irish Republic amends its constitution and drops its territorial claim on Northern Ireland, November.

North–south and British–Irish bodies are established, November.

Martin McGuiness becomes minister for education and announces reduction in viability criteria for integrated and Irish-medium schools.

UNESCO report on integrated education is published.

One integrated primary school opens: Spires IPS in Magherafelt, County Londonderry.

ACT's fifteenth conference: a private seminar for clergy entitled: 'The work of a joint Anglican–Roman Catholic school'.

2000
Secretary of state Peter Mandelson, suspends devolution and restores direct rule, February.

Saville Inquiry into Bloody Sunday opens, March.

Devolution is restored: unionists agree to return to Stormont if the arms issue is dealt with while the assembly functions, May.

IRA weapons dump is inspected by General de Chastelain, June.

Drumcree march is banned by the Parades Commission and final prisoner releases are made under the Good Friday Agreement, July.

Department of Education, Northern Ireland is renamed Department of Education.

One integrated primary school opens: Millennium IPS in Carryduff, Belfast.

2001
IRA decommissioning begins, January.

First Minister Trimble resigns after DUP gains in the general election, July.

Three Irish republicans accused of technology exchange with FARC terrorists are arrested in Colombia, August.

Clashes outside Holy Cross School, north Belfast, September.

RUC becomes Police Service of Northern Ireland (PSNI), November.

Burns review on post-primary selection is published.

One primary school transforms to integrated status: Carnlough, County Antrim.

2002
IRA break-in at Castlereagh police headquarters, March.

Police raid the Sinn Féin office in Stormont over alleged

One integrated post-primary school opens: Sperrin Integrated College, Magherafelt, County Londonderry.

intelligence gathering, October.
John Reid, Northern Ireland secretary of state, suspends devolution, October.

2003 During visit by Prime Minister Tony Blair and Taoiseach Bertie Ahern to Hillsborough, Gerry Adams informs David Trimble that the IRA will disband, March.
US President George W. Bush visits Northern Ireland, April.
Prime Minister Tony Blair postpones assembly elections, May.
Independent Monitoring Commission on paramilitaries starts work, October.
Third act of IRA decommissioning takes place; unionists reject it as insufficient, October.
DUP and Sinn Féin emerge as the two largest parties in assembly elections, November.

ACT gives £200,000 to NICIE to support the communications team and outreach workers involved with groups of parents setting up new schools.
One integrated primary school opens: Maine IPS, Randalstown, County Antrim.
Two primary schools transform to integrated status: Round Tower IPS, County Antrim, and Glengormley IPS, in the outskirts of Belfast.
ACT disbands and holds a farewell dinner for Sister Anna Hoare, returning to her religious community in England, having worked tirelessly for reconciliation in Northern Ireland for over 20 years.

2004 Talks at Leeds Castle to seek agreement on the restoration of a power-sharing executive, September.
Gerry Adams meets Hugh Orde, chief constable, PSNI, for the first time, September.
Bloody Sunday inquiry closes 'hearings' stages of its work, November.
£26.5-million robbery from Northern Bank in Belfast, December.

One integrated post-primary college opens: Armagh Integrated College.
Two primary schools transform to integrated status: Glencraig IPS, Holywood, and Groomsport IPS, both in County Down.
Four integrated primary schools open: Drumlins IPS, Ballynahinch, County Down; Roe Valley IPS, Limavady, Co. Londonderry; Phoenix IPS, Cookstown, County Tyrone, and Lir IPS, Ballycastle, County Antrim.

2005 Chief Constable Hugh Orde informs the public that the IRA are responsible for the Northern Bank robbery, January.
Robert McCartney is killed by the IRA outside a Belfast bar, January.
IRA declares an end to the 'armed struggle', July.
General de Chastelain's report on decommissioning claims that IRA arms are now beyond use, September.
A shared future: policy and strategic framework for good relations in Northern Ireland is published, March.

One primary school transforms to integrated status: Groarty IPS, County Londonderry.

2006 Prime Minister Tony Blair visits Northern Ireland and Peter Hain, Northern Ireland secretary of state, sets 24 November deadline to assembly members to 'power share', April.
The Independent Monitoring Commission reports that the IRA appear to have decommissioned their weapons, October.
Joint summit in Scotland leads to St Andrew's Agreement (on the restoration of devolved

The integrated-schools movement celebrates the twenty-fifth anniversary of the opening of Lagan College. There are now 61 integrated schools with 18,733 pupils in Northern Ireland.
Two primary schools transform to integrated status: Crumlin IPS, Belfast, and Ballycastle IPS, County Antrim.
One integrated post-primary college opens: Rowallane Integrated College, Saintfield, County Down.

government), October.
'Pledge of office' agreed between Ian Paisley (DUP), first minister designate, and Martin McGuinness (Sinn Féin), deputy first minister designate, November.

One integrated primary school opens: Clogher Valley IPS, Fivemiletown, County Tyrone.
Lir IPS, Ballycastle, closes.
Groomsport IPS closes owing to falling enrolments, June.

2007   In assembly elections DUP and Sinn Féin increase their representation, March.
The new Northern Ireland assembly meets and new executive is formed, May; Prime Minister Tony Blair and Taoiseach Bertie Ahern attend when oath of office is taken at Stormont, 8 May
British military campaign in Northern Ireland, codenamed Operation Banner, officially ends, July.
UVF, Red Hand Commandos and UDA issue a statement declaring an end to their armed campaign, stating that they would retain their weapons but put them 'beyond use', November.

One integrated primary school opens: Rowandale, Moira, County Down.

2008   The International Monitoring Commission produces a report stating that the Continuity IRA must be regarded as a 'very serious threat', November.

One primary school transforms to integrated status: Cliftonville IPS, Belfast.
Blackwater Integrated College is established by an amalgamation of Down Academy and Rowallane Integrated College.
Hilden Integrated PS closes in December owing to falling enrolments.

2009   Real IRA murder two British soldiers and injure two more in Massereene, County Antrim – the first British army fatalities in Northern Ireland since 1997, March.
Continuity IRA murder a police officer in Craigavon, County Armagh – the first police fatality in Northern Ireland since 1998, March.
Despite an encouraging visit to Belfast by US secretary of state, Hillary Clinton, the main parties at Stormont fail to agree on the devolution of policing and justice powers, October.

Research paper, *Churches and Christian ethos in integrated schools*, initiated by ACT, is launched at Lagan College. It was produced by Macaulay Associates, commissioned by NICIE and funded by IEF.
Initial work on a website containing the archive of ACT papers commences.

APPENDIX 2

Letter informing principals of meeting regarding Sunday-school classes for Catholic children, 1973

Dooks
My Lady's Mile
Holywood

12 November 1973

Dear

A meeting of parents of Catholic children attending non-Catholic schools will be held in the Windsor Hotel, Knocknagoney, on Tuesday, 27 November at 7.45 p.m.

In the circumstances which prevail in the province, we do not want to go around knocking on doors and saying, 'Are you a Catholic? Is your child attending a non-Catholic school?' We are nonetheless keen to help anyone who needs help and are trying to get Sunday schools for Catholic children established.

If, therefore, you know of any Catholic children attending your school, we will be most grateful if you will tell their parents about the meeting. If anyone wants to know who is running this meeting, you can tell them it is just an ad-hoc group of Catholic parents – we have no other official title. Thank you.

Thank you
Yours sincerely

Cecilia F. Linehan
CONVENOR

APPENDIX 3

Speech made by Bettie Benton at the peace meeting
in Grosvenor Hall, Belfast on 11 September 1974

Madam Chairman, first of all I would like to say what a pleasure it is to be here
this evening among so many people seeking peace.

We all long for peace now, a lasting peace. I belong to the All Children Together
movement and I don't think we can talk about peace and reconciliation without
talking about the children – our children. We want a peace that will ensure a
future for our children – a future where all will work together for the good of the
whole community – one community instead of two, one people.

Our children are our hope for the future; they are the citizens of tomorrow.
But can you tell me how we can become one community, one people, when our
children continue to grow up separately and are educated separately?

Madam Chairman, you issued a press statement on Sunday after the meeting
in which you said something about how blind we have been through not knowing
each other and thus misunderstanding each other. We believe that the children
should mix together where the parents desire it, and where better than in school?
During school years little friendships are formed which often last a lifetime and
this is very valuable. We know that many parents desire this, but some of them
live in areas where they are afraid to speak out.

It is nonsense that the first time many of us meet each other is in our first job.
This is too late, too late.

We would know each other if we had gone to school together. So, why not see
if our children can get to know each other? Then perhaps they'll not
misunderstand each other as we have.

And so I say to you tonight: if we are talking peace then we must also talk about
getting all our children together.

APPENDIX 4

Letter to Catholic parents asking them to consider making ACT interdenominational, 1974

174 Groomsport Road
Bangor
Co. Down

Tel. Bangor 4168

15 May 1974

Dear Parent,

There will be a meeting in the Dempsey Room, Royal Hotel, Bangor, on Thursday, 23 May 1974 at 8.15 p.m.

Many people have been in contact with Mrs Cecilia Linehan since her articles appeared in the newspapers and there is much to report to you.

Shared schools

We feel that this is something that ACT should look into. ACT believes that parents should have the right to 'freedom of choice' regarding the school to which they send their children. Vatican II (*Declaration on Christian education*, Section 6) says, 'Parents who have the primary and inalienable right and duty to educate their children must enjoy true liberty in their choice of schools.' ACT seeks discussion with the hierarchy, not confrontation.

On the suggestion of 'shared schools', we feel this could help towards reconciliation in Northern Ireland. If you are agreeable, we can set up a 'working party' of Catholics and others in the education field. They would produce proposals to be presented to our hierarchy for consideration and also to the other churches and, of course, the minister of education. These proposals would take into account the wishes of the parents regarding denominational R.E. for their children in the schools, the two cultures, which must be accommodated if the system is to work, and many other aspects.

We feel now that as well as pursuing our own immediate problem directly with the hierarchy and the Vatican, we should also broaden our base to include sincere people of other denominations who are anxious to work with us.

Fr James Good, the eminent theologian, in a letter to us today, says, 'Keep up the good work.' He enclosed a photostat of his article on Bishop Philbin which appeared in *Hibernia* on 10 May 1974. It is reassuring to know, at this time, that we have friends, especially among the clergy, who feel that we must be given every encouragement.

Yours sincerely,

Bettie Benton
HON. SECRETARY

Please don't miss this very important meeting.

APPENDIX 5

Recommendation passed at close of one-day seminar on interdenominational schools, Saturday, 30 November 1974

1 That this conference recognises the need for a third, interdenominational sector in the education system in Northern Ireland, and calls on the government, the education and library boards and the churches to initiate public discussions with a view to setting up such a system.

2 That where new schools are being planned, the Department of Education, the boards and the churches should consult with the parents in the area before commencing negotiations.

3 That this conference being committed to the concept of Christian love, first shown in a family, requests the churches:
    a. To increase their pastoral care to the family.
    b. To initiate the preparation of a joint curriculum of religious education.

Cecilia Linehan
CHAIRMAN, ACT
DECEMBER 1974, CIRCULATED JANUARY 1975

APPENDIX 6

ACT submissions to the Department of Education and Science in Westminster and other bodies, 1977–2000

1977	Reorganisation of secondary education in Northern Ireland
1977	Daycare and education for the under fives
1978	The Working Party on the Administrative and Legislative Aspects of Reorganising Secondary Education
1979	The report of the Working Party on the Management of Schools in Northern Ireland
1979	The report of the Working Party on Voluntary Schools
1979	The Review of Higher Education Group (Department of Education and Science)
1980	Voluntary maintained schools and centralised responsibility (separate discussion paper)
1980	The future structure of teacher education in Northern Ireland (interim report)
1982	The future of higher education in Northern Ireland
1982	The improvement of community relations: the contribution of schools
1982	Fair Employment Act re. exemption of teachers
1983	Schools and demographic trends
1983	Education and the arts (Department of Education and Science)
1984	Draft Education and Libraries (Northern Ireland) Order 1983
1988	Education reform in Northern Ireland: proposals for reform
1989	Proposals for draft Education Reform (Northern Ireland) Order 1989
1990	ACT proposal for Standing Advisory Council on R.E. (SACRE) for Northern Ireland
1990	Submission to the Churches' Religious-Education Core-Curriculum-Drafting Group
1991	Response to the proposals of the Churches' Religious-Education Core-Curriculum-Drafting Group
1992	The Opshal report – Initiative '92
1993	Response to the consultative document 'Educational administration in Northern Ireland'

1994   Submission to British-Irish Interparliamentary Body Committee D (Culture, Education and the Environment)

1994   Response to Department of Education, Northern Ireland, 'Strategic analysis of the educational service'

1995   Response to Department of Education, Northern Ireland, 'Educational administration in Northern Ireland: proposals for change'

1996   Submission on the transformation of schools (to controlled integrated status)

1998   Submission to the Working Party on the Future Development of Integrated Education

2000   Response to Department of Education. Northern Ireland consultation paper, 'Towards a culture of tolerance: education for diversity'

2000   Response to 'Learning for tomorrow's world: towards a new strategic plan for educational services in Northern Ireland'

APPENDIX 7

Opinion polls on community choice regarding integrated schools in Northern Ireland, 1967–2008

1 In 1967 and 1968, two surveys carried out in Northern Ireland by National Opinion Poll found that:

> 64% of adults favoured integrated schools.
> 65% of youths favoured integrated schools.
> 69% of Catholics favoured integrated schools.

2 Six years later, in 1973, an opinion poll carried out by the *Sunday Times/Fortnight* found the following results in reply to the question, 'How would you feel about your children, or children you know, going to a school attended by pupils and taught by teachers, some of whom were Catholic and some Protestant?

	P.	R.C.	All
Strongly in favour	28%	34%	31%
In favour	31%	30%	31%
Don't mind/willing to accept	29%	21%	24%
Against	10%	3%	10%
Strongly against	3%	10%	3%

3 Further evidence of the state of public opinion is given in the following table from a report, to be published shortly, on a survey funded by the Social Science Research Council of attitudes in a stratified random sample of 2,416 adults in Northern Ireland in 1972. The statement put to respondents was: 'If a Catholic school and a Protestant school in this area decided to get together now and make a joint school for both religions, I would like my children to go to it.

	P.	R.C.	All
Agree very much	62.2%	75.4%	67.2%
Agree a little	15.2%	12.6%	14.2%
Don't know	5.2%	4.3%	4.84 %
Disagree a little	4.4%	2.5%	3.7%
Disagree very much	12.9%	5.2%	10.1%

4   In 1980 another *Fortnight* poll found once again that there is substantial demand among both Protestant and Catholics for those who wished to be given a real chance to send their children to integrated schools. In this poll the first statement was: 'The government should insist that there should be mixed primary and secondary schools in each area to which both Catholic and Protestant children could go as well as unmixed schools.'

	P.	R.C.	All
Agree strongly	20%	23%	21%
Agree	40%	39%	40%
Neither agree nor disagree	15%	15%	15%
Disagree	17%	15%	17%
Disagree strongly	7%	7%	7%

The second question was, 'If there was an integrated school near your home as well as an unmixed Catholic or state school, how would you feel about sending your children to the integrated school?'

	P.			R.C.			All
	ABC1	C2	DE	ABC1	C2	DE	
Definitely send to integrated	25	20	15	19	25	17	20
Prefer to send to integrated	14	13	8	23	13	17	14
Wouldn't really mind	41	37	37	30	25	38	36
Prefer to send to unmixed	12	15	17	16	25	19	17
Definitely send to unmixed	8	14	22	12	9	8	13

Comment

These opinion polls, taken in 1967, 1968 and 1973, show that a majority of people in both sections of the community wanted shared schools. The *Sunday Times/Fortnight* poll shows that 86 per cent of people in Northern Ireland wanted shared schools for their children.

Yet an analysis of the present school population shows approximately 99.5 per cent of Protestant children in non-Roman Catholic schools and 98 per cent of Catholic children in Catholic schools.

The divide is almost complete. Only 13 per cent of the people wish to see Catholic and Protestant children divided so. Yet this 13 per cent appear to be able to deprive a majority of parents in Northern Ireland of the right to have their children playing together and learning together in school.

2003   Millward Brown Ulster Survey

In reply to the question, 'How important is integrated education to peace and reconciliation in Northern Ireland?' the 2003 Millward Brown Ulster survey received the following answers.

Very important	62%
Fairly important	20%
Neither important nor unimportant	8%
Fairly unimportant	2%
Very unimportant	2%
Don't know	5%

2008   Millward Brown Ulster Survey

In the 2008 Millward Brown Ulster survey all 1,001 respondents placed a very high importance on integrated education in terms of its contribution to mutual respect and understanding. When asked, 'How important or unimportant is integrated education in promoting mutual respect and understanding in Northern Ireland?', 63 per cent saw it as 'very important' and a further 21 per cent saw it as 'fairly important'.

When asked, 'How important or unimportant is integrated education in promoting a shared and better future for Northern Ireland?', once again the general public placed similar importance on integrated education, with 63 per cent of all respondents stating that integrated education was 'very important'. A further 21 per cent said it was 'fairly important'.

Support for sharing and collaboration between schools
A huge 79 per cent of parents and grandparents with children of school age or younger supported schools sharing facilities with the nearest school, even if that school was from a different type (sector). When asked, 'Irrespective of the school type you would prefer, would you support or oppose the school your children or grandchildren attend partnering, sharing facilities or collaborating with other nearby schools even if they are a different type?' this idea was strongly supported by 38 per cent of respondents and supported by 41 per cent, with only 7 per cent opposing it.

Support for joint management of schools by churches
Very interestingly, when asked, 'Would you support or be opposed to the establishment of a jointly managed church school – that is, a school whose management is shared between the Catholic and Protestant churches?' just over two thirds (67 per cent) of parents and grandparents with children/grandchildren of school age or younger supported the establishment of such a school. Only 17 per cent opposed this suggestion. (It was strongly supported by 31 per cent, supported by 36 per cent, opposed by 12 per cent, neither supported nor opposed by 10 per cent and strongly opposed by 5 per cent. Six per cent of respondents didn't know.)

APPENDIX 8

Main provisions of the Education (Northern Ireland) Act 1978

The bill drafted by the All Children Together movement to facilitate the voluntary integration of schools in Northern Ireland became law on 26 May 1978.

The act is entitled
An act to facilitate the establishment in Northern Ireland of schools likely to be attended by pupils of different religious affiliations or cultural traditions. The act, an enabling measure, arises out of the particular position of schools in Northern Ireland (see appendix) and is to allow the development of integrated education by consent.

The act suggests two routes to integrated schools:
Where two-thirds of the Protestant church representatives on the management committee of a state school request that the school should become integrated. Where the trustees (e.g. Roman Catholic Church) of a voluntary school request that the school should become an integrated school, the views of parents of pupils at the school shall be ascertained.

Procedure
Measures are laid down to indicate the procedure to be adopted by the area boards and the Department of Education.

Views of parents
> Briefly, this section of the act requires that the views of parents with children at the school are to be obtained 'in such a way that their identity is not revealed'. Where at least three-quarters of the parents are prepared to share the school, the area board shall request the Department of Education to establish it as an integrated school. Thus for the first time we have enshrined in the law governing schools the concept of parental consultation.

Integrated school-management committees
> The next step will be the establishment of the new management structures. The composition of the new management committees will be as follows:

Churches – Jointly	Parents	Education Board
33.1/3%	33.1/3%	33.1/3%

Churches and parents share equally in management.

Appendix

1   Management committees of state-controlled primary and secondary schools are at least 50 per cent representative of 'transferors'. Protestant churches, in the main, have transferred schools in the past and the *de facto* position is that most state schools have at least 50 per cent Protestant church management as a continuing right even in new schools.

Composition of state (controlled) schools' management committees

Education Board	Parents	Protestant Churches
25%	25%	50%

2   Management committees of voluntary Roman Catholic secondary schools are two-thirds representative of the trustees – i.e. the Roman Catholic Church. No Roman Catholic schools have been transferred and these schools are largely managed by the clergy with virtually no parent involvement.

Composition of Catholic (maintained) schools' management committees

Education Board	Catholic Church
33.3%	66.6%

3   Both types of school are open to all but Roman Catholic schools do not greatly attract Protestant pupils and as the state school presents an image of Protestant church control it does not attract Roman Catholic pupils. The result is that neither type of school management presents a proper model for integration.

    In the most recent research published, it has been shown that at least 98 per cent of pupils and teachers are segregated by religion. Two thirds of adults favour integrated education.

APPENDIX 9

Integrated schools: ACT appeals to the churches, June 1978

The Education (Northern Ireland) Bill has now passed through both houses of parliament and has received the royal assent. The act will create a new type of management structure for schools in Northern Ireland for pupils of different religious affiliations or cultural traditions. This management structure gives equal representation to the parents, the education and library boards and the churches.

However, the act will remain unused on the statute book unless the churches here respond to the opportunities it offers to share in a Christian way in the education of young people who are already one in Christ.

The All Children Together movement is making a strong appeal to the churches to take the necessary steps to enable parents who so wish to bring their children together in schools.

Protestant churches

The main Protestant churches, which have half the places on state-school management committees, have repeatedly supported the principle of integrated education at their synods, assemblies and conferences. We appeal to them now to get their representatives on the committees of the schools that already have a minority of Catholic pupils, or where the local community favours integrated education, to take the initiative and request the area board to place the school under an integrated school-management committee.

Catholic Church

We make the same appeal to the trustees of Catholic schools, and urge them to take the initiative, as the Catholic Church has in Tanzania, England and other countries, to join other Christian churches in creating shared Christian schools in Northern Ireland.

Goodwill between the main churches

One of the main principles on which the act is based is goodwill between the main churches. It is founded on trust that, if the main groups of churches are involved together in the management of a school, they will between them have sufficient goodwill to agree what should be done and to make the arrangements that will enable the children in the school who belong to their church to be suitably instructed in its particular tenets.

Gradual development of voluntary integration

There are two aspects of integration as we see it. The first is the structure of the school: management committee, teaching staff, pupils and parents. Only when all these are integrated will we have truly integrated schools. The new act provides the legal framework for such schools to develop. Once the church representatives on the committee of a school have taken the initiative, the legal and administrative machines will start moving. But they are not likely to move fast.

Difficult issues will arise, especially over teacher appointments. Reasonable people, committed to integration, will work out reasonable solutions; but it will not be done easily, nor quickly.

The second aspect is the education given in the school. All too easily it could carry on quite unaffected by the installation of a new management committee: the minority pupils would simply be 'assimilated', not 'integrated'. Real integration will make demands on the content and process of the education provided. That education must be widened to include the dearly held elements of both the cultures of our society, so that neither group of parents feels cheated of part of their cultural tradition.

APPENDIX 10

ACT milestones

1972   ACT is formed.

1972   'Guidance for parents', ACT's first publication, is produced.

1974   ACT is formally constituted.

1974   ACT's first public conference, 'Interdenominational schools: why? how? and the way ahead', is held.

1976   ACT's first policy document, 'ACT on shared schools', is published.

1977   ACT drafts the Education Bill; it has its first reading as a private member's bill.

1978   The first breakthrough in legislation on integrated schools, the Education (Northern Ireland) Act 1978, is enacted.

1979   The International Year of the Child; the ACT Charitable Trust is set up

1980   The first proposals for founding schools are drawn up.

1981   Lagan College, Belfast, Northern Ireland's first integrated secondary school, is founded.

1984   Lagan College is the first integrated school to be recognised by the government and receives grant aid.

1985   Forge Integrated Primary School, Belfast, Northern Ireland's first integrated primary school, opens.

1986   All Children's Integrated Primary School, Newcastle, the first integrated school outside Belfast, opens.

1987   ACT takes the first step in seeking coordinated funding.

1988 onwards   New integrated schools open province-wide and receive support from ACT.

1990   The Education Reform (Northern Ireland) Order 1989 is enacted.

APPENDIX 11

'ACT on shared schools': an All Children Together discussion document, June 1976

At a press conference held on Monday, 14 June 1976, at the Corrymeela Centre, Belfast, the All Children Together movement launched an important discussion document entitled 'ACT on shared schools'.

It suggests a new kind of shared community management, initially in schools which are already 'mixed'. These shared schools would offer a wider choice to parents, rather than the present 'dual' system of controlled (Protestant) and maintained (Catholic) schools.

The document is the result of many months of research and is the consensus of the views expressed to us regarding the form of shared schooling desired by the majority of parents in Northern Ireland. It is hoped that it will dispel any fears of 'forced integration' or interference with the right of parents to opt for 'separate' education for their children.

We would urge the education authorities and the churches to give careful consideration to this document and to invite wider discussion on the whole issue.

At a time when the reorganisation of secondary education seems imminent we feel that the religious and cultural integration of our children should also be taken into account.

Copies of the document are available from the address given below.

Elizabeth Benton
HONORARY SECRETARY
14 JUNE 1976

All Children Together
A new movement in Northern Ireland

> I do not know of any measures which would prepare the way for a better feeling in Ireland, than uniting children at an early age and bringing them up in the same school, leading them to commune with one another and to form those little intimacies and friendships which often subsist through life.
>
> DR JAMES DOYLE, ROMAN CATHOLIC BISHOP OF KILDARE AND LEIGHLIN, 1826

- WE BELIEVE and support these views expressed 150 years ago.
- WE BELIEVE that the high degree of religious segregation in the Northern Ireland education system is an obstacle to the solution of Northern Ireland's problems.
- WE BELIEVE that parents have the fundamental right to choose the kind of education that shall be given to their children.
- WE BELIEVE that the existing educational system of Northern Ireland permits excessive representation of the churches and their clergy in both Catholic (maintained) and Protestant (controlled) schools and that such high representation is unnecessary from an educational viewpoint.
- WE BELIEVE the essential role of the clergy in schools is in the religious education of their children.

Aims

The All Children Together movement seeks changes in the education system of Northern Ireland that will make it possible for parents who so wish to secure for their children an education in shared schools acceptable to all religious denominations and cultures in which the churches will provide religious education and pastoral care.

Definition of a shared school

WE BELIEVE a shared school to be one in which those of differing religious and cultural backgrounds share at all levels in management, staffing and pupils.

Types of shared schooling already exist in the province. We do not see that it would be necessary or practical to build new schools in order to provide parents with this choice.

1   **Finance**

WE BELIEVE that shared schools should be entirely financed from public funds through the area boards. Indeed, we believe that all schools should be financed entirely by area boards. This would place no extra burden on the budget as 'dual' schooling is completely uneconomical and probably outweighs the 15 per cent of initial building costs presently borne by the voluntary bodies.

2   **Composition of management committee**

WE BELIEVE that the 'four-and-two' system should be adopted, giving the local education authority – that is, the area board – a one-third stake in the management committee, representatives of parents and the local community making up the other two-thirds.

3   **Church involvement in the management of shared schools**

WE BELIEVE that integration is prevented in the main by a church view. We see clearly that the churches are naturally concerned about their influence on religious education. It seems to us that this is the issue which is causing major concern, although an equally serious concern is the difference in culture between the two sides of our community.

Ideally, we consider that clergy should be on management committees as persons chosen by the community or parents' representatives, not as 'church representatives with a continuing right'.

We believe that it is possible to develop such a system of management in some areas now, where sharing in the community is already established. This could be initiated by a voluntary stepping down of some of the clerical representatives to allow for greater representation from the local community.

We see a much more specific and important role for the clergy – in the provision of religious education, pastoral care and worship.

4   **Staffing**

WE BELIEVE that as shared schools will have a mixture of children from different religious and cultural backgrounds, the staff, both professional and ancillary, should reflect the same community spirit.

Appointments to senior posts

WE BELIEVE appointments to senior posts could be made by a joint committee of the area board and the school-management committee.

5   **Religious education**

WE BELIEVE that no hard and fast rules for individual schools should be laid down by the area boards concerned. Here is where the invaluable experience and expertise of the churches must be used to the full. The clergy of each denomination should be encouraged to be part of the school in the area where they have most to offer – i.e., the field of religious education.

The manner in which religious education is conducted may vary from school to school. The following options may be listed.

a   Since Christianity is the religion of our people a common religious-education syllabus could be devised, covering the large part of Christian belief that is common to all denominations.

b   Children could join together for classes in common religious education for a number of periods in the week.

c   Denominational instruction could be given in consultation with the appropriate church authorities.

d   Worship together should unite clergy, teachers, children and, at times, parents.

WE BELIEVE that teachers of religious education should be committed Christians and should be willing to teach the subject. This should obviate the distress felt by some teachers at the moment, who feel compelled to take classes in religious education, for which they have little enthusiasm. Furthermore, it should reassure parents and clergy who feel that commitment to religious practice may be diminished in a shared school.

Teachers of religious education bear a tremendous responsibility and much depends on each teacher's own attitude. It is a true saying that 'religion is caught, not taught'. Teaching staff should be able to attend courses to enable them to cope with the difficult task of communicating Christian belief to children today.

Historical and cultural studies

The two cultures in Northern Ireland have had their loyalties slanted in different directions. Only recently has there been any talk of 'rooting' them here. Schools reinforce this orientation by curriculum, sport etc. without ostensibly planning to do so.

We have much to be proud of in our past. Our contribution to the culture, religion and development of places other than Ireland is recorded in history. It is a fact that many of the planters coming here were really coming back to their ancestral homes. Ireland, in a sense, planted Scotland to some degree, particularly in St Columba's time, although a Dalriada had already been established there before that. We gave Scotland her name.

Along with Scotland, Wales, the Cornish peninsula, the Isle of Man, southern Ireland and Brittany in France, we belong to the Celtic race.

WE BELIEVE that the introduction of a comprehensive curriculum in Celtic studies would encourage an integrated ethnic pride and help to establish a shared identity. Within this curriculum would be social history, historical geography, environment studies, religion, music and the arts and linguistics.

Achievement of our aims

1   To demand that the Department of Education and the area boards introduce shared schools now, in development areas, in rural areas where duplication may already be uneconomical and especially in areas where sharing already exists at all levels throughout the community.
2   To press for integrated teacher-training colleges – the only section of post-school education in Northern Ireland that remains segregated.
3   To oppose the establishment of sectarian nursery schools.
4   To seek to change the present legislation, which in effect perpetuates a sectarian system of education.
5   To urge the Department of Education and the area boards to consult with parents on educational matters and before taking decisions regarding new schools.

6   To press for more involvement of parents and teachers in the management of schools.

7   To promote a new curriculum involving a common pattern of religious and moral education, and of historical and cultural studies.

8   To seek cooperation with local clergy in the provision of religious education and pastoral care.

General comment

The All Children Together movement is not advocating the closure of any schools nor the imposition of a uniform pattern of education within the province, but since three opinion polls taken over the last ten years have shown a majority of Catholics and a majority of Protestants to be in favour of shared schooling for their children, we feel this demand must be met. We are conscious of the depression felt by many parents who long to see integrated schooling but feel they are powerless against church and state authorities.

1   Parents' rights

The rights of parents are laid down in:

a   Education and Library (Northern Ireland) Order 1972, Article 34: 'pupils to be educated in accordance with the wishes of their parents'.

b   The *Universal declaration of human rights*, 1948, Article 26.3: 'parents have a prior right to choose the kind of education that shall be given to their children'.

c   Vatican II *Declaration on Christian education*, Section 6: 'parents who have the primary and inalienable right and duty to educate their children must enjoy true liberty in their choice of schools'.

d   The European Convention for the Protection of Human Rights.

It must be abundantly clear, therefore, that this movement has never been, nor will ever be, against Catholic schools. As we have said over and over again, how could we as parents deprive others of that which they wish for their children, namely freedom of choice in schools? Nor do we rejoice in the fact that the traffic appears to be in one direction only at the moment – Catholic children going to state schools.

However, since the aim of this movement is the creation of shared schools for those who want them, we must make reference to comments made to us by Protestant parents who are very keen to see their children going to schools with Catholic children, but fear the present Catholic system because of what they see as clerical monopoly in management. The introduction of parents' representatives on management committees would undoubtedly help the situation.

The presence of Protestant clergymen at the level of 50 per cent on the management committees of state schools deters many Catholic parents who also wish to see their children going to school with Protestant children. We are aware that in some areas the number of clergymen may be higher than 50 per cent. This leads some Catholics to say that they are not state schools, they are Protestant schools. Again, a reduction of clerical representatives would be taken as a sign of great goodwill in many areas.

2   The Department of Education

The Department of Education appears to be very reluctant at the moment to encourage those who provide schools to share when the opportunity arises. We do not feel that they adhere strictly to their own policy when they accept schemes submitted to them both from area boards and voluntary authorities where there is ample evidence of duplication. We feel that maintaining the status quo appears to be more important than avoiding unnecessary duplication and wastage of taxpayers' money – and this in these days of severe financial cutbacks.

The most recent example in this field was the acceptance by the department of plans for expansion in the nursery sector. While welcoming the expansion of nursery education, we deplore the construction of 'dual' nursery schools and the extension of the segregated system even to our three to four year olds. Prior to 1968 there were no segregated nursery schools. Why now?

3   The churches

The movement realises that there will be no progress towards a shared system of schooling unless the churches are in sympathy with it.
We ask the churches:

a To involve themselves in dialogue and discussion with us and with each other.
b To accept that, as lay people, we are also members of our respective churches and capable of having responsibility.
c To share with us as parents what has traditionally been the churches' responsibility in the past, namely the control of schools for the young.
d To consider urgently the establishment of adult centres for religious education on an interdenominational basis.

  i To encourage research into and debate about:
  ii The effectiveness and efficiency of church schools.
  iii The use of teachers and schools for evangelisation.
  iv The return of the churches to doctrinal teaching.

In conclusion

This movement is committed to helping all parents who wish to have shared schools for their children achieve that possibility.

While there have been many calls for pilot schemes to be set up, we would like to point to the many sections of the educational system where integration has always been accepted:

- Nursery schools (to 1968).
- Technical colleges.
- Government training institutes.
- Schools for handicapped children.
- Queen's University.

There are also a small number of primary schools where children of both communities are accommodated. A precedent has been created already. Do we need a pilot scheme?

We feel that everyone in the field of education should recognise that change is inevitable and that inquiry into a system which has lasted over 50 years is quite healthy and natural. Schools constantly take on different forms when viewed historically. As long as change is slow and by consent it should not be feared.

We feel that as much consideration should be given to the religious and cultural integration of our children as is currently being given to the reorganisation of secondary education. Indeed, we would hope that change in one direction will not be introduced without consideration of change in the other.

We do not seek change for change's sake; we seek change for our children's sake.

APPENDIX 12

Response to the Churches' Religious-Education Core-Curriculum Drafting Group, November 1990

13 University Street,
Belfast BT7 1FY
Northern Ireland
Telephone: (0232) 327335
(24 Hr. Answering)

19 Nov. 1990

Rev. H. KcKelvey
Hon. Sec.
Churches' R.E. Core-Curriculum-Drafting Group
283 Kingsway
Dunmurry
BT17 9AE

Dear Rev. McKelvey,
Further to my phonecall, I can now enclose a submission from All Children Together to the Churches' R.E. Core-Curriculum-Drafting Group.

The document was drawn up by the directors of ACT and contains some of our thinking on the rationale, which we, as advocates of integrated education by consent, would like to see embodied in a joint R.E. syllabus. The cooperation by Christians of differing denominations in this important task is very dear to our hearts. Indeed, we have long looked forward to it.

In the light of the movement's experience, through our annual seminars, the development of R.E. courses and the establishment of a Christian ethos in integrated schools, we would very much like the opportunity to give oral evidence to the working group, if your group thought it would be of benefit. Our written submission is just a summary of our views and, particularly in the programmes of study, we have touched only briefly on any possible content.

We look forward to hearing from you in the not-too-distant future and, in the meantime, our very best wishes and our prayers go with you in this most important task.

I am enclosing some copies of our latest information sheet.

Yours sincerely
Sr Anna
HON. SEC.

1   **The aims and objectives of All Children Together**
Founded in 1974, All Children Together was established for the advancement of integrated education by consent in Northern Ireland in order to make it possible for parents who so wish to secure for their children an education in planned shared schools acceptable to people of differing religious affiliations and cultural traditions and in which there will also be provision for religious education and pastoral care.

2   **Introduction**
a All Children Together (subsequently to be referred to as ACT in this paper) welcomes the cooperation between the four main churches the working group represents and wishes the working group well in its deliberations.
b ACT hopes that the particular needs of the other denominations in Northern Ireland, both Christian and non-Christian, will be provided for in the proposals.
c In addition, ACT hopes that the working group will adopt the principle that religious education should be an essential part of the complete education of any individual, regardless of personal belief.
d Since the conflict in Northern Ireland is quasi-religious, we believe the working group has a rare opportunity in the drawing up of an R.E. core curriculum, with its attendant skill areas, aims and objectives, to affect the mindset of each child of school age by correcting myths and encouraging a more harmonious outlook.
e ACT notes that the integrated schools are not represented on the working group, but is confident that the group will take into consideration the needs of such schools. Indeed, despite the exemption clause in Para. 13 (1)b of the order, which refers to the teaching of R.E. in controlled integrated schools, ACT believes the integrated schools would wish to be included in the development of an agreed R.E. core curriculum for the province.

3   **Suggested aims and objectives of an R.E. core curriculum in Northern Ireland (for a variety of key stages)**
• To develop in pupils an understanding of the main tenets of the world's great religions.
• To help pupils to appreciate the good in religions other than Christianity.
• To foster in pupils pleasure in the concept that we are all part of a worldwide brotherhood.
• To encourage in pupils the ability and the desire to see good in others, especially in others on this island.
• To enable pupils to understand that we all sprang from an honourable Celtic church in Ireland.

- To appreciate the great missionary role and achievements of the saints and scholars of that time in our history and their influence in Europe.
- To acknowledge the role of 'accident of birth' in denominational affiliation.
- To lead pupils to understand that Catholics and Protestants belong to the same religious family, viz. Christianity.
- To make clear to pupils in the Northern Ireland context that Christ's second commandment applies to everyone.

4   **Some proposed content for the core curriculum**

   a ACT believes that in the core curriculum pupils should be required to learn about the beliefs and values that distinguish the great world religions from each other – different founders, different holy books, different tenets etc. In a transnational context pupils should be taught how Catholics and Protestants belong to the same religion and that there is more to unite than to divide us.

   b However, the historical and doctrinal divisions that do exist between Catholics and Protestants should be explained honestly and objectively and correct terminology (e.g. schism, heresy) should be used as required.

   c Although a major concern of religious education should be with all religions, the core curriculum should focus particularly on religion as practised in the society in which pupils live.

   d ACT acknowledges the centrality of the Bible in R.E. However, we believe that unless the core curriculum has a convincing rationale and relevance for pupils, R.E. will falter and fail. It is for this reason that we advocate a more experimental approach, based on the biblical foundation of Christ's two great commandments and the importance of reconciliation.

   e In the report of the Fifth Working Party on Social Questions, appointed jointly by the Irish Council of Churches and by the Irish hierarchy of the Roman Catholic Church, the following statement was made:

> The teaching of Religion in schools of both traditions must have explicitly and deliberately an Ecumenical dimension. The stereotypes which each community may have inherited regarding the religious beliefs and practices of the other must be firmly rejected and replaced by exact and sympathetic understanding.

ACT concurs fully with this statement and believes firmly that the single most important contribution an R.E. core curriculum could make would be to provide a framework within which the reconciling power of the gospel will be freed to illuminate and challenge claims to orthodoxy which are often used as an excuse for not examining the other community's beliefs or practices.

5   **Religious education and history**

a ACT hopes the working group will respond seriously and imaginatively to the challenge made to it by the history working group in its proposals (2.12). ACT considers that a study of Ireland from the fifth to the ninth century is of particular importance.

b This is such a critical period in the history of this island and in the development of Christianity here and in Europe that we consider it essential that it should be studied by all pupils in the province during the statutory school years.

c We note that this period is well documented as an optional history study unit in Key Stage 2 of the history programme of study. However, we believe that as the religious divisions in our province arise, in the main, from Scots Presbyterianism and Irish Catholicism, the understanding of the religious links between Ulster and Scotland, and our common Celtic ancestry, merit detailed study. We would therefore urge the working group to include the study of this period in the core R.E. curriculum.

6   **The weak position of religious education within the school curriculum**

a ACT hopes that by being bold and imaginative in its approach, the working group will lay firm foundations for the revitalising of R.E. in schools. It is generally recognised that the subject is in a perilous state. It is being squeezed out of the place it rightly deserves in the centre of the curriculum. We believe that the reasons why the subject is held in such low esteem at present are as follows:

  i The subject is not inspected by the Department of Education and therefore not regarded as an academic subject.

  ii There are too few qualified teachers.

The role of DENI in inspecting R.E.

b ACT believes that part of the key to remedying the entire situation lies within the scope of the working group, which can prescribe an essential core element of the R.E. curriculum to be studied in all grant-aided schools, with adequate resources for teachers and opportunities for INSET. We believe that this section of the R.E. curriculum at least should be inspected by the DENI inspectorate. To leave it to individual boards of governors to decide whether to have R.E. inspected or not, as the present order suggests, seems to us to be a sure way of guaranteeing that R.E. will remain the Cinderella of the school curriculum.

c We appreciate the sensitivities that exist regarding this whole area within the province. We recognise also that essential denominational instruction will be required in some schools and by some parents. The responsibility for the testing or inspection of this will remain, rightly, with the church/diocesan authorities concerned. This does not invalidate the recommendation made in the preceding paragraph.

Support for teachers

d The difficulties faced in the past by teachers who wished to adopt an ecumenical approach to the teaching of R.E. without an agreed core curriculum or the collaboration of the churches have been considerable. An agreed core curriculum in R.E. would concentrate the minds of teachers and clergy on the content of what they are teaching, the methods used to impart that knowledge, their interpretation of the facts and the effects on the children.

e Conversely, we ask that special consideration be given to teachers who, having taught for many years in a segregated system of education, feel uncomfortable with having to discuss, in a classroom situation, topics which may have been totally outside their own tradition and identity.

7   **Religious education and the cross-curriculum themes**

a ACT believes that there is no other subject on the curriculum which can contribute to the cross-curricular themes as extensively and significantly as religious education.

b It is our hope that the R.E. core curriculum will provide many opportunities for work in the fields of health education (H.E.) and careers education (C.E.) as well as in cultural heritage (C.H.). It has definite potential also for inclusion in the field of economic awareness (E.A.), and even information technology (I.T.).

c We feel that an imaginative core curriculum in R.E., highlighting its potential contribution right across the school curriculum, will do a great deal to enhance its status.

8   **Religious education and resources**

a ACT hopes the opportunity will be taken to build on all the good curriculum-development work done in R.E. in recent years, especially those developments relevant to EMU and cultural heritage, notably John Greer's Religion in Ireland project, the Irish Council of Churches and Irish Commission for Justice and Peace 'looking at churches and worship', the materials of the Schools Cultural-Studies project and, most recently, the Religion in Ireland: Yesterday, Today and Tomorrow project.

b ACT believes that R.E. work generally will benefit greatly from a wider use of so-called 'ordinary material'. For example, many young people do not understand the hurt and fear caused by sectarian songs and slogans. On the more positive side, we think a greater use of our considerable talents in poetry, music, literature and drama within the study of R.E. will make the subject more interesting and relevant.

9   **Religious education and worship**

a We appreciate that it is within the remit of the working group to comment on the arrangements for religious education, which consists both of what is taught and what is 'caught', and we hope that all schools will be encouraged to find time for worship together, uniting clergy, teachers, pupils and, at times, parents.

Conclusion

For too long, responsibility for the interpretation of the gospel of Jesus Christ to our children has been left in the hands of people presenting their own denominational or individual religious attitudes in Northern Ireland and the political situation in which we live. This is understandable but not justifiable. *Religious education can only be justified on the curriculum of Northern Ireland's schools if it is being effective as a reconciling influence rather than as a dividing one.*

We end with a quotation from Bishop Ndola of Zambia, speaking at the Plenary Session of the Vatican Secretariat for Promoting Christian Unity, November 1979:

> ECUMENISM should be present in Catechesis. In particular, local churches who (like ourselves in Africa) live in a pluralistic society have a responsibility in developing an ecumenical religious education programme, especially in State schools and Institutes of Higher Education.

ALL CHILDREN TOGETHER
20 NOVEMBER 1990

APPENDIX 13

Enrolments in integrated schools in Northern Ireland, September 2008

SCHOOL/COLLEGE	LOCATION	OPENED	2003	2004	2005	2006	2007	2008
Lagan College	Belfast	1981	1,020	1,040	1,124	1,150	1,150	1,200
Forge CIPS*	Belfast	1985	212	226	213	230	250	249
Hazelwood College	Belfast	1985	721	744	740	804	810	845
Hazelwood IPS*	Belfast	1985	456	452	455	455	454	456
All Children's CIPS	Newcastle	1986	211	208	211	199	203	203
Bridge IPS	Banbridge	1987	411	410	414	408	413	409
Mill Strand IPS*	Portrush	1987	180	181	210	190	196	192
Windmill IPS*	Dungannon	1988	217	222	231	230	228	234
Braidside IPS*	Ballymena	1989	336	345	351	346	351	370
Enniskillen IPS*	Enniskillen	1989	235	243	261	235	239	240
Omagh IPS*	Omagh	1990	239	232	276	291	300	325
Portadown IPS*	Portadown	1990	223	222	218	220	228	234
Brownlow CIC	Craigavon	1991	377	410	410	434	439	450
Carhill CIPS	Garvagh	1991	41	46	42	44	55	40
Corran IPS*	Larne	1991	199	190	189	201	212	208
Oakgrove IPS*	L'derry	1991	460	452	445	467	451	441
Acorn IPS*	Carrickfergus	1992	229	229	229	230	254	260
Oakgrove IC	L'derry	1992	852	876	849	846	800	850
Cranmore IPS*	Belfast	1993	211	193	215	208	223	209
Loughview IPS*	Belfast	1993	348	368	415	437	435	420
Saints and Scholars IPS*	Armagh	1993	240	250	275	272	274	258
Erne IC	Enniskillen	1994	341	332	362	375	419	415
Shimna IC	Newcastle	1994	495	492	514	511	509	510
Cedar IPS*	Crossgar	1995	213	216	211	217	220	225
Drumragh IC	Omagh	1995	563	519	493	525	610	580
Integrated College	Dungannon	1995	489	483	467	462	467	430
Newbridge IC	Loughbrickland	1995	498	514	502	504	500	500
Portaferry CIPS	Portaferry	1995	84	84	86	83	80	73
Hilden CIPS	Hilden	1996	69	69	60	47	35	0
North Coast IC	Coleraine	1996	527	522	512	534	535	495
Oakwood IPS*	Derriaghy	1996	206	192	224	230	231	232
Rathenraw CIPS	Antrim	1996	111	105	101	94	84	82

SCHOOL/COLLEGE	LOCATION	OPENED	2003	2004	2005	2006	2007	2008
Slemish IC	Ballymena	1996	677	681	690	720	710	720
Annsborough CIPS*	Castlewellan	1997	42	46	50	55	62	54
Malone IC	Belfast	1997	799	797	800	791	790	797
Strangford IC	Carrowdore	1997	466	486	469	488	505	526
Ulidia IC	Carrickfergus	1997	500	522	529	530	540	540
Bangor Central CIPS	Bangor	1998	498	531	537	561	561	560
Down Academy CIC	Downpatrick	1998	304	297	300	300	240	0
Forthill CIC	Lisburn	1998	891	867	867	867	873	880
Kilbroney CIPS	Rostrevor	1998	88	96	93	93	105	105
Kircubbin CIPS	Kircubbin	1998	126	119	111	103	102	121
Priory CIC	Holywood	1998	446	477	489	418	420	445
Spires IPS	Magherafelt	1999	163	183	188	201	200	202
Millennium IPS*	Carryduff	2000	97	105	155	195	208	218
Carnlough CIPS	Carnlough	2001	27	37	41	41	52	48
Sperrin IC	Magherafelt	2002	115	196	268	353	403	442
Glengormley CIPS*	Glengormley	2003	185	150	160	155	155	167
Maine IPS*	Randalstown	2003	17	30	48	86	104	117
Round Tower CIPS*	Antrim	2003	120	134	195	187	216	245
Armagh IC	Armagh	2004		50	108	153	140	61
Lir IPS	Ballycastle	2004		17	26	0	0	0
Drumlins IPS	Ballynahinch	2004		12	22	37	61	83
Glencraig CIPS	Holywood	2004		186	210	225	230	253
Groomsport CIPS	Groomsport	2004		21	21	25	0	0
Phoenix IPS	Cookstown	2004		17	42	54	80	105
Roe Valley IPS	Limavady	2004		25	44	72	101	126
Groarty CIPS	L'derry	2005			43	40	36	31
Ballycastle CIPS*	Ballycastle	2006				100	124	129
Clogher Valley IPS	Fivemiletown	2006				12	20	23
Crumlin CIC	Crumlin	2006				352	350	400
Rowallane IC	Belfast	2006				40	86	0
Rowandale IPS	Moira	2007					18	34
Kindle CIPS	Ballykinlar	2007					36	0
Blackwater IC	Downpatrick	2008						340
Cliftonville CIPS	Belfast	2008						182
TOTAL			16,575	17,149	17,811	18,733	19,183	19,589

*denotes a pre-school unit, including reception classes, nurseries and playgroups

Lir IPS closed in June 2005 following the successful transformation of Ballycastle PS.
Groomsport CIPS closed in June 2006 owing to decreasing enrolments.
Kindle CIPS closed in August 2008.

Hilden CIPS closed in December 2008.
Blackwater IC came about as the result of a merger between Rowallane IC and Down Academy.

These figures include all children being educated in integrated schools, including pre-school provision and those with statements of special educational needs, which explains any discrepancy with the official Department of Education figures.

61 schools
    16 grant-maintained integrated colleges
    4 controlled integrated colleges
    23 grant-maintained integrated primary schools
    17 controlled integrated primary schools
    1 independent primary – Clogher Valley IPS

APPENDIX 14

ACT seminars and conferences, 1974–99

1974   Interdenominational schools: why? how? and the way ahead
1976   Religious education in shared schools (this had to be cancelled because two of the main speakers, who were Catholic, were prevented from coming to Belfast by episcopal pressure)
1978   Shared schools in action
1978   Agreed syllabi in religious education
1979   Cooperation in higher education (teacher training)
1979   The case for a shared curriculum
1980   Sharing and integration: English, Welsh and Scottish models and practice
1982   Shared schools in action
1983   Education across the religious and educational divide
1986   Into the future: the role of integrated education
1990   Changes and challenges: a study of the new Education Reform (Northern Ireland) Order 1989
1991   Children, churches and culture (part 1): religious education and chaplaincy
1991   Children, churches and culture (part 2): our common cultural heritage
1999   Private seminar for clergy on the work of an existing joint Anglican–Roman Catholic school in England

APPENDIX 15

An international list of joint Roman Catholic–Anglican schools and third-level colleges

1 St Columba College, Andrew's Farm, South Australia
2 Gaelscoil an tSlí Dála, Ballaghmore, County Laois, Republic of Ireland
3 The Doane Stuart Schools, Albany, New York, United States of America
4 St Aidan's Church of England High School and St John Fisher Catholic High School, Harrogate, North Yorkshire, United Kingdom
5 St Cuthbert Mayne School, Torquay, Devon, United Kingdom
6 St Bede's School, Redhill, Surrey, United Kingdom
7 Roehampton University, London, United Kingdom
8 Trinity School, Teignmouth, Devon, United Kingdom
9 Liverpool Hope University, Liverpool, United Kingdom
10 St Augustine of Canterbury School, Taunton, Somerset, United Kingdom
11 St Edward's Royal Free Ecumenical Middle School, Windsor, Berkshire, United Kingdom
12 St Francis Xavier School, Richmond, North Yorkshire, United Kingdom
13 The Bishops' Church of England and Roman Catholic Primary School, Chelmsford, Essex, United Kingdom
14 St Edward's School, Poole, Dorset, United Kingdom
15 All Saints Inter-Church Primary School, March, Cambridgeshire, United Kingdom
16 Emmaus Church of England and Roman Catholic Primary School, Liverpool, United Kingdom
17 St Michael's Catholic and Church of England High School, South Yorkshire, United Kingdom
18 The Academy of St Francis of Assisi, Liverpool, United Kingdom
19 St Joseph's Catholic and Anglican High School, Wrexham, Wales, United Kingdom
20 Christ College, Cheltenham, Gloucestershire, United Kingdom

APPENDIX 16

Forge directors' diary of developments, 1990–2

February 1990
The Department of Education had advised FIPS not to wait for the new order to become law as this might take some time. Mr Roy of the Department of Education also wanted a letter from ACT stating their asking price for the property. Cecil Linehan was to explain the situation to ACT. She said that ACT did understand but were under pressure from Nuffield. The loan from Nuffield with which ACT purchased the school in 1987 was interest free for two years. Nuffield now wanted the loan repaid and interest was due.

April 1990
A letter was sent by the solicitors to FIPS directors regarding agreeing the price of the Balmoral Avenue premises, confirming names of trustees to whom property should be transferred and pointing out that they (the Department of Education) had queried the use of the limited company as a suitable vehicle for transfer. They now accepted this as possible but it would have to be resolved with the Department of Education.

July 1990
A letter from the Department of Education said that the site had been valued at £325,000 and they were now recommending going ahead with the vesting procedures.

10 September 1990
The solicitors wrote to ACT and said that FIPS would purchase the premises from ACT and pay the interest due. It was agreed that the chairman and the treasurer should go to the bank man with a copy of the letter from the Department of Education regarding the £325,000 valuation and explain the situation.

17 September 1990
An emergency meeting was called to discuss the solicitors' letter of 10 September 1990 and ACT's request for a rent grant. There was disquiet over ACT's demand for the grant. Cecil Linehan explained that FIPS would not lose any money through this as any rental payments made to ACT could be claimed back from BELB. Nuffield had written to say that repayment of the £110,000 would complete the legal repayment of the loan but that FIPS had

had the benefit of the loan interest free for years, during which time the property had increased substantially. In view of this they felt that FIPS should consider making a donation to the integrated funds and, in particular, to schools that had not repaid their loans on time and were now carrying heavy interest costs.

December 1990
The FIPS directors felt that ACT should receive all expenses incurred but were not in favour of a further payment for hidden costs. This had never been discussed before. FIPS directors might consider a donation when all finances were being sorted out. Great concern was expressed about the financial situation. Margaret Kennedy said that Mr McCormack of the Department of Education had said that 100 per cent would be available from 1 April 1991 and that this would save FIPS £48,000 – 15 per cent of the purchase price.

March 1991
Deliberations and anxieties about the correct path to follow were ongoing. ACT's hard expenses were received on 4 February 1991; they would not pursue soft expenses and would honour their commitments to Forge.

June 1991
A letter between the Department of Education and FIPS advised not to proceed any further in the acquisition of the property at 4 Balmoral Avenue. A letter of 25 July 1990 referred to the transfer of the property as a maintained school, qualifying for 85 per cent of capital expenditure. A letter between ACT and the solicitor said that he thought the the Department of Education letter of 6 June 1991 was a 'scare' and should not be regarded as a negative. He added that he thought FIPS should be seeking a meeting with the Department of Education at the highest level. Meanwhile, the overdraft reached £6,000.

July 1991
A letter from Forge to BELB said that CIS had been granted conditionally.

September 1991
A joint meeting of the Board of Governors and the Board of Directors requested a meeting with the minister. Nothing happened.

October 1991
The Board of Directors heard from the Department of Education that they would not accept a proposal for a larger school on this site. The Board of Governors had withdrawn its application for increase in enrolment to 400.

February 1992
The overdraft had reached £13,723. The bank manager refused to extend it; no more cheques could be written.

March 1992
A letter between BELB and ACT said that BELB was required to provide premises for the school. BELB sought a lease for one year, to be renewed, to enable it to carry out an investment appraisal.

Acknowledgements

Most sincere thanks are due to members of ACT, other activists in the Northern Ireland integrated-education movement and representatives of charitable trusts who provided useful documentation and helped to explain events and developments in conversation, interviews, notes and e-mails. In particular the author would like to thank: Wallis Johnson; Bettie Benton; Brian Garrett; John Kennedy; Jill McIvor; Yvonne Friers; Brian Lambkin; Helen McHugh; Colm Cavanagh; Msgr Barry Wimes; the late Tom Linehan; and members of the committee who steered this book towards publication – Cecil Linehan, Margaret Kennedy, Thelma Sheil, Bill Brown and the late Basil McIvor. He is also grateful for the assistance of the staffs of the Integrated Education Fund, the Northern Ireland Council for Integrated Education, St Bede's joint Anglican–Roman Catholic School in Redhill, BBC Northern Ireland, Belfast Central Library, the Linen Hall Library and the Public Record Office of Northern Ireland.

Abbreviations

ACT	All Children Together
BELTIE	Belfast Trust for Integrated Education
NAGIE	North Armagh Group for Integrated Education
SUTIE	South Ulster Trust for Integrated Education
FIPS	Forge Integrated Primary School
CIS	Controlled Integrated Primary School
IEF	Integrated Education Fund
DENI	Northern Ireland Department of Education
NIO	Northern Ireland Office
NICIE	Northern Ireland Council for Integrated Education
BELB	Belfast Education and Library Board
SEELB	South Eastern Education and Library Board
SELB	Southern Education and Library Board
WELB	Western Education and Library Board
NEELB	North Eastern Education and Library Board

Bibliography

This book is based primarily on the All Children Together papers, which are due to be lodged in the Public Record Office of Northern Ireland. Though placed in box files, they have yet to be calendared and fully referenced.

The author also had access to the late Basil McIvor's files of press cuttings. A single, but large, file on integrated education in PRONI (press mark ED/32/B/1/12/1) informed much of Chapter 4.

BOOKS, ARTICLES, REPORTS

Akenson, D.H., 'Pre-university education, 1921–84' in J.R. Hill (ed.), *A new history of Ireland*, vii: *Ireland, 1921–1984* (Oxford: Clarendon Press, 2003).

Akenson, D.H., 'Pre-university education, 1870–1921' in W.E. Vaughan (ed.), *A new history of Ireland*, vi: *Ireland under the union ii: 1870–1921* (Oxford: Clarendon Press, 1996).

Akenson, D.H., *Half the world from home: perspectives on the Irish in New Zealand, 1860–1950* (Wellington: Victoria University Press, 1990).

Akenson, D.H., 'Pre-university education, 1782–1870' in W.E. Vaughan (ed.), *A new history of Ireland*, v: *Ireland under the union i: 1801–1870* (Oxford: Clarendon Press, 1989).

Akenson, D.H., *A mirror to Kathleen's face: education in independent Ireland, 1922–60* (Montreal and Kingston: McGill-Queen's University Press, 1975).

Akenson, D.H., *Education and enmity: the control of schooling in Northern Ireland, 1920–50* (Newton Abbot: David and Charles Ltd for the Institute of Irish Studies, Queen's University, Belfast, 1973).

Akenson, D.H., *The Irish education experiment: the national system of education in the nineteenth century* (London: Routledge and Kegan Paul and Toronto: University of Toronto Press, 1969).

Akenson, D.H., 'National education and the realities of Irish life, 1831–1900', *Éire-Ireland*, iv (winter 1969), pp. 42–52.

Allport, G., *The nature of prejudice* (Cambridge, Mass: Addison-Wellesley, 1954).

Atkinson, N., *Irish education: a history of educational institutions* (Dublin: Allan Figgis, 1969).

Bardon, J., 'The plantation and the royal schools: Ulster before 1608' in T. Duncan (ed.), *The 1608 royal schools celebrate 400 years of history, 1608–2008* (Aghalee: the 1608 Royal Schools, 2007).

Bardon, J., *A history of Ulster* (Belfast: Blackstaff Press, 1992).

Bardon, J., *Belfast: an illustrated history* (Belfast: Blackstaff Press, 1982).

Bell, H.V., *Diligence and skill: 100 years of education at Belfast Institute* (Belfast Institute of Further and Higher Education, 2006).

Brown, M., *Public opinion survey: integrated education in Northern Ireland* (Belfast: Northern Ireland Council for Integrated Education, 2003).

Cairns, E., *Caught in the crossfire: children and the Northern Ireland conflict* (Belfast: Appletree Press, 1987).

Carson, T. and C. Jamison, *Integrate to accumulate: beyond conflict, how a shared school system fuels social and economic growth* (Toronto: Alexandrian Press, 2006).

Catholic Church: Irish Episcopal Conference, *Directory on ecumenism in Ireland* (Dublin: Veritas, 1976).

Caul, L. (ed.), *Schools under scrutiny: the case of Northern Ireland* (London: Macmillan, 1990).

Chadwick, P., *Schools of reconciliation: issues in joint Roman Catholic–Anglican education* (London and New York: Cassell, 1994).

Connolly, S.J., 'Mass politics and sectarian conflict, 1823–30' in W.E. Vaughan (ed.), *A new history of Ireland, v: Ireland under the union i: 1801–1870* (Oxford: Clarendon Press, 1989), pp. 74–80.

Connolly, S.J. 'Catholicism in Ulster' in P. Roebuck (ed.), *Plantation to partition: essays in Ulster history in honour of J.L. McCracken* (Belfast: Blackstaff Press, 1981).

Darby, J., P. Murray, S. Dunn, S. Farran and J. Harris, *Schools apart? Education and community in Northern Ireland* (Belfast: New University of Ulster, 1977).

Department of Education, Northern Ireland, *Integrated education: a framework for transformation* (Belfast: Department of Education, 1996).

Department of Education, Northern Ireland, *Education in Northern Ireland: proposals for reform* (Belfast: Department of Education, Northern Ireland, 1988).

Department of Education, Northern Ireland, *Schools and demographic trends: a backcloth to planning* (Belfast: Department of Education, 1981).

Dunn S., J. Darby and K. Mullan, 'Integrated schools in Northern Ireland', *Oxford Review of Education*, xv, no. 2 (1989).

Dunn S., J. Darby and K. Mullan, 'The role of education in the Northern Ireland conflict', *Oxford Review of Education*, xii, no. 3 (1986).

Dunn S., J. Darby and K. Mullan, *Schools together?* (Coleraine: Centre for the Study of Conflict, University of Ulster, 1984).

Farren, S., *The politics of Irish education 1920–65* (Belfast: Institute of Irish Studies, Queen's University, 1995).

Fisk, R., *The point of no return: the strike which broke the British in Ulster* (London: Times Books, 1975).

Flannery, A., *Vatican Council II: the conciliar and post-conciliar documents* (Wilmington: Scholarly Resources, 1975).

Fraser, G. and V. Morgan, *In the frame: integrated education in Northern Ireland: the implications of expansion* (Coleraine: Centre for the Study of Conflict, University of Ulster, 1999).

Fraser, M., *Children in conflict* (London: Secker and Warburg, 1973).

Gallagher, T.M., *Education and religion in Northern Ireland: the majority – minority review no. 1* (Coleraine: Centre for the Study of Conflict, University of Ulster, 1989).

Gallagher, T.M. and S. Dunn, 'Community relations in Northern Ireland: attitudes to contact and integration' in P. Stringer and G. Robinson (eds.), *Social attitudes in Northern Ireland* (Belfast: Blackstaff Press, 1991).

Gallagher, T.M., A. Smith and A. Montgomery, *Integrated education in Northern Ireland, report 1: participation, profile and practice* (Coleraine: UNESCO Centre, University of Ulster, 2003).

Harris, M., *The Catholic Church and the foundation of the northern state* (Cork University Press, 1993).

Higher Education Review Group, *The future structure of teacher education in Northern Ireland: an interim report of the Higher Education Review Group* (Belfast: HMSO, 1980).

Independent Strategic Review of Education, *Schools for the future: funding, strategy, sharing: report of the Independent Strategic Review of Education* (Bangor: Department of Education, 2006).

Irish Council of Churches and Roman Catholic Church Joint Group on Social Questions, *Violence in Ireland: a report to the churches* (Belfast: Christian Journals, 1976).

Irwin, C.J., 'Integrated education: from theory to practice in divided societies', *Prospects: Quarterly Review of Comparative Education*, xxii, no. 1 (March 1992).

Irwin, C.J., *Education, peace building and human rights* (Belfast: Institute of Irish Studies, Queen's University, 1994).

Irwin, C.J., *Integrated education: a moral issue: first call for children* (New York: UNICEF, 1992).

Irwin, C.J., *Education and the development of social integration in divided societies* (Belfast: Northern Ireland Council for Integrated Education, 1991).

Kavanagh, C.M., 'Integrated schools and their impact on the local community' in C. Moffat (ed.), *Education for a change: integrated education and community relations in Northern Ireland* (Belfast: Fortnight Educational Trust, 1993).

Lambkin, B., *Opposite religions still? Interpreting Northern Ireland after the conflict* (Aldershot: Avebury, 1996).

Lemon, E., 'The transformation process viewed from the staffroom' in C. Moffat (ed.), *Education together for a change: integrated education and community relations in Northern Ireland* (Belfast: Fortnight Educational Trust, 1993).

Liechty, J., *Roots of sectarianism in Ireland: chronology and reflections* (Belfast: Irish Inter-Church Meeting, 1993).

Linehan, C., 'Reconciliation in Northern Ireland: the future: the role of education' in E. Hanna (ed.), *Proceedings of the Summer School of the Social Studies Conference* (Dublin: SSC Publications, 1987).

Mawhinney, B., *In the firing line: politics, faith, power and forgiveness* (London, HarperCollins, 1999).

Mawhinney, B. and R. Wells, *Conflict and Christianity in Northern Ireland*, Grand Rapids: Eerdmans, 1975).

McEwen, A., *Public policy in a divided society: schooling, culture and identity in Northern Ireland* (Aldershot: Ashgate, 1999).

McEwen, A. and J. Salters, *Integrated education: the views of parents*, Belfast: Queen's University, 1992).

McGaffin, P., 'The development of an integrated school' in Leslie Caul (ed.), *Schools under scrutiny: the case of Northern Ireland* (London: Macmillan, 1990).

McGonigle, J., A. Smyth and T.M. Gallagher, *Integrated education in Northern Ireland, report 3: the challenge of transformation* (Coleraine: UNESCO Centre, University of Ulster, 2003).

McIvor, B., *Hope deferred: experiences of an Irish unionist* (Belfast: Blackstaff Press, 1998).

Moffat, C., 'The transformation option' in *Education together for a change: integrated education and community relations in Northern Ireland* (Belfast: Fortnight Educational Trust, 1993).

Montgomery, A., G. Fraser, C. McGlynn, A. Smith and T. Gallagher, *Integrated education in Northern Ireland: integration in practice, report 2*, Nuffield Foundation, 2008 (gtcni.openrepository.com/gtcni/bitstream/2428/6018/1/Integration %20in%20Practice.pdf) (1 September 2009).

Morgan V., S. Dunn, E. Cairns and G. Fraser, *Breaking the mould: the roles of parents and teachers in the integrated schools in Northern Ireland* (Coleraine: Centre for the Study of Conflict, University of Ulster, 1992).

Murray, D., *Worlds apart: segregated schools in Northern Ireland* (Belfast: Appletree Press, 1985).

Northern Ireland assembly official report, iii, no. 3 (30 April 1974).

Northern Ireland assembly official report, iii, no. 7 (8 May 1974).

O'Connor, F., *A shared childhood: the story of integrated schools in Northern Ireland* (Belfast: Blackstaff Press and Integrated Education Fund, 2002).

O'Leary, C., S. Elliott and R.A. Wilford, *The Northern Ireland assembly 1982–1986: a constitutional experiment* (London: C. Hurst & Co. and Belfast: Queen's University Bookshop, 1988).

Osborne, R.D., R. Cormack and R.L. Miller (eds), *Education and policy in Northern Ireland* (Belfast: Queen's University of Belfast and the University of Ulster Policy Research Institute, 1978).

Parkes, S.M., 'Higher education, 1793–1908' in W.E. Vaughan (ed.), *A new history of Ireland*, vi: *Ireland under the union ii: 1870–1921* (Oxford: Clarendon Press, 1996).

Pollak, A. (ed.), *A citizens' inquiry: the Opshal report on Northern Ireland* (Dublin: Lilliput, 1993).

Sacred Congregation for Catholic Education, *The Catholic school* (Rome: Vatican Polyglot Press, 1977).

Shea, P., *Voices and the sound of drums: an Irish autobiography* (Belfast: Blackstaff Press, 1981).

Smith, A., 'Education and the conflict in Northern Ireland' in S. Dunn (ed.), *Facets of the conflict in Northern Ireland* (London: Macmillan, 1995).

Smith, A., *Extending inter-school links: an evaluation of contact between Protestant and Catholic pupils in Northern Ireland* (Coleraine: Centre for the Study of Conflict, University of Ulster, 1990).

Smith A., and A. Robinson, *Education for mutual understanding: the initial statutory years* (Coleraine: Centre for the Study of Conflict, University of Ulster), 1990.

Spencer, A.E.C.W., *Arguments for an integrated school system in education and policy in Northern Ireland* (Belfast: Policy Research Institute, 1987).

Spencer, A.E.C.W., 'Integration and segregation in the Northern Ireland educational system: Lagan College and its context', *Queen's News* (November 1982).

Spencer, T., 'All children apart' in *Fortnight: An Independent Review for Northern Ireland*, no. 176 (May 1980).

Trew, K., 'Evaluating the impact of contact schemes for Catholic and Protestant children' in J. Harbison (ed.), *Growing up in Northern Ireland* (Dublin: University Press, 1989).

Warm, D., and S. Bailie, *An exploratory study of the pattern of pupil recruitment to an integrated school* (Belfast: Hazelwood College/Northern Ireland Council for Integrated Education, 1994).

Whyte, J., *Interpreting Northern Ireland* (Oxford: Clarendon Press, 1990).

Wilson, D., and S. Dunn, *Integrated schools information for parents* (Coleraine: Centre for the Study of Conflict, University of Ulster, 1989).

Wright, F., *Integrated education and new beginnings in Northern Ireland* (Coleraine: Corrymeela Press, 1991).

NEWSPAPERS AND PERIODICALS

ACT-LETT: News from All Children Together, i–iv (1977–1995)
Belfast News Letter
Belfast Telegraph
Church of Ireland Gazette
Daily Telegraph
Education Times
Evening Press
Irish News
Irish Times
Newsweek
Sunday Independent
Sunday News
Sunday Times
The Tablet
The Times

OTHER MANUSCRIPT SOURCES

Donnelly, F.M., 'Transforming integrated education: an historical and contemporary analysis of developments in integrated education' (M.Ed. dissertation, University of Ulster, Jordanstown, 1998).
Holywood parish, weekly bulletin (unpublished, 19 February 1978).
Linehan, C., 'All Children Together: the struggle of Catholic parents to have their children educated with Protestant children in Northern Ireland' (M.Phil. dissertation, Irish School of Ecumenics/Trinity College, Dublin, 2005).
McGlynn, C., 'The impact of post-primary integrated education in Northern Ireland on past pupils' (D.Ed. thesis, University of Ulster, Jordanstown, 2001).
Sheil, T., 'The story of All Children Together and the founding of Lagan College' (B.Ed. thesis, Ulster Polytechnic, Jordanstown, 1982).

Notes

INTRODUCTION

1 B. Mawhinney, *In the firing line: politics, faith, power and forgiveness* (London, HarperCollins, 1999).
2 Ibid., p. 95; quotation from B. Mawhinney and R. Wells, *Conflict and Christianity in Northern Ireland* (Grand Rapids: Eerdmans, 1975).
3 N. Scott, DENI circular (one page only) numbered 'DENI 1982/21'.
4 Mawhinney, 1999, p. 96.
5 Ibid., p. 103.
6 B. Mawhinney, address to meeting of All-Party Parliamentary Committee on Northern Ireland, June 2008.

CHAP 1

1 D.H. Akenson, 'Pre-university education, 1782–1870' in W.E. Vaughan (ed.), *A new history of Ireland*, v: *Ireland under the union i: 1801–1870* (Oxford: Clarendon Press, 1989), pp. 527–31.
2 Ibid., pp. 529–30.
3 Ibid., p. 533.
4 S.J. Connolly, 'Mass politics and sectarian conflict, 1823–30' in W.E. Vaughan (ed.), *A new history of Ireland*, v: *Ireland under the union i: 1801–1870* (Oxford: Clarendon Press, 1989), pp. 74–80.
5 J. Bardon, *A history of Ulster* (Belfast: Blackstaff Press, 1992), p. 226.
6 S.J. Connolly, 'Catholicism in Ulster' in P. Roebuck (ed.), *Plantation to partition: essays in Ulster history in honour of J.L. McCracken* (Belfast: Blackstaff Press, 1981), p. 169.
7 J. Liechty, *Roots of sectarianism in Ireland: chronology and reflections* (Belfast: Irish Inter-Church Meeting, 1993), p. 27.
8 Akenson, 1989, p. 534.
9 Ibid., pp. 536–7.
10 J. Bardon, 'The plantation and the royal schools: Ulster before 1608' in T. Duncan (ed.), *The 1608 royal schools celebrate 400 years of history, 1608–2008* (Aghalee: The 1608 Royal Schools, 2007), pp. 13–14.
11 D.H. Akenson, 'Pre-university education, 1870–1921', in W.E. Vaughan (ed.), *A new history of Ireland*, vi: *Ireland under the union ii: 1870–1921* (Oxford: Clarendon Press, 1996), pp. 523–6.
12 H.V. Bell, *Diligence and skill: 100 years of education at Belfast Institute* (Belfast Institute of Further and Higher Education, 2006), pp. 22–6.
13 S.M. Parkes, 'Higher education, 1793–1908' in W.E. Vaughan (ed.), *A new history of Ireland*, vi: *Ireland under the union ii: 1870–1921* (Oxford: Clarendon Press, 1996), p. 569.

14 D.H. Akenson, *Education and enmity: the control of schooling in Northern Ireland, 1920–50* (Newton Abbot: David and Charles Ltd for the Institute of Irish Studies, Queen's University, Belfast, 1973), p. 41.
15 Ibid., p. 66.
16 Ibid., p. 52.
17 Ibid., pp. 79 and 82.
18 Ibid., p. 108.
19 Ibid., p. 114.
20 J. Bardon, *Belfast: an illustrated history* (Belfast: Blackstaff Press, 1982), p. 250.
21 Akenson, 1973, p. 168.
22 *Belfast News-Letter*, 9 November 1946.
23 Ibid.
24 P. Shea, *Voices and the sound of drums: an Irish autobiography* (Belfast: Blackstaff Press, 1981), p. 162.
25 J. Bardon, *A history of Ulster* (Belfast: Blackstaff Press, 1992), pp. 595–6.

CHAP 2

1 *Belfast Telegraph*, 30 April 1974.
2 B. McIvor, *Hope deferred: experiences of an Irish unionist* (Belfast: Blackstaff Press, 1998), p. 97.
3 Ibid., p. 75.
4 Ibid., p. 111.
5 Ibid., p. 112.
6 Ibid., p. 113.
7 *Belfast Telegraph*, 30 April 1974.
8 McIvor, 1998, p. 114.
9 *Belfast News Letter*, 1 May 1974.
10 *Irish Press*, 4 May 1974.
11 *Belfast News Letter*, 1 May 1974.
12 *Irish Times*, 6 May 1974.
13 *Irish Times*, 10 May 1974.
14 *Irish Times*, 1 May 1974.
15 *Belfast Telegraph*, 8 May 1974.
16 Ibid.
17 Ibid.
18 *Sunday News*, 5 May 1974.
19 *Irish Times*, 1 May 1974.
20 *Irish Times*, 1 May 1974; *Irish News*, 1 May 1974.
21 *Belfast Telegraph*, 3 May 1974.
22 *Irish Times*, 9 May 1974; McIvor, 1998, pp. 114–17.
23 *Northern Ireland assembly official report*, iii, no. 3 (30 April 1974).
24 *Northern Ireland assembly official report*, iii, no. 7 (8 May 1974).
25 Ibid.
26 *The Times*, 10 May 1974.
27 Ibid.
28 Ibid.
29 *Irish Times*, 10 May 1974.

30   Ibid.
31   Ibid.
32   *Irish Times*, 6 May 1974.
33   Ibid.
34   R. Fisk, *The point of no return: the strike which broke the British in Ulster* (London: Times Books, 1975), p. 140; Bardon, 1992, pp. 707–11.
35   McIvor, 1998, p. 121.
36   Ibid., p. 116.
37   Ibid., p. 122.

CHAP 3

1   Speaking at a peace meeting in the Grosvenor Hall, Belfast, 11 September 1974, 'ACT information leaflet 002' (ACT papers, 1974).
2   T. Sheil, 'The story of All Children Together and the founding of Lagan College' (B.Ed. thesis, Ulster Polytechnic, 1982), p. 12.
3   'ACT information leaflet 001' (ACT papers, 1974).
4   Sheil, 1982, p. 13.
5   C. Linehan, 'All Children Together: the struggle of Catholic parents to have their children educated with Protestant children in Northern Ireland' (M.Phil. thesis, Irish School of Ecumenics/Trinity College, Dublin, 2003), p. 33.
6   T. Sheil, pers. comm., February 2008.
7   Linehan, 2003, p. 34.
8   Ibid.
9   Sheil, 1982, p. 14.
10   A. Flannery, *Vatican Council II: the conciliar and post-conciliar documents* (Wilmington: Scholarly Resources, 1975), p. 726.
11   Ibid., p. 732.
12   Ibid., p. 803.
13   Linehan, 2003, p. 37.
14   *The Tablet*, 11 June 1977.
15   Ibid.
16   *Belfast Telegraph*, 22 March 1977.
17   *The Tablet*, 11 June 1977.
18   *Daily Telegraph*, 22 March 1977.
19   *The Tablet*, 11 June 1977.
20   Linehan, 2003, p. 38.
21   Ibid.
22   Ibid.
23   Ibid.
24   Linehan, 2003, p. 40.
25   Holywood parish, weekly bulletin (unpublished, 19 February 1978); Linehan, 2003, p. 48.
26   Sheil, 1982, p. 14.
27   *Irish News*, 23 February 1978.
28   *Evening Press*, 22 February 1978.
29   *Irish Times*, 14 March 1978.
30   *Irish Times*, 15 May 1981.
31   The case came to court in Dublin in May 1981 (High Court, no. 2936P, 1978). The bishop was awarded damages of IR£12,000, which was generally regarded as a derisory sum for a Catholic bishop in an Irish court in the 1980s. *Irish Times*, 13–16 May 1981.
32   Linehan, 2003, p. 44.
33   *Belfast Telegraph*, 9 April 1974.
34   Ibid.
35   B. Brown and M. Kennedy, pers. comm., February 2008.
36   C. Linehan, pers. comm., February 2008.
37   Ibid.
38   Ibid.
39   ACT, early document (ACT papers, n.d.).
40   See Appendix 11.
41   'Parents have a prior right to choose the kind of education that shall be given to their children', United Nations, *Universal declaration of human rights* (1948, www.un.org/en/documents/udhr/) (1 September 2009), Article 26.3.
42   'Parents who have the primary and inalienable right and duty to educate their children must enjoy true liberty in their choice of schools', *Declaration on Christian education*, Section 6 in Flannery, 1975, p. 731.
43   'Pupils to be educated in accordance with the wishes of their parents', Education and Libraries (Northern Ireland) Order 1972 (Belfast: HMSO, 1972), Article 34, p. 26.
44   G. Allport, *The nature of prejudice* (Cambridge, Mass: Addison-Wellesley, 1954), p. 489.
45   C. Linehan, pers. comm., February 2008.
46   *Irish Times*, 11 November 1974.
47   Sr Agnes Devlin was prevented (perhaps by episcopal censure) from coming to the conference so Tony Spencer stood in for her and gave very interesting examples of how Catholic religious education was delivered outside the Catholic school system in England, Australia, New Zealand and the USA.
48   Allport, 1954, p. 489.
49   The full text of 'ACT on shared schools' is reproduced in Appendix 11.
50   ACT conference papers (ACT papers, 1976).
51   *Belfast Telegraph*, 30 March 1976.
52   'Aborted conference April '76' in 'All Children Together: background information' (ACT papers, 1978).
53   Ibid.
54   Ibid.
55   All seminars held from 1974 to 2001 and the topics they covered are listed in Appendix 14.
56   Sheil, 1982, p. 18.
57   A full list of these submissions and the bodies to which they were submitted is contained in Appendix 6.
58   Bound copies of the 27 published editions of *ACT-LETT* are available for consultation in the Linen Hall Library, 7 Donegall Square North, Belfast.
59   Sheil, 1982, cover page.

CHAP 4

1   R. Darlington, 'Note for the record – shared schools: meeting with Cardinal Conway, Bishop Philbin and Bishop Daly' (PRONI, Shared schools: inquiry into

integrated education, ED/32/B/1/12/1, 5 August 1976).

2 *Education Times*, 15 August 1974.

3 Ibid.

4 Ibid.

5 Ibid.

6 Ibid.

7 Ibid.

8 Ibid.

9 C. O'Leary, S. Elliott and R.A. Wilford, *The Northern Ireland assembly 1982–1986: a constitutional experiment* (London: C. Hurst & Co and Belfast: Queen's University Bookshop, 1988), p. 39.

10 K.P. Bloomfield to A.C. Brooke (PRONI, Shared schools: inquiry into integrated education, ED/32/B/1/12/1, 15 January 1975).

11 Ibid.

12 Later in 1979, Lord Chilver was asked to chair an inquiry into the possibility of amalgamating the state (Stranmillis) and Catholic (St Mary's and St Joseph's) colleges of education in Belfast. The establishment and the work of the inquiry led to furious reaction from the Catholic authorities, including the circulation of letters of objection at Sunday masses. Higher Education Review Group, *The future structure of teacher education in Northern Ireland: an interim report of the Higher Education Review Group* (Belfast: HMSO, 1980).

13 K.P. Bloomfield to A.C. Brooke (PRONI, Shared schools: inquiry into integrated education, ED/32/B/1/12/1, 15 January 1975).

14 Ibid.

15 Northern Ireland Office press statement (PRONI, Shared schools: inquiry into integrated education, ED/32/B/1/12/1, 18 September 1975).

16 PRONI, Shared schools: inquiry into integrated education, ED/32/B/1/12/1, 22 January 1976.

17 Ibid.

18 *Belfast Telegraph*, 7 June 1976.

19 Ibid.

20 B. Benton to R. Moyle (PRONI, Shared schools: inquiry into integrated education, ED/32/B/1/12/1, 20 June 1976).

21 Department of Education, Northern Ireland to ACT (PRONI, Shared schools: inquiry into integrated education, ED/32/B/1/12/1, 8 July 1976).

22 Ibid., 5 July 1976.

23 Ibid., 30 July 1976.

24 Ibid.

25 Ibid., 16 July 1976.

26 *Irish News*, 23 July 1976.

27 Ibid.

28 Ibid.

29 'Note for the record: meeting with representatives of All Children Together' (PRONI, Shared schools: inquiry into integrated education, ED/32/B/1/12/1, 22 July 1976).

30 Ibid.

31 T. Cowan, minute (PRONI, Shared schools: inquiry into

32 Ibid.

33 J. Pitt-Brooke, minute (PRONI, Shared schools: inquiry into integrated education, ED/32/B/1/12/1, 30 July 1976).

34 *Belfast Telegraph*, 22 July 1976.

35 *Irish News*, 23 July 1976.

36 Ibid.

37 Ibid.

38 R. Darlington, 'Shared schools' (PRONI, Shared schools: inquiry into integrated education, ED/32/B/1/12/1, 5 August 1976).

39 H. Young to Cardinal W. Conway (PRONI, Shared schools: inquiry into integrated education, ED/32/B/1/12/1, 23 July 1976).

40 J. Pitt-Brooke, 'Note for the record – shared schools' (PRONI, Shared schools: inquiry into integrated education, ED/32/B/1/12/1, 30 July 1976).

41 Ibid.

42 Ibid.

43 Ibid.

44 Bishop Basil Butler, auxiliary bishop of Westminster; Rev. John Harriott, Jesuit and assistant editor of *The Month*; Bishop Charles Grant, bishop of Northampton; and Rev. Michael Hollings, a parish priest in Southall.

45 Pitt-Brooke, 30 July 1976.

46 Ibid.

47 Ibid.

48 Ibid.

49 I.M. Burns to J. Pitt-Brooke (PRONI, Shared schools: inquiry into integrated education, ED/32/B/1/12/1, 9 August 1976).

50 P. Carvill, 'Comprehensive education: integration' (PRONI, Shared schools: inquiry into integrated education, ED/32/B/1/12/1, 5 August 1976).

51 Ibid.

52 Ibid.

53 A. Brooke, 'Confidential/secretary of state/shared schools' (PRONI, Shared schools: inquiry into integrated education, ED/32/B/1/12/1, presented 1 September 1976).

54 Ibid.

55 Ibid.

56 Ibid.

57 *Irish News*, 29 September 1976.

58 Ibid.

59 'House of Commons, 28 October 1976', cutting (PRONI, Shared schools: inquiry into integrated education, ED/32/B/1/12/1, 28 October 1976).

60 'Résumé of discussions with Lord Melchett' (PRONI, Shared schools: inquiry into integrated education, ED/32/B/1/12/1, 21 October 1976).

61 Ibid.

62 'House of Commons, 28 October 1976', 1976.

63 A. Brooke, memorandum (PRONI, Shared schools: inquiry into integrated education, ED/32/B/1/12/1, November 1976).

64 D.K. Middleton, minute (PRONI, Shared schools: inquiry into integrated education, ED/32/B/1/12/1, November 1976).
65 *Irish Times*, 29 December 2007; 'Note for the record' (PRONI, Shared schools: inquiry into integrated education, ED/32/B/1/12/1, November 1976).
66 Ibid.
67 William Ross was the unionist MP for Derry city between 1974 and 1983.
68 Ibid.
69 *The Times*, 9 June 1977.
70 Ibid.
71 Ibid.
72 Ibid.

CHAP 5

1 *ACT-LETT*, i, no. 2 (May 1977), p. 4.
2 *ACT-LETT*, i, no. 1 (January 1977), pp. 2–4.
3 Ibid., p. 6.
6 Ibid., p. 1.
5 R. Moyle to honorary secretary, ACT (PRONI, Shared schools: inquiry into integrated education, ED/32/B/1/12/1, 8 July 1976).
6 'House of Commons, 22 January 1976', cutting (PRONI, Shared schools: inquiry into integrated education, ED/32/B/1/12/1, 22 January 1976).
7 *ACT-LETT*, i, no. 2 (May 1977), pp. 3–5.
8 Only government measures affecting Northern Ireland could be introduced into the House of Commons by orders in council – and integrated education was not likely to be on the government's agenda. See McIvor, 1998, p. 140.
9 *ACT-LETT*, i, no. 3 (January 1978), pp. 1–2.
10 Ibid., pp. 3–4.
11 Ibid.
12 B. Brown, pers. comm.
13 *ACT-LETT*, i, no. 4 (May 1978), pp. 1 and 3.
14 *ACT-LETT*, i, no. 8 (June 1980), p. 3.
15 B. Brown, pers. comm.
16 M. Kennedy, pers. comm.
17 Ibid.
18 *Irish Press*, 10 April 1977; *Catholic Herald*, 16 April 1977; *ACT-LETT*, i, no. 2 (May 1977), pp. 3–4.
19 M. Kennedy, pers. comm.
20 *ACT-LETT*, i, no. 6 (June 1979), p. 5.
21 Minutes, ACT executive meeting (ACT papers, 26 June 1978), p. 2.
22 *ACT-LETT*, i, no. 6 (June 1984), pp. 2–3.
23 *ACT-LETT*, i, no. 4 (May 1978), p. 3.
24 *ACT-LETT*, i, no. 8 (June 1980), p. 8.
25 T. Spencer, 'All children apart' in *Fortnight: An Independent Review for Northern Ireland*, no. 176 (May 1980), pp. 9–10.
26 Ibid.
27 Ibid.
28 *ACT-LETT*, i, no. 8 (June 1980), p. 1.
29 *Sunday Independent*, 13 July 1980.

CHAP 6

1 *ACT-LETT*, i, no. 10 (June 1981), p. 4.
2 See also *ACT-LETT*, i, no. 2 (May 1977), pp. 1–2.
3 Minutes, ACT executive meeting (ACT papers, 10 March 1981), p. 3.
4 *ACT-LETT*, i, no. 10 (June 1981), p. 4.
5 Ibid.
6 Ibid.
7 Ibid.
8 B. Brown, pers. comm., 2006.
9 W. Johnson, pers. comm., May 2005.
10 Ibid.
11 *ACT-LETT*, i, no. 10 (June 1981), p. 3.
12 Ibid.
13 *ACT-LETT*, ii, no. 1 (February 1982), p. 1.
14 *ACT-LETT*, ii, no. 2 (June 1982), p. 3.
15 Cited in *ACT-LETT*, ii, no. 3 (March 1983), p. 1.
16 *ACT-LETT*, ii, no. 3 (March 1983), pp. 2–4.
17 Ibid.
18 Ibid.
19 B. Lambkin, address to 'Planned shared schools' seminar, ACT, 6 March 1982, reprinted in *ACT-LETT*, ii, no. 3 (March 1983), p. 4.
20 Ibid., p. 4.
21 Ibid., pp. 5–7.
22 *ACT-LETT*, ii, no. 6 (June 1984), p. 7.
23 Ibid., p. 2.
24 *ACT-LETT*, ii, no. 7 (January 1985), p. 1.
25 Ibid.
26 *ACT-LETT*, ii, no. 7 (January 1985), p. 2.
27 Ibid.
28 Ibid.
29 Ibid.
30 *ACT-LETT*, ii, no. 1 (February 1982), p. 1.
31 Ibid.

CHAP 7

1 English Anglican-Roman Catholic Committee, 'Joint church schools', 2000. (www.cofe.anglican.org/info/ccu/england/catholics/jointschools.rtf) (1 September 2009), p. 1.
2 P. Chadwick, *Schools of reconciliation: issues in joint Roman Catholic–Anglican education* (London and New York: Cassell, 1994), p. 61.
3 Ibid., pp. 62–3.
4 Ibid., p. 73.
5 Ibid., p. 70.
6 Ibid., p. 73.
7 Ibid., p. 74.
8 Ibid., p. 75.
9 Ibid., p. 77.
10 Ibid.
11 A. Lawrence, address to 'Shared schools in action' seminar, ACT, 15 April 1978.
12 Ibid.
13 Canon E. Elliott, address to 'Shared schools in action' seminar, ACT, 15 April 1978.

14 Ibid.
15 C. Linehan, address to 'Shared schools in action' seminar, ACT, 15 April 1978.
16 Ibid.
17 Higher-Education Review Group, 1980.
18 M. Bradbury, address to 'Cooperation in education' seminar, ACT, 31 March 1979.
19 Ibid.
20 *ACT-LETT*, ii, no. 1 (February 1982), p. 2
21 *ACT-LETT*, ii, no. 6 (June 1984), p. 4.
22 A report produced by the fifth working party appointed by the Irish Council of Churches and the Roman Catholic Church Joint Group on Social Questions, *Violence in Ireland: a report to the churches* (Belfast: Christian Journals, 1976).
23 Ibid., p. 86.
24 *ACT-LETT*, ii, no. 6 (June 1984), p. 4.
25 Ibid., pp. 4 and 7.
26 Answer from Cardinal Cahal Daly in a radio phone-in in 1984, note on relations with the churches (ACT papers, n.d.).
27 Catholic Church: Irish Episcopal Conference, *Directory on ecumenism in Ireland* (Dublin: Veritas, 1976).
28 *ACT-LETT*, ii, no. 8 (June 1985), p. 3.
29 B. Brown, pers. comm., 2006.
30 *Newsweek*, May 1984.
31 Second Vatican Council, *Declaration on Christian education*, 1965.
32 Sacred Congregation for Catholic Education, *The Catholic school* (Rome: Vatican Polyglot Press, 1977), p. 14.
33 Document referred to as 'Catholic hierarchy, 1976'.

CHAP 8

1 Co-chairpersons' report, first annual general meeting of Foyle Trust for Integrated Education, December 1991, cited in C.M. Kavanagh, 'Integrated schools and their impact on the local community' in C. Moffat (ed.), *Education for a change: integrated education and community relations in Northern Ireland* (Belfast: Fortnight Educational Trust, 1993), p. 31.
2 Minutes, ACT executive meeting (ACT papers, 11 September 1984).
3 Minutes, ACT executive meeting (ACT papers, 26 September 1984).
4 Bettie Benton to Tony Spencer ('Tony Spencer' file, ACT papers, 28 September 1984), p. 1.
5 Ibid.
6 Minutes, ACT executive meeting (ACT papers, 26 September 1984).
7 C. Linehan, 'Inaccuracies in Mr Spencer's paper relating to All Children Together's "failure" to appoint a development officer' (ACT papers, 1984), p. 4.
8 W. Johnson, pers. comm., May 2002.
9 Ibid.
10 T. Spencer, 'The All Children Together movement and

proposed school closures in Northern Ireland' (ACT papers, 1983), p. 10.
11 Ibid.
12 Ibid.
13 Ibid.
14 Ibid.
15 Ibid.
16 Ibid.
17 Minutes, ACT executive meeting (ACT papers, 28 October 1984).
18 M. Connolly to ACT trustees (ACT papers, 22 October 1984), p. 1.
19 Ibid., p. 2.
20 Minutes, ACT executive special meeting (ACT papers, 9 November 1984), p. 6.
21 Ibid., p. 7.
22 Minutes, joint meeting of Lagan College Ltd directors and ACT Charitable Trust trustees, (ACT papers, 4 December 1984), p. 5.
23 Ibid., p. 5.
24 Ibid., p. 6.
25 Ibid.
26 Press release, joint appeal by Lagan College and ACT (ACT papers, 10 December 1984).
27 D. Haughey, honorary secretary, ACT, to trusts and Department of Education, Northern Ireland (draft, ACT papers, 13 February 1988), p. 1.
28 Sr Anna Hoare, 'Historical résumé (which you mainly know)' (ACT papers, 1988), p. 1.
29 Ibid.
30 J. McKenna to C. Linehan, 1988 ('NICIE' file, ACT papers, 24 February 1988).
31 D. McFerran to J. Mulvenna ('NICIE' file, ACT papers, 19 February 1988).
32 Ibid.
33 *ACT-LETT*, iii, no. 2 (July 1986), p. 4.
34 *ACT-LETT*, iii, no. 3 (February 1987), p. 5.
35 Ibid.
36 Ibid.
37 *ACT-LETT*, iii, no. 4 (July 1988), p. 2.
38 Ibid.
39 Co-chairpersons' report, 1991, p. 31.
40 *Belfast Telegraph*, 16 October 1993.

CHAP 9

1 Proverb, reputedly often quoted by the fourth earl of Shaftesbury.
2 Elliott Duffy Garrett, ACT's solicitors.
3 B. Benton to FIPS Board of Directors ('Forge' file, ACT papers, 28 November 1990).
4 A. Montgomery, G. Fraser, C. McGlynn, A. Smith and T. Gallagher, *Integrated education in Northern Ireland: integration in practice, report 2*, Nuffield Foundation, 2008 (gtcni.openrepository.com/gtcni/bitstream/2428/6018/1/Integration%20in%20Practice.pdf) (1 September 2009).

[5] Education Reform (Northern Ireland) Order, 1989 (Belfast: HMSO, 1989), Article 95 (1b).

[6] K. Brown to C. Linehan ('Forge' file, ACT papers, 20 March 1996).

[7] S. Lee to B. McIvor ('Forge' file, ACT papers, 30 April 1991).

[8] B. Benton to S. Lee ('Forge' file, ACT papers, 17 May 1991).

[9] Ibid.

[10] Muir and Addy, accountants, to B. Benton ('Forge' file, ACT papers, 3 June 1992).

[11] B. Lockhart to Elliott Duffy Garrett ('Forge' file, ACT papers, 4 September 1993).

[12] M. Brown to B. Deeny of Elliott Duffy Garrett ('Forge' file, ACT papers, 3 September 1993).

[13] Full text of the letter sent by the CEO of BELB, Gerry Moag, in October 1993:

Dear Parents

You will be aware of the difficulties which the board has had in obtaining planning permission for the new site for Forge Primary School in the grounds of Wellington College. These difficulties have created an air of uncertainty about the move from the present site at Balmoral Avenue and this I very much regret.

Following the agreement between All Children Together and a private developer for the sale of the premises currently occupied by the Forge Controlled Integrated Primary School, the Belfast Education and Library Board drew up a programme for the provision of new accommodation for the school. Unfortunately difficulties in relation to obtaining planning permission have caused a major delay in the planned timetable.

I am, however, pleased to advise you that planning permission has now been granted for the location of the school at the new site and that as a result building work should commence very shortly. As a result Forge Primary School will remain in Balmoral Avenue until the end of the present school term and it will re-open in January on its new site. Further details about this will of course be given to parents nearer the time.

The Belfast Education and Library Board appreciates the help and co-operation of All Children Together in delaying the completion date of the proposed sale and in allowing the school to remain in occupation of Balmoral Avenue premises until 31 December 1993. By permitting the children to remain at Balmoral Avenue, All Children Together has assisted the board in achieving its objective of minimising the potential disruption to the school, children, staff and parents, associated with the move to the new accommodation.

[14] Minutes, FIPS directors' meeting ('Forge' file, ACT papers, 8 July 1990).

[15] C. Linehan to ACT Directors ('Forge' file, ACT papers, 10 April 1992).

[16] B. Garrett to M. Brown ('Forge' file, ACT papers, 2 June 1993).

[17] S. Frizzell to B. Benton ('Forge' file, ACT papers, 25 August 1993).

[18] M. Brown to Elliott Duffy Garrett ('Forge' file, ACT papers, 7 June 1993).

[19] Frizzell to Benton, 25 August 1993.

[20] C. Duffy to C. Linehan ('Forge' file, ACT papers, 4 December 1995).

[21] P. Smith QC to Elliott Duffy Garrett ('Forge' file, ACT papers, 2 May 1996).

[22] Minutes, ACT meeting (ACT papers, 15 May 1996).

[23] C. Linehan to B. Garrett ('Forge' file, ACT papers, 1993).

[24] Ibid.

[25] C. Linehan to Nuffield Foundation ('Forge' file, ACT papers, 24 June 1996).

[26] C. Linehan to R. Marshall ('Forge' file, ACT papers, 20 July 1966).

[27] Ibid.

CHAP 10

[1] Quoted in B. Mawhinney, *In the firing line: politics, faith, power and forgiveness* (London: HarperCollins, 1999), p. 95.

[2] Ibid., p. 95.

[3] Ibid., pp. 95–6.

[4] Ibid., p. 96.

[5] Ibid.

[6] Ibid.

[7] Ibid., p. 97.

[8] Ibid.

[9] Ibid., p. 98.

[10] Ibid.

[11] Department of Education, Northern Ireland, *Education in Northern Ireland: proposals for reform* (Belfast: Department of Education, Northern Ireland, 1988), p. 6.

[12] Ibid.

[13] Education Reform (Northern Ireland) Order 1989 (Belfast: HMSO, 1989), Article 64 (1).

[14] *ACT-LETT*, iii, no. 1 (April 1991), p. 1.

[15] *ACT-LETT*, iii, no. 5 (September 1989), p. 1.

[16] Mawhinney, 1999, p. 99.

[17] Ibid., pp. 98–9.

[18] 'Memorandum on the need for an Integrated Schools Advisory Commission, suggested by Basil McIvor' (ACT papers, February 1986), p. 1.

[19] Cited in B. Benton, 'Some thoughts on the future of ACT' ('1988' file, ACT papers, 28 November 1988), p. 2.

[20] D. McFerran to C. Linehan (ACT papers, 19 September 1988).

[21] Ibid., pp. 1–2.

[22] D. McFerran, report to ACT (ACT papers, 22 September 1988), pp. 1–2.

[23] Ibid., p. 2.

[24] Ibid.

[25] DENI minutes, meeting with Dr B. Mawhinney, minister for education ('Basil's paper' file, ACT papers, 8 May 1990), p. 2.

26 Ibid.
27 B. Benton to B. Mawhinney ('Basil's paper' file, ACT papers, 14 June 1990).
28 S. Peover to Sr A. Hoare ('Basil's paper' file, ACT papers, 17 July 1990).
29 M.T. Donnelly to B. Benton ('Basil's paper' file, ACT papers, 9 April 1991), p. 1.
30 Ibid.
31 S. Quinn to B. Benton, enclosing minutes, 'Meeting with representatives of "All Children Together" (ACT), Thursday 30 May 1991', [PS] 20146 ('ACT/NICIE 1986–1995' file, ACT papers, 19 June 1991), pp. 1–2.
32 Ibid., p. 3.
33 Ibid., p. 4.
34 ACT directors to S. Quinn ('ACT/NICIE 1986–1995' file, ACT papers, 31 May 1991), p. 1.
35 DENI, press release (ACT papers, 3 June 1991), p. 1.
36 B. Benton, C. Linehan and B. Brown, report to ACT on meeting with Lord Belstead at Rathgael House, 3 June 1991 (ACT papers, n.d.).
37 Ibid.
38 Ibid., pp. 2–3.
39 Ibid., p. 3.
40 Minutes, ACT directors' meeting (ACT papers, 28 June 1991), p. 1.
41 Ibid.
42 Lord Belstead to B. Benton ('Ombudsman' file, ACT papers, 28 July 1991), p. 1.
43 Jill McIvor, ombudsman, to C. Linehan and B. Benton (ref. PC 185/9118, February 1992), p. 1.
44 Parliamentary Commissioner Act (NI) 1969: statement of complaint (case no. PC 73/92, 1992), p. 2.

CHAP 11
1 B. Brown, address to launch of Warrington Project, October 1993, reprinted in *ACT-LETT*, iv, no. 3 (May 1994), p. 1.
2 Nominating ACT for the 1995 UNESCO prize for peace education.
3 P. McGaffin, 'The development of an integrated dchool' in Leslie Caul (ed.), *Schools under scrutiny: the case of Northern Ireland* (London: Macmillan, 1990), pp. 57–70.
4 Submission from ACT to Churches' Religious-Education Core-Curriculum-Drafting Group (ACT papers, November 1991).
5 Mawhinney, 1999, pp. 103–04.
6 Ibid.
7 A. Pollak (ed.), *A citizens' inquiry: the Opshal report on Northern Ireland* (Dublin: Lilliput, 1993). (Following the sudden death of Torkel Opsahl in 1993, the report became popularly known as the Opsahl report.)
8 Brown, 1993, p. 1.
9 *ACT-LETT*, iv, no. 3 (May 1994), p. 1.
10 P. Chadwick, *Schools of reconciliation: issues in joint Roman Catholic–Anglican education* (London and New York: Cassell, 1994).
11 Dr Colin Irwin is a research fellow in the Institute of Irish Studies at the University of Liverpool and in the Institute of Governance at Queen's University, Belfast. He was the principal investigator on the project entitled 'Peace building and public policy in Northern Ireland' funded by the Rowntree Trust. As part of the Northern Ireland peace process he conducted eight public-opinion polls in collaboration with the political parties elected to take part in the Stormont talks. Since then he has extended his work to include the Balkans and Middle East (www.peacepolls.org) (1 September 2009).
12 C. Irwin, '1995 UNESCO Prize for Peace Education: draft nomination: All Children Together and Lagan College on behalf of all integrated schools in deeply divided societies', ('Colin Irwin: UN/UNESCO 1992–1995' file, ACT papers), pp. 1–2.
13 Higher Education Review Group, 1980.
14 *ACT-LETT*, iv, no. 6 (autumn/winter 1995), p. 2.
15 'Ulidia Integrated College: totally confidential – update on Funding situation as of May 1999' (fax 01960 370919, ACT papers, May 1999), pp. 1–2.
16 See Appendix 11.
17 C. Moffat, 'The transformation option' in *Education together for a change: integrated education and community relations in Northern Ireland* (Belfast: Fortnight Educational Trust, 1993), pp. 113–21.
18 E. Lemon, 'The transformation process viewed from the staffroom' in Moffat (ed.) 1993, pp. 122–3.
19 Ibid., p. 122.
20 Ibid., p. 124.
21 *ACT-LETT*, iv, no. 5 (spring/summer 1995), p. 6.
22 Lemon, 1993, p. 130.
23 Department of Education, Northern Ireland, *Integrated education: a framework for transformation* (Belfast: Department of Education, 1996).
24 'Integrated education could be in danger', press release (ACT papers, July 1996), p. 1.
25 ACT to Department of Education, Northern Ireland (ACT papers, 24 August 1996).
26 F. Donnelly, 'Transforming integrated education: an historical and contemporary analysis of developments in integrated education' (M.Ed. thesis, University of Ulster, Jordanstown, 1998).
27 Ibid.
28 Ibid.
29 Minutes, ACT annual general meeting (ACT papers, 19 June 1997), p. 4.
30 Minutes, ACT directors' planning meeting (ACT papers, 9 October 1997), pp. 1–2.
31 M. Kennedy, 'The closing years' (unpublished, MS in possession of J. Bardon, 2008), p. 3.
32 M. Kennedy, address to twenty-sixth annual general meeting, ACT (ACT papers, 8 February 2001).

[33] M. Kennedy, address to twenty-eighth annual general meeting, ACT (ACT papers, 15 January 2003).

[34] M. Kennedy to M. Wardlow (ACT papers, 28 January 1993).

[35] Ibid.

[36] M. Kennedy, address to farewell dinner for Sr Anna, Canada Room, Queen's University, Belfast, 2003.

[37] Ibid.

EPILOGUE

[1] D.H. Akenson, *The Irish education experiment: the national system of education in the nineteenth century* (London: Routledge and Kegan Paul and Toronto: University of Toronto Press, 1969). This probably has more detail than most readers will be looking for. Economical summaries are D.H. Akenson, 'National education and the realities of Irish life, 1831–1900', *Éire-Ireland*, iv (winter 1969), pp. 42–52, 'Pre-university education, 1782–1870', in W.E. Vaughan (ed.), *A new history of Ireland*, v: *Ireland under the union i: 1801–1870* (Oxford: Clarendon Press, 1989), pp. 532–7, and 'Pre-university education, 1870–1921', in W.E. Vaughan (ed.), *A new history of Ireland*, vi: *Ireland under the union ii: 1870–1921* (Oxford: Clarendon Press, 1996), pp. 523–38.

[2] Since historians of Ireland necessarily keep a watching brief on how history gets written, I will include for them the following residual details. The original author of the two essays was to be Dr Tarlach Ó Raifeartaigh, a very good amateur historian who had taken the tasks on with serious intent, unlike many of Moody's other original contributors. (The early plan had been for Ó Raifeartaigh to do the nineteenth-century essay as well.) He had been head civil servant of the Republic's Department of Education and in 1968 had become chairman of the Higher-Education Authority, and in 1973 chairman of the Advisory Committee on Cultural Relations in the Department of Foreign Affairs. The Higher-Education Authority was a secondary source of funding for the *A new history of Ireland*, which explains why, when Theo Moody suggested that he put Ó Raifeartaigh's name as co-author on one of the essays that I submitted, I said no and took this as a lesson in academic ethics, as defined in Dublin.

[3] D.H. Akenson, *A mirror to Kathleen's face: education in independent Ireland, 1922–60* (Montreal and Kingston: McGill-Queen's University Press, 1975).

[4] D.H. Akenson, *Education and enmity: the control of schooling in Northern Ireland, 1920–50* (Newton Abbot: David and Charles Ltd for the Institute of Irish Studies, Queen's University, Belfast, 1973). Incidentally, the essay that was in final form for *A new history of Ireland* in 1974 was published somewhat latterly: 'Pre-university education, 1921–84', [with appendices by Sean Farren and John Coolahan] in J.R. Hill (ed.), *A new history of Ireland*, vii: *Ireland, 1921–1984* (Oxford: Clarendon Press, 2003), pp. 711–56. The entire *A new history of Ireland* project was completed three decades late with the publication of the volume on prehistoric and early Ireland in 2005.

[5] The last chapter of *Education and enmity* departed from the usual historian's format and suggested some policy changes for the future, most importantly, 'some hopeful careful experiments in integration'. In the 1980s, Brian Lambkin wrote to me that he and some associates had encountered that last chapter while in training college, and they had decided to make integration their mission. Here Brian was being characteristically generous, but I would be quite pleased to have had any part in encouraging integrated schooling.

[6] On New Zealand's educational evolution, see D.H. Akenson, *Half the world from home: perspectives on the Irish in New Zealand, 1860–1950* (Wellington: Victoria University Press, 1990), pp. 159–90.

[7] Independent Strategic Review of Education, *Schools for the future: funding, strategy, sharing: report of the Independent Strategic Review of Education* (Bangor: Department of Education, 2006), p. 112.

Index

322 ALL CHILDREN TOGETHER

Ulster Women's Unionist Council, 18
Ulster Workers' Council strike, 1974, xi, 35–6, 52, 54
Unitarian Church, 5
United Education Committee of the Protestant
    Churches, 13, 14, 17
United Nations, vii, 222
United Nations Educational, Scientific and Cultural
    Organisation (UNESCO), 222
United Nations: Universal declaration of human
    rights, 53, 157
United States of America, 3, 20, 83, 132, 133, 215,
    221, 242, 244, 247
University of Ulster, 55
University Street, Belfast, 237
Unsworth, John, 241
UTV, 128
UVF, 9, 20, 36

Vane-Tempest-Stewart, Charles S.H. *See*
    Londonderry, Lord.
Vatican II. *See* Second Vatican Council.
Vietnam, 229
Vietnam War, 20

Wallace, John, 30
Walmesley, Charles. *See* Pastorini.
Wardlow, Michael, 243
Warrenpoint, Co. Down, 14
Warrington Project, 1993, 220–21
Warrington, Cheshire, 220–21

Wates Foundation, 167
Waugh, Eric, 177
Wellington College, Belfast, 191
Wells, Ronald, x, 196
Westacres, County Armagh, 229
Western Education and Library Board (WELB), 92
Westminster, xii, 2, 6, 15, 22, 23, 67, 78, 93, 98, 101
Westminster, diocese of (Catholic), 59, 60
Whig Party, 2
Whitehead, County Antrim, 225, 227
Whitelaw, William, x, 22
Williams, Rev. Robert, 59
Willibands, Cardinal Jan, 146
Wilson, Dorothy, 173
Wilson, Fr Des, 50, 55
Wilson, Harold, 35, 67
Wilson, Sr Winifred, 59, 60, 61
Wilton, William, 18
Wimbledon, London, 142
Windmill Integrated Primary School, Dungannon,
    166, 175, 176
Wisconsin, USA, 132
Wolfenden, Sir John, 24
Wolff, Virginia, 238
World War I, 9
World War II, x, 16, 20
Worthington, Tony, 226, 227

York Lane, Belfast, 173
Young, Hugo, 79–80, 83